D0475342

THE CHRONICLE OF JAZZ

THE CHRONICLE OF JAZZ

MERVYN COOKE

For my parents

Acknowledgments

This book would not have been possible without the unstinting support of the staff at Thames & Hudson. Thanks are also due to my old friend Roland Robertson, without whose influence I might never have delved into this extraordinary music in the first place, and to George Double and Charlie Furniss for teaching me more about jazz than I could ever hope to teach them.

Frontispiece Saxophonist Courtney Pine, who inspired a creative surge in British jazz during the 1980s.

Right King Oliver and his Creole Jazz Band at the time of their pioneering recordings in 1923: (l. to r.) Honoré Dutrey (trombone), Baby Dodds (drums), King Oliver (cornet), Louis Armstrong (slide trumpet), Lil Hardin (piano), Bill Johnson (banjo), and Johnny Dodds (clarinet).

Oxford University Press is a department of the University of Oxford. It furthers the University's objective of excellence in research, scholarship, and education by publishing worldwide. Oxford is a registered trade mark of Oxford University Press in the UK and in certain other countries

Published in the United States of America by
Oxford University Press
198 Madison Avenue, New York, NY 10016, United States of America

First published in the United Kingdom in 1997 by
Thames & Hudson Ltd, 181A High Holborn, London WC1V 7QX
This updated and revised edition 2013

Designed by Adam Hay

Library of Congress Cataloging-in-Publication Data

Cooke, Mervyn.
The chronicle of jazz / Mervyn Cooke.—Revised and expanded edition.
pages cm
Includes bibliographical references and index.
ISBN 978-0-19-934100-9 (hardback : alk. paper) 1. Jazz—Chronology. 2. Jazz—History and criticism. I. Title.
ML3506.C69 2013
781.6509—dc23
2013019617

ISBN: 9780199341009

Printed and bound in China by Asia Pacific Offset Ltd
9 8 7 6 5 4 3 2 1

DAGUERRE
Chicago

CONTENTS

A CENTURY OF JAZZ

Note Terms that appear in SMALL CAPS are listed in the Glossary; pp. 261–63.

"Jazz became many things – frenetic, destructive, hysterical, decadent, venal, alcoholic, saccharine, Lombardish, vapid – it has enriched stuffed bellies; it has corrupted the innocent; it has betrayed and it has traduced; but, everywhere and in all its forms, something jazz acquired at the moment of its origin has profoundly touched all its hearers. What was this thing that set folks dancing and smiling from the slums of New Orleans to all the capitals of the earth?"

Alan Lomax (1950)

The extraordinarily varied nature of jazz can only be understood by considering the exhilarating rapidity with which it established itself at the forefront of the modern musical world. Like cinema, that other major American contribution to twentieth-century culture, jazz is now well into its second century of existence. Over the course of its first century jazz adopted and transformed many of the technical innovations of earlier classical music with astonishing speed, compressing four centuries of musical expertise into a dazzling array of styles and structures. The result was an audience appeal that still ranges from the mass pop market to an intellectual cliquishness even more exclusive than that of the 1960s avant-garde in art. Along with these achievements, jazz has managed to summarize most of our instinctive feelings about music and reshape the art for the future.

The story of jazz is one of lively interactions and tensions between performers and composers of widely differing temperaments. The chronological diary at the heart of this book vividly illustrates the exciting and often unpredictable nature of these creative encounters, tracing the history of jazz from its largely disreputable beginnings, through the height of its popularity in the Swing Era, to its gradual evolution into a serious art music capable of sustaining intellectual and emotional interest on a par with any other modern art form. Never far below the story's surface are the racial tensions that sparked off the early development of jazz. Slaves transported from West Africa to the New World took their musical traditions with them, and adapted their tribal work songs and dances to sustain them in their forced labors (• p. 17). Fundamental elements of jazz were born when the dynamic rhythmic language and expressive pitch-bending of African vocal music became fused with structures and harmonies borrowed from the European music favored by white slave owners. After universal emancipation in 1865, black religious music (which also synthesized techniques of African and European origin) paved the way for the two genres that would directly lead to the early jazz style: RAGTIME and the BLUES, both of which appeared in the 1890s.

Ragtime (• p. 20) – "white music played black," as it has been aptly described – derived from white dance forms such as the polka and MARCH, and superimposed a SYNCOPATED rhythmic style reminiscent of black BANJO music and plantation songs on simple harmonic structures built from western CHORDS. More adventurous ragtime composers (including some white musicians) began to borrow elements from the blues, a vocal form characterized by a greater degree of IMPROVISATION and distinctive tonal colorings retained from African music (• p. 27). Ragtime began to disappear around 1920, although it had already influenced classical composers such as Claude Debussy (• p. 24) and Igor Stravinsky (• p. 43). Its style formed the basis for later jazz piano playing and spawned the Harlem STRIDE school of the 1920s and 1930s (• p. 46). The blues, which continued to flourish in its own right and led both to the BOOGIE-WOOGIE style of piano playing and ultimately to rock 'n' roll in the 1950s, donated to jazz the universally popular TWELVE-BAR harmonic progression, as well as a new emphasis on improvisation.

Below The banjo, based on traditional West African prototypes, was typical of the homemade musical instruments to which slaves had to resort. It remained popular in jazz until the 1930s, when it was supplanted by the more versatile guitar.

Ragtime pianists usually eked out a living in brothels and saloons, some of the few employment opportunities open to black musicians after emancipation. Another source of work was provided by the celebrated brass bands that appeared in funeral processions in southern cities such as New Orleans (• p. 29) and flourished due to the availability of cheap secondhand instruments abandoned by Civil War military bands. Band marches borrowed the ragtime idiom, often to "jazz up" classical pieces such as Chopin's Funeral March. When this style merged with rougher blues elements, early ensemble jazz in the DIXIELAND style (• p. 37) was born.

Jazz recordings first appeared in 1917 and began to proliferate after 1923, by which time the centers of musical activity had moved to Chicago and New York. The growing popularity of dances such as the Charleston led to the development of a livelier style, with its headier tempos and snappier rhythms. In the 1920s jazz developed further at the hands of many brilliant pioneers, including Jelly Roll Morton (• p. 45) and Louis Armstrong (• p. 57). With the work of Duke Ellington at Harlem's Cotton Club in 1927–32, jazz at last found a composer worthy of being hailed as equal in intellectual stature to his counterparts in the field of classical music. Ellington produced a stream of tightly organized masterpieces in the three-minute format ideally suited to the technical limitations of 78rpm recordings. He then broke new ground by constructing pieces of considerably greater length.

Above A 1920s jazz band in Berlin, where the new music flourished until the Nazi Party attempted to suppress it in the 1930s (● p. 81).

Right Duke Ellington at the keyboard, in a characteristically suave mood. Coming from a middle-class background, Ellington combined social respectability with phenomenal compositional talent and in the process raised the intellectual standing of jazz in the 1930s.

Above A poster by Charles Lévy, designed in 1879 for the Folies Bergère in Paris, reveals how the stereotyped view of black minstrel shows prevalent in the USA was exported wholesale to Europe.

Below right This painting by Edward Burra (1905–76), entitled *The Band*, depicts a group that includes a sousaphone to the left of the drummer. This derivative of the tuba was named after the "March King," John Philip Sousa. Both instruments were retained from New Orleans marching bands and replaced by the double bass during the 1920s.

In spite of its growing intellectual respectability during the 1930s, jazz had still not quite succeeded in shedding its early links with sex and low living. The music continued to be tarnished by an inevitable association with illicit drinking during the Prohibition years (1919–33) and, later, with the addiction to hard drugs that caused the premature and often impecunious deaths of many a talented musician. Jazz seemed more respectable in Europe, which had not endured social problems of such magnitude as those in the US arising from slavery and racial disharmony. From the early 1930s onward many American jazz musicians opted to emigrate to France, where greater social status and appreciative audiences made them welcome.

In the 1930s the three strands of art music, popular music and jazz came closer together than they had ever been before – or have been since. The growing commercial success of jazz ensured that it became the pop music of the immediate prewar years, while the distinguished SYMPHONIC JAZZ cultivated by composers such as George Gershwin and Aaron Copland (• p. 55) seemed destined to fuse highbrow and lowbrow into a cogent and enduring synthetic idiom. With Benny Goodman's and John Hammond's concerts at Carnegie Hall in 1938 (• p. 91), jazz at last proved itself to be an art form worthy of appreciation by critics, scholars and audiences in full evening dress.

Predominant in these years was the SWING band, its extended instrumentation exploiting the contrast between massed saxophone and brass sections as a background to exciting improvised passages performed by featured soloists, many of whom became international stars. The most successful swing bands were based in New York, although some originated in Kansas City (• p. 64), where Bennie Moten's work influenced the young Count Basie (• p. 87). Alongside the HOT and inventive style of the black swing bands, white ensembles, such as that led by Paul Whiteman (• p. 55), produced a restrained yet suavely polished dance music. The virtuosity and commercial success of the more enterprising white bands, notably those led by Benny Goodman (• p. 84) and Glenn Miller (• p. 107), were spectacular, and did much to spur on the growth of jazz in Europe.

White commercialization of jazz seemed at its height in the later 1930s, and the attempts of black musicians to regain the artistic initiative ultimately led to the decline of the swing band after World War II. The "BEBOP" (or bop) revolution began around 1941 when rebellious musicians like Charlie Parker (• p. 136), Dizzy Gillespie (• p. 219), and Thelonious Monk (• p. 155) began experimenting with a new style in which outmoded harmonic progressions were replaced by more startling CHORD sequences, and melodic IMPROVISATIONS became increasingly characterized by distortion, fragmentation and metrical ambiguity. Traditionalists lamented the alarmingly esoteric and abstract nature of bop. It was described by poet and jazz critic Philip Larkin as "bloodless note patterns," and Duke Ellington likened it to "playing scrabble with all the vowels missing." The modernistic forcefulness of this new sound in jazz (later to become the HARD BOP of Art Blakey and countless imitators) was allied to a political need to reclaim jazz for the black Americans who had invented it in the first place: as with modernism in the other arts, the deliberate inaccessibility of the idiom protected it from a casual audience.

Left A scene at the Moulin Rouge club in Vienna in 1925 vividly illustrates the inextricable link between jazz and the sheer hedonism of its early years.

Below A young couple dance the jitterbug in Harlem in the 1930s, to the accompaniment of Erskine Hawkins's popular swing band.

Above Trumpeter Donald Byrd, photographed by William Claxton in 1959, in a picture that says it all: a solitary black musician communes with his instrument, while the body language of the white onlookers ranges from indifference to grudging curiosity.

After his early work in bop, Miles Davis (• p. 217) rapidly established himself as the most creative figure in postwar jazz. His achievement in developing not one but several new styles has remained unparalleled, and has largely accounted for the profusion of possibilities available to the contemporary jazz musician. Seeking first to temper the unfortunate aggressiveness of bop, Davis initiated the COOL style in the late 1940s (• p. 121), in which dark instrumentation was coupled with a laid-back mood and sophisticated harmonies. This new restraint proved to be influential on the emerging WEST COAST style (• p. 134), which grew up in Los Angeles in the 1950s and was dominated by white musicians. Next came Davis's experiments with MODAL JAZZ (• p. 147), which abandoned CHORD progressions altogether and consisted of extended IMPROVISATION on unchanging groups of notes. Davis's SIDEMEN in the 1950s included pianist Bill Evans (• p. 157) and tenor saxophonist John Coltrane (• p. 160), both of whom later revolutionized the styles associated with their instruments.

A serious crisis in the mid-1960s was caused by the wholesale defection of a new generation of potential jazz fans to the relatively fresh pop and rock markets. Disaster was partly averted by Davis's canny synthesis of rock and jazz elements into a new hybrid style: FUSION (• p. 171). This became the characteristic (and largely electronic) sound of jazz in the 1970s, and scored exactly the commercial success jazz then so desperately needed to survive. Fusion also rescued jazz from the avant-garde dead end into which the eccentric talents of performers such as saxophonist Ornette Coleman (• p. 150) seemed in danger of leading it in the 1960s. Radical departures from fundamental concepts in earlier jazz included the rejection of TONALITY, a move not likely to guarantee popularity. The growth of avant-garde jazz paralleled that of avant-garde classical music prominent in the same period, but was potently symbolic in likening its lack of formal constraints to the spiritual and political freedom that African Americans still found it necessary to demand.

By the early 1980s, fusion seemed to have run its course and many musicians who had made their names in the synthetic arena returned to playing a brand of jazz that (sometimes self-consciously) resurrected elements borrowed from earlier styles. Since the 1940s, when the obsolete genres of RAGTIME and DIXIELAND were systematically revived by both performers and scholars, jazz has had its own "classic" idioms that survive in a healthy state today. Sometimes these early genres are pursued authentically in liberal doses of musical nostalgia, and in other cases they are modified from a modern perspective in a kind of jazz "neo-classicism." The virtuoso trumpeter Wynton Marsalis (• p. 197) has been an outspoken advocate of this return to wholesome musical values, lamenting the commercialism behind the entire jazz-rock fusion movement.

But jazz has always had a concern for popularity at its very heart, and attempts to place it on an elitist pedestal have historically been doomed to failure. Ever since the 1930s, when Louis Armstrong was criticized for "selling out" to commercial interests, the feud between the elitists and the populists in jazz has sometimes been vitriolic. And Marsalis's own commercial success was, ironically enough, partly secured by the untiring promotional efforts of CBS (and later Sony) – the same company that pushed Miles Davis in the direction of fusion four decades ago.

The plurality of jazz styles with which the often perplexed listener is surrounded today is almost as diverse as that in classical music: in little more than a century, jazz has caught up with its illustrious musical forebears, both in quality and quantity. As they have in the past, jazz musicians today move in and out of each other's spheres of influence, the only difference now being the international flavor these migrations have acquired. Styles continue to be transmitted and transformed through an exciting process of musical osmosis that, in essence, is comparable to that which spawned the beginnings of jazz not so very long ago.

Below Wynton Marsalis, a prodigious talent who assured jazz a continuing audience of young enthusiasts during the problematic 1980s.

Opposite The only surviving photograph of the legendary cornetist Buddy Bolden (back row, third from left), a famous image often printed back-to-front in an attempt to correct the left-handed positions of the string players.

Origins: West African musical traditions, kept alive by slaves on US plantations in the nineteenth century, gradually coalesce with the tonality and structures of European classical music to create an exciting new American art form.

-1916

1895–1905

Black composers and their white imitators popularize a new style of light music based on catchy rhythms and appealing melodies. This "ragtime" is refined by the capable hands of Scott Joplin, who hopes to turn it into an art form. As it begins to merge with the rougher blues style, the beginnings of jazz are heard.

THE RAGTIME ERA BEGINS

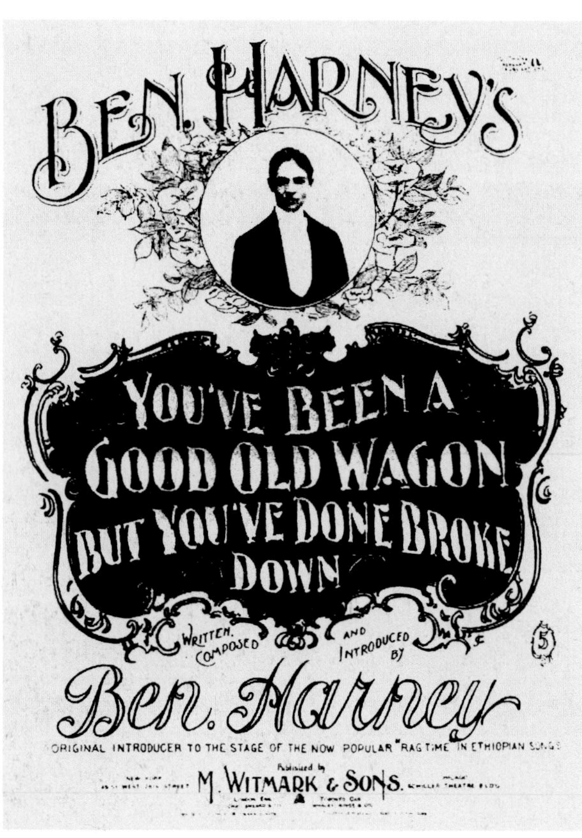

Above A landmark publication in the early development of ragtime: Ben Harney's song "You've Been a Good Old Wagon."

"Ragtime is a certain type of syncopation and only certain tunes can be played in that idea. But jazz is a style that can be applied to any type of tune. I started using the word in 1902 to show people the difference between jazz and ragtime."

Jelly Roll Morton

Jazz Events

1895

February

The Czech composer Dvořák, director of the National Conservatory in New York, publishes an article in *Harper's New Monthly Magazine* entitled "Music in America." He causes considerable controversy by advising American composers to build their future music on the basis of Negro folk melodies.

- Ben Harney composes his RAGTIME song "You've Been a Good Old Wagon," and has it published in Louisville, Kentucky. He later styles himself the "Inventor of Ragtime."
- Scott Joplin (● p. 21) publishes two songs in Syracuse, New York.

1896

3 August

Ernest Hogan (who was himself black) copyrights his ragtime "coon" song "All Coons Look Alike to Me," published by Witmark & Sons in New York. The title sets the racist tone of the genre, which rapidly grows in popularity.

5 August

Ben Harney copyrights "You've Been a Good Old Wagon" and issues a revised version under the Witmark imprint.

- Scott Joplin publishes his first instrumental pieces in Temple, Texas. They are both MARCHES, one (*The Great Crush Collision*) inspired by a railway accident.

1897

January

William H. Krell, a white composer, publishes his *Mississippi Rag* in Chicago. It is the first RAG for solo piano to appear in print.

December

Tom Turpin publishes his *Harlem Rag* in St. Louis, the first piano rag by a black composer to appear in print. At least twenty more rags by other composers are published in this year.

- Ben Harney issues his *Rag Time Instructor*.
- The first recordings of ragtime are made for the newly introduced disc-playing gramophone, in versions for solo BANJO and orchestrations for band.
- New prostitution legislation regulates the red-light district in STORYVILLE, New Orleans, where brothels have been conducting their business legally since 1857. Storyville soon becomes an important center for early jazz musicians (● p. 23).

1895–1905

PLANTATION ROOTS

Hundreds of thousands of African slaves were relocated to North America between the sixteenth and mid-nineteenth centuries, torn away from their tribal homes by European traders. Although the importation of slaves to America became illegal in 1808, domestic slavery continued to flourish in the southern states until Abraham Lincoln became President. He forced the issue, and the bloody four-year Civil War between the industrialized northern states and the secessionist southern confederacy began in 1861. Slavery was finally abolished by the Thirteenth Amendment to the US Constitution in 1865. If freed slaves rejoiced at the news, their elation would prove short-lived: severe problems rooted in violent racism and strict segregation continued to blight black Americans for more than a century afterward.

In the popular imagination, jazz was born directly out of the hardships and repression of slavery and emancipation. Slaves had from the earliest years been systematically deprived of their cultural heritage, including their rich African musical traditions. On the cotton and rice plantations of the Deep South, slaves were forbidden to touch any musical instruments that might be used for secret communication, including drums or loud wind instruments. However, resourceful musicians produced homemade instruments such as the banjo, which was based on a type of West African lyre. Although slaves from the same tribe were split up and dispersed to weaken their morale, African workers from disparate backgrounds soon forged a common musical language through work songs and FIELD HOLLERS.

Unaccountably anxious to please their masters, many slaves began to learn European musical styles and became proficient on Western instruments, such as the violin, in order to perform popular white dance music. When white entertainers began imitating what they saw as quaint black music-making (their faces duly blackened with burnt cork or boot polish), the MINSTREL SHOW was born. After emancipation, many black musicians – including early jazz practitioners – started their careers in minstrelsy. Other genres that arose from black music-making and proved influential on the development of early jazz included religious music based on European hymns (SPIRITUALS, later supplanted by GOSPEL) and the secular BLUES (• p. 27).

World Events

1894

- Accession of Czar Nicholas II, Russia

1895

- Birth of cinema
- Discovery of X-rays
- Creation of Rhodesia

1896

- Racial segregation upheld by US Supreme Court
- Gold rush in Alaska
- Revival of Olympic Games in Greece
- Marconi demonstrates radio technology

1897

- Queen Victoria's Diamond Jubilee
- Discovery of electrons

"Jazz came to America three hundred years ago in chains."

Paul Whiteman (1926)

Above left William Aiken Walker's painting *Plantation Economy in the Old South* (*c.* 1876) presents a typical scene on a cotton plantation, and seems to suggest that, even after the Civil War, life in America's Deep South carried on much as before. Walker was born in Charleston, South Carolina, which later gave its name to the most famous jazz composition of the 1920s (• p. 58).

TRACES OF AFRICA

While several characteristics of jazz reveal affinities with techniques common in West African music, these have frequently been overemphasized by commentators keen to promote the image of jazz as an exclusively black phenomenon: jazz could not have developed in the way it did without the wholesale borrowing of European HARMONY (a concept alien to African music) undertaken by black musicians under strong white influences. Although the harmonic dimension of jazz is thoroughly Western, its harmonies are distinctively colored by BLUE NOTES, which probably originated in the African technique of "bending" pitches for expressive effect. Blue notes flatten the third, fifth, and seventh degrees of the Western major SCALE, and this undoubtedly dictated the choice of harmonies underlying the TWELVE-BAR BLUES, which later became the most important harmonic sequence in jazz (• p. 27).

In terms of structure, jazz reflects African influences in its widespread adoption of CALL-AND-RESPONSE patterns. In slave work songs, passages for a solo lead voice were answered by a choral response from the workers. The solo passages might be elaborated by a process of melodic IMPROVISATION, the characteristic that most obviously differentiates jazz from classical music. The "dirty" vocal tone of plantation singing was directly carried over into jazz where, in contrast to the pure sounds favored in classical music, a singer's or player's idiosyncrasies are prized for their unique expressive effect.

But it is in the sphere of RHYTHM that jazz's debt to African music is most clearly detected. Observers of slave music in the nineteenth century noted the unorthodox use of SYNCOPATION in their melodies. Deprived of drums, slaves habitually used the regular pulsation of hand-claps or axe-blows to set up a solid rhythmic foundation above which they could sing in catchy CROSS-RHYTHMS. This technique, ultimately a simplification of the complex POLYRHYTHMS in African music, soon became the basis for the exciting rhythms so characteristic of jazz.

Above Tom Anderson's "Arlington Annex," a leading establishment located at the junction of Basin and Iberville Streets in Storyville, New Orleans. In the background is Lulu White's Mahogany Hall.

World Events

1898

- War between Spain and USA
- Discovery of radium
- Opening of Paris Métro

1899

- Boer War commences

1900

- Chinese Boxer rebellion
- Oscar Wilde dies

"A wave of vulgar, filthy, and suggestive music has inundated the land. Nothing but ragtime prevails, and the cakewalk with its obscene posturings, its lewd gestures."

Musical Courier (1899)

Left Ragtime composer Tom Turpin's *Harlem Rag*, published in 1897.

Jazz Events

1898

- Will Marion Cook and Paul Lawrence Dunbar stage their revue *Clorindy: The Origin of the Cakewalk* on Broadway, and subsequently take it on tour to London.

1899

Summer

The publisher John Stark visits the Maple Leaf Club in Sedalia, Missouri, and hears its resident pianist, Scott Joplin, perform his *Maple Leaf Rag*. Stark signs a contract with Joplin on **10 August**, pays him an advance of $50 for the piece and immediately publishes it. It sells over one hundred thousand copies within a year of publication.

- Joplin publishes his *Original Rags* in Kansas City. The title page describes it as "picked by Scott Joplin," a reference to the figurations borrowed from BANJO music that characterize the RAGTIME style.
- Irving Jones publishes his song "I Don't Understand Ragtime" in New York.
- Baltimore pianist Eubie Blake composes his RAG *Sounds of Africa*.

1900

23 January

A CUTTING CONTEST between ragtime pianists is held at New York's Tammany Hall. The winner, Mike Bernard, receives the title "Champion Ragtime Pianist of the World."

May

Banjo player Vess Ossman performs *A Bunch of Rags* in London, where he attends a recording session. This year he also participates in two New York recording sessions.

- John Stark moves his business from Sedalia to St. Louis, and Joplin follows.
- Tom Turpin opens his Rosebud Café in St. Louis, which becomes a meeting place for jobbing pianists.
- John Philip Sousa takes his famous band on a European tour, performing ragtime arrangements at the Paris Exposition.

1895–1905

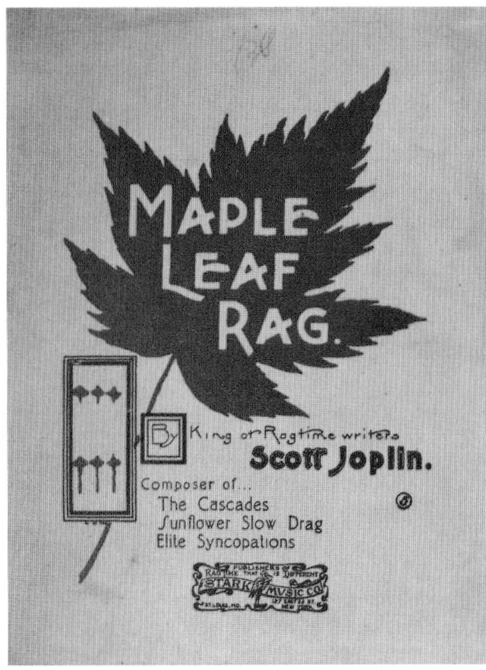

Above The title page of Scott Joplin's *Maple Leaf Rag* (1899).

RAGTIME

The popularity of SYNCOPATION in black music of the 1890s is apparent in RAGTIME, which derives its name from the image of "ragged" rhythmic patterns. Unlike the BLUES (and unlike later jazz), ragtime was pre-composed and circulated in printed form. It reflected the higher musical aspirations of the new generation of black musicians seeking to broaden their horizons after emancipation: along with their widespread commercial success, composers of ragtime such as Scott Joplin ultimately hoped that they would create a new black American classical music.

The ragtime style first appeared in songs with BANJO (later piano) accompaniment, but became famous when adapted for solo piano. Its pianistic origins lie in nineteenth-century salon music, especially in the work of Louis Moreau Gottschalk, who based some of his pieces on slave melodies; its sectionalized, repetitive structures were borrowed from the MARCH idiom popularized by John Philip Sousa, composer of *The Stars and Stripes Forever.* A typical ragtime texture consists of regular "oom-pah" patterns set up by the pianist's left hand (sometimes termed "boom-chick" after the alternating bass-drum and cymbal strokes in march RHYTHM), over which the right hand plays a highly syncopated melodic line. The HARMONY of ragtime may seem tame when compared with classical music of the same era, but the importation of BLUE NOTES from the blues (• p. 27) marked the next step toward the early jazz style.

Ragtime disappeared in the early 1920s when it was rapidly supplanted in popularity by New Orleans jazz, but it enjoyed revivals in the 1940s (• p. 116) and 1970s (• p. 181). It also directly spawned the most important of early jazz piano styles – the Harlem STRIDE school (• p. 46) of the 1920s.

Jazz Events

1901

January
A ragtime CUTTING CONTEST is held at Tomlinson Hall, Indianapolis, Indiana.

7 June
The Sousa Band records an orchestrated version of Gottschalk's piano piece *Pasquinade*. Originally composed around 1860, the work was a clear stylistic precursor of ragtime.

- Charles Booth records J. Bodewalt Lange's *Creole Belles* for the newly formed Victor recording label. This is the first ACOUSTIC RECORDING of a piano RAG to be commercially issued.
- The American Federation of Musicians votes to suppress ragtime.

1902

16 June
The Sousa Band records the NOVELTY ragtime number *Trombone Sneeze* under the direction of its composer, Arthur Pryor.

July
Lincoln Park opens in New Orleans and becomes a center for performances by ragtime and early jazz ensembles.

- Scott Joplin publishes *The Entertainer: A Ragtime Two-Step* (• p. 181), and composes his ballet *The Ragtime Dance*.
- The eccentric composer Charles Ives, an insurance salesman who also happens to be a musical genius, begins a set of four *Ragtime Dances* for piano or small orchestra. He is the first American classical composer to respond positively to the ragtime craze.
- Tony Jackson, a famous PROFESSOR (i.e., piano player who can read music) in STORYVILLE, composes his ragtime *Naked Dance*.
- The revue *Joyeux Nègres* is staged at the Nouveau Cirque, Paris.
- Decades later, Jelly Roll Morton claimed to have invented jazz single-handedly in this year – even though in 1902 he was only twelve years old!

1903

18 February
Scott Joplin registers the copyright of his unpublished (and now lost) ragtime opera *A Guest of Honor*, and takes it on tour.

- Eubie Blake publishes his first piano rags.
- *Maple Leaf Rag* is issued by Stark as a song, with lyrics by Sydney Brown.
- The Sousa Band performs at the British Royal court, and tours Prussia and Russia.

1904

22 February
Louis Chauvin wins the annual cutting contest organized by Tom Turpin at his Rosebud Café in St. Louis.

- Scott Joplin composes his rag *The Cascades* for the St. Louis World's Fair.
- Cornetist Buddy Bolden (• p. 25) is becoming established in New Orleans as the leading exponent of a musical style that fuses elements from ragtime and the blues: in a word, "jazz."

1905

- Joplin's *Bethena: A Concert Waltz* transforms the ragtime style into triple METER.
- Joseph Lamb publishes his first compositions, not yet in the rag idiom.
- Stark moves his company to New York, which is becoming established as the major music publishing center.
- Jerome H. Remick founds his publishing house in Detroit and New York, going on to publish over three hundred ragtime pieces.
- A black newspaper in Indianapolis strikes out against the racism of coon songs, and declares: "Composers should not set music to a set of words that are a direct insult to the colored race."
- Jelly Roll Morton (• p. 45) claimed to have composed his *Jelly Roll Blues* in this year.

SCOTT JOPLIN: THE ENTERTAINER

The most famous composer of piano rags was born in 1868, the son of an ex-slave who worked the railroads and his banjo-playing wife. Joplin learned classical music from an immigrant German teacher and forged a career for himself as a pianist, appearing at the Chicago World's Fair in 1893. He settled in Sedalia, Missouri, where he was employed as house pianist at the Maple Leaf Club. It was here that he was discovered in 1899 by publisher John Stark, whose edition of Joplin's *Maple Leaf Rag* met with such commercial success that the two men moved to St. Louis and prospered. Stark's publishing house also promoted the work of Joseph Lamb (1887–1962) and James Scott (1886–1918) who, together with Joplin, became established as the so-called Missouri School of "classic" ragtime composers. They did their best to keep ragtime restrained and refined, but were ultimately swept into obscurity by the jazz craze. Stark's company went out of business in 1922, but not before he published many of the finest hits of the ragtime era.

Joplin's rags include the famous *Pineapple Rag* and *The Entertainer*, both of which show his mastery of an essentially limited genre. Later in his career, he attempted to branch out into more ambitious compositional projects, such as ragtime ballet and opera. After moving in 1907 to New York, which was rapidly becoming the center of the popular-music industry, Joplin channeled his energies into the creation of what was to be his final stage work, an opera with an all-black cast entitled *Treemonisha*. Published at his own expense and performed privately in Harlem in 1915, the work flopped badly and the composer's resulting nervous breakdown and deep-seated bitterness precipitated his early death in 1917. It was 1972 before *Treemonisha* was rescued from obscurity and given a public performance (• p. 178). Shortly afterward, Joplin's complete works were published and the composer was awarded a posthumous Pulitzer Prize.

World Events

1901

- Death of Queen Victoria and accession of Edward VII
- Picasso's first exhibition, Paris
- Assassination of President William McKinley, USA
- Nobel Prizes instituted
- Giuseppe Verdi dies

1902

- Émile Zola dies
- Boer War ends

1903

- Wright brothers' first flight, USA
- Paul Gauguin dies

1904

- Antonin Dvořák dies
- Anton Chekhov dies
- Completion of Trans-Siberian Railway

1905

- Civil unrest in Russia
- Einstein's theory of relativity
- Norway gains independence from Sweden
- End of Russo-Japanese war

Above A pensive study of Scott Joplin, who aimed to transform ragtime into a kind of black classical music.

Above left A photograph from the first professional production of Joplin's opera *Treemonisha*, performed at Houston Grand Opera in 1975.

1906–9

As the ragtime craze peaks and begins to influence composers of classical music, New Orleans establishes itself as the cradle of the emerging jazz style.

NEW ORLEANS: THE MUSICAL MELTING POT

"**He was the blowingest man ever lived since Gabriel. They claim he went crazy because he really blew his brains out through the trumpet.**"

Jelly Roll Morton on Buddy Bolden

Jazz Events

1906

26 March
Buddy Bolden attacks his mother-in-law and is placed under medical supervision.

- James Scott meets Scott Joplin in St. Louis. John Stark publishes Scott's *Frog Legs Rag*, and Joplin prepares an orchestral version.
- Stark publishes Joplin's ballet *The Ragtime Dance* in a truncated version for solo piano.
- Jelly Roll Morton composes his *King Porter Stomp* which, more than two decades later, becomes a smash hit in the Swing Era (• p. 83).
- New Orleans trumpeters Freddie Keppard and Bunk Johnson begin to make names for themselves.

1907

13 March
Buddy Bolden is arrested and, three months later, committed to an asylum for the insane. His promising career is cut short, and the first jazz legend passes into obscurity without having entered the recording studio.

- Joseph Lamb meets Joplin and Stark; the latter publishes Lamb's *Sensation Rag*.
- As part of a growing migration northward and eastward, pianist Tony Jackson heads for Chicago and Scott Joplin moves to New York.
- Jelly Roll Morton later claimed to have invented SCAT singing in this year.

Left Canal Street, New Orleans, *c.* 1905.

FUNKY BUTT HALL: NEW ORLEANS AND STORYVILLE

Although the term "funky" is today associated with musical earthiness, its original meaning was strong bodily odor. The aptly named Funky Butt Hall was one of numerous houses of pleasure in New Orleans that provided employment for RAGTIME and early jazz musicians. It was located on the outskirts of the red-light district known as STORYVILLE, bordered by Canal Street and the railroad, which offered various services to visiting sailors and doubtless many others.

"The District," as it was universally known, was named after Alderman Story who boldly initiated legislation in 1897 regulating prostitution in the city. The region comprised thirty-eight blocks, and was sufficiently well organized to issue its own consumers' guide, known as *The Blue Book* (published by Tom Anderson). Over two thousand women plied their trade in the "Tenderloin," as it was also known, and Creole musicians could find plenty of work in ragtime bands, as solo pianists, or in other small groups. Men from fairly respectable backgrounds, including Jelly Roll Morton and Sidney Bechet (• p. 43), worked there in secret, not wanting their families to know. (Morton's grandmother discovered the truth, however, and slung her grandson, then only fifteen, out of their house.) Other notable musicians who started their careers in Storyville include King Oliver (• p. 48) and Louis Armstrong (• p. 57). Many famous early jazz compositions took their titles from streets in the region ("Basin Street Blues"), or from the names of specific establishments ("Mahogany Hall Stomp" was Armstrong's tribute to Lulu White's sporting house).

Storyville was a haven particularly for ragtime pianists. According to Clarence Williams, the PROFESSORS who entertained clients on honky-tonk instruments sometimes doubled as pimps, conveniently observing professional activities as they played. Two of the best-known pianists were Kid Ross at Lulu White's (one of the most lavishly appointed venues of all, catering for the affluent and priding itself on Miss Lulu's "lifelong study of music and literature"), and Tony Jackson at Gypsy Schaeffer's. Morton recalled that Jackson's ***Naked Dance*** was a ragtime favorite, played at a rapid tempo to accompany the girls' nude dancing on a small stage while onlookers sipped champagne.

In 1917, Storyville was closed down following pressure from the US Navy. The closure was one factor encouraging musicians to migrate northward to Chicago (• p. 65) in search of work, although an exodus from the South had already been in progress for some time because of increasing economic depression in the region. Storyville's mythical status as the colorful progenitor of early jazz has probably led to its importance having been overstressed: much fine music was developed at more salubrious establishments elsewhere in the city and, indeed, elsewhere in America.

World Events

1906

- Eruption of Mount Vesuvius, Pompeii
- San Francisco and Chile earthquakes
- British suffragettes imprisoned
- Deaths of Paul Cézanne and Henrik Ibsen

1907

- British reject proposal for Channel Tunnel
- Death of Edvard Grieg
- Rudyard Kipling receives Nobel Prize for Literature
- First wireless broadcast of classical music, New York

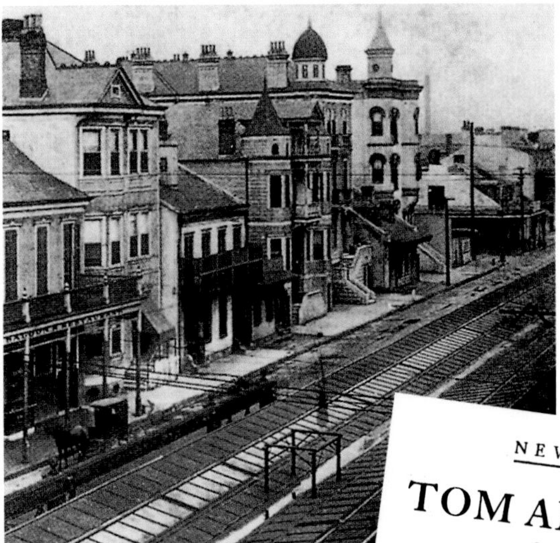

Above Basin Street, New Orleans, showing the adjacent railroad and (at far left) part of Tom Anderson's Annex.

Right Music and sex are the prime commodities on offer in this 1906 advertisement for Anderson's establishment.

NEVER CLOSED
TOM ANDERSON'S
Annex
COR. BASIN & IBERVILLE STS.
NOTED THE STATES OVER *for* BEING THE BEST CONDUCTED CAFE *in* AMERICA

PRIVATE ROOMS *for the* FAIR SEX
MUSIC NIGHTLY
PHONES: 2253-Y & 2993-W
BILLY STRUVE, *Manager*

1906–9

Jazz Events

1908

18 December
First performance of French composer Claude Debussy's piano suite *Children's Corner*, which emulates the RAGTIME idiom in its "Golliwogg's Cakewalk."

- Scott Joplin, his relationship with Stark deteriorating, publishes his *Pineapple Rag* with the Seminary Music Co. in New York. He also issues his *School of Ragtime: Six Exercises for Piano* this year.
- George Botsford composes his NOVELTY *Black and White Rag*, published in New York by Jerome H. Remick. In the 1970s, it becomes a hit as the theme tune to the BBC television snooker program *Pot Black*, in a virtuoso arrangement by Winifred Atwell.
- Freddie Keppard begins to take his New Orleans band on tour. Other early jazz figures becoming prominent at around this time include cornetist Joe "King" Oliver (• p. 48), also based in New Orleans.

1909

15 June
The Victor Dance Band records Botsford's *Black and White Rag* in New York.

- The band of the US Marines records Joplin's *Maple Leaf Rag*. Joplin publishes *Solace: A Mexican Serenade* in New York.
- Ragtime publication and the output of instruments from piano manufacturers both peak.
- Charles Ives completes his Piano Sonata No. 1, incorporating an outrageously jazzy section. This prophetic work, in which jazz elements are surrealistically distorted, is not performed in public until 1949.

Above The front cover of James Scott's *Frog Legs Rag*, published by John Stark in 1906.

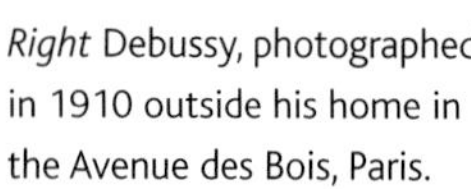

Right Debussy, photographed in 1910 outside his home in the Avenue des Bois, Paris.

DEBUSSY DISCOVERS RAGTIME

The development of classical music in the nineteenth century was dominated by composers working in Germany and Austria, and was seen by many at the turn of the century to have reached its height in the operas of Richard Wagner. Although in his youth Claude Debussy (1862–1918) had been an ardent admirer of Wagner's music, the French composer eventually broke away from Austro-German musical techniques by cultivating an innovative style of musical impressionism. In the process, he laid the foundations for the extraordinary diversity in composition that characterizes twentieth-century music.

Debussy probably heard ragtime when the famous band led by John Philip Sousa appeared at the 1900 Paris Exposition as part of a European tour. The crisp clarity of the idiom must have appealed to Debussy's growing sense of anti-romanticism, and he went on to emulate the ragtime style in three piano pieces. The best known of these is "Golliwogg's Cakewalk" (part of his *Children's Corner* suite, completed in 1908), which includes an incongruous quotation from Wagner's opera *Tristan und Isolde*. Debussy returned to the ragtime style in two later piano preludes: "Minstrels" (1910) and "General Lavine – excentric" (1913), the latter inspired by the antics of a clown from the Médrano Circus. Debussy's music, and that of his younger contemporary Maurice Ravel, came in turn to influence a later generation of jazz musicians. The advanced harmonies of French impressionism, which included the emphasis of attractive 7th, 9th, and 11th CHORDS in unconventional ways, became the staple harmonic vocabulary of both big-band and bop idioms (• p. 97), while Debussy's pioneering modal techniques exerted a major influence on the work of Miles Davis and Bill Evans in the 1950s (• p. 147).

World Events

1908

- Alcohol banned in North Carolina and Georgia, USA
- Assassination of King Carlos I of Portugal
- Death of Nikolai Rimsky-Korsakov

1909

- Alcohol banned in Tennessee, USA
- Louis Blériot flies across English Channel
- Joan of Arc canonized
- Robert Peary reaches North Pole

THE FIRST LEGEND OF JAZZ: BUDDY BOLDEN

The figure of Buddy Bolden, the cornetist who is reputed to have been the most influential of the early jazz musicians, is shrouded in mystery: only one photograph of him survives (above). In 1907 he was committed to the state lunatic asylum in Jackson, Louisiana, for smashing a jug on his mother-in-law's head, and he died in the same institution in 1931 – never having recorded his performances for posterity.

A builder by trade, Bolden had devoted his energies almost entirely to music by the turn of the century (retaining, however, some strength for his inveterate womanizing and carousing, and for the alcoholism that led to his mental breakdown). His ensemble of six instrumentalists reflected the standard FRONT LINE and RHYTHM SECTION format of early New Orleans groups (• p. 37).

Bolden is said to have imbued the ragtime style with elements borrowed from the rougher, improvised BLUES, and to have developed the improvised melodic embellishments so characteristic of New Orleans jazz. He played at such a piercingly loud volume, it reportedly caused parts of his instrument to eject themselves into mid-air.

Bolden's manner of playing was later reproduced by his protégé Bunk Johnson during the 1940s revival of early jazz styles (• p. 116), although by then it must have been virtually impossible to strip away the accumulated musical developments of four decades and achieve a truly authentic imitation.

Above The first page of Debussy's rag-influenced "Golliwogg's Cakewalk," clearly showing the "oom-pah" figurations in the left hand and syncopated melody in the right.

Jazz Events

1910

- John Stark moves his company back to St. Louis from New York.
- Scott Joplin's *Pineapple Rag* is issued as a song, with lyrics by Joe Snyder.
- King Oliver plays professionally in STORYVILLE.
- James Reese Europe (• p. 41) founds the Clef Club, an association for black musicians based in New York.
- Claude Debussy again emulates the RAGTIME style in "Minstrels" (*Préludes pour piano,* Book II).

The blues, widely disseminated by the work of W. C. Handy, strengthens its influence on early jazz as the popularity of ragtime begins to decline.

THE IMPACT OF THE BLUES

Above An advertisement for James Reese Europe's Clef Club, founded in 1910 to promote the interests of black musicians.

Right Europe attempts to conduct members of his Clef Club Orchestra (who seem to have no intention of playing!) in a publicity shot dating from c. 1914. The cluster of posed banjos in the foreground is notable.

W. C. HANDY AND THE BLUES

Unlike ragtime, the BLUES was IMPROVISED music and did not initially circulate in printed form. The genre ultimately derived from plantation songs, and may be considered a secular counterpart of the SPIRITUALS popularized in the black church at around the same time. Originally sung unaccompanied, the CALL-AND-RESPONSE patterns typical of slave music were soon incorporated in the genre by the trading of melodic phrases between a solo voice and a single accompanying instrument, usually guitar (a format retained in the modern country blues).

By the turn of the century, a typical blues would be based on a melancholy text organized in verses of three lines (of which the first two were identical, and the third rhymed with them). The following example comes from a blues song recorded in the 1930s by Robert Johnson, one of the finest singers to hail from the Mississippi Delta:

> I got stones in my pathway and my road seems dark at night,
> I got stones in my pathway and my road seems dark at night,
> I have pains in my heart, they have taken my appetite.

Other examples, such as those regularly sung by Bessie Smith (• p. 67), were more lighthearted, and often featured extensive sexual innuendo and a broad vein of comedy.

Since no examples of blues singing were recorded until the 1920s, it is impossible to reach definite conclusions about the genre's stylistic origins. It seems incontrovertible, however, that the improvised vocal melody would from the outset have been characterized by BLUE NOTES (• p. 18). These probably inspired the simple harmonies that later became standardized as the TWELVE-BAR BLUES progression fundamental to much later jazz, since these CHORDS are often extended to include the blue dominant-seventh notes.

The first published examples of the blues were copyrighted by the bandleader W. C. Handy, who issued his *Memphis Blues* in 1912 and *St. Louis Blues* two years later. Handy's pre-composed piano accompaniments, replacing the improvised guitar parts of live blues performances, show how the blues and ragtime styles were already beginning to merge in anticipation of the birth of jazz. During the 1920s, the blues became a recognized sub-genre of jazz through the wide circulation of recordings made by singers such as Mamie Smith (• p. 44), Ma Rainey (• p. 53), and Bessie Smith, who earned herself the nickname "Empress of the Blues." It also spawned the development of the BOOGIE-WOOGIE style of piano playing, which enjoyed a popular revival in the 1940s.

Left W. C. Handy at the piano in later life. Almost blinded in a subway accident in 1943, he died in 1958 – the year in which Nat King Cole portrayed him in the Paramount biopic *St. Louis Blues*.

Jazz Events

1911

May
Scott Joplin publishes, at his own expense, his RAGTIME opera *Treemonisha* in New York.

7 June
Irving Berlin's song "Alexander's Ragtime Band" (• p. 29), published by Ted Snyder & Co., is recorded in New York. It is a phenomenal success, but is detested by classic ragtime composers for what they see as its commercial dilution of the idiom.

- Trombonist Kid Ory and clarinetist Sidney Bechet (• p. 43), among other musicians based in New Orleans, begin to establish their reputations.

1912

August
W. C. Handy publishes his *Memphis Blues: A Southern Rag*, which begins to popularize the blues.

- Jerome H. Remick publishes an important anthology of orchestrated ragtime.
- Singer Bessie Smith joins F. S. Wolcott's "Rabbit Foot Minstrels."
- Kid Ory is leading his own band in New Orleans, where Armand Piron succeeds Freddie Keppard as leader of the Olympia Orchestra and hires King Oliver.
- James P. Johnson, later to become the "Father of STRIDE Piano" (• p. 46), turns professional and plays as a cinema pianist at the Nickelette in New York.
- Drummer Louis Mitchell forms his Southern Symphony Quintet in New York.
- Recordings are made of calypso music from Trinidad.

1910–13

Jazz Events

1913

1 January
Twelve-year-old Louis Armstrong is arrested for firing a shot in the air during a fit of high spirits in New Orleans.

29 December
James Reese Europe records RAGTIME arrangements in New York with his Society Orchestra, which becomes the first black ensemble to record.

- Freddie Keppard takes his Original Creole Orchestra on tour.
- Mamie Smith starts singing in New York clubs.
- As the popularity of ragtime begins to dwindle, Artie Matthews publishes his first *Pastime Rag* and Luckey Roberts composes his *Junk Man Rag*.
- Canon Newboldt of St. Paul's Cathedral, London, preaches that ragtime is "indecent . . . suggestive of evil and destructive of modesty."
- The word "jaz" [*sic*] appears in print for the first time. In an article published in the *San Francisco Bulletin*, it is defined as "anything that takes manliness or effort or energy or activity or strength of soul."

World Events

1910

- Marie Curie isolates radium
- Eruption of Mount Etna, Sicily
- Deaths of Leo Tolstoy, Mark Twain, and King Edward VII

1911

- Civil War in Mexico
- Roald Amundsen reaches South Pole
- Italy at war with Turkey
- Death of Gustav Mahler

1912

- Sinking of the *Titanic*
- Unrest in the Balkans
- First Pathé newsreels
- Deaths of August Strindberg and Jules Massenet

1913

- Balkan wars escalate
- Igor Stravinsky composes *The Rite of Spring*

"Those parades were really tremendous things. The drums would start off, the trumpets and trombones rolling into something like 'Stars and Stripes' . . . You see, whenever a parade would get to another district the enemy would be waiting at the dividing line. If the parade crossed that line it meant a fight, a terrible fight . . . Sometimes it would require a couple of ambulances to pick up the people that was maybe cut or shot occasionally . . . And [there was] always plenty to eat and drink, especially for the men in the band, and with bands like Happy Galloway's, Manuel Perez's, and Buddy Bolden's we had the best ragtime music in the world. There was so many jobs for musicians in these parades that musicians didn't ever like to leave New Orleans."

Jelly Roll Morton

Right The arrow indicates the young Louis Armstrong, participating in the brass band of the Colored Waifs' Home in New Orleans, *c.* 1913.

MARCHING BANDS

New Orleans at the turn of the century was a flourishing hub of musical activity. Predominant among black ensembles were the celebrated marching bands, which provided music for funeral ceremonies and other outdoor events. Many early jazz musicians gained their formative musical experiences by playing in these groups, which offered one of the few sources of paid employment to black musicians.

A typical band comprised cornets, trombones, clarinets, tubas, and drums. Not surprisingly, these instruments (all cheaply available secondhand) were soon favored in the make up of early jazz ensembles. Somber music accompanied the procession to the cemetery, but an exuberant version of ragtime – a style itself originally based on MARCHES (• p. 20) – would be performed on the return trip and at the prolonged feasting afterward.

Right The Onward Brass Band in New Orleans, *c.* 1913. From 1903 to 1930 this celebrated ensemble was led by cornetist and cigar-maker Manuel Perez (far left), who also played at Storyville's Mahogany Hall.

Above Front cover of Irving Berlin's hit song "Alexander's Ragtime Band," published in 1911.

TIN PAN ALLEY

By the last decade of the nineteenth century, New York had become the powerful center of the music-publishing industry in the United States. The publishers, whose premises were largely concentrated on "Tin Pan Alley" (West 28th Street), were quick to capitalize on the growing popularity of VAUDEVILLE. They employed song PLUGGERS to promote their recent merchandise, and from the 1920s onward they fostered the fashion for musical comedies on Broadway. Both George Gershwin and Irving Berlin started their careers as humble song pluggers before going on to establish themselves as two of the finest popular songwriters of their era, alongside Jerome Kern and Cole Porter. All four composers contributed innumerable STANDARDS to the jazz repertoire.

Relations between jazz musicians and the publishers of Tin Pan Alley were not always cordial, however. Berlin's hit song "Alexander's Ragtime Band" (• p. 27) was disliked by ragtime composers, in spite (or perhaps because) of its popularity; and Kern heartily detested attempts to "jazz up" his songs (• p. 55), commenting that "no author would permit pirated editions of his work in which his phraseology and punctuation were changed." For impoverished jazz musicians, Tin Pan Alley often provided a welcome source of immediate income: it was by no means uncommon for musicians to compose a song or two in a taxi en route to a publisher's, the manuscript ready on arrival for an instant sale.

ON THE VERGE OF JAZZ

"FULL OF ORIGINALITY"
THE "JELLY ROLL" BLUES
(FOX-TROT)
BY
FERD MORTON
AUTHOR OF "THE "JELLY ROLL" BLUES" SONG

Ragtime enjoys its final flowering in a spate of recordings on piano rolls, while a white band from New Orleans takes Chicago by storm and ushers in the jazz craze.

Jazz Events

1914

- Louis Mitchell's Southern Symphony Quintet visits London to play their version of RAGTIME. They return to England in the following year after a tour of the USA.
- Fifteen-year-old George Gershwin leaves the New York High School for Commerce and begins work for Jerome H. Remick's publishing firm on Tin Pan Alley for $15 per week. His activities as a song PLUGGER lead to a deep empathy for popular song styles.
- W. C. Handy publishes his *St. Louis Blues* and *Yellow Dog Rag*. The latter was originally entitled *Yellow Dog Blues*, an indication of the interchangeability of the two genre labels in this period.
- Edward Kennedy "Duke" Ellington composes his *Soda Fountain Rag*.
- James P. Johnson hears Eubie Blake play in Atlantic City, New Jersey.
- The *Ragtime Review* begins monthly publication.

1915

15 September

Jelly Roll Morton publishes *Jelly Roll Blues*, the first work in a genuine jazz style to appear in print. Morton claims publication is necessary to introduce the new idiom to musicians outside New Orleans.

- In New Orleans, clarinetists Jimmie Noone and Johnny Dodds begin to make their names.
- Scott Joplin stages his ragtime opera, *Treemonisha*, in Harlem at his own expense, and receives only a lukewarm response.
- Luckey Roberts composes his tango *Spanish Venus*, an early example of what Morton terms the "Latin tinge" in jazz (• p. 114).
- Joseph Lamb composes his romantic *Ragtime Nightingale*, a piece that demonstrates ragtime's indebtedness to nineteenth-century classical piano music.
- John Stark issues his orchestral anthology *Standard High-Class Rags*.
- Joe Jordan plays ragtime in London.

Far left Although he allegedly composed it in 1905, Morton did not copyright his *Jelly Roll Blues* until 1915.

Opposite The premises of Jerome H. Remick & Co. on Tin Pan Alley, where Gershwin worked between 1914 and 1917.

Below The teenage George Gershwin during his time as a song plugger at Remick's publishing house.

MUSIC PUBLISHERS
45
WHITNEY WARNER
DETROIT MUSIC NEW YORK
WHITNEY WARNER
MUSIC
PRINTER
PPER
MUSIC PUBLISHERS.
LIPPER.
JEROME H. REMICK & COMPANY
NEW YORK CLIPPER
WILLIAM
MORRIS
45
MUSIC
PUBLISHERS
MUSIC
PUBLISHERS
JEROME H. REMICK & COMPANY.
WHITNEY WARNER PUBLISHING CO.
THOMAS YOUNG JR
THOMAS YOUNG JR

RAGS ON ROLLS

Recording technology before the advent of the electrical process in the 1920s was a primitive affair. Performers played into a large horn that transmitted the vibrations of their music directly to a needle cutting a groove on a wax master (a revolving cylinder or rotating disc). This process, developed independently by Thomas Edison and Alexander Graham Bell in the 1880s, resulted in recordings of wildly varying quality and limited sensitivity to dynamic contrasts.

Pianists generally preferred to record using the medium of the PIANO ROLL, which became popular at the turn of the century. A live performance at the keyboard was recorded as a series of perforations on a roll of paper, which could then be "read" by a special player-piano (i.e., pianola), which converted the pattern on the roll into a close approximation of the original mechanical action of the keys. Numerous RAGTIME pieces were preserved in this manner, including the only known recordings by Scott Joplin (• p. 21). The clattering action of the pianola was well suited to the reproduction of fast, virtuosic pieces, and this may have been one factor behind the development of a more exciting ragtime style, which left the restrained "classic" ragtime of Joplin and his associates far behind and culminated in the exuberant music of the Harlem STRIDE school.

A piano roll did not necessarily provide a faithful reproduction of a live performance, however. Technicians could easily add extra notes in the workshop and, in some cases, the entire "performance" could be fabricated without the use of a keyboard. The pianola system rapidly declined after the arrival of electrical recording in 1925 (• p. 59), when performers such as James P. Johnson (• p. 46) abandoned the old method in favor of live studio recordings.

Right A selection of original labels for piano rolls, with part of the roll for James P. Johnson's *Caprice Rag* shown above. This was released in 1917, along with Johnson's *Innovation* and *After To-Night*. Wilbur Sweatman's *Down Home Rag* dates from c. 1912, and Roy Bargy's novelty *Omeomy* from 1920; Gershwin recorded his *Rialto Ripples* in 1916 (• p. 89).

Jazz Events

1916

3 March
Johnny Stein's Dixie Jass Band appears at Schiller's Café on East 31st Street, Chicago. Stein is deposed as leader in June, whereupon the group renames itself the Original Dixieland Jass Band under cornetist Nick LaRocca (• p. 37).

1 May
Stein's Dixie Jass Band is reviewed in the *Chicago Herald*.

9 October
The Chicago Piano Players' Social Club holds a ragtime CUTTING CONTEST and ball.

- Scott Joplin embarks on a substantial series of recordings on piano rolls, including *Maple Leaf Rag*. Nervous illness following the failure of *Treemonisha* forces him to enter Manhattan State Hospital for treatment.
- Luckey Roberts makes his recording debut, becoming the first black artist to record in the stride style.
- James P. Johnson begins cutting piano rolls for the Aeolian piano manufacturing company in New York.

THE TRUMPET FAMILY

Many might argue, with some justification, that the trumpet has been the most influential instrument in the history of jazz (pianists and saxophonists would doubtless disagree). Certainly the predominance of the trumpet – and its mellower cousin, the cornet – in the New Orleans marching bands (• p. 29) allowed it to assume the principal melodic role in early jazz ensembles. The earliest jazz practitioners, such as Buddy Bolden (• p. 25), stimulated the development of novel performance techniques that had scarcely been dreamt of during the trumpet's limited treatment in classical music. Jazz trumpeters employed a variety of contrasting timbres for expressive effect, including the GROWL and experimentation with a variety of MUTES, first undertaken by King Oliver (• p. 48). The instrument's range dramatically increased, and in the work of Louis Armstrong (• p. 57) it showed itself capable of dazzling virtuosity.

The size of the trumpet section in the big bands of the 1930s and 1940s swelled to four or five. Meanwhile, solo performers such as Roy Eldridge followed on from Armstrong's example and cultivated increasingly rapid figurations and piercingly high notes, both characteristics of BEBOP trumpet playing epitomized in the work of Dizzy Gillespie (• p. 219). Aware of the natural agility of the competing saxophone, trumpeters did their best to keep up with the escalating pace of jazz in the later 1940s and 1950s, until Miles Davis (• p. 217) turned away from vacuous pyrotechnics to espouse a restrained, emotionally neutral idiom characterized by an absence of VIBRATO. This development influenced the emergence of COOL jazz (• p. 121), and in particular the playing of Chet Baker (• p. 210). Davis also introduced the haunting sound of the HARMON MUTE, which was later adopted by many other soloists.

Also important was the flugelhorn, a relative of the bugle with a range identical to that of the cornet. Although used in jazz as early as the 1930s, the flugelhorn's mellow tone came into its own during the boom in cool jazz in the 1950s, when both Davis and Baker temporarily adopted it. Perhaps the most impressive exponent of the instrument was Thad Jones, who led one of the most exciting big bands of the 1960s (• p. 162) and whose popular composition "A Child is Born" derived much of its character from the rich and expressive tone of his instrument. There have been few influential developments in trumpet technique since the 1960s, although Don Cherry's use of a tiny "pocket" trumpet is noteworthy.

World Events

1914

- Assassination of Archduke Franz Ferdinand of Austria and beginning of World War I
- Foundation of American Society of Composers, Authors, and Publishers

1915

- Gallipoli campaign
- Nurse Edith Cavell shot by Germans
- Deaths of Rupert Brooke and Alexander Scriabin

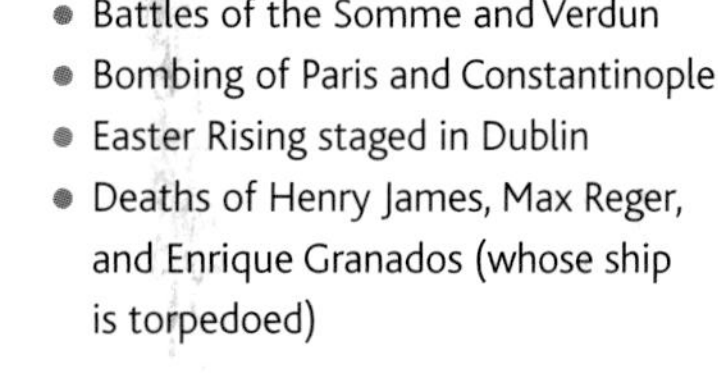

1916

- Battles of the Somme and Verdun
- Bombing of Paris and Constantinople
- Easter Rising staged in Dublin
- Deaths of Henry James, Max Reger, and Enrique Granados (whose ship is torpedoed)

Left A modern trumpet in B^b (front), with its close cousins the cornet (right) and flugelhorn (left).

Opposite Jelly Roll Morton's Red Hot Peppers, photographed in Chicago in 1926 (l. to r.): Andrew Hilaire (drums), Kid Ory (trombone), George Mitchell (cornet), Johnny Lindsay (bass), Jelly Roll Morton (piano), Johnny St. Cyr (banjo), and Omer Simeon (clarinet).

From New Orleans to the East Coast:
An exodus of musicians from old New Orleans spreads jazz throughout the USA, first to Chicago and then New York, while some enterprising performers cross the Atlantic to stimulate the growing European demand for the new music.

1929

1917

The spectacular success of the first jazz record, cut by the Original Dixieland Jass Band from New Orleans, threatens to sweep ragtime aside.

ALL THAT JAZZ

Jazz Events

27 January
The Original Dixieland Jass Band, a white group from New Orleans, performs in Manhattan.

30 January
The Original Dixieland Jass Band records two SIDES in a trial session for Columbia. The company declines to issue the tunes, which would have been the first recorded jazz.

2 February
The word "jazz" (often spelled "jass" in these early years) appears in print in *The New York Times*.

26 February
The Original Dixieland Jass Band records "Livery Stable Blues" and "Dixieland Jass Band One-step" in the studios of Victor. Further recordings follow in **August**, **September**, and **November**.

February
Louis Mitchell's Syncopating Sextette appears in Glasgow. His Seven Spades appear in London later in the year.

7 March
Victor issues the two sides recorded by the Original Dixieland Jass Band in February. These are the first jazz recordings to be made available to the public, and the witty farmyard-animal imitations in "Livery Stable Blues" help the release to become an instant commercial success.

March
George Gershwin leaves Jerome H. Remick & Co. to work on Broadway.

Above The New Orleans Rhythm Kings, Chicago, 1923. At the far right is Voltaire de Faut (C-melody saxophone), who recorded a fine duet with Jelly Roll Morton in May 1925. Morton, although not in this photograph, played piano for N.O.R.K. recordings made in July 1923.

Left The Original Dixieland Jass Band, Chicago, 1917: Henry Ragas (piano), Larry Shields (clarinet), Eddie Edwards (trombone), Nick LaRocca (cornet), and Tony Sbarbaro (drums).

DOWN SOUTH IN DIXIE

The first band to make recordings billed as "jazz" was in many ways untypical of early groups, not least because it comprised five white men under the leadership of cornetist Nick LaRocca. The quintet hailed from New Orleans and derived its style from the music played there by black ensembles, achieving a rapid rise to prominence through spirited performances that incorporated novelty instrumental effects such as animal imitations. The group's success was an early (and by no means only) example of the white commercialization of black music, and their recordings appear embarrassingly crude alongside the finesse of comparable black groups who recorded in the early 1920s.

Firmly based on the sectionalized structure and syncopated MARCH rhythms of RAGTIME, with increasing use of the TWELVE-BAR BLUES progression, the New Orleans ensemble style is correctly termed DIXIELAND only when performed by white groups (the term derives from the nickname "Dixie," used to describe the southern secessionist states in the Civil War). Dixieland music sometimes incorporated improvised BREAKS, an important development away from the pre-composed nature of ragtime. The normal arrangement included three solo melody instruments – cornet, clarinet, and trombone – which simultaneously performed different embellished versions of the melody. This elaboration constituted another notable departure from traditional ragtime. The melodic embellishments were supported by a RHYTHM SECTION – a bass instrument (tuba or double bass), HARMONY instrument (BANJO, guitar, or piano), and simple drum kit (typically bass drum, side drum, and suspended cymbal).

White groups were generally less adept at handling IMPROVISATION, BLUE NOTES, and SWUNG RHYTHM than their black counterparts, although the New Orleans Rhythm Kings (who made recordings in 1922–25) represented a tangible improvement on the primitive idiom of the Original Dixieland Jass Band. Both groups had disbanded by 1925, by which time black ensembles had gained the ascendancy they merited.

JASS OR JAZZ?

The exact etymology of the word "jazz" (which first appeared in print in a San Francisco newspaper in 1913) is impossible to establish, but its early connotations were undoubtedly sexual. The most likely derivation is from "orgasm," which in slang usage was shortened to "jasm" or "jism." The word "jass" had become synonymous with fornication, and its original application to the new musical genre was decidedly uncomplimentary (e.g., "that godawful jass music"). Around 1915, several bands provocatively adopted the expletive in their names, and it immediately caught on. Legend has it that the Original Dixieland Jass Band changed the spelling because pranksters often deleted the letter "j" from their posters!

The following alternative (and less convincing) etymological derivations have been proposed:

- Jasmine (the practice of adding it to perfumes in New Orleans led to the phrase "jassing it up")
- *Jaser* (a verb in the French dialect spoken in Louisiana, meaning "to chatter")
- *Yas* or *jasi* (African words for acting energetically, or out of character)
- Jas. or Chas. (i.e., abbreviations for James and Charles)
- Jasper (a famous dancing slave in New Orleans in the 1820s)
- Jasbo (referring to Jasbo Brown, a black musician in Chicago)

Below The front cover of a Victor Records catalog issued in March 1917 lists the variety of spellings to which the word "jazz" was subjected in these early years.

Special List
New Victor Records
Jass Band and other
Dance Selections
The Original Dixieland Jass Band
SPELL it Jass, Jas, Jaz or Jazz—nothing can spoil a Jass band. Some say the Jass band originated in Chicago. Chicago says it comes from San Francisco—San Francisco being away off across the continent. Anyway, a Jass band is the newest thing in the cabarets, adding greatly to the hilarity thereof.
They say the first instrument of the first Jass band was an empty lard can, by humming into which, sounds were produced resembling those of a saxophone with the croup. Since then the Jass band has grown in size and ferocity, and only

1917

"The word [jazz] never lost its association with those New Orleans bordellos. In the 1920s I used to try to convince Fletcher Henderson that we ought to call what we were doing 'Negro music.' But it's too late for that now."

Duke Ellington, 1976

Jazz Events

1 April
Death of Scott Joplin (• p. 21) in New York.

18 May
Erik Satie's ballet *Parade*, based on a scenario by Jean Cocteau (with set designs by Picasso), is given its first performance in Paris by Diaghilev's Ballets Russes. The score uses the RAGTIME idiom and quotes from a song by Irving Berlin in a section depicting "a little American girl."

21 September
W. C. Handy's Orchestra of Memphis embarks on a series of recordings in New York, including (on **25 September**) their interpretation of "Livery Stable Blues."

12 November
The US Navy closes down the red-light district of STORYVILLE, New Orleans. Many ragtime and jazz musicians leave the city to seek employment elsewhere.

- Clarinetist Sidney Bechet settles in Chicago and plays with King Oliver and Freddie Keppard.

Right Costume designs by Picasso for Erik Satie's ballet *Parade*, first staged in 1917.

World Events

16 March
Czar Nicholas II abdicates, Russia

6 April
US enters World War I

31 July
Third battle for Ypres

26 September
Death of Edgar Degas

6 November
Passchendaele captured by British and Canadian forces

7 November
Lenin's Bolsheviks assume power in Russia after the October Revolution

10 December
The Vatican forbids Roman Catholics to dance the tango

1918

RAGTIME GOES ABROAD

Already outmoded in the US, ragtime enjoys a final flowering in Europe and influences classical composer Igor Stravinsky.

Jazz Events

February–March
James Reese Europe tours twenty-five French cities with "The Hellfighters," the RAGTIME band of the 369th US Infantry.

25 March
The Original Dixieland Jazz Band (• p. 37) records four SIDES in New York, including Nick LaRocca's hit "Tiger Rag." They make further recordings later in the year.

28 September
First performance of Russian composer Igor Stravinsky's music-theater piece *The Soldier's Tale*, which includes a movement entitled "Ragtime" (• p. 43).

November
Louis Armstrong (• p. 57) begins work in bands performing on the Mississippi riverboats, including a famous group led by Fate Marable that performs on vessels sailing out of St. Louis. In this year Armstrong also replaces King Oliver (who moves to Chicago) in Kid Ory's band, based in New Orleans.

December
The Louisiana Five record on the Emerson label in New York.

- Jelly Roll Morton (• p. 45), who is working in California, copyrights his *Frog-i-More Rag*.

Above Louis Armstrong (third from right) in Fate Marable's band on the steamboat *SS Capitol*, St. Louis, 1919. Marable is seated at the keyboard (third from left); to his right is Johnny St. Cyr, who would later play banjo in groups led by King Oliver and Armstrong, along with drummer Baby Dodds (far right).

Above Giant Mississippi steamships, with their floating ballrooms, provided an important employment opportunity for early black jazz bands.

EUROPE IN EUROPE

As the jazz craze took hold at the end of World War I, the ragtime style enjoyed its final heyday at the hands of James Reese Europe (1881–1919). His early career was spent as a director of musical comedies in New York, where he promoted the work of the ragtime songwriter Ernest Hogan (• p. 16) and formed the Clef Club, one of the first associations specifically designed to cater to the interests of black musicians. His Society Orchestra, which included violins and mandolins, made history as the first black group to make recordings (in 1913), and it performed colorful and witty orchestrated versions of popular RAGS, MARCHES, and CAKEWALKS. Europe's work is especially notable for its unusual and expressive instrumentation, which foreshadowed later developments in jazz.

Europe's fame spread to Europe when he crossed the Atlantic on tour with the all-black military band of the 369th US Infantry ("The Hellfighters"), which met with great success when it played in French cities during a six-week period in February and March 1918. An equally successful tour of America was brutally curtailed in the following year when Europe was stabbed to death by his drummer in circumstances that remain obscure.

Above Europe hired singer Noble Sissle and ragtime pianist Eubie Blake as members of his Society Orchestra during World War I. Sissle and Blake were later responsible for the hit show *Shuffle Along* (• p. 47).

World Events

18 February
German offensive against Russia

25 March
Claude Debussy dies in Paris

16 July
Czar Nicholas II executed

27 July
Opera critic Gustav Kobbé killed in his boat in a freak accident with a US Navy seaplane

17 October
Yugoslavia achieves independence from Austro-Hungarian Empire

9 November
Kaiser Wilhelm II abdicates, Germany

11 November
Armistice ends World War I

"The best qualification for a jazzist is to have no knowledge of music and no musical ability beyond that of making noises either on piano, or clarinet, or cornet or trap drum."

Review of the Original Dixieland Jazz Band's London show in the *Performer*, 10 April 1919

JAZZ ON TOUR

Dixieland causes a sensation in London. The jazz craze soon sweeps across Europe, where New Orleans clarinetist Sidney Bechet goes on tour and stays for three years.

"When you're really playing ragtime [i.e., jazz], you're feeling it out, you're playing to the other parts, you're waiting to understand what the other man's doing, and then you're going with his feeling, adding what you have of your feeling."

Sidney Bechet, *Treat it Gentle*, 1960

Left Sidney Bechet, pioneer of the soprano saxophone, pictured in the late 1940s.

Jazz Events

20 January
Drummer Sonny Greer first plays with Duke Ellington (• p. 63) and remains with him until 1951. Ellington later declares, "Greer was not the world's best reader of music, but he was the world's best percussion reactor. When he heard a ping he responded with the most apropos pong."

7 April
The Original Dixieland Jazz Band (• p. 37) performs at London's Hippodrome, where they are soon sacked. They move on to the Palladium and a nine-month spell at the Hammersmith Palais, and make an appearance before King George V at Buckingham Palace.

10 May
James Reese Europe is killed in the middle of a high-profile national tour of the US. This year, his band records more than twenty SIDES in New York.

26 May
La La Lucille, George Gershwin's first full-length musical comedy, opens at the Henry Miller Theater, New York.

June
Will Marion Cook tours Europe with his Southern Syncopated Orchestra, having hired Sidney Bechet in Chicago before their departure. Bechet decides to remain in Europe.

October
Swiss conductor Ernest Ansermet, who has heard Bechet perform in London, describes him as a "genius" in an article published in the *Revue Romande*.

8 November
First performance of Igor Stravinsky's *Piano-Rag-Music* for solo piano.

29 December
All VAUDEVILLE theaters are closed in the Soviet Union, following a decree from the Council of People's Commissars stating that light music is a corrupting influence.

BECHET ABROAD

Clarinetist Sidney Bechet was one of the legendary figures of New Orleans jazz, and one of the music's most wayward and idiosyncratic personalities. Sceptical about the importance of STORYVILLE as a catalyst in the music's origins (• p. 23), he recalled that outdoor parties and CUTTING CONTESTS in New Orleans were more significant occasions on which musicians traded creative ideas.

Bechet played with Will Marion Cook in Chicago and New York before embarking on a tour of Europe in 1919 with Cook's Southern Syncopated Orchestra. It was while in London that he bought himself a soprano saxophone, which became his preferred instrument. His playing was distinguished by an unusually intense VIBRATO, and a gift for appealing melodic invention. Deported from England after a brawl, he worked briefly in France before returning to the US in 1922. Two years later he enjoyed a spell playing with Duke Ellington's orchestra, during which he influenced the emerging talent of alto saxophonist Johnny Hodges.

In 1925 Bechet moved to Paris (• p. 59), where he served an eleven-month prison sentence following a firearms incident in 1929. With the rise of the new SWING music in the 1930s, his talent seemed in danger of being eclipsed by changing fashions, but he continued to make musical innovations, including a novel attempt to record as a one-man band (• p. 98).

The timely revival of early jazz styles in the late 1940s rescued him from a slide into oblivion, and he was again hailed as one of the giants of New Orleans jazz. A triumphant reception in Paris at the 1949 Salle Pleyel Jazz Festival (• p. 121) inspired him to move back to Europe in 1951 to spend his remaining eight years in France.

In his autobiography, Bechet provided a vivid description of an attempt by the French critic Hugues Panassié (• p. 80) to record HOT jazz in New York in around 1938. Apparently unaware that jazz musicians tend not to give of their best early in the morning after the night before, Panassié was surprised when the musicians rolled into the studio obviously inebriated:

"Tommy [Ladnier, on trumpet], he showed up dead drunk. James P. Johnson, he just stretched himself on the piano and passed out. Some of the musicianers [*sic*] didn't know how many fingers they'd got on each hand . . . Tommy knew the records weren't what they could have been and he wanted to say something to appease Panassié, who was sitting in the corner holding his head – something he thinks will fit the occasion. So he pulled himself up and called out, 'Vive la France!' and then fell almost flat on his face."

Below Picasso's front-cover design for the piano reduction of Stravinsky's *Ragtime for Eleven Instruments*.

World Events

5 January
Nazi Party formed in Germany

17 January
Pianist Ignacy Paderewski becomes Prime Minister of Poland

23 February
Mussolini forms Italian Fascist Party

15 June
Alcock and Brown fly nonstop across the Atlantic

28 June
Treaty of Versailles signed

27 July
Chicago race riots

3 December
Death of Pierre-Auguste Renoir

STRAVINSKY'S "STOLEN" RAGS

The Russian composer Igor Stravinsky (1882–1971), a self-styled musical "kleptomaniac" whose genius could transform almost any compositional source material into a highly original work of art, began to borrow from RAGTIME in 1918 when he included a ragtime-style dance in his music-theater piece *The Soldier's Tale*. Stravinsky's friend, the Swiss conductor Ernest Ansermet, had visited the US two years before and brought back the sheet music for various RAGS, and it was Ansermet's glowing reports of Sidney Bechet's clarinet playing in London in 1919 that stimulated Stravinsky to compose his *Three Pieces for Clarinet* of the same year.

Stravinsky wrote two more works in this period that were heavily influenced by ragtime. His *Piano-Rag-Music* for solo piano, conceived for Arthur Rubinstein in 1919, demonstrates how the CROSS-RHYTHMS and OSTINATOS typical of ragtime complemented Stravinsky's own compositional preoccupations at the time. In *Ragtime for Eleven Instruments*, first performed in 1920 (• p. 44), his unorthodox instrumental ensemble included the distinctive cimbalom, a folk instrument from Eastern Europe played with hammers, which was used by the composer to represent the clattering of a honky-tonk piano.

Stravinsky was for a time interested in mechanical pianos, and in 1945 he composed his *Ebony Concerto* for Woody Herman in emulation of the big-band style that was then fashionable.

1920

Mamie Smith's recording debut marks the start of a widespread demand for female blues singers, while Paul Whiteman's band begins to be renowned for its successful brand of white dance music.

BRANCHING OUT FROM DIXIE

Jazz Events

January
The Original Dixieland Jazz Band (• p. 37) records in London.

27 April
First performance of Igor Stravinsky's *Ragtime for Eleven Instruments* at the Aeolian Hall, London, conducted by British composer Arthur Bliss. Stravinsky's score features a front cover designed by Picasso (• p. 43).

10 August
Mamie Smith records "Crazy Blues" for Okeh in New York; it is the first BLUES to be cut by a black singer. She goes on to record further blues SIDES in the autumn.

- In Chicago King Oliver forms his own band, which will later become the famous Creole Jazz Band.
- Bandleader Paul Whiteman makes his first recordings in New York. His disc coupling "Whispering" and "Japanese Sandman" goes on to sell over one million copies.
- John Stark publishes the last of Artie Matthews's five *Pastime Rags*.
- James P. Johnson (• p. 46) meets George Gershwin (• p. 89), and later reports that they enjoy "lots of talks about our ambitions to do great music on American themes."

Left Mamie Smith and her Jazz Hounds in 1920, with stride pianist Willie "The Lion" Smith at the keyboard.

MISTER JELLY ROLL

For jazz to develop from its tentative beginnings into an intellectually satisfying and commercially viable art form, two things were needed by musicians: an ability to create varied and coherent musical structures, and a keen business instinct. Ferdinand "Jelly Roll" Morton (whose nickname apparently referred to part of his anatomy) combined both attributes at a crucial stage in the music's evolution. A product of STORYVILLE, he began his career as a brothel pianist and later branched out into pimping and managing a hotel, a casino, and a boxing agency. The height of his musical achievements came in the mid-1920s when he worked and recorded in Chicago, enjoying the firm support of Melrose Brothers (his white publishers).

In 1926 Morton founded his finest group, The Red Hot Peppers, consisting of a standard New Orleans instrumentation (• p. 37), in which the piano was a featured solo instrument. The band was unusually well organized, with its members receiving regular fees for both recordings and rehearsals (the latter were by all accounts rigorous, and resulted in committed performances that displayed keen attention to every detail of the music). Morton's compositions were mostly based on the sectionalized structure of RAGTIME, and achieved a pleasing balance between passages for the full band using the COUNTERPOINT typical of the New Orleans style, as well as solo CHORUSES and BREAKS. In addition to being a STRIDE pianist of considerable accomplishment, Morton also promoted his talents as a singer and would later claim that he was one of the earliest exponents of both blues and SCAT vocal styles.

At the end of the 1920s, when the SWING music of the big bands rapidly swept the New Orleans style aside, Morton lost his position of ascendancy. His career was revived in 1938 by Alan Lomax, who edited his memoirs and encouraged him to make a series of historically valuable retrospective recordings for the Library of Congress in Washington, DC. While Morton's music may seem today to lack some of the improvisational spontaneity of later jazz styles, his importance as the first musician to approach jazz from an intellectual point of view and to seek to improve its artistic standing is incalculable. And his flamboyant personality and repeated attempts to claim sole responsibility for the early development of jazz proved legendary.

Right US Government officials disposing of illicit alcohol during the 1920s.

"In your broadcast of March 26, 1938, you introduced W. C. Handy as the originator of jazz . . . and blues. By this announcement you have done me a great injustice . . . It is evidently known, beyond contradiction, that New Orleans is the cradle of jazz, and I, myself, happened to be the creator in the year 1902."

Jelly Roll Morton, letter to Robert Ripley, 1938

World Events

16 January
Prohibition comes into effect, USA

25 January
Death of Amadeo Modigliani

February
Escalation of Russian Civil War

28 August
Nineteenth Amendment guarantees women the right to vote, USA

2 October
Death of Max Bruch

15 November
First performance of Gustav Holst's *The Planets* suite

Left Jelly Roll Morton poses for a New York publicity shot in 1929, just before his music was finally eclipsed by the popularity of the fashionable swing bands.

The Harlem "stride" school of piano playing grows in popularity, preserving a clear link with the outmoded ragtime style but delighting in greater virtuosity and jazziness.

STRIDING AHEAD

Left This uncharacteristically somber portrait of James P. Johnson, taken in 1921, scarcely reflects the infectious effervescence and virtuosity of the "stride" piano style he perfected in the 1920s.

HARLEM STRIDE

When Jelly Roll Morton (• p. 45) made his historic retrospective recordings in 1938, he demonstrated how he habitually jazzed up Scott Joplin's *Maple Leaf Rag* during his early years in New Orleans. This tendency to elaborate existing rags by adding melodic embellishments and increasing the tempo was further encouraged during the 1910s by the popularity of PIANO ROLLS, and was much lamented by the composers of "classic" RAGTIME. It led to a brand of piano jazz referred to as the Harlem STRIDE school, named after its principal center of development (the black enclave of New York City) and the characteristic "striding" motion of its left-hand split CHORDS. Although in this technique and in its sectionalized structure the new style remained indebted to ragtime models, it was considerably "jazzier" than ragtime in its increased use of BLUE NOTES, IMPROVISATION, and SWUNG RHYTHM.

Stride pianists developed a formidable skill, especially impressive in the accuracy of their leaping left hands, and considered themselves to be the elite of the jazz world. They dressed well (homburgs and cigars were de rigueur, even while playing) and were often well educated in classical music, which influenced their compositions. Willie "The Lion" Smith, for instance, wrote stride pieces with impressionistic titles that reflected his knowledge of piano music by Edvard Grieg and Claude Debussy (• p. 24). All jazz pianists before the development of BEBOP in the 1940s were initially schooled in the stride style, which remains the most technically challenging of all jazz keyboard idioms and continued to be promoted by performers such as Dick Hyman and Ralph Sutton.

The greatest of the first generation of stride pianists was undoubtedly James P. Johnson, universally known as "The Father of Stride Piano" and best remembered as the composer of the catchy "Charleston" (• p. 58). His most influential piece was *Carolina Shout*, which the young Duke Ellington attempted to learn by slowing down his pianola's mechanism in order to copy the fingering patterns preserved on a piano roll made by its composer in 1918. Johnson's protégé, Thomas "Fats" Waller, learned *Carolina Shout* in a similar way, and went on to ensure that the popularity of the stride style continued into the 1930s.

For his part, Johnson became increasingly preoccupied with the composition of ambitious (and now largely forgotten) concert works in a SYMPHONIC JAZZ idiom, including the "Negro Rhapsody" for piano and orchestra premiered by Waller at Carnegie Hall (• p. 64) in 1928, and a *Harlem Symphony* (1932). Unlike many of his contemporaries, however, Johnson adapted his jazz style to changing fashions with some success and continued to record and compose stage shows well into the 1940s.

Right Zez Confrey (inset) appeared with Paul Whiteman's band at the famous 1924 concert, which launched Gershwin's *Rhapsody in Blue* (• p. 55).

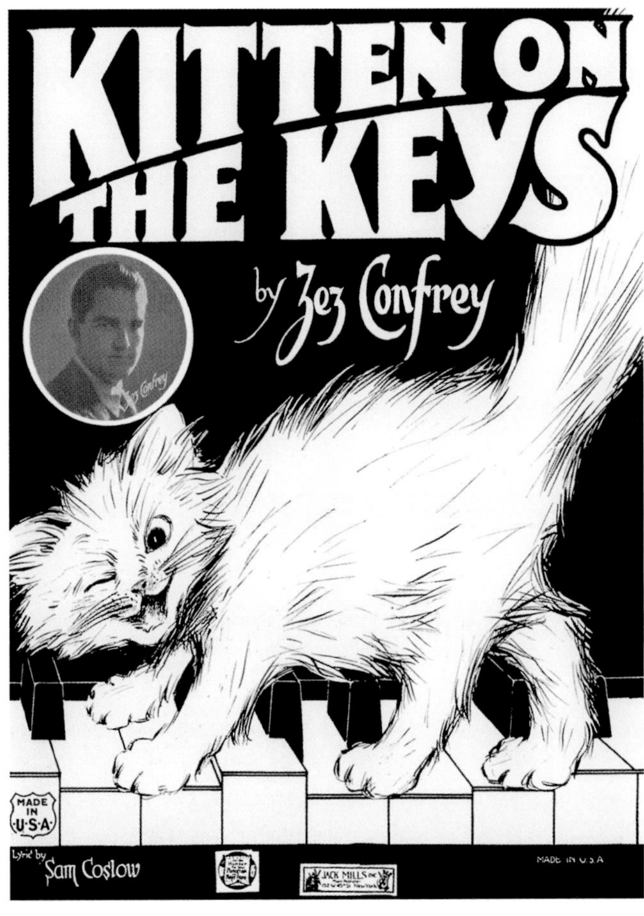

World Events

9 February
End of Russo-Polish War

Spring
Crisis over German postwar reparations

4 May
French army enters the Ruhr

29 July
Hitler elected leader of Nazi Party

2 August
Death of Enrico Caruso

4 October
Russia refused entry to League of Nations

16 December
Death of Camille Saint-Saëns

Jazz Events

January
The town of Zion, Illinois, bans jazz performances, considering the music to be a sinful pursuit.

20 April
Ragtime pianist Tony Jackson (• p. 23) dies in Chicago.

June
King Oliver (• p. 48) takes his band to San Francisco, where they remain until December.

18 October
James P. Johnson records the first version of his stride solo *Carolina Shout*, which later has an enormous influence on major figures such as Fats Waller (• p. 105) and Duke Ellington (• p. 63).

- Singer Mamie Smith continues her prolific output in the recording studio, cutting nearly thirty SIDES in this year alone.
- Fletcher Henderson (• p. 71) becomes musical director of Harry Pace's Black Swan, the first label to be run by black entrepreneurs, in Harlem.
- Eubie Blake and Noble Sissle stage their show *Shuffle Along*, which runs for 504 performances on Broadway. Blake also records his *Charleston Rag* under the title *Sounds of Africa*.
- James Scott publishes a RAG with a title designed to draw attention to the improvisational liberties increasingly taken by pianists: *Don't Jazz Me Rag – I'm Music*.
- Zez Confrey scores a hit with his piano NOVELTY, *Kitten on the Keys*.

Below The program for a performance of Blake and Sissle's *Shuffle Along* in January 1922.

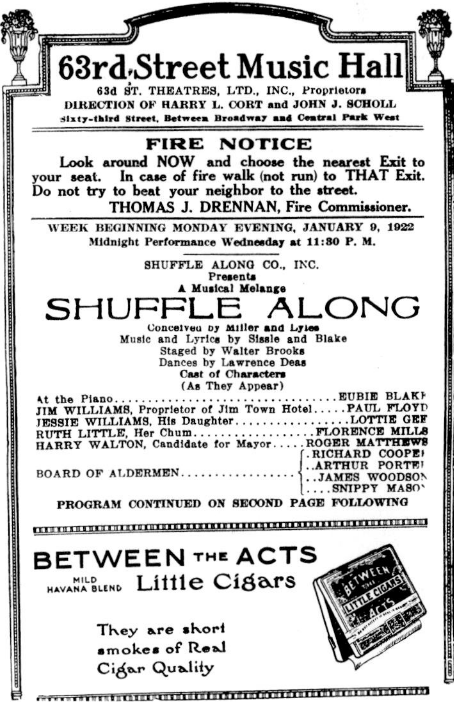

63rd Street Music Hall
63d ST. THEATRES, LTD., INC., Proprietors
DIRECTION OF HARRY L. CORT and JOHN J. SCHOLL
Sixty-third Street, Between Broadway and Central Park West

FIRE NOTICE
Look around NOW and choose the nearest Exit to your seat. In case of fire walk (not run) to THAT Exit. Do not try to beat your neighbor to the street.
THOMAS J. DRENNAN, Fire Commissioner.

WEEK BEGINNING MONDAY EVENING, JANUARY 9, 1922
Midnight Performance Wednesday at 11:30 P. M.

SHUFFLE ALONG CO., INC.
Presents
A Musical Melange
SHUFFLE ALONG
Conceived by Miller and Lyles
Music and Lyrics by Sissle and Blake
Staged by Walter Brooks
Dances by Lawrence Deas
Cast of Characters
(As They Appear)

At the Piano.................................EUBIE BLAK
JIM WILLIAMS, Proprietor of Jim Town Hotel.....PAUL FLOYD
JESSIE WILLIAMS, His Daughter................LOTTIE GE
RUTH LITTLE, Her Chum.................FLORENCE MILLS
HARRY WALTON, Candidate for Mayor.....ROGER MATTHEWS
BOARD OF ALDERMEN.................. .RICHARD COOPE / ..ARTHUR PORTE / ..JAMES WOODSO / ....SNIPPY MASO

PROGRAM CONTINUED ON SECOND PAGE FOLLOWING

King Oliver and Kid Ory establish their reputations in Chicago and Los Angeles, as ragtime suffers its death throes.

KING OLIVER IN CHICAGO

THE KING OF CREOLE JAZZ

In the summer of 1922 at Chicago's Lincoln Gardens, cornetist Joe "King" Oliver and his Creole Jazz Band brought the New Orleans style of small-ensemble jazz to its first artistic high point. The following April, they began recording their fine performances for posterity. Oliver's early days in STORYVILLE were typical of many first-generation jazz musicians, as was his migration northward in search of more rewarding work. By the time of his first recordings, he had assembled an impressive lineup of New Orleans performers.

The FRONT LINE comprised Oliver (first cornet), Louis Armstrong (second cornet), Johnny Dodds (clarinet), and Honoré Dutrey (trombone), who together created splendid examples of the decorative COUNTERPOINT essential to the New Orleans style. This quartet was supported by a solid RHYTHM SECTION made up of Lil Hardin (piano), Baby Dodds (drums), and Bill Johnson (BANJO). The Creole Jazz Band's success proved to be short-lived: the Dodds brothers quit in 1924, and Armstrong, who married Hardin that year, soon followed suit. In 1927, in an attempt to adapt his output to the growing popularity of big-band jazz, Oliver formed a larger group in New York that met with little success. He made his last recordings in 1931, and died in oblivion seven years later.

In his brief moment of glory, however, Oliver accomplished two lasting achievements. He developed the timbral potential of the cornet and trumpet by experimenting with various forms of MUTE and other novel techniques, and his solos (notably that in "Dippermouth Blues," which extended across three CHORUSES) exerted a strong influence on the trumpeters who followed him – in particular Bubber Miley, who developed certain aspects of Oliver's playing into Duke Ellington's famous "jungle" style (• p. 63). In addition, Oliver brought the style of New Orleans ensemble jazz to such a peak of refinement that it became difficult to see how the music could continue to progress in the same direction. Not surprisingly, the subsequent virtuosity and improvisational brilliance of Armstrong and the sophisticated orchestrations of the big bands soon took jazz along new and contrasting paths.

1922

Right A sketch by Jean Cocteau celebrating Le Boeuf sur le Toit, a jazz club that opened in Paris at the end of 1921 and was soon frequented by composers of the stature of Satie and Ravel.

Opposite King Oliver (third from left), pictured with his Creole Jazz Band in San Francisco on 12 June 1921. Louis Armstrong joined the band in the following year, and in 1924 married its pianist, Lil Hardin (fourth from left).

World Events

18 March
Mahatma Gandhi imprisoned

29 July
Greeks threaten to invade Constantinople

18 October
Foundation of BBC

23 October
Isadora Duncan's suggestive dancing banned in Boston

31 October
Mussolini seizes power in Rome

- Discovery of Tutankhamun's tomb, Egypt
- James Joyce's novel *Ulysses*

"As Oliver's recordings . . . recede further into the historical past, each succeeding generation will undoubtedly find it harder to relate to them. Forty years or so of solo-oriented jazz make it difficult for people to understand the collective music-making conception the Creole Jazz Band represented, and, of course, the antique sound of the old acoustical Gennett, Okeh, and Paramount recordings is strange to modern ears. For me, they have a lovely sound all their own, as nostalgic and personal as the sound of a Model T."

Gunther Schuller, 1968

Jazz Events

24 January
A private performance is mounted in Chelsea, London, of William Walton's entertainment *Façade*. Setting the nonsense poetry of Edith Sitwell to jazzy music, the production creates a scandal in the English capital.

Spring
Kid Ory's Sunshine Orchestra makes its first recordings under the name Spikes' Seven Pods of Pepper in Los Angeles. The two SIDES issued ("Ory's Creole Trombone" and "Society Blues") are the first to be cut by a black ensemble playing in the New Orleans style.

July
King Oliver invites Louis Armstrong (● p. 57) to join his Creole Jazz Band, which is now playing at Chicago's Lincoln Gardens.

29 August
The New Orleans Rhythm Kings make their first recordings at Gennett's Richmond studios under the name Friar's Society Orchestra. Their repertoire includes several numbers made famous by the Original Dixieland Jazz Band (● p. 37).

21 October
Fats Waller (● p. 105) makes his first recordings.

- William "Count" Basie (● p. 87) records his first piano solos.
- Mamie Smith records a further twenty sides this year. Her band, the Jazz Hounds, now includes saxophonist Coleman Hawkins, whom she meets on a trip to Kansas City.
- Europe's first jazz club, Le Boeuf sur le Toit ("The Bull on the Roof"), opens in Paris.
- As RAGTIME is supplanted by the new jazz craze, John Stark's ragtime publishing house goes out of business.
- German classical composer Paul Hindemith mimics ragtime and popular dance music in his solo piano work, *Suite "1922."*

1923

Fine recordings by black artists start to dominate the market and set new performance standards. The craze for the vocal blues intensifies, and French composer Milhaud breaks controversial new ground by adapting jazz for a classical ballet score.

FIRST FLOWERING

Above Bessie Smith, arguably the greatest of the female blues singers.

Jazz Events

16 February
Bessie Smith (• p. 67) cuts her first recording, "Downhearted Blues," in New York. It sells over three-quarters of a million copies within six months, and she signs a nine-year contract with Columbia.

5 and 6 April
King Oliver's Creole Jazz Band (• p. 48), now appearing at Chicago's Lincoln Gardens, makes its first recordings. These include "Dippermouth Blues," and are cut at the Gennett Studios in Richmond, Indiana. The band includes Louis Armstrong (second cornet), the Dodds brothers (clarinet and drums), and Lil Hardin (piano).

22 and 23 June
King Oliver's band records seven SIDES for the Okeh label of the General Phonograph Corporation. Eight more Okeh sides follow in **October**.

17 July
Having settled in Chicago in May, Jelly Roll Morton makes several recordings at the Gennett studios with the New Orleans Rhythm Kings, and as solo pianist in "King Porter Stomp" and (on **18 July**) "Grandpa's Spells."

30 July
Sidney Bechet makes his first extant recordings with pianist Clarence Williams, who has also engaged Bessie Smith.

Summer
Fletcher Henderson (• p. 71) forms the Fletcher Henderson Orchestra and opens at the Club Alabam in the Nora Bayes Theater, West 44th Street, New York City.

September
Pianist Bennie Moten makes his first recordings for Okeh with a six-piece band from Kansas City.

Autumn
Bandleader Elmer Snowden's Washingtonians open at the Kentucky Club on Broadway, with Duke Ellington as pianist. Its lineup soon expands with the addition of Joe "Tricky Sam" Nanton (trombone) and Bubber Miley (trumpet).

RACE TO RECORD

The success of the early Original Dixieland Jazz Band recordings did not immediately establish a new market within the recording industry. The full commercial potential of jazz discs was only realized in 1920 when Mamie Smith's best-selling sides revealed an extensive black audience, who (contrary to popular white belief) could evidently afford gramophones. From 1921, so-called RACE RECORDS of jazz performances were aimed exclusively at black consumers. This divisive categorization persisted until World War II, although in practice many fine recordings by black artists had been circulated in general recording catalogs since the 1920s.

In 1923 there was a sudden increase in both the quality and quantity of jazz recordings, as many great black performers entered the recording studio for the first time. Among them were Bessie Smith, King Oliver, Sidney Bechet, Bennie Moten, Freddie Keppard, Louis Armstrong, and Jelly Roll Morton. Their performances were preserved through the ACOUSTIC process (• p. 32). Problems of balance were enormous, and it is likely that in some areas (especially drumming, which was all but curtailed in the studio) these tracks differed significantly from live renderings; when European musicians attempted to copy the early recordings, these eccentricities were faithfully reproduced. After 1925 the widespread adoption of electrical recording techniques, in which an amplified electrical input from a microphone was transmitted to the cutting needle, revolutionized the industry and allowed recordings to be made on location.

Above The Gennett recording studio at Richmond was in reality a glorified railway shed. Attempted takes were frequently interrupted by the noise of passing freight trains.

Right Freddie Keppard in Chicago, *c.* 1918. Along with King Oliver, Keppard was one of the most influential and widely traveled of the early jazz cornetists.

Right Founded in 1917, the Gennett company had issued no fewer than 6,000 recordings by the end of 1926. "Wolverine Blues" was cut in the Richmond studio on 13 March 1923 and "Canal Street Blues" on 6 April.

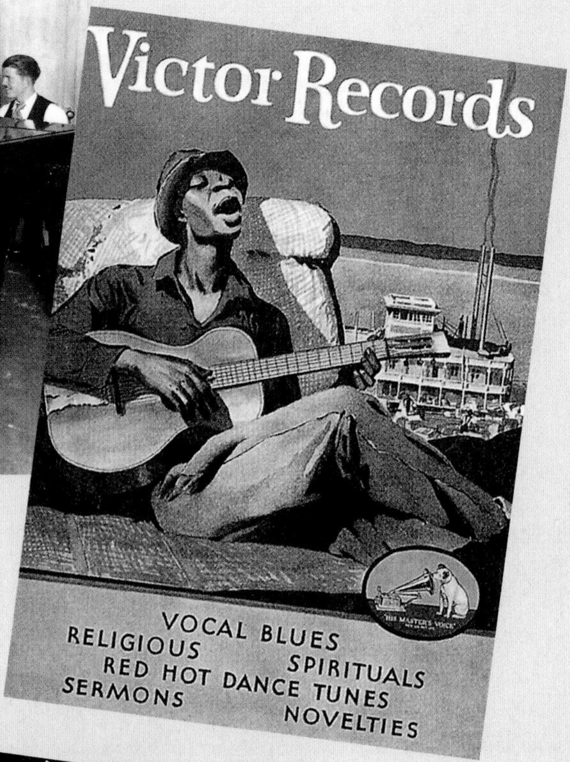

1923

WHITE LABELS, BLACK MUSIC

The Victor company manufactured recordings of John Philip Sousa's band (• p. 20) and James Reese Europe's RAGTIME orchestra (• p. 41) early in the century and went on to issue the first Original Dixieland Jazz Band SIDES in 1917. With these successes, Victor stole the limelight from their rivals at Columbia. But it was Columbia who soon capitalized on the growing demand for recorded jazz by producing several series of RACE RECORDS from 1923 onward. These two labels dominated record production in later years: Victor recorded Jelly Roll Morton in 1926 and Duke Ellington in 1927 before being taken over by the Radio Corporation of America (RCA) in 1929. Meanwhile, Columbia, controlled from 1938 by the Columbia Broadcasting System (CBS), secured an international market for the big bands of the Swing Era and made a millionaire out of Miles Davis in the 1960s.

But in these pioneering years it was the small independent labels that did most to promote the new music. The Okeh label shot to prominence by issuing the Mamie Smith record in 1920, and set up an extensive race series in 1921 that issued recordings by King Oliver, Louis Armstrong, and Bennie Moten before it became part of Columbia in 1926. The two Gennett studios in Chicago and Richmond, Indiana (the latter a notoriously cramped shed next to a railway line; • p. 51) recorded the New Orleans Rhythm Kings in 1922 and added Jelly Roll Morton and King Oliver to their race catalog in the following year. The Paramount label issued race records by Ma Rainey, King Oliver, and Freddie Keppard, and the Vocalion company (a subsidiary of New York's Aeolian piano manufacturers) established a race series in 1926, marketing performances by Duke Ellington and King Oliver.

Left and above Catalogs of "race records" issued by Okeh (1926) and Victor (1929).

Above left Trumpeter Wingy Manone (sitting on piano), recording with the San Sue Strutters for Okeh in Chicago in 1925.

Jazz Events

25 October
Darius Milhaud's ballet *La Création du Monde* opens in Paris with set designs by Fernand Léger. Based on black folklore, the work is heavily indebted to jazz and boldly synthesizes elements borrowed from baroque COUNTERPOINT and the BLUES.

November
Columbia launches its first race records, including sides by King Oliver and Bessie Smith.

December
Singer Ma Rainey records eight blues sides in Chicago for Paramount Records.

- James P. Johnson (● p. 46) visits London as director of a touring musical revue. In this same year, his first Broadway musical, *Runnin' Wild*, completes 213 performances and contains the hit number "Charleston" (● p. 58).
- French composer Maurice Ravel begins work on his Violin Sonata, which includes a movement entitled "Blues."

World Events

4 January
First network radio broadcast, USA

11 January
French and Belgian forces occupy the Ruhr

31 August
Italy occupies Corfu

1 September
Earthquake in Tokyo kills 100,000

29 October
Mustafa Kemal forms first Turkish Republic

11 November
Hitler arrested after failed Munich *Putsch*

Above Representative labels from discs manufactured by Victor and Okeh.

Right Set design by Léger for Milhaud's jazz-inspired ballet *La Création du Monde* (1923).

1924

JAZZ IN THE CONCERT HALL

George Gershwin and Paul Whiteman collaborate on *Rhapsody in Blue*, a pioneering excursion into the realms of symphonic jazz, which is adopted by other American classical composers in an energetic wave of nationalism.

Jazz Events

12 February
First performance of George Gershwin's *Rhapsody in Blue* at New York's Aeolian Hall, with the composer at the piano and the Paul Whiteman band accompanying. It is billed as "An Experiment in Modern Music," and the phenomenal success of this "jazz concerto" stimulates other composers to cultivate an American nationalist idiom often labeled SYMPHONIC JAZZ.

18 February
Bix Beiderbecke's recording debut, with The Wolverines, at the Gennett studios.

February
The Dodds brothers quit King Oliver's Creole Jazz Band (• p. 48), having discovered that Oliver has been retaining their earnings. Louis Armstrong (• p. 57) marries the band's pianist, Lil Hardin.

June
Louis and Lil Armstrong quit King Oliver's band.

Summer
Fletcher Henderson's orchestra (• p. 71) moves to the Roseland Ballroom, New York.
• Count Basie (• p. 87) joins the New York group Katie Krippen and Her Kiddies (with whom Fats Waller has recently appeared) in the touring show *Hippity Hop* on the Columbia burlesque circuit. He earns $40 per week, an amount that is soon doubled.

7 October
Louis Armstrong makes his first recording with the Henderson Orchestra.

November
Duke Ellington (• p. 63) makes his first recordings as leader of The Washingtonians.

December
Jelly Roll Morton (• p. 45) records a duet version of "King Porter Stomp" with King Oliver.

Above left George Gershwin at the piano, *c.* 1925. Looking on is Walter Damrosch, who conducted the first performances of Gershwin's Piano Concerto in 1925 and *An American in Paris* in 1928.

Above King Oliver's Creole Jazz Band, 1923 (l. to r.): Johnny Dodds (clarinet), Baby Dodds (drums), Honoré Dutrey (trombone), Louis Armstrong (cornet), King Oliver (cornet), Lil Hardin (piano), and Johnny St. Cyr (banjo).

Below Paul Whiteman and his orchestra posing for a publicity shot in January 1938.

Above The poster announcing the "New Typically American Compositions," which were performed during Whiteman's "Experiment in Modern Music" on 12 February 1924.

AN EXPERIMENT IN MODERN MUSIC

The RAGTIME craze had inspired several European composers to experiment with styles that attempted to fuse elements from popular and classical music, but it was not until the mid-1920s that American composers began to emulate their example by exploring a creative synthesis between the new HOT jazz and art music. The concept of jazz for the concert hall was promoted by the bandleader Paul Whiteman, whose polished orchestrations later formed the basis for the big-band arrangements of the Swing Era.

In 1923 Whiteman asked George Gershwin (• p. 89) to compose something for a concert promoting American music to be held at the Aeolian Hall, New York, on Lincoln's birthday (12 February). Having virtually forgotten about the request, it was only when Gershwin read in the *New York Tribune* that Rachmaninov would be at the concert and that he himself was "reported to be at work on a jazz concerto" that he was spurred into action with only five weeks remaining. He later commented that the resulting *Rhapsody in Blue* was conceived "as a sort of musical kaleidoscope of America – of our vast melting pot, of our incomparable national pep, our blues, our metropolitan madness."

Legend has it that the score was still unfinished on the day of the concert, and that Gershwin improvised large sections of the solo piano part. Some critics found *Rhapsody in Blue* crude, but reluctantly admitted its claim to originality. The work's phenomenal success stimulated widespread interest in the new genre of symphonic jazz, and Gershwin went on to produce finer specimens such as *An American in Paris* (1928) and the opera *Porgy and Bess* (1935). He clearly saw symphonic jazz as the strongly nationalistic musical style for which American classical composers had long been searching.

When Aaron Copland returned from his studies in Paris, he immediately followed up Gershwin's lead with a succession of jazz-inspired works, including *Music for the Theater* (1925) and a Piano Concerto (1927). In an article entitled "Jazz Structure and Influence", published in 1927, Copland predicted that jazz might become "the substance not only of the American composer's foxtrots and Charlestons, but of his lullabies and nocturnes." Copland later moved away from an overtly jazzy style (although he composed a Clarinet Concerto for Benny Goodman (• p. 84) in 1950), but his brash and exciting early works directly influenced his protégé Leonard Bernstein, who brought the symphonic jazz trend to a new peak of sophistication with his Symphony No. 2 (1949) and *Prelude, Fugue, and Riffs* (1955).

World Events

21 January
Lenin dies, USSR

6 April
Fascists win Italian general election

4 November
Gabriel Fauré dies

29 November
Giacomo Puccini dies

- Cecil B. de Mille's film *The Ten Commandments*
- The British Empire Exhibition results in the construction of Wembley Stadium, London

Jazz Events

1 December
Gershwin's musical *Lady, Be Good!*, his first with lyrics provided entirely by his brother Ira, opens at the Liberty Theater. Among its hits later to become jazz STANDARDS are the title song and "Fascinatin' Rhythm."

22 December
Sidney Bechet (• p. 43) and Louis Armstrong record Clarence Williams's composition "Cake Walking Babies from Home" in New York for Gennett. Their group, the Red Onion Jazz Babies, is named after a New Orleans club.

- Jerome Kern, worried that hit songs from his musical *Sitting Pretty* would be distorted in jazz IMPROVISATIONS, describes jazz as a "debasement of all music."
- Belgian lawyer and critic Robert Goffin (• p. 74) organizes jazz parties in Brussels.

1925

Louis "Satchmo" Armstrong brings the early jazz style to its climax in a series of innovative recordings featuring virtuoso improvisations. Discs achieve better sound quality through developments in electrical recording techniques.

SATCHMO

Jazz Events

8 January
Louis Armstrong and Sidney Bechet (● p. 43) rerecord "Cake Walking Babies" for Okeh with Clarence Williams's Blue Five (● p. 53).

14 January
Bessie Smith (● p. 67) and Louis Armstrong record their celebrated version of W. C. Handy's "St. Louis Blues" for Columbia in New York.

29 May
Fletcher Henderson (● p. 71) and Armstrong record "Sugarfoot Stomp," Don Redman's big-band arrangement of King Oliver's "Dippermouth Blues," in New York.

May
Jelly Roll Morton (● p. 45) records a duet IMPROVISATION on his "Wolverine Blues" with clarinetist Voltaire de Faut, Chicago.

World Events

3 January
Mussolini commences dictatorship in Italy

14 February
Germany lifts ban on Nazi Party

25 March
First electrical recording of classical music by pianist Alfred Cortot for the Victor company, USA

April
Paris Exposition des Arts Décoratifs launches Art Deco style

Left Louis Armstrong in 1933. Taken in London during his European tour (● p. 77), the picture captures this singular performer's sense of humor and inimitable style.

"Louis Armstrong would improvise on the same theme for a full half hour, taking twenty choruses in a row. Often he would be quite motionless as he played or sang – his eyes closed, like a man carried out of the world; tears would roll down his cheeks. His imagination seemed inexhaustible; for each new chorus he had new ideas more beautiful than those he had produced for the preceding chorus. As he went along, his improvisation grew hotter, his style became more and more simple – until at the end there was nothing but the endless repetition of one fragment of melody – or even a single note insistently sounded and executed with cataclysmic intonations."

Hugues Panassié, *Le Jazz Hot* (1934)

Left Louis Armstrong (at the piano) with his Hot Five in 1925, during the time of their early recordings. The other members of the group are (l. to r.): Johnny St. Cyr (banjo), Johnny Dodds (reeds), Kid Ory (trombone), and Lil Hardin Armstrong (pianist).

LOUIS ARMSTRONG: HOT FIVE AND SEVEN

Louis Armstrong (dubbed "Satchmo," from satchel mouth) began as a cornetist in early bands led by Kid Ory in New Orleans (1918), King Oliver in Chicago (1922–24), and Fletcher Henderson in New York (1924), before returning to Chicago in 1925 to form his own Hot Five. This group, known as the Hot Seven when tuba and drums were added, recorded on the Okeh label, and their technical brilliance exerted a profound influence on the development of jazz.

By 1925 Armstrong had changed from playing cornet to the brighter trumpet, and shown himself to be equally accomplished as a singer. Among the best-known Hot Five and Seven recordings are "Heebie Jeebies" (1926), an early example of SCAT singing, and "West End Blues" (1928), with its virtuosic introductory trumpet cadenza and impressive TRUMPET STYLE piano solo by Earl Hines (• p. 125). Armstrong and Hines also collaborated in a duet recording of "Weather Bird," demonstrating an instinctive rapport between the two men that is unparalleled either before or since.

Armstrong was the first great innovator in jazz. He was responsible for the increased prominence of improvisation, and he developed the concept of an extended improvised solo based on the CHORD CHANGES of a song, always shaping his extemporized melodic lines with an innate sense of proportion and growth. In earlier jazz forms such as DIXIELAND (• p. 37), improvisation was confined to brief two-bar BREAKS between phrases: after Armstrong, the melodic ingenuity of the soloist assumed an unprecedented importance.

He considerably expanded trumpet technique, hitting notes higher than any played before and employing tricks such as the RIP for added excitement. He was the first in jazz to demonstrate consistent LICKS: apart from the rip, he frequently ended long notes with a rich VIBRATO and tended to terminate phrases with characteristic melodic formulae. His singing was as innovative as his playing, his vocal improvisations shaped with the same instinctive sense of melodic structuring. And in his unwavering grasp of SWING he generated rhythmic excitement like no one before him.

In the 1930s Armstrong was based in New York and appeared as a highly paid featured soloist with various big bands. When he joined the books of hard-hitting agent Joe Glaser in 1935, his sellout to the lucrative world of popular song and Hollywood films seemed complete. Many lamented what they saw as a defection to commercial interests and regretted his abandonment of fundamental artistic values. Miles Davis, while admiring Armstrong's playing, found his habitual impersonation of a grinning black minstrel racially unacceptable.

In 1947 Armstrong formed his "All Stars" and began to record again in the New Orleans style, which was then enjoying a revival. He also embarked on a series of high-profile international trips organized by the US State Department, which led to a new nickname: "Ambassador Satch."

1925

The Girl of the straight legs. "It's a pity you don't Charleston, Audrey. Your knees are simply made for it."

Above A New York dancing competition devoted to the Charleston during 1926. Composed by James P. Johnson, the original "Charleston" melody had featured in the hit stage show *Runnin' Wild* three years before.

Left Inspired by the growing craze for dancing the Charleston, a *Punch* cartoon from 1925 satirizes the dance's knock-kneed stance.

Far left Robj porcelain figures of jazz musicians, c. 1925.

Jazz Events

June
James P. Johnson (• p. 46) cuts a PIANO ROLL of his most famous composition, "Charleston (South Carolina)," a hit number from his Broadway musical *Runnin' Wild.* First recorded in 1923 and dedicated to the sailors from Charleston who attended Johnson's performances, the piece becomes highly popular worldwide as a lively dance that epitomizes the epoch for subsequent generations.

12 November
Having quit the Fletcher Henderson Orchestra and moved back to Chicago, Louis Armstrong makes his first recording with his Hot Five for Okeh.

20 November
Aaron Copland's jazzy score *Music for the Theater* is performed in Boston. Just returned to America after a spell of compositional study in Paris, Copland is anxious to cultivate a distinctively American musical style.

3 December
Premiere of George Gershwin's Piano Concerto in F Major in New York. The score is a more substantial and satisfying investigation of SYMPHONIC JAZZ than *Rhapsody in Blue*, but does not achieve the widespread popularity of the earlier work.

- Introduction of electrical recordings, in which a microphone and electrical amplification are employed.
- The Original Dixieland Jazz Band (• p. 37) disbands.
- Fats Waller (• p. 105) gives lessons in jazz organ playing (for accompanying silent films) to the twenty-one-year-old Count Basie (• p. 87) on the Wurlitzer pipe organ at Harlem's Lincoln Theater.
- The *Revue Nègre* (with a band that includes Sidney Bechet) visits Paris, where its star dancer Josephine Baker subsequently remains to join the *Folies-Bergère*.
- F. Scott Fitzgerald writes "The Children of Jazz" (*Tales of the Jazz Age*).

Left Poster by Paul Colin for the *Revue Nègre*, staged in Paris in 1925 and starring erotic dancer Josephine Baker. Racial stereotyping continued to persist in artworks associated with black American jazz, both in the USA and Europe.

Below left The first page of the autograph manuscript of Aaron Copland's *Music for the Theater* (1925). The concert in which this work was first performed also included Darius Milhaud's *Ballad* for piano and orchestra, with Milhaud himself appearing as soloist. The Milhaud–Copland pairing was entirely appropriate, since both composers were early pioneers of symphonic jazz.

World Events

1 July
Erik Satie dies

8 August
Ku Klux Klan march in Washington, DC

1 December
France, Germany, Italy, and the UK sign the Treaty of Locarno

3 December
Border established between Northern Ireland and the Irish Free State

- F. Scott Fitzgerald's novel *The Great Gatsby*

1926

Louis Armstrong's spellbinding talents continue to flourish, while the compositional skills of Jelly Roll Morton raise the art of jazz to a new intellectual level.

THE NEW VIRTUOSITY

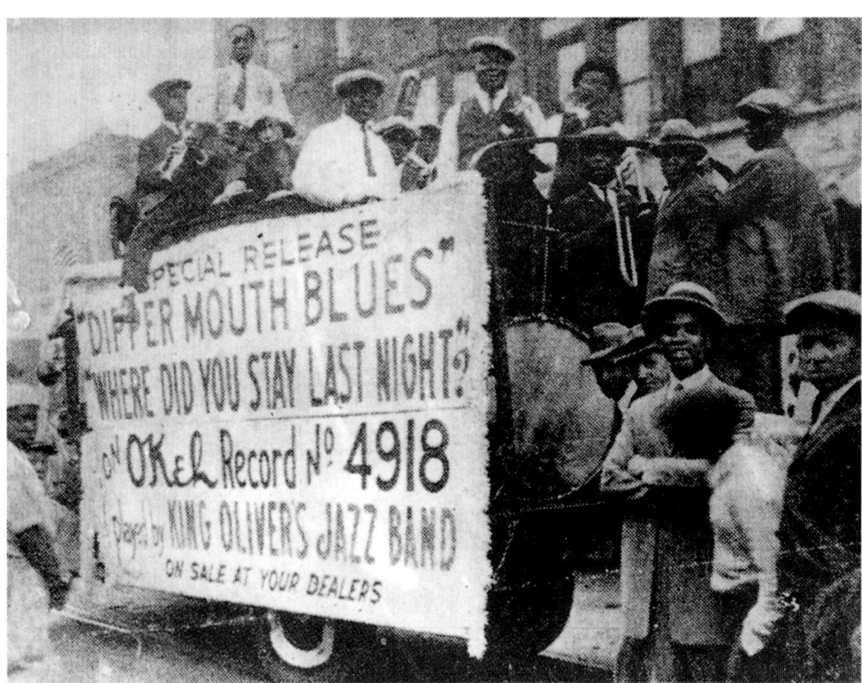

Above King Oliver and his Creole Jazz Band "tailgating" on State Street, Chicago, to promote their Okeh recording of "Dippermouth Blues" in 1923.

Jazz Events

January
The Melody Maker and British Metronome magazine begins publication in London.

28 February
Louis Armstrong records his first song, "Heebie Jeebies," pioneering the use of SCAT singing and propelling his Hot Five to stardom. In this year, he switches from cornet to trumpet.

14 May
Fletcher Henderson's band records "The Stampede" in New York, featuring tenor saxophonist Coleman Hawkins.

15 and 21 September
In Chicago, Jelly Roll Morton's Red Hot Peppers (• p. 35) record some of their finest SIDES, including "Black Bottom Stomp" and "Dead Man Blues." Members of his band receive $5 per rehearsal and $15 per take. Further recordings are made on **16 December**, including "Grandpa's Spells."

November
Fats Waller (• p. 105) records organ solos in New York.

Autumn
Bix Beiderbecke (• p. 73) joins the Jean Goldkette orchestra.

- Paul Whiteman and his orchestra tour Europe to promote George Gershwin's *Rhapsody in Blue* (• p. 55).
- Sidney Bechet plays in Moscow with Benny Peyton's Jazz Kings.
- Duke Ellington hires trombonist Joe "Tricky Sam" Nanton, who models his GROWL style on Bubber Miley's innovations in trumpet playing. Ellington records with The Washingtonians, later restyled The Kentucky Club Orchestra.
- André Coeuroy and André Schaeffner publish their book *Le jazz* in Paris, the first critical monograph on the subject to appear in print.

Left Trombonist Tommy Dorsey, who played with Paul Whiteman's and Jean Goldkette's bands before teaming up with his clarinetist brother Jimmy to form the short-lived Dorsey Brothers Orchestra in 1934. The brothers were to collaborate again between 1953 and Tommy's death in 1956.

World Events

27 January
First television unveiled by John Logie Baird

3 May
General strike, UK

6 December
Death of Claude Monet

25 December
Hirohito becomes Emperor of Japan

- Fritz Lang's epic film *Metropolis*

TROMBONE

As a stalwart fixture of the New Orleans marching bands (• p. 29), the trombone was assured a prominent place in jazz from the outset. It was quickly adopted as part of the three-strong FRONT LINE and used in melodic flourishes alongside the clarinet and trumpet. The early "tailgate" style of trombone playing (so called because the trombonist would stand at the rear of an open truck when the band was mobile) was championed by Kid Ory and characterized by robust GLISSANDOS made possible by the instrument's slide mechanism, which also permitted effective pitch-bending of BLUE NOTES.

The number of trombones in SWING bands increased from one in the 1920s to no fewer than four by the 1940s, thus allowing arrangers to introduce more complex harmonies in their brass writing. Big bands led by solo trombonists include those of Glenn Miller (• p. 107), Tommy Dorsey, and Jack Teagarden.

The valve trombone is operated by a mechanism similar to that found on the trumpet. It was promoted as an instrument of supple lyricism and considerable agility by Juan Tizol (who played with Duke Ellington's orchestra between 1929 and 1944), and by Bob Brookmeyer in the 1950s. The slide trombone's technical difficulties did not, however, prevent it from achieving continued prominence in the BEBOP and HARD BOP styles, thanks to the dexterity of musicians like J. J. Johnson and Kai Winding. More radical technical advancements were made by the German player Albert Mangelsdorff, who exploited the avant-garde technique of MULTIPHONICS, in which CHORDS are generated by singing notes into the mouthpiece while playing.

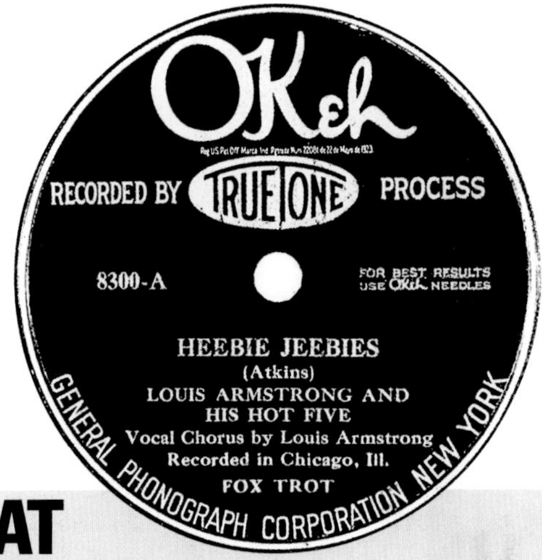

SCAT

The precise origins of scat singing are unknown, although it almost certainly thrived in New Orleans long before either Jelly Roll Morton or Louis Armstrong first employed it. Morton, with characteristic conceit, claimed to have invented the technique, even though Armstrong was the first to record it (and is said by some to have hit upon the style by accident when he dropped his sheet music in rehearsal but continued to sing *ex tempore*).

Armstrong's celebrated "Heebie Jeebies" (recorded in 1926) is an early but fine example of the use of nonsense syllables in an improvised vocal line, which is the essential characteristic of scat: the voice, in effect, becomes another instrument when divorced from meaningful words, and can even be used to imitate the melodic style of instrumental IMPROVISATIONS.

After Armstrong's popular success with the technique, it was promoted by bandleader Cab Calloway, and from the 1940s onward it was widely adopted as an ideal vehicle for vocal improvisations in the more angular melodies of bebop. (It may have been a specific pair of scat nonsense syllables that christened the new style "bebop.") The finest virtuoso of scat was without doubt Ella Fitzgerald (• p. 195), and the technique has remained popular to the present day in widely differing musical contexts.

HARLEM, CHICAGO, AND KANSAS CITY

In the work of Duke Ellington, jazz achieves greater musical sophistication. Jean Goldkette and Paul Whiteman lead the finest white dance bands of the time, while Aaron Copland and George Gershwin produce masterpieces of symphonic jazz. Leading musicians converge on New York, the new capital of the jazz world.

Above The program cover for a typical Cotton Club show in 1938.

Jazz Events

1927

28 January
Premiere of Aaron Copland's jazz-influenced Piano Concerto, played by the composer and the Boston Symphony Orchestra under Serge Koussevitzky.

7 May
Louis Armstrong (● p. 57) makes his first recordings with his Hot Seven (i.e., Hot Five, plus drums and tuba).

June
Jelly Roll Morton's Red Hot Peppers (● p. 35) continue their successful series of recordings in Chicago.

9 September
Bix Beiderbecke (● p. 73) records his impressionistic piano solo *In a Mist*, reflecting the influence of Debussy (● p. 24).

18 September
Jean Goldkette's orchestra is dissolved, forcing Beiderbecke to seek work elsewhere. He finds it in **November** with the Paul Whiteman band.

October
Release of the first "talkie" motion picture, *The Jazz Singer,* starring Al Jolson.

4 December
Duke Ellington begins his residency at the Cotton Club in Harlem, increasing the size of his band from six to eleven players. New names include Barney Bigard (clarinet) and Harry Carney (baritone saxophone). "Black and Tan Fantasy," "Creole Love Call," and "East St. Louis Toodle-oo" (the band's signature tune) are among the masterpieces recorded by Ellington this year.

December
Armstrong's Hot Five record "Hotter Than That" and "Struttin' With Some Barbeque" in Chicago.

World Events

1927

24 March
USA and UK use military force in China

21 May
Charles Lindbergh makes solo flight across the Atlantic

14 September
Isadora Duncan dies when her scarf is caught in the wheels of a car

25 November
Eleven-year-old Yehudi Menuhin plays a concerto with the New York Symphony Orchestra

DUKE ELLINGTON AT THE COTTON CLUB

In 1923, Edward Kennedy "Duke" Ellington first began to make his mark in New York with his band The Washingtonians, which took its name from his home city. He soon assembled a remarkable corpus of talented instrumentalists, whose qualities he exploited not only by showcasing them in dynamic solo passages, but also by joining them in astonishingly varied and colorful combinations of a kind never before heard in jazz. These achievements, in addition to Ellington's expertise as an originator of intellectually satisfying musical structures, made him the most celebrated and critically acclaimed of all jazz composers.

Ellington's orchestra began its four-year residency at Harlem's famous Cotton Club in 1927, providing music for sumptuous stage routines in which exotically dressed black dancers performed for an exclusively white audience. The band developed a new style of "jungle" music for these dances, which featured a GROWL technique of brass playing developed by trumpeter Bubber Miley and trombonist Joe "Tricky Sam" Nanton. Ellington's other notable SIDEMEN in these early years were alto saxophonist Johnny Hodges (famous for his sensuous tone), baritone saxophonist Harry Carney (whose agility on his potentially ponderous instrument was phenomenal), and clarinetist Barney Bigard (who personified a direct link with old New Orleans). In 1929, the virtuoso Cootie Williams succeeded Miley as principal trumpet.

A succession of popular radio broadcasts from the Cotton Club brought Ellington national fame, and his name became known around the globe after the successes of "Mood Indigo" (1930) and "It Don't Mean a Thing (If It Ain't Got That Swing)" (1932). In 1933, he took his band on their first tour of Europe. By this time singer Cab Calloway had succeeded Ellington at the Cotton Club, and Calloway was in turn succeeded by Jimmie Lunceford in 1934. Racial unrest in Harlem in the following year forced the club to close down temporarily, but it reopened in a different location in the autumn of 1936 and remained in business for a further four years. In the 1980s, the legendary venue inspired a movie by director Francis Ford Coppola (• p. 203).

Other important nightspots in Harlem during the heyday of the Cotton Club were Connie's Inn (which hosted performances by Louis Armstrong, Fletcher Henderson, and Fats Waller between 1929 and 1931), Small's Paradise (haunt of STRIDE pianists Willie "The Lion" Smith and James P. Johnson), and the Savoy Ballroom (just one block away from the original Cotton Club on Lenox Avenue).

Below Ethel Waters sings in the routine "Stormy Weather" at the Cotton Club in 1933. Ellington is conducting, standing in front of Sonny Greer's impressive drum kit.

Below Duke Ellington poses with his famous orchestra, including saxophonists Johnny Hodges and Harry Carney (front row, second and third from right) and brass players Joe "Tricky Sam" Nanton (back row, far left) and Cootie Williams (front row, second from left), *c.* 1931.

KANSAS CITY

Jazz owed part of its origins to the RAGTIME music emanating from St. Louis at the turn of the century, and the state of Missouri again became important for the music's continuing evolution during the 1920s, when large ensembles in Kansas City began playing a distinctive brand of jazz.

The style originated in the popular orchestrated versions of ragtime, but also benefited from a mixture of BLUES elements alongside a new technique of repeated thematic fragments called the RIFF. This ultimately provided the foundation for the big-band music of the Swing Era (• p. 71). Bennie Moten's band, which recorded between 1923 and 1932, and Walter Page's Blue Devils from Oklahoma City both featured the gifted young pianist Count Basie (• p. 87), who formed his own band from Moten's dispersed members and took New York by storm in 1936. Later products of Kansas City include bop giant Charlie Parker (• p. 136) and, more recently, guitarist Pat Metheny (• p. 199).

In 1995, director Robert Altman revisited the city (his own birthplace) to film a reconstruction of the heady period around 1934 when the SWING style was emerging there. Altman assembled a pool of over twenty leading contemporary jazz musicians on the set of his Hey Hey Club to recreate the JAM SESSIONS of the era, and described the resulting movie, *Kansas City*, as "a jazz memory."

Above Bennie Moten (seated, right) shows a new arrangement to the young Count Basie at the Pearl Theater, Philadelphia, *c.* 1931. Singer Jimmy Rushing stands between them.

Right Poster advertising Bennie Moten's gig at the Golden Slipper in Dayton, Ohio, on 30 September 1930.

Jazz Events

1927

- Russian pianist Leopold Teplitsky returns from the US with stocks of American jazz recordings, performing parts and instruments, and sets up "official" jazz activities in Leningrad on behalf of the Commissariat of Public Enlightenment.
- Jazz elements are used in two classical operas first performed in Germany during this year: Ernst Krenek's *Johnny Strikes Up* (Leipzig, **10 February**) and Kurt Weill's *The Rise and Fall of the City of Mahagonny* (Baden-Baden, **17 July**).
- Fats Waller (• p. 105) sells some of his compositions to Fletcher Henderson (• p. 71). Legend has it that Waller asks for, but does not receive, payment in the form of hamburgers (to which he is addicted).

1928

23 January
Clarinetist Benny Goodman (• p. 84) makes his first recordings.

14 March
Fletcher Henderson's band record their interpretation of Jelly Roll Morton's "King Porter Stomp," which becomes a hit under Goodman seven years later (• p. 83).

27 April
James P. Johnson's *Yamekraw: A Negro Rhapsody* is performed at Carnegie Hall by his protégé Fats Waller and an orchestra conducted by W. C. Handy (• p. 27). The "Father of STRIDE Piano" devotes increasing energy to works for the concert hall.

May
Alto saxophonist Johnny Hodges joins the Duke Ellington band.

28 June
Louis Armstrong's Hot Five record "West End Blues," opening with a spectacular trumpet cadenza from Armstrong that is soon widely imitated.

July
Count Basie joins Walter Page's Blue Devils in Kansas City.

17 October
Duke Ellington's Cotton Club orchestra records "The Mooche" in New York at one of six recording sessions held over the year.

5 December
In Chicago, Armstrong and Earl Hines record their virtuosic duet "Weather Bird." Hines forms a big band at the Grand Terrace Café, which remains there under his leadership for ten years.

13 December
First performance of George Gershwin's symphonic poem *An American in Paris,* New York.

- Belgian gypsy guitarist Django Reinhardt (• p. 75) loses the use of two fingers of his left hand in a caravan fire.
- Jelly Roll Morton and Louis Armstrong both move to New York.

1928

11 January
Death of Thomas Hardy

May
Japanese troops in China

3 July
First television sold, USA

12 August
Death of Leoš Janáček

1 September
King Zog becomes first monarch of Albania

15 September
Alexander Fleming discovers penicillin

- D. H. Lawrence completes *Lady Chatterley's Lover*

CHICAGO

Many musicians from New Orleans and other southern cities had migrated northward to the Windy City in search of employment since the 1910s, and by 1922 Chicago was home to such revered performers as Jelly Roll Morton, King Oliver, and Louis Armstrong, who recorded many of their early masterpieces in the city's studios. But by the end of the 1920s, Chicago was beginning to lose its status as the focal point for jazz.

Important venues during the 1920s included the Apex Club on East 35th Street (which featured the music of New Orleans clarinetist Jimmie Noone from 1926), the Coliseum on East 15th Street (famous for hosting CUTTING CONTESTS between rival bands), the Dreamland Café, Friar's Inn, Lincoln Gardens, and the Savoy Ballroom. Some of these were closely linked to local gangster organizations, and were heavily involved in the supply of illicit alcohol during Prohibition (1919–33). Figures such as the notorious Al Capone built empires through establishments known as "speakeasies," which sold bootleg liquor. Where there is alcohol, jazz is generally not far away, and a severe government clampdown on Chicago speakeasies in 1928 was one reason behind the new migration of musicians eastward to New York. By this time, the Big Apple was widely regarded as jazz's future city-of-opportunity.

Thanks to the tenacious efforts of performers such as Earl Hines (• p. 125), who remained for a decade at Chicago's Grand Terrace under the watchful eye of the Mafia, the city nevertheless remained firmly on the jazz map during the Swing Era, and new venues sprang up in the 1940s that helped to promote the developing bop style. Simultaneously, Chicago became one of the most important centers for the postwar growth of a powerful urban brand of blues, and in the 1960s the city again became prominent as the home of the radical FREE JAZZ (• p. 150).

Above left In the 1920s, the Coliseum was the venue for an annual show that celebrated Chicago's status as "the radio hub of the world."

Above Fletcher Henderson (far left) with his orchestra in 1927. Coleman Hawkins sits in the center of the front row.

1929

EMPRESS OF THE BLUES

Singer Bessie Smith, at the pinnacle of her career, appears in a Hollywood movie about W. C. Handy. Stride and boogie-woogie piano styles suffer a temporary setback with the murder of Pine Top Smith and the imprisonment of Fats Waller.

Above Bessie Smith, seen here in 1928. Her impassioned renderings of blues repertoire exerted a colossal influence on the next generation of jazz singers.

Jazz Events

28 January
Duke Ellington's recording of "Tiger Rag" breaks new ground by lasting over six minutes and occupying both SIDES of a 78rpm disc.

1 March
Fats Waller records some of his recent STRIDE compositions for solo piano, including "Handful of Keys." "Ain't Misbehavin'," from his hit stage show *Hot Chocolates*, featuring Louis Armstrong (who records the song on **22 July**), is recorded in a piano version on **2 August**. Waller is jailed this year for failing to keep up with his alimony payments. He also takes part in a mixed-race recording session at which he is forced to play behind a screen to segregate him from the white musicians.

15 March
Twenty-four-year-old BOOGIE-WOOGIE pianist Pine Top Smith is shot dead during a fight at a performance in a masonic lodge in Chicago. His composition "Pine Top's Boogie Woogie" is the first known use of the term.

June
Bessie Smith appears with an all-black cast in the Warner Bros. film *St. Louis Blues*, a biopic concerning the life of W. C. Handy (• p. 27), directed by Dudley Murphy. The musical direction is by Handy himself, supported by James P. Johnson's band (• p. 46).

October
Count Basie (• p. 87) records in Chicago with Bennie Moten's band from Kansas City.

7 November
Pianist Mary Lou Williams (• p. 196) records with Andy Kirk's Twelve Clouds of Joy in Kansas City.

29 November
Cootie Williams replaces Bubber Miley in the Ellington band, which makes a short film entitled *Black and Tan Fantasy*. Puerto Rican valve trombonist Juan Tizol also joins the band this year.

- Sidney Bechet (• p. 43) is arrested in France following a shooting incident, and subsequently deported.
- The journal *Musik-Echo* is founded in Berlin.
- Jean Cocteau begins poetry readings with jazz accompaniment in Paris.

World Events

6 January
Yugoslavia formed under King Alexander I

14 February
Valentine's Day Massacre, Chicago

16 May
First Academy Awards ceremony, Hollywood

19 August
Death of Serge Diaghilev

24 October
Wall Street stock market crash

- Cartoon characters Tin-Tin and Popeye created

BESSIE SMITH

Bessie Smith's appearance in *St. Louis Blues* came at a time when she was one of the most prolific recording artists in New York. Like many vocalists, she had begun her career in MINSTREL SHOWS and VAUDEVILLE before branching out to combine her talents with many of the day's finest jazz instrumentalists. Her early successes through work for the Theater Owners' Booking Association (the acronym T.O.B.A. was alternatively rendered as "Tough on Black Asses") brought her to the attention of pianist Clarence Williams, with whom she recorded "Downhearted Blues" in 1923. Further recordings with COMBOS led by Fletcher Henderson (• p. 71) and others followed, and her commercial success was secured by her popular stage shows *Harlem Frolics* and *Mississippi Days*.

Smith is today widely regarded as the finest jazz BLUES singer of all time. Her recordings, which spanned a period of some ten years, represent the first coherent attempt to import the spontaneous, often powerfully expressive style of raw blues singing into mainstream jazz. Her repertoire included examples of both the intensely melancholy and lighthearted blues styles (the latter often colored by heavy sexual innuendo). She developed a "dirty" GROWL tone that influenced many vocalists and instrumentalists, including Louis Armstrong (with whom she recorded a famous rendering of "St. Louis Blues" in 1925), Billie Holiday (• p. 131), and the brass players of Duke Ellington's orchestra (• p. 63).

Several factors combined to bring Smith's shining career to a sorry end. Her addiction to alcohol (a substance which, before it lost out to hard drugs, caused the premature demise of many musicians during Prohibition) coincided with a slump in the recording industry during the Depression. Her contract with Columbia lapsed in 1931 and was not renewed, and she made no recordings at all after 1933, although her singing continued to be well received in live performances.

On 25 September 1937 Smith was severely injured in an automobile accident and died within hours. The legend that she was refused admittance to a whites-only hospital, and expired before being admitted to an institution that accepted blacks, seems to have been concocted for political reasons.

Right The original poster advertising Bessie Smith's appearance in the 1929 Warner Bros. movie *St. Louis Blues*.

Below left A painting by Archibald J. Motley, Jr. (1891–1981), entitled *Blues* (1929).

ST. LOUIS BLUES

Originally published in 1914, W. C. Handy's *St. Louis Blues* quickly became one of the most popular STANDARDS in the growing repertoire of jazz pieces based on the TWELVE-BAR BLUES. Bessie Smith and Louis Armstrong recorded their superb interpretation on 14 January 1925, with an understated chordal accompaniment provided on the harmonium by Fred Longshaw. The absence of drums, coupled with Longshaw's fluctuating pulse, allowed the soloists an unusual degree of expressive freedom as they spontaneously reshaped Handy's simple theme, responding intuitively to each other's ideas.

Bessie's raw, earthy singing is a fine example of the "dirty" tone so characteristic of female blues singers in the 1920s. Each of her two-measure phrases is followed by a two-measure answering phrase from Armstrong's cornet (a CALL-AND-RESPONSE pattern typical of much early jazz): Armstrong skillfully imitates the tone quality and pitch-bending of the singer. Many more BLUE NOTES are sung and played than exist in Handy's printed score – especially that which flattens the third degree of the SCALE, repeatedly emphasized by Bessie to darken the mood.

The passionate spontaneity of this celebrated recording contrasts sharply with another interpretation cut in the same year by Paul Whiteman's dance orchestra, full of harmonic sophistication and colorful instrumentation but entirely pre-composed. A few years later, Bessie Smith strengthened her association with Handy's tune when she performed it in the movie *St. Louis Blues* in June 1929, backed by a full choir and jazz band led by stride pianist James P. Johnson.

Opposite Dorothy Dandridge dances atop Count Basie's piano in the movie *Hit Parade of 1943*, while his band nestles in a giant mock-up of a grand piano.

Swing: White musicians quickly capitalize on the success of black band arrangements to create a swinging style of jazzy dance music that will survive until the end of World War II and achieve global popularity.

–1945

DANCE BANDS

The suave, pre-composed music of white dance bands in New York begins to merge with the black big-band sound to create an exciting new style that becomes the pop music of the 1930s.

Jazz Events

1930

9 October
Louis Armstrong records "Body and Soul" in New York.

16 October
Percussionist Lionel Hampton records his first vibraphone solo in a session with Armstrong, and decides to devote himself to this hitherto unexploited instrument.

17 October
Duke Ellington's orchestra (• p. 63) records "Mood Indigo," one of nearly forty SIDES recorded by the band this year.

- Ted Lewis's DIXIELAND ensemble plays at the Kit Kat Restaurant, London, with Jimmy Dorsey (clarinet) and Muggsy Spanier (trumpet).
- Paul Whiteman and his orchestra star in the movie *The King of Jazz* (Universal).

Left Lionel Hampton, who established the vibraphone as a jazz solo instrument in the Benny Goodman Quartet (1936–40) and went on to compose the wartime hit "Flying Home" in 1942.

VIBRAPHONE

Having started out as a drummer, Lionel Hampton recorded a vibraphone solo in 1930 and subsequently became this neglected instrument's first virtuoso. Invented during World War I and superficially similar to the xylophone, the vibraphone has metal bars laid out in a keyboard arrangement. Each bar is suspended above its own tubular resonator, which contains an electrically driven fan that produces an oscillating tone. Hampton promoted the vibraphone as a solo instrument in his work with the Benny Goodman Quartet, then went on to lead his own big band, which turned out to be the longest surviving ensemble in the history of jazz, remaining active into the 1980s.

Another notable exponent of the instrument was Red Norvo, who, in the 1940s and 1950s, demonstrated that it could be employed equally well in the widely differing styles of SWING, BEBOP, and WEST COAST. Milt Jackson gave the instrument an intellectual respectability in his intricate work with the Modern Jazz Quartet (• p. 129), and Gary Burton added further sophistication in the 1960s by developing the technique of holding two beaters in each hand and striking four notes simultaneously to make a chord.

Below A modern Yamaha vibraphone. Note the instrument's sustaining pedal, and the tubular resonators that increase in size toward the bottom of the range.

Left The photograph on this LP reissue of Fletcher Henderson's music shows his band at Atlantic City in 1931, at the time when they were appearing at Connie's Inn in New York. In the back row are Coleman Hawkins (second from left) and Rex Stewart (fourth from left).

World Events

1930

18 February
Planet Pluto discovered

2 March
Death of D. H. Lawrence

29 March
Chicago musicians oppose choice of American national anthem

4 May
Gandhi arrested, India

14 September
Nazi election successes

ALL YOU GOTTA DO IS SWING

The big-band jazz that, in a diluted and commercialized form, became the pop music of the 1930s had essentially very little in common with the New Orleans style it supplanted. Some of the earliest practitioners originated in Kansas City (• p. 64) as part of a local development that climaxed in the definingly HOT sound of the Count Basie band (• p. 87). However, it was the popularity of the polished dance music being produced in New York that formed the backbone of the big-band style.

White dance bands had absorbed most of the important features of early jazz (principally BLUE NOTES, SYNCOPATION, and SWUNG RHYTHM), but avoided extended IMPROVISATION in favor of a high degree of PRE-COMPOSITION – an essential ingredient where a large number of performers is involved. The elaborate improvised COUNTERPOINT of the New Orleans style gave way to a new technique, which soon became a cliché, of presenting a melody in a BLOCK-CHORD harmonization. These parallel harmonies would usually be assigned to a single instrumental family (i.e., REEDS or brass), and might be rapidly traded from one group to the other in a pattern of RIFFS (yet another manifestation of the CALL-AND-RESPONSE concept).

The black pianist and arranger Fletcher Henderson created the finest dance music of his day, and provided a model for much later swing music. Henderson's band appeared at Broadway's Club Alabam and then at the Roseland Ballroom in the mid-1920s, and for a time numbered Louis Armstrong (• p. 57) among its members. By 1927, the Henderson orchestra comprised three trumpets, two trombones, three saxophones (which could double on clarinets as required), and a standard four-piece RHYTHM SECTION. It was only when Benny Goodman (• p. 84) bought Henderson's arrangements for his own (white) band seven years later that the popularity of the swing style rapidly spread across America. The size of the big bands grew with their commercial success, so that by the 1940s a typical lineup might include four trumpets, three trombones, and as many as five saxophones.

The work of Duke Ellington's orchestra (• pp. 63 and 182) from the late 1920s to the 1940s stands out as undoubtedly the most artistically satisfying example of the big-band style. While Ellington's music was rooted in the technical innovations of the Swing Era, and included some of the most commercially successful compositions of the period – notably "It Don't Mean a Thing (If It Ain't Got That Swing)" – his interest in pre-composed structures produced highly original and coherent musical forms that were felt by many to warrant direct comparison with the output of classical composers.

1930–31

Jazz Events

1931

20 January and 11 June
Duke Ellington again breaks with convention by recording two versions of his extended composition "Creole Rhapsody": each fills both sides of a 78rpm disc. Singer Ivie Anderson joins the band this year.

13 March
Fats Waller (• p. 105) records "I'm Crazy 'Bout My Baby."

6 August
Bix Beiderbecke dies of pneumonia at the age of thirty-eight, New York.

17 September
RCA demonstrates the first $33^{1}/_{3}$ rpm long-playing disc.

4 November
Buddy Bolden (• p. 25) dies, Jackson, Louisiana.

- Chick Webb's band is established at the Savoy Ballroom, Harlem.
- Lil Hardin separates from Louis Armstrong and forms an all-female band.
- French composer Maurice Ravel includes jazz elements in his Piano Concerto in G Major.
- Hungarian composer Mátyás Seiber teaches jazz at the Hoch Conservatory, Frankfurt.

Above Paul Whiteman and his orchestra as they appeared in the movie *The King of Jazz* (1930).

Left Bix Beiderbecke in the early 1920s: a musical genius driven to an early grave by alcoholism.

"The word jazz in its progress toward respectability has meant first sex, then dancing, then music. It is associated with a state of nervous stimulation . . ."

F. Scott Fitzgerald, *Echoes of the Jazz Age*, 1931

BIX AND THE DANCE BANDS

Of the white dance bands that brought a diluted brand of jazz to a wider audience in the 1920s and helped to form the basis for the emerging big-band style, the most accomplished were those led by Jean Goldkette and Paul Whiteman. Goldkette had the good sense to employ the talented cornetist Bix Beiderbecke as a featured soloist. Beiderbecke was the first white performer to be widely regarded by black musicians as a genuine jazz talent. After an apprenticeship in the New Orleans style, he joined Goldkette in 1926, and then went to work with Paul Whiteman's orchestra in the following year. Beiderbecke left Whiteman in 1929 and played sporadically with the Dorsey brothers and other bands until his premature death two years later, which was accelerated by alcoholism – an all too frequent menace during the years of Prohibition.

Praised for his velvety tone and understated lyricism, Beiderbecke was in many ways the opposite of Louis Armstrong. His keen interest in classical music led him to compose a Debussy-inspired piano piece, *In a Mist* (1927), and in Whiteman he found a kindred spirit. There is no doubt that the increasing use of techniques from classical music by both Goldkette and Whiteman did much to stimulate a more sophisticated conception of jazz composition. From an early stage Whiteman also showed himself to be a pioneer of the hybrid SYMPHONIC JAZZ (• p. 55).

Below Bix (seated, center) at New York's Bronx Zoo in 1927, surrounded by other members of Jean Goldkette's dance band. The exotic instrument draped around the standing attendant is, in fact, a live snake!

World Events

1931

23 January
Death of Anna Pavlova

14 April
Spain becomes Republic

1 May
Empire State Building opens, New York

13 June
German banks collapse

18 September
Japan invades Manchuria

3 October
Carl Nielsen dies

- Massive worldwide unemployment
- William Walton's oratorio *Belshazzar's Feast*

"It is my firm belief that what is still known as 'jazz' is going to play a considerable part in the serious music of the future . . . The music of my race is something more than the American idiom. It is the result of our transplantation to American soil and was our reaction in the plantation days to the tyranny we endured. What we could not say openly we expressed in music."

Duke Ellington, "The Duke Steps Out," *Rhythm*, March 1931

1932

ROBERT GOFFIN

AUX FRONTIÈRES DU JAZZ

Préface de PIERRE MAC ORLAN

PREMIÈRE ÉDITION
illustrée de 60 photographies.

"LES DOCUMENTAIRES"
EDITIONS DU SAGITTAIRE
(ANCIENNES ÉDITIONS KRA)
20, Rue Henri-Regnault, 20
PARIS-XIV.

Left The cover of Robert Goffin's groundbreaking book, *Aux Frontières du Jazz*.

PARIS

France becomes the leading country in European jazz, producing the first critical books on the subject and launching the hugely successful Hot Club in Paris.

Racial prejudices continue to mar objective musical criticism in the 1930s, as shown by the following bigoted response to Louis Armstrong's London appearance:

"Armstrong is the ugliest man I have ever seen on the music hall stage. He looks and behaves like an untrained gorilla. He might have come straight from some African jungle and then, after being taken to some slop tailors for a ready made dress suit, been put straight on the stage and told to 'sing'."

Hannen Swaffer, *Daily Herald*, 25 July 1932

Jazz Events

2 February
Duke Ellington records "It Don't Mean a Thing (If It Ain't Got That Swing)," the first jazz composition with the word SWING in its title. In this year, he appears in a concert at Columbia University organized at the suggestion of the Australian composer Percy Grainger.

6 March
Death of John Philip Sousa.

20 May
Former Ellington trumpeter Bubber Miley dies, New York.

August
Vocalist Adelaide Hall records with pianist Art Tatum (• p. 125) in New York.

Summer
Louis Armstrong's first tour to Europe includes a visit to London.

9 December
The Fletcher Henderson orchestra (• p. 71) records "New King Porter Stomp" for John Hammond in New York.

- Fats Waller (• p. 105) plays in Paris.
- Belgian lawyer Robert Goffin publishes his book *Aux Frontières du Jazz* in Paris.
- The Hot Club de France, Europe's first jazz club, is founded in Paris by French critic Hugues Panassié, together with Elwyn Dirants and Jacques Ozenfant.

World Events

2 January
Japanese form a Manchurian Republic

28 January
Japanese attack Shanghai

6 May
President Doumer assassinated, France

June–August
Nazi power escalates, Germany

12 August
Monarchist coup, Seville

- Aldous Huxley's novel *Brave New World*
- Olympic Games in Los Angeles
- British physicist John Cockcroft splits the atom, Cambridge, UK

LE HOT CLUB DE FRANCE

In Paris in 1932, a group of like-minded jazz aficionados formed the Hot Club de France under the presidency of the French writer and critic Hugues Panassié, who also edited the club's influential journal (*Jazz-hot*) when it was launched in 1935. The Hot Club, the first organization of its kind in Europe, became famous after 1934 when it promoted its own jazz quintet (violin, three guitars, and bass), featuring violinist Stephane Grappelli and guitarist Django Reinhardt. A wider circulation for the quintet's work was secured by the Swing record label, founded in 1937 by Panassié and Charles Delaunay (son of the painters Robert and Sonia). Swing also recorded the music of touring American musicians, such as saxophonists Coleman Hawkins and Benny Carter.

Apart from a separation during the war years when Reinhardt performed in occupied Europe while Grappelli remained in England (• p. 92), the two played together until Reinhardt's death in 1953. In temperament, they could hardly have been more different. Grappelli came from a comfortable middle-class background, and initiated the use of the violin as a solo jazz instrument through dedicated hard work born of classical training. Reinhardt, on the other hand, hailed from Belgian gypsy stock (a fire in his caravan had crippled his left hand). He was an unpredictable and undisciplined genius, difficult to work with even at the best of times.

The instinctive musical rapport between the two men in performance was electrifying, and they generated a new brand of small-ensemble jazz at a time when big bands were at the height of fashion across the globe. Both players brought out qualities in their instruments never before seen in jazz, and exerted considerable influence on subsequent violinists and guitarists. Reinhardt's disability compelled him to play novel harmonies that might, arguably, not have been discovered had his fingers been capable of their full function. In the 1990s, the octogenarian Grappelli was still performing with as much verve as he had in his youth (and in much the same style), notably in partnership with British guitarist Martin Taylor – forty-eight years his junior.

Above This fine study of Django Reinhardt, taken by William Gottlieb in the 1940s, clearly shows the guitarist's disfigured left hand.

Left The Quintette du Hot Club de France, *c.* 1934, featuring the talents of Stephane Grappelli (far left) and Django Reinhardt (center).

1933

European jazz is stimulated by visits from Louis Armstrong and Duke Ellington at a time when the Nazi Party in Germany seems bent on suppressing it. In America, singer Billie Holiday emerges just as Bessie Smith ends her recording career.

SATCHMO AND THE DUKE IN EUROPE

Jazz Events

21 March
Art Tatum (• p. 125) records his first piano solo, "Tiger Rag," which is thought by some to be a piano duet.

March
The Berlin radio station Funkstunde bans jazz broadcasts in deference to Nazi doctrine.

2 June
Duke Ellington and his orchestra sail from New York to Southampton to begin their first European tour, which includes a two-week appearance at the London Palladium and a visit to the Salle Pleyel, Paris. In **February**, the band recorded the Duke's most recent hit, "Sophisticated Lady."

15 July
Trumpeter Freddie Keppard dies, Chicago.

July
Louis Armstrong returns to London as part of his ongoing European tour.

24 November
Bessie Smith (• p. 67) makes her last four recordings.

27 November
Billie Holiday makes her first recording ("Your Mother's Son-in-Law") with Benny Goodman (• p. 84) for English Columbia, earning $35.

December
A CUTTING CONTEST for tenor saxophonists in Kansas City (• p. 64) is won by Lester Young. Other contenders include Ben Webster, Herschel Evans, and Coleman Hawkins.

• Eubie Blake and Noble Sissle take their show *Shuffle Along of 1933* on tour to Los Angeles, where it collapses and leaves seventeen-year-old pianist Nat King Cole (• p. 125) without a job. He finds one the following year with the Royal Dukes in Chicago, where he is influenced by Earl Hines at the Grand Terrace Café.

Above Guy Arnoux's *Couples Dancing to Jazz* (1920).

Left Duke Ellington as he liked to appear in the 1930s: every bit as elegant and sophisticated as his highly acclaimed music.

JAZZING IN EUROPE

On 19 January 1919, *The Times* in London, finally recognizing the existence of jazz, described the new music as "one of the many American peculiarities that threaten to make life a nightmare." Less than three months later, the Original Dixieland Jazz Band descended on the city fresh from their spectacular successes in Chicago and New York. They created a sensation: their appearance at the Hippodrome caused such a wildly enthusiastic response from the audience that they were immediately (and somewhat perversely) dismissed by the management. Undaunted, the band moved on to the London Palladium and the Hammersmith Palais, and even performed for King George V at Buckingham Palace.

A burgeoning craze for HOT dance music intensified when Paul Whiteman visited England in 1923 and 1926, and when Louis Armstrong and Duke Ellington did so in 1932–33. Many British big bands enjoyed success during the 1930s, including one led by Jack Hylton, who persuaded Coleman Hawkins to come to England in 1934. But British shortsightedness soon began to rear its ugly head. The late 1920s brought vociferous demands for the jobs of native musicians to be protected from a feared invasion by immigrant Americans, and thus began the sorry tale of extensive anti-American action by the Musicians' Union that resulted in a regrettable musical insularity until horizons broadened in the 1950s (• pp. 84 and 134).

The situation was much more positive elsewhere in Europe. In France – the country in which Debussy, Satie, and Stravinsky had all fallen under the spell of RAGTIME before 1918 – the arrival of the spectacularly erotic black dancer Josephine Baker (• p. 59) in the mid-1920s gave a new impetus to Parisian nightlife. Baker also visited Berlin in 1925 and 1927, and Paul Whiteman toured from Paris to Berlin in 1926 with *Rhapsody in Blue* (• p. 55). Jack Hylton appeared regularly in France and Germany in the late 1920s and early 1930s. An informal jazz festival was organized in 1932 in Belgium, where enthusiasts had been trying to emulate the New Orleans style for many years.

The arrival in Paris of major stars such as Fats Waller (1932), Duke Ellington (1933), and Louis Armstrong (1934) further intensified popular interest in American jazz, and with the foundation of the Hot Club de France (• p. 75) the position of Paris as the jazz capital of Europe was secured. It was here, not in America, that the first significant books on jazz were published: Hugues Panassié's *Le Jazz Hot* (1934) and Charles Delaunay's *Hot Discography* (1936). It was only the rise to power of Hitler's Nazi Party (• p. 81) that threatened to impede the rapid progress of jazz throughout Continental Europe.

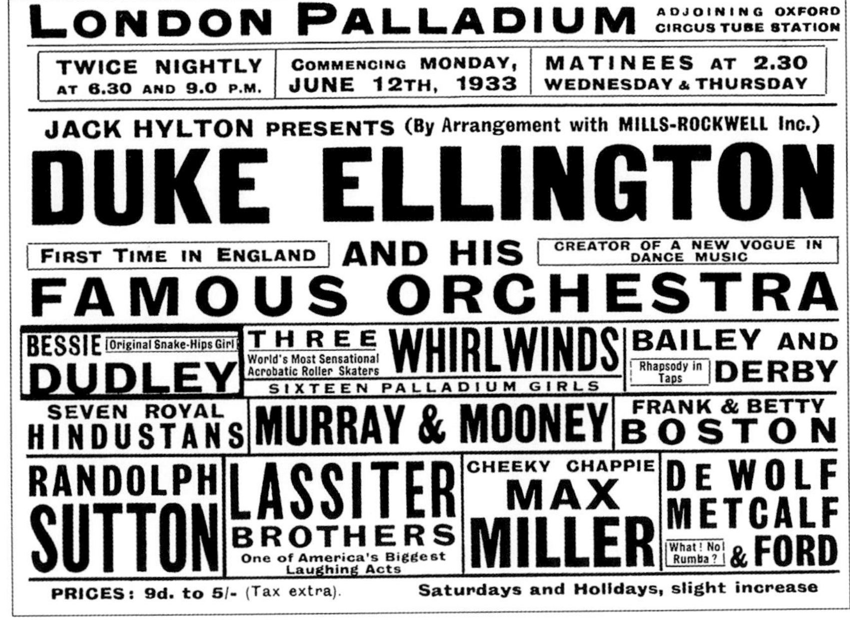

World Events

30 January
Hitler becomes Chancellor of Germany

1 March
Political arrests begin, Germany

4 March
President Roosevelt initiates US economic recovery

20 March
Establishment of Dachau concentration camp

1 April
Jewish finances appropriated by Nazi government

4 July
Gandhi imprisoned

5 December
End of Prohibition, USA

- Ernest Schoedsack's movie *King Kong*

Below Billie Holiday (left), sporting her trademark gardenias in her hair, and the formidable Bessie Smith (right), pictured toward the end of her singing career in the 1930s.

1934

STOMPIN' AT THE SAVOY

Chick Webb's band, with teenage vocalist Ella Fitzgerald, delights audiences in New York. Fletcher Henderson begins his association with Benny Goodman, who is unwittingly poised on the brink of international stardom.

Jazz Events

30 March
Coleman Hawkins arrives in England to work with Jack Hylton and his band, having quit Fletcher Henderson's orchestra earlier in the month. Lester Young becomes his temporary replacement.

18 May
Drummer Chick Webb records "Stompin' at the Savoy" with his band. He soon employs sixteen-year-old vocalist Ella Fitzgerald (• p. 195), who wins two talent competitions in Harlem this year.

June
Benny Goodman's band (• p. 84) opens at Billy Rose's Music Hall, New York.

July
The journal *Down Beat: The Contemporary Music Magazine* is launched in Chicago.

November
Henderson's band folds due to financial difficulties. He sells some of his best arrangements to Goodman, whose band has just successfully auditioned for an NBC radio show.
• As part of his prolific series of piano recordings on the Victor label, Fats Waller (• p. 105) cuts "Honeysuckle Rose" and "Alligator Crawl."

2 December
The Quintette du Hot Club de France, including Django Reinhardt and Stephane Grappelli (• p. 75), gives its first public performance at the École Normale de Musique de Paris.

Above Django Reinhardt (left) looks on in mock horror as Stephane Grappelli exchanges his violin for Reinhardt's guitar. This picture dates from 1948, some fourteen years after their first appearance with the Quintette du Hot Club de France in Paris.

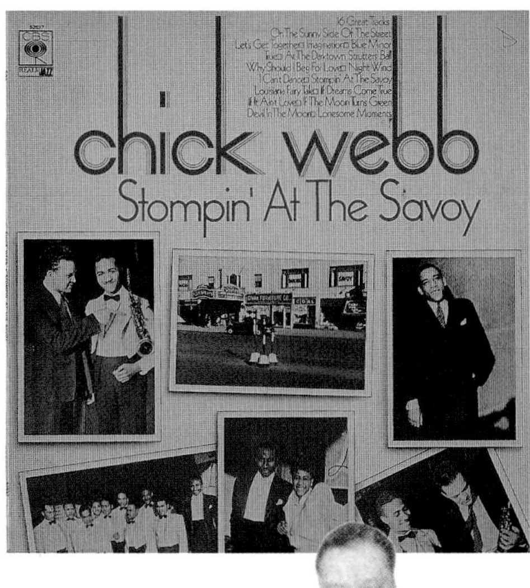

Left CBS's LP reissue of classic Chick Webb recordings from the 1930s.

Below James P. Johnson (at the piano) with his Small's Paradise band, pictured in New York in 1934.

World Events

23 February
Edward Elgar dies

23 May
Outlaws Bonnie Parker and Clyde Barrow shot dead, USA

25 May
Gustav Holst dies

May
First Glyndebourne opera festival, UK

10 June
Frederick Delius dies

23 June
Italian troops invade Albania

25 July
Nazi coup fails in Austria

19 August
Hitler begins dictatorship

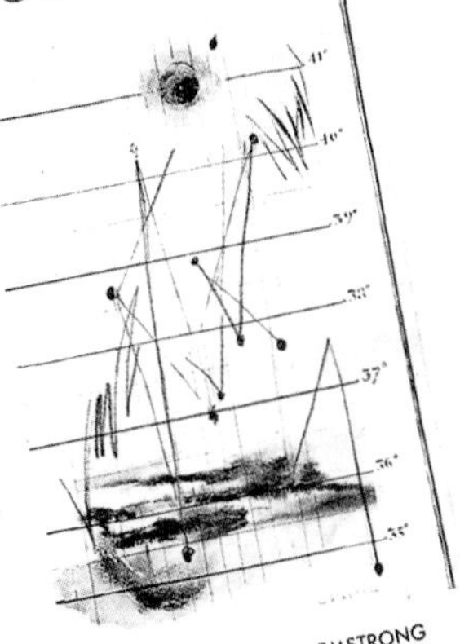

Jazz Events

- Jimmie Lunceford's band replaces Cab Calloway's at the Cotton Club, Harlem (• p. 63).
- The Dorsey Brothers Orchestra is founded by Jimmy (clarinet) and Tommy (trombone).
- Louis Armstrong appears at the Salle Pleyel, Paris.
- Duke Ellington and Billie Holiday appear in the film *Symphony in Black* at Paramount studios.
- Hugues Panassié publishes *Le Jazz Hot* in Paris, the first critical study of the music to appear in print.
- Soviet composer Dmitri Shostakovich composes his first *Suite for Jazz Orchestra*.

Above The exterior of the Cotton Club during Cab Calloway's residency there from 1931 to 1934.

Far left Hugues Panassié, president of the Hot Club de France (1935–46), published his first book in 1934 and remained a staunch traditionalist in later life.

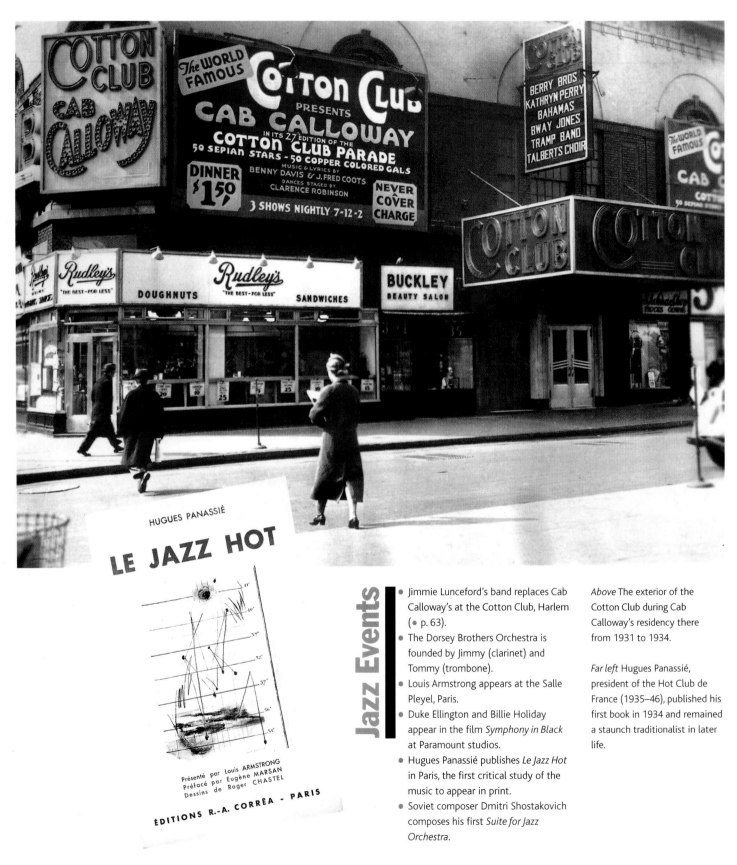

JAZZ UNDER THE NAZIS

Since its inception, jazz has been distinguished by a freedom of musical expression (sometimes politically symbolic) that ultimately derives from the performer's individuality. This essential trait was hardly likely to endear the music to the rulers of totalitarian regimes, which can function effectively only through the suppression of personal freedoms. In both Soviet Russia and Nazi Germany, jazz came to be seriously discredited. In Hitler's Germany, it was perceived as the loathsome product of blacks and Jews, both ethnic groups that needed to be eradicated from society in order to preserve the purity of the Aryan master race. The fact that jazz was largely an American import made it even more distasteful to the Nazis, especially when the US joined the Allies in fighting against Germany at the end of 1941.

The heady nightlife of Berlin in the 1920s, in which jazz played an important role, had attracted numerous foreign musicians (• p. 77). There were several German bands who imitated the style of HOT recordings from America with some success, including multi-instrumentalist Stefan Weintraub and his Syncopators, who wisely failed to return to Germany from a world tour in 1933 when the Nazis came to power. In that year, propaganda minister Joseph Goebbels set up the *Reichskulturkammer* to keep a watchful eye on cultural activities, and his control of broadcasting permitted him gradually to replace American-style jazz with an anodyne dance music designed to keep both public and troops happy. Meanwhile, Jewish musicians were increasingly prevented from plying their trade.

In 1937, Goebbels proclaimed that all music recorded by non-Aryan musicians was to be banned. Several regional authorities prohibited the live performance of jazz in 1938–39. The only authentic jazz on German airwaves featured in the notorious propaganda broadcasts by Lord Haw-Haw, where it was included solely as bait to entice listeners from enemy countries (• p. 96). Jazz nevertheless continued to be enjoyed covertly in Berlin, Leipzig (which opened an influential "Hot Club"), and elsewhere. In Hamburg, the flamboyant "Swings" espoused both Anglo-American mannerisms and proscribed SWING music with courageous openness, and as a consequence many of them were sent to concentration camps. Favorite American numbers continued to be played wherever possible, however, often with their famous titles heavily disguised (in occupied Paris, for example, Gershwin's "Lady Be Good" was rendered as "Les Bigoudis," or "The Hair-Rollers!") Even Luftwaffe pilots on bombing missions to England habitually tuned their radio receivers to the BBC's jazz broadcasts from London in an attempt to catch up on the outlawed music.

Jazz could be performed with greater ease in the Nazi-occupied countries of western Europe. In France, Belgium, Holland, and Denmark, regulations were sufficiently relaxed to permit recordings, which, although prohibited from sale in Germany, circulated freely in the country of origin. Thus Django Reinhardt (• p. 75) continued to promote his career in France, in spite of his anxieties concerning Nazi attempts to liquidate those of gypsy blood (• p. 105).

Above The decadent Berlin nightlife as portrayed by painter Otto Dix in 1927, before the Nazi attempt to eradicate hot jazz from German culture.

Top Ludwig Tersch's savage front cover design for H. S. Ziegler's catalog *Entartete Musik* ("Degenerate Music"), published in 1938 at the height of the Nazi proscription of jazz.

KINGS OF SWING

Benny Goodman's spectacular success in Los Angeles creates a world market for big-band jazz. Symphonic jazz is further developed as a vehicle for American musical nationalism in Gershwin's folk opera *Porgy and Bess*.

Above A jazz party at Tony's Tavern, Chicago, on Valentine's Day, 1935. Guests of honor are Duke Ellington and Louis Armstrong (fifth and sixth from left).

Right The journal *Jazz-hot*, first published in 1935 as the official organ of the Hot Club de France, was issued monthly until the beginning of World War II. Publication resumed in 1945, and from 1950 continued alongside the separate *Bulletin du Hot Club de France*.

Jazz Events

March
First publication of the journal *Jazz-hot: revue internationale de la musique de jazz,* Paris.

2 April
Bennie Moten dies, Kansas City. Count Basie forms his Barons of Rhythm with members of Moten's band, and the new group appears at Club Reno, Kansas City.

April and May
STRIDE pianist Willie "The Lion" Smith is rediscovered in a series of recordings for Decca, New York.

12 June
Ella Fitzgerald (● p. 195) records "I'll Chase the Blues Away" and "Love and Kisses" with Chick Webb, in her first appearance on disc.

1 July
Benny Goodman (● p. 84) records Jelly Roll Morton's "King Porter Stomp" in an arrangement by Fletcher Henderson (● p. 71). This month Goodman begins recording with a mixed-race trio that includes Teddy Wilson (piano) and Gene Krupa (drums).

2 and 31 July
Billie Holiday (● p. 131) records seven SIDES with Teddy Wilson in New York, including "What a Little Moonlight Can Do."

21 August
Benny Goodman's American coast-to-coast tour climaxes with a sensationally successful performance at the Palomar Ballroom, Los Angeles, which intensifies public interest in the SWING-band style.

12 September
Duke Ellington (● p. 63) records his second extended score, "Reminiscin' in Tempo," filling all four sides of two 78rpm discs.

Autumn
Stephane Grappelli and Django Reinhardt (● p. 75) record together in Paris.
● Louis Armstrong, back in New York after his tours of Europe and now on the books of commercially aggressive agent Joe Glaser, reenters the recording studio.

World Events

January–February
Italian military activity in Africa

18 June
Anglo-German naval agreement

29 August
Queen Astrid of Belgium killed in car crash

15 September
Anti-Semitic laws passed, Germany

2 October
Italy invades Ethiopia

24 December
Death of Alban Berg

● T. S. Eliot's play *Murder in the Cathedral*

Below Ella Fitzgerald performs at New York's Savoy Ballroom in 1940, shortly after assuming the leadership of Chick Webb's band.

POPULIST AND CLASSICIST: BENNY GOODMAN

A sudden decline in the fortunes of Fletcher Henderson's dance orchestra (• p. 71), when his tenor saxophonist Coleman Hawkins left to work for Jack Hylton in Britain, coincided with the meteoric rise to prominence of the twenty-five-year-old Jewish clarinetist Benny Goodman in 1934. Initially based in Chicago, Goodman moved to New York in 1928 – a year in which many notable musicians gravitated eastward to the Big Apple. He successfully auditioned for an NBC radio show in November 1934 with a newly formed big band and, at the suggestion of record producer John Hammond (• p. 209), bought a number of band arrangements from Henderson to augment his then meager repertoire. The combination of Henderson's exciting and intricate orchestrations with the professionalism and commercial potential of Goodman's new band propelled big-band jazz into the limelight, and initiated a rage for SWING music that lasted well into the 1940s.

All this happened virtually overnight. In August 1935, after a dispiriting season in New York, Goodman took his band to California and played to a packed Palomar Ballroom in Los Angeles, where the crowd went wild with excitement (as did those listening in to the live radio broadcast from the venue). Goodman instantly became a household name. He was dubbed the "King of Swing," and gained such nationwide prestige that he appeared at New York's Carnegie Hall (• p. 91) three years later. His band included flamboyant drummer Gene Krupa and agile trumpeter Harry James, both of whom left in 1938 to lead their own bands after personality clashes with the often intractable Goodman. Henderson joined the band as full-time staff arranger in 1939, and in the following year Goodman formed a new group that included guitarist Charlie Christian (• p. 99). He continued to produce big-band jazz of impeccable quality, and shrewdly hired BEBOP soloists in the later 1940s when it seemed evident that jazz was moving in a new direction.

Alongside his cultivation of a polished big-band sound, Goodman worked with smaller groups that were prophetic of developments in jazz after World War II. In 1935 he set up a trio with Krupa on drums and the dexterous Teddy Wilson at the keyboard. Since Wilson was black and the other two members white, this was a bold statement in a period when mixed-race groups were still severely frowned upon in America. In the following year, the black vibraphonist Lionel Hampton (• p. 70) was added to the group to create a quartet.

Goodman was also the first jazz musician to pursue a parallel career in classical music, recording the Clarinet Quintet by Mozart in 1938 (• p. 90) and commissioning concert works from internationally distinguished composers such as Béla Bartók, Benjamin Britten, Paul Hindemith, and Aaron Copland. That he was able to achieve all this remains an eloquent testament to his faultless technique, which has been the envy of every jazz clarinetist since.

Never easy to work with, Goodman had an absentminded and sometimes irritable personality, and his inveterate musical perfectionism did not endear him to all his players. Pianist Jess Stacy recalled the leader's obsession with the accurate tuning of instruments, and even Goodman's own daughter declared that she was terrified of playing classical music for her father. He could also be devious: one of Goodman's star vocalists remained convinced that he had asked her to marry him just to ensure her continued commitment to the band at the height of her popular success.

Jazz Events

10 October
George Gershwin's three-act opera *Porgy and Bess* opens at the Alvin Theater, New York; its plot, adapted from the novel by DuBose Heyward, is set among the black community of Charleston, South Carolina. Although not a striking success at first, the opera later becomes renowned as a landmark in the development of SYMPHONIC JAZZ and contributes a number of songs to the repertory of jazz STANDARDS.

12 October
A meeting of German radio-station directors in Munich hears Nazi government plans for a total broadcasting ban on jazz.

- Britain's Ministry of Labour, under pressure from the Musicians' Union, decrees that American musicians are to be banned from appearing in the UK until mutually satisfactory terms are agreed with the American Federation of Musicians.

Left Benny Goodman in the mid-1930s: the first performer to forge a dual career in jazz and the classics.

Above The cast assembles in Catfish Row to depart for a picnic in the original 1935 production of Gershwin's celebrated opera *Porgy and Bess* (Act 2, Scene 1). This scene includes the songs "I Got Plenty o' Nuttin'" and "Bess, You is My Woman Now."

Left Benny Goodman and his quartet rehearse for a radio broadcast in 1938 (l. to r.): Lionel Hampton (vibraphone), Goodman (clarinet), Teddy Wilson (piano), and Gene Krupa (drums).

1936

The big-band era now in full swing, Count Basie injects a powerful blues flavor into the music. Recordings by young vocalists Billie Holiday and Ella Fitzgerald are soon heavily in demand.

BILLIE AND ELLA

Jazz Events

January
Count Basie signs a contract with Decca to record twenty-four SIDES per annum, for a yearly fee of $750 (with no royalties). Lester Young rejoins the Basie band this year after brief spells with Fletcher Henderson and others.

January–February
A series of recordings in Chicago by Albert Ammons and Meade Lux Lewis heralds a revival of interest in BOOGIE-WOOGIE.

February
Charlie Green, a jobbing trombonist who recorded with Bessie Smith, Fletcher Henderson, and Chick Webb, dies from exposure on a Harlem street.

17 March
Nineteen-year-old Ella Fitzgerald stands in for Billie Holiday (her senior by only two years) with Teddy Wilson's band in a New York recording session.

30 June
Holiday and Wilson record "I Cried for You," which sells fifteen thousand copies.

28 July
Young pianist Nat King Cole (● p. 125) makes his first recordings with the Solid Swingers, a band led by his brother Eddie (on bass) in Chicago.

21 August
Benny Goodman adds vibraphonist Lionel Hampton (● p. 70) to his trio to record "Moonglow," the first in a celebrated series of quartet sessions.

9 October
Count Basie records for Vocalion in Chicago at the instigation of John Hammond, who has heard the band's broadcasts from Kansas City.

- Duke Ellington (● p. 63) provides music for the Marx Brothers' movie *A Day at the Races*.
- In Paris Charles Delaunay publishes *Hot Discography*, the first jazz discography to appear in print.
- The English translation of Hugues Panassié's pioneering critical study *Le Jazz Hot* (● p. 80) is published in New York and London.

World Events

20 January
King George V dies, UK

28 January
Dmitri Shostakovich's opera *Lady Macbeth* banned by Stalin in USSR

26 February
Volkswagen introduced, Germany

18 April
Death of Ottorino Respighi

7 May
Germany occupies the Rhineland

17 July
Spanish Civil War begins

1 August
Olympic Games open in Berlin

1 November
Berlin and Rome form Axis

18 November
General Franco established, Spain

10 December
Abdication of Edward VIII, UK

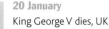

Left A bird's-eye view of Count Basie's band at the Apollo Theater, New York, in January 1939.

CLARINET

The clarinet was a favored instrument in New Orleans during the early days of jazz, flourishing both at the hands of untutored black musicians and through an extension of the European tradition of classical clarinet playing in which many Creole performers were schooled. The best of the latter, notably Sidney Bechet (• p. 43) and Barney Bigard (• p. 62), combined their considerable technical facility with a flair for the extemporized melodic embellishments characteristic of New Orleans jazz. This school of playing culminated in the fluent improvising of later bandleader clarinetists, principally Artie Shaw and Benny Goodman (• p. 84).

During the Swing Era, the clarinet lost out to the growing popularity of the saxophone (• p. 93), both as a featured solo instrument and in big-band arrangements. For a time, REED players were expected to play saxophone and clarinet, since both have similar single-reed mouthpieces and some shared fingering techniques (related to the "Boehm" system).

After the advent of BEBOP, very few important clarinet soloists emerged. One exception was Buddy DeFranco, who met with a mixed critical reception. Rare ancillary instruments, such as the contrabass clarinet played by Anthony Braxton, were employed in the experimental FREE JAZZ of the 1960s (• p. 150), largely for their novelty value. At the hands of Eddie Daniels, however, the standard clarinet was revived as a versatile participant in the easygoing post-FUSION style produced on the GRP label (• p. 214). The clarinet achieved a fresh prominence in jazz from the 1990s onwards, and was a distinctive participant in the modern blending of Jewish klezmer music and jazz.

Right Bandleader Artie Shaw, c. 1940, pictured beneath a B♭ clarinet (right) and bass clarinet (left), the latter rarely used as a solo instrument in jazz until the work of Eric Dolphy and others in the 1960s.

Left Count Basie's laconic and understated keyboard playing formed an effective contrast to the extrovert brilliance of his virtuoso big band.

THE COUNT FROM NEW JERSEY

In the spring of 1936, pianist William "Count" Basie was leading his Barons of Rhythm band at Club Reno in Kansas City (• p. 64). By happy chance, John Hammond (• p. 209) heard a broadcast from the venue and persuaded Basie to bring the band to New York, where its energetic "southwest" manner of playing soon enthralled audiences. Basie's early experience with Bennie Moten and Walter Page in Missouri had influenced his cultivation of a big-band style that was far more entrenched in the BLUES than that of his white competitors. His band's powerful sense of SWING and greater improvisational spontaneity demonstrated how much jazzier a good black band could sound when compared with the polished but sometimes pedestrian performances of Goodman and others. Basie's orchestra exploited the WALKING BASS and characteristic rhythmic patterns of the swing style to the full, creating an unfailing sense of musical momentum with techniques that could, however, all too easily become stale clichés.

A spell in 1937 at New York's Roseland Ballroom, former stomping ground of Fletcher Henderson, cemented the band's reputation. That same year it also recorded the hit tune "One O'Clock Jump," which embodied a masterful treatment of a simple but catchy RIFF. Now expanded from its original nine members to no fewer than sixteen, the band included a formidable saxophone section that thrived on the creative tension between its two tenor players, Lester Young and the ill-fated Herschel Evans (• p. 92). Young espoused a light tone full of air and grace, while Evans was one of the most impassioned melodists of his generation. Basie himself contributed piano solos that seemed to leave their STRIDE origins far behind. This former protégé of Fats Waller (• p. 105) now began to rely on a bare minimum of notes, delivered with an unerring sense of timing and a delicacy of touch that at times sat oddly alongside the invigorating style of his band.

1937

PIANO TRIO

Virtually all imported jazz records are banned in Germany in a year that sees the birth of the piano trio and the deaths of George Gershwin and Bessie Smith.

Above Nat King Cole (far right) poses with his innovative piano trio.

Jazz Events

13 March
Billie Holiday (• p. 131) makes her debut with Count Basie's band in Scranton, Pennsylvania. She stays with the group until early the following year, but contractual restrictions prevent her from recording with them.

28 April
Coleman Hawkins records with Django Reinhardt (• p. 75) and Benny Carter in Paris.

14 May
Duke Ellington records the exotic "Caravan," composed by his trombonist Juan Tizol. On **20 September**, he records his radical extended composition "Diminuendo and Crescendo in Blue," which is not successful until revived in 1956 (• p. 138).

June
Count Basie's band (• p. 87) broadcasts from the Savoy Ballroom, Harlem, and appears at the Apollo Theater. On **7 July** they record "One O'Clock Jump," which becomes their hit signature tune.

6 July
Benny Goodman (• p. 84) records "Sing, Sing, Sing (With a Swing)" in Los Angeles, fusing the original Louis Prima tune with "Christopher Columbus" to create an extended piece that causes a sensation at Carnegie Hall (• p. 91) the following year.

11 July
George Gershwin dies from a brain tumor at the age of thirty-eight, in Hollywood.

26 September
Bessie Smith (• p. 67) dies from severe injuries in a motor accident.

September
Nat King Cole (• p. 125) creates a new ensemble – the piano trio – by forming a group with Oscar Moore (guitar) and Wesley Prince (bass). The trio, based in Los Angeles, performs live for three years before committing their music to disc.

December
Nazi propaganda minister Joseph Goebbels prohibits the sale of "non-Aryan" recordings in Germany, effectively outlawing all jazz recorded by black and Jewish artists. A list of proscribed compositions is circulated.

GEORGE GERSHWIN

Gershwin's untimely death in 1937 robbed the musical world of a unique talent. Unlike his compatriot Aaron Copland (• p. 55), Gershwin had approached the challenge of creating SYMPHONIC JAZZ from a grounding in popular rather than classical music, and had scored an early success with *Rhapsody in Blue* in 1924.

The son of immigrant Russian Jews (his real surname was Gershovitz), Gershwin began his career modestly at the age of fifteen by working as a song PLUGGER in a New York publishing house (• p. 30). He became a highly competent STRIDE pianist and recorded numerous PIANO ROLLS (• p. 32), but first found fame as a composer of popular musical comedies on Broadway, beginning with *La La Lucille* in 1919. Five years later, his older brother Ira joined him as librettist, usually adding words to themes George had already composed. Together they created a stream of brilliant songs that rapidly reached a wide international audience. The series of Broadway musicals on which they collaborated from 1924 onward spawned a number of independent hits, including "Fascinatin' Rhythm" (from *Lady, Be Good!,* 1924) and "I Got Rhythm" (from *Girl Crazy,* 1930). Gershwin's "American folk opera," *Porgy and Bess* (• p. 85), although only achieving a limited success on Broadway in 1935, included several songs – "Summertime," "It Ain't Necessarily So," "I Got Plenty o' Nuttin'," and "I Loves You, Porgy" – that became jazz STANDARDS.

By this stage in Gershwin's career, the acclaim he had received in the concert hall with his groundbreaking symphonic jazz caused him to regard his work as a composer with more seriousness. For a time he even contemplated studying formally with French composer Maurice Ravel, who is reputed to have told Gershwin when they met, "Why be a second-rate Ravel when you can be a first-rate Gershwin?" Another report records that when Gershwin asked Ravel for lessons, the Frenchman replied with his own sly question: "How much do you earn from your composing?" When Gershwin revealed to Ravel the extent of his income, Ravel simply said "You teach me!"

World Events

26 April
Germans bomb the Basque town of Guernica

6 May
Airship *Hindenburg* explodes, New Jersey

12 May
Coronation of George VI, UK

28 July
Japanese capture Peking

October
Duke and Duchess of Windsor meet Hitler

8 November
Japanese secure Shanghai

25 December
Arturo Toscanini's inaugural concert with NBC Symphony Orchestra, USA

29 December
Irish Free State renamed Eire

• Dmitri Shostakovich's Fifth Symphony

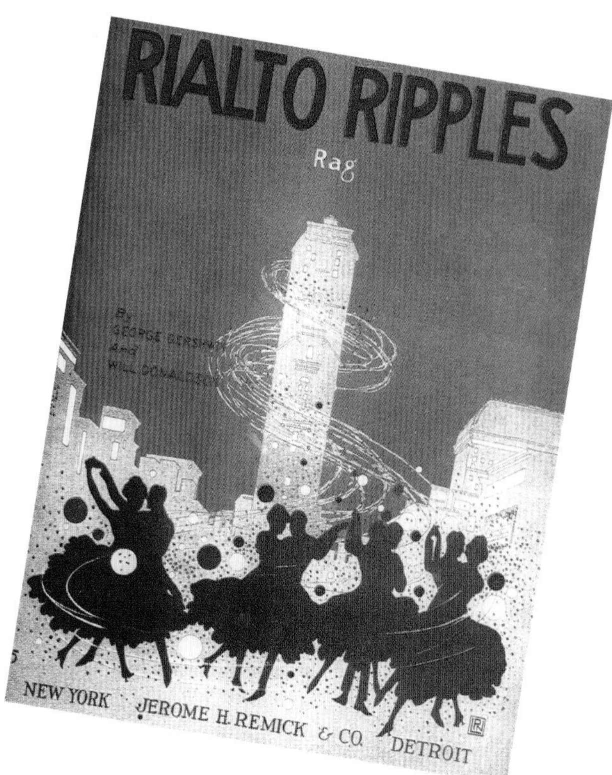

Above "Rialto Ripples," cocomposed with Will Donaldson, was recorded on piano roll by Gershwin in 1916.

Above left George Gershwin at the piano.

Left Blind keyboard virtuoso Art Tatum, pictured in the late 1940s.

NEW RESPECTABILITY

Benny Goodman's and John Hammond's concerts at Carnegie Hall raise jazz to the same social status as classical music. Jelly Roll Morton is discovered languishing in Washington, DC, and the early history of jazz begins to be documented in earnest.

DUKE ELLINGTON: PRELUDE TO A KISS

Duke Ellington's instrumental recording of his song "Prelude to a Kiss" on 9 September 1938 encapsulated the composer's sophisticated artistry in a hauntingly beautiful three-minute composition. Deriving in style from the "mood" music that Ellington penned during his earlier Cotton Club days, the thirteen-piece orchestral arrangement perfectly absorbs each player's distinctive sonorities within the band's complex musical fabric.

Supported by the elusive CHROMATIC HARMONY for which Ellington was famous, Lawrence Brown's expressive trombone melody threads its circuitous and unpredictable way through the rich orchestral backdrop. The theme is developed in a concentrated solo from Johnny Hodges's sensuous alto saxophone (complete with his trademark "smears"), a duet between Brown and baritone saxophonist Harry Carney, and a solo from trumpeter Wallace Jones. Following the horn solos, the saxophone section inverts the texture, with the melody low in register and the accompanying chords floating high above.

Duke Ellington himself then takes center stage as piano soloist. In its use of parallel chord voicings – already heard in the introduction – his solo reveals the influence of impressionist composers such as Debussy. Interspersed with the piano phrases are parenthetical echoes and decorative paraphrases from the other instruments – a subtle and complex texture of a kind unique to Ellington's work in this period. Finally, Brown's trombone returns the listener to the opening theme as this miniature masterpiece draws to its close.

Jazz Events

16 January
Benny Goodman's band introduces jazz to New York's bastion of classical music, Carnegie Hall. The event, which is sold out, includes a sequence of pieces illustrating the history of jazz and a JAM SESSION involving musicians from the Benny Goodman (• p. 84), Duke Ellington (• p. 63), and Count Basie (• p. 87) bands. After the concert, the bands of Count Basie and Chick Webb compete informally at the Savoy Ballroom.

18 January
Eddie Condon makes the first recordings on Milt Gabler's new Commodore record label.

February
Gene Krupa quits Benny Goodman to lead his own band.

March
Art Tatum (• p. 125) plays in Soho, London.

10 April
King Oliver (• p. 48) dies, Savannah, Georgia. He has made no recordings since 1931 and has spent two years in retirement, eking out a living as a poolroom janitor.

May–July
Jelly Roll Morton (• p. 45), brought out of retirement by Alan Lomax, makes a historic series of retrospective recordings for the Library of Congress, Washington, DC.

24 July
Artie Shaw's orchestra records its popular interpretation of Cole Porter's "Begin the Beguine" in New York.

August
In Britain on tour, Fats Waller (• p. 105) appears in Glasgow.
• The Quintette du Hot Club de France records in London.

November
Benny Goodman continues to develop his alternative career as a classical clarinetist by giving a recital in New York's Town Hall. This year he also records Mozart's Clarinet Quintet with the Budapest String Quartet and commissions Hungarian composer Béla Bartók to write his chamber work *Contrasts*.

15 December
The Benny Goodman band records Alec Templeton's "Bach Goes to Town: Prelude and Fugue in Swing," a witty composition fusing Baroque contrapuntal techniques with SWING.

23 December
At Carnegie Hall, John Hammond (• p. 209) mounts a concert illustrating the history of jazz, "From Spirituals to Swing," featuring BLUES pianists Pete Johnson, Albert Ammons, and Meade Lux Lewis, Count Basie's band, the Benny Goodman sextet, Sidney Bechet (• p. 43), and James P. Johnson (• p. 46).

- Trumpeter Harry James quits Benny Goodman at the end of the year to form his own orchestra in Philadelphia.
- In New York, Winthrop Sargeant publishes his study *Jazz, Hot and Hybrid,* one of the earliest critical books on jazz in English.

World Events

12 March
Germany annexes Austria

3 May
Fascist summit, Rome

August–September
Neville Chamberlain negotiates with Hitler

1 October
Germany annexes Sudetenland

21 October
Japanese capture Canton

9–10 November
Kristallnacht: night of Nazi violence against Jews in Germany and Austria

- Walt Disney's cartoon *Snow White and the Seven Dwarfs*

6D
PRICE
5FR
15¢
Paul Smith
A NEW CATALOGUE OF RECENT RECORDINGS AND RARE, OUT-OF-PRINT, OLD TIME GOOD ONES BY OUTSTANDING SWING VIRTUOSI
COMMODORE CLASSICS IN SWING

Above right Goodman's epoch-making appearance at Carnegie Hall in January 1938. His band includes Gene Krupa on drums, who quit soon after to become a leader in his own right.

Left Famous for recordings made by Billie Holiday, Coleman Hawkins, and many musicians from Chicago in the 1940s, the Commodore label later benefited from reissue programs undertaken by Columbia, Telefunken, and Mosaic.

HOW TO GET TO CARNEGIE HALL

January 1938 marked a significant turning point in the history of jazz. Benny Goodman's appearance at New York's Carnegie Hall was the first occasion on which jazz was performed at a prestigious concert hall, rather than in nightclubs and ballrooms. The event's sellout success ensured that paying audiences would continue to enjoy professionally organized jazz concerts at classical venues in years to come. It is not surprising that this tradition was initiated by a white band; Goodman's mixed-race trio and quartet could only be included in the program as a VAUDEVILLE-style interlude. But Goodman integrated musicians from Count Basie's and Duke Ellington's black bands into the show, and from 1943 Ellington's own orchestra made annual appearances at the historic venue, performing a series of large-scale "symphonic" works (• p. 104). Billie Holiday's two concerts at Carnegie Hall in 1948 broke all their box-office records.

Goodman carefully organized his 1938 concert to demonstrate the historical evolution of jazz styles, and included a parody of the Original Dixieland Jazz Band's crude early recordings (• p. 37) along with a spirited tribute to Louis Armstrong (• p. 57), as well as a lengthy jam session on Fats Waller's "Honeysuckle Rose." (When asked how long he required for an intermission, the nonplussed Goodman replied, "How long does Mr Toscanini take?") Goodman's second appearance at Carnegie Hall, on 6 October 1939, with markedly different musicians, featured a lighthearted satirical interpretation of "T'Ain't What You Do, It's the Way that You Do It" – which aped the styles of certain of his competitors – and his pseudo-Baroque hit "Bach Goes to Town."

In 1978, the sixty-nine-year-old Goodman fronted a much younger band in a concert at Carnegie Hall held to celebrate the fortieth anniversary of his original appearance. The program on that night included a powerful rendering of Jelly Roll Morton's "King Porter Stomp," in the same arrangement by Fletcher Henderson (• p. 71) that had become virtually the signature tune of the Swing Era four decades earlier (• p. 83).

1939

WAR

As big-band jazz, exemplified by Glenn Miller's polished performances, becomes the pop music of World War II, the tenor saxophone acquires a new prominence at the hands of Lester Young and Coleman Hawkins. The foundation of the Blue Note label inspires a revival of boogie-woogie and other blues-oriented styles.

Jazz Events

9 February
Herschel Evans dies from heart disease at the age of thirty in New York.

February
STRIDE pianist Willie "The Lion" Smith records eight of his compositions for Commodore, including "Echoes of Spring" and "Rippling Waters," which both reveal his debt to classical and impressionist composers.

21 March
Duke Ellington's orchestra records "Something to Live For" by Billy Strayhorn, with the composer appearing as pianist. It is the beginning of a long and fruitful association between the two men (• p. 182).

23 March
Duke Ellington and his band sail to Le Havre for a concert tour of France, Holland, and Denmark. Knowing of Hitler's antipathy toward jazz, they pass anxiously through Nazi Germany.

March
A new band led by trombonist Glenn Miller (• p. 107) plays at the Glen Island Casino, New York. Moving on to play at Meadowbrook, New Jersey, the band becomes well known through regular radio broadcasts.

4 April
Glenn Miller records his "Moonlight Serenade."

20 April
Billie Holiday (• p. 131) records the anti-racist song "Strange Fruit" with the Café Society band. With its graphic description of a lynching scene, it proves highly controversial and is banned by several radio stations.

April
Teddy Wilson leaves the Benny Goodman Quartet (• p. 84) to form his own big band.

16 June
Bandleader Chick Webb dies, Baltimore, Maryland. His orchestra is taken over by his protégée Ella Fitzgerald (• p. 195), who leads it until 1942.

1 August
Glenn Miller records the phenomenally successful "In the Mood." On the same day, guitarist Charlie Christian is hired by Benny Goodman (• p. 209).

3 September
Britain's declaration of war on Nazi Germany finds the Quintette du Hot Club de France (• p. 75) on tour in London. All members of the group except Stephane Grappelli return to France and continue to perform there after the Nazi invasion in May 1940.

Above The record cover of Commodore's long-playing reissue of the piano compositions originally recorded by Willie "The Lion" Smith on 78s in 1939.

SAXOPHONE: BODY AND SOUL

When Coleman Hawkins ("Bean" to his associates) recorded his intense rendition of "Body and Soul" on 11 October 1939, he brought the saxophone's lyrical powers to a peak that, some would argue, has never been surpassed. By this time, the saxophone family had long been almost exclusively associated with jazz, although when invented in around 1840 by Adolphe Sax the instruments had been intended for classical music. Apart from a few cases of its use by composers such as Maurice Ravel, Alban Berg, and Sergey Rachmaninov, the saxophone rarely appeared in the classical orchestra during the first half of the century. When George Gershwin (• p. 55) and Aaron Copland incorporated saxophones in the orchestration of their SYMPHONIC JAZZ scores in the 1920s, the instrument's blend of seductive warmth and brassiness – deriving from the combination of a single-REED mouthpiece and metal body – was already indelibly associated with jazz.

Debate continues over precisely when the saxophone became an independent jazz solo instrument, but it appears prominently in numerous recordings from the early 1920s. Early players in New Orleans directly adapted clarinet style; many were proficient on both instruments (• p. 87). The finest exponent of this approach was Sidney Bechet (• p. 43), who promoted the B♭ soprano saxophone in a series of recordings after 1923. Another New Orleans musician, Barney Bigard (• p. 63), adapted his clarinet-playing style for use on the B♭ tenor saxophone, but it was not until Coleman Hawkins, Lester Young, and Ben Webster that the tenor saxophone realized its full potential. From the lushness of Webster and lightness of Young to the later aggressive reediness of John Coltrane, an astonishing range of tone colors was revealed.

The E♭ alto saxophone, on the other hand, had established itself as a solo voice at an early stage in the hands of Jimmy Dorsey, and later in the elegant playing of Duke Ellington's saxophonist Johnny Hodges. The saxophone section in a typical big band of the Swing Era comprised two altos, two tenors, and a baritone; the work of Glenn Miller's saxophones is the most striking example of the dense parallel harmonies they created. The baritone saxophone has been less popular as a solo instrument, although the work of Gerry Mulligan was an outstanding feature of the WEST COAST school from the 1950s. In Duke Ellington's orchestra, Harry Carney showed how the baritone was capable of considerable fluency and delicacy.

After the innovations of Charlie Parker (• p. 136) in the 1940s, alto and/or tenor saxophone soloists became indispensable members of bop and HARD BOP ensembles. Many players became proficient on more than one member of the saxophone family: John Coltrane (• p. 160) and Wayne Shorter played both tenor and soprano, Parker's disciple Sonny Stitt played the alto, tenor, and baritone, and the SOUL-jazz performer Grover Washington, Jr. played soprano, alto, and tenor. The ethereal sonorities that the soprano instrument can deliver have, since the work of Shorter with Weather Report (• p. 175), become one of the most striking modern developments in saxophone playing.

Left and above The two most widespread members of the saxophone family: tenor in B♭, and alto in E♭.

Above The Squadronaires performing at the Stoll Theatre in aid of the Musicians' Social and Benevolent Fund in 1943.

Right Tenor saxophonist Coleman Hawkins at the time of his hit "Body and Soul," which set a new standard of melodic lyricism.

Jazz Events

5 September
Lester Young records his "Lester Leaps In" with Count Basie (• p. 87) for Vocalion, New York.

11 October
Coleman Hawkins records "Body and Soul" for Victor in New York, setting a new standard of improvisational sophistication for the saxophone. At the end of the year, a *Down Beat* readers' poll declares Hawkins the best tenor saxophonist.

November
Artie Shaw suddenly retires, just one year after scoring a tremendous success with his "Begin the Beguine."

22 December
Ma Rainey dies, Rome, Georgia.

- The Royal Air Force big band, "The Squadronaires," is formed in Britain to provide entertainment for servicemen.
- Drummer Art Blakey (• p. 139) appears with the Fletcher Henderson orchestra, shortly before Henderson disbands the group and joins Benny Goodman's big band as staff arranger.
- The Blue Note record company is founded by German emigrés Alfred Lion and Francis Wolff in New York.
- In New York, Frederic Ramsey, Jr. and Charles Edward Smith publish *Jazzmen: The Story of Hot Jazz Told in the Lives of the Men who Created It*, which promotes a new awareness of jazz history and helps revive DIXIELAND and RAGTIME in the 1940s.

World Events

28 January
Death of W. B. Yeats

28 March
Spanish Civil War ends with Franco's capture of Madrid

March
German army occupies Bohemia, Moravia, Slovakia, and Lithuania

27 April
Military conscription introduced in UK

30 April
New York World's Fair

22 May
Hitler and Mussolini agree their "Pact of Steel"

23 August
USSR agrees a policy of non-aggression with Germany

1 September
German troops invade Poland

3 September
Britain and France declare war on Germany

17 December
German battleship *Graf Spee* scuttled near Montevideo

- James Joyce finishes *Finnegans Wake*
- *Gone with the Wind* released

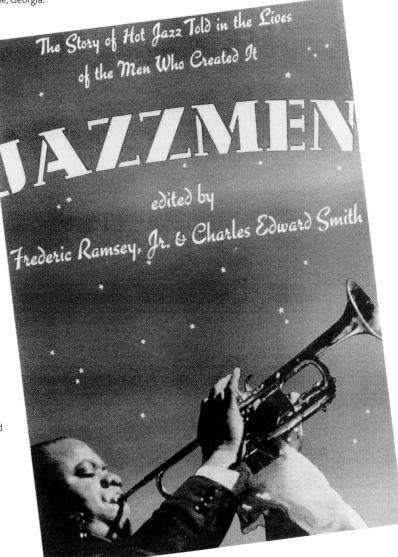

Right Ramsey and Smith's book *Jazzmen* did much to foster public interest in the early history of jazz, which had been severely neglected until the late 1930s.

SEEDS OF REVOLUTION

A new generation of performers evolve the bebop style, which is ideally suited to small ensembles and soon comes to influence and coexist with the big-band format.

Jazz Events

January
Lord Haw-Haw (the notorious wartime traitor, William Joyce) begins to make regular broadcasts of anti-British propaganda from Berlin. Jazz, which is now banned in Germany (● p. 81), is used in the broadcasts as bait to lure English-speaking listeners to tune in.

26 February
Lionel Hampton's newly formed big band (● p. 70) records "Flying Home" in Chicago.

February
Duke Ellington hires Ben Webster as tenor saxophonist. Ellington also records his masterpieces "Ko-Ko" (**6 March**), "Concerto for Cootie" (**15 March**), and "Cottontail" (**4 May**).

1 May
Benny Goodman (● p. 84) performs Mozart's Clarinet Concerto under the direction of conductor Leopold Stokowski. In **July**, illness forces him to dissolve his band for three months.

8 August
Clarinetist Johnny Dodds dies, Chicago.

15 September
Down Beat publishes a transcription of the first CHORUS from Coleman Hawkins's recording of "Body and Soul" (● p. 95).

November
Cootie Williams leaves the Duke Ellington band, and is replaced by Ray Nance (trumpet/violin).

6 December
Nat King Cole's trio (● p. 88) records "Gone With the Draft," a humorous song about conscription that soon becomes uncomfortably topical.

13 December
Django Reinhardt (● p. 75) records "Nuages" in Nazi-occupied Paris.

December
Lester Young leaves Count Basie's band (● p. 87) to form his own small COMBO.

- Under new management, Minton's Playhouse in New York becomes the venue for much exciting new jazz. Performers appearing here include pianist Thelonious Monk (● p. 155), trumpeter Dizzy Gillespie, and drummer Kenny Clarke.
- The American Society of Composers, Authors, and Publishers issues a ban at the end of the year preventing the broadcast of ASCAP works (● p. 103). The boycott results in the growth of the rival organization Broadcast Music, Inc. (BMI).

Left Dizzy Gillespie's *Ol' Man Rebop* (with its early spelling of what would later become "bebop") was an HMV LP reissue of ten sides cut in the period 1946–49.

Above left Max Roach, resident drummer at Monroe's Uptown House, was a vital influence on the rhythmic sophistication of the emerging bop style.

MINTON'S PLAYHOUSE

Above Owner Teddy Hill (far right) poses outside his famous club with (l. to r.) house pianist Thelonious Monk and trumpeters Howard McGhee and Roy Eldridge.

In 1938, saxophonist Henry Minton established a club on Harlem's West 118th Street in a rundown former dining room, and engaged Thelonious Monk as house pianist in the following year. In 1940 the management of the venue passed to Teddy Hill, another saxophonist who had been in a band with James P. Johnson (• p. 46). Monk and resident drummer Kenny Clarke provided the backbone for a historic series of after-hours informal JAM SESSIONS with visiting instrumentalists that laid the foundations for the BEBOP style, which soon spread throughout the jazz world and replaced the outworn music of the big bands with an innovative and exciting musical language.

Two of the most prominent of the guest artists at Minton's were trumpeter Dizzy Gillespie (• p. 219), a former SIDEMAN of Teddy Hill's and pioneer of Latin jazz, and alto saxophonist Charlie Parker (• p. 136). In the early 1940s both men played in bands led by Earl Hines (• p. 125) and Billy Eckstine, in addition to pursuing their informal but vastly influential stylistic explorations at Minton's Playhouse (similar jam sessions were also conducted at Monroe's Uptown House on West 134th Street). Unfortunately, recording boycotts at the time meant that no bop numbers were recorded during its formative phase (• p. 103), although a few poor-quality private recordings of the seminal jam sessions afford a tantalizing glimpse of the atmosphere at Minton's and Monroe's, and reveal guitarist Charlie Christian (• p. 99) to have been a crucial influence on the development of the new style.

World Events

11 February
USSR attacks Finland

9 April
Germany invades Norway and Denmark

10 May
Winston Churchill becomes prime minister, UK

15 May
Holland falls to Germany

3 June
Evacuation of British forces, Dunkirk

10 June
Italy declares war on Britain and France

14 June
Germany occupies Paris

Summer
Battle of Britain

DROPPING BOMBS

Although it seemed radical at the time, bebop, or "bop," as it is usually abbreviated (the name was derived either from syllables commonly used in SCAT singing or from the offbeat accents of the drumming techniques characteristic of the style), was in many respects a logical development from the more conservative jazz of the early 1940s. Its most effective outlet was the small ensemble, which was more economically viable than the ailing big bands, but it retained the WALKING BASS, prominent use of RIFFS, and some of the characteristic rhythmic patterns of the SWING-band idiom.

Bop drummers such as Kenny Clarke and Max Roach adapted their accompaniments to create a high degree of unpredictability, injecting the music with powerful syncopated accents (especially on bass drum, a procedure known as "dropping bombs"). Latin rhythms also increasingly crept into the drumming, doubtless reflecting the influence of Dizzy Gillespie (• p. 114). Drummers now began to be promoted from merely keeping time to performing as full-fledged soloists. The FRONT LINE instruments, principally trumpet and saxophone, improvised long and elaborate solos, typically framed by a UNISON statement of the HEAD theme (which was invariably pithy, highly syncopated, and often fragmentary in nature). Solo melodic IMPROVISATIONS reached a peak of virtuosity, combining sheer speed with exciting DISSONANCES, the notes sometimes passing by so rapidly that the traditional sense of SWUNG RHYTHM became an impossibility. As with the new drumming style, angularity and unpredictability were the order of the day. Bop HARMONY, strikingly developed by Thelonious Monk, became a complex affair in which the TWELVE-BAR BLUES progression was supplemented with numerous additional and substitute chords.

In its formative years, the sometimes self-conscious complexity of bop served a clear extra-musical purpose: it discouraged a casual audience and allowed ensembles to exclude undesirable players, unversed as they were in the novel idiom, from participating in jam sessions. The motivation behind this aggressive stance (which often produced aggressive music) was partly political, since bop musicians wished to wrest the creative initiative back from the white performers who had scored such a considerable commercial success with big-band jazz – hence the boppers' preoccupation with improvisation and BLUES elements, both of which had been neglected by many popular white musicians. Players in the early bop groups emphasized their exclusivity by the wearing of goatees and berets (and, in Monk's case, a wide variety of hats), and by using "hip" language. In part, the eccentric image was intended to present bop practitioners as the new musical intellectuals, rather than purveyors of mindless dance music for the masses.

After Parker and Gillespie, the foremost advocates of the new style included saxophonist James Moody, who worked closely with Gillespie and helped take bop to Europe in the late 1940s. (Gillespie and Moody were renowned for the hilarious mock disagreements and brawls that they staged during performances.) Younger players, such as alto saxophonist Julian "Cannonball" Adderley, helped see bop safely through the changeable decades of the 1950s and 1960s, during which it sprang a stylistic offshoot – HARD BOP. Both idioms continued to be influential in the 1980s and beyond, largely due to the work of Art Blakey.

ENTER BIRD

The bebop revolution gathers pace with the emergence of alto saxophonist Charlie Parker, nicknamed "Bird" – one of the most prodigious and tragic figures in the history of jazz.

Jazz Events

15 February
In Los Angeles, Duke Ellington's band records Billy Strayhorn's "Take the 'A' Train," which is adopted as the band's new signature tune. Ellington's musical *Jump for Joy*, with a plot concerning the need for racial harmony, opens in Los Angeles this year.

18 April
Sidney Bechet (• p. 43) plays five different instruments to create one-man-band recordings of "The Sheik of Araby" and "Blues of Bechet," early examples of OVERDUBBING.

30 April
Charlie Parker makes his first recording, "Swingmatism," with Jay McShann in Dallas, and begins to participate in the famous JAM SESSIONS at Minton's Playhouse (• p. 97), which result in the birth of the BEBOP style.

April
Trumpeter Roy Eldridge joins Gene Krupa's orchestra as featured soloist.

Right The sheet music for Billy "Sweetpea" Strayhorn's perennially popular "Take the 'A' Train," recorded by Duke Ellington in 1941.

Above right Sidney Bechet indulging his taste for musical eccentricity at a one-man-band session in April 1941.

May–June
Pete Johnson and Albert Ammons continue their series of BOOGIE-WOOGIE recordings on the Blue Note label.

10 July
Jelly Roll Morton (• p. 45) dies, Los Angeles.

July
End of the American Society of Composers, Authors, and Publishers' broadcasting boycott (• p. 103).

7 August
Billie Holiday (• p. 131) records "I Cover the Waterfront" in New York with Teddy Wilson and his orchestra.

October
Radio stations in Nazi Germany begin broadcasting light dance music in an attempt to find a popular substitute for outlawed jazz.

- Stan Kenton (piano) founds his Artistry in Rhythm Orchestra in California.
- Charles Mingus (bass) plays with Louis Armstrong's band. (He is thrown out two years later for making anti-segregation remarks during a tour of southern states.)

GUITAR

The short career of guitarist Charlie Christian, who died from tuberculosis in 1942, coincides with the instrument's evolution from its relatively insignificant role as a member of the RHYTHM SECTION to solo status. In traditional New Orleans jazz and dance bands of the late 1920s, the guitar had been only an occasional participant: the brighter, metallic sound of the BANJO was generally preferred to provide buoyant, strummed chords in the background, and perhaps contribute a spiky solo passage on occasion. The guitar gradually replaced the banjo in the early 1930s, partly because its comparatively delicate sonority made it a more appropriate partner to the double bass, which had quickly ousted the tuba as the supplier of the all-important bass line.

The dance bands of Paul Whiteman and Jean Goldkette (• p. 73) both employed Eddie Lang, the first guitarist to perform solos regularly. Lang died while having his tonsils removed in 1933, just as he was embarking on a promising career as Bing Crosby's accompanist. Lang also recorded duo SIDES in the late 1920s with violinist Joe Venuti (• p. 101), and it was a similar pairing of guitar and violin that was responsible for furthering the career of the most colorful early virtuoso of the guitar, Django Reinhardt (• p. 75). Both Lang and Reinhardt deserve credit for developing the instrument's melodic potential by learning how to improvise extended single lines, often at exceptionally fast speeds.

By the late 1930s, the first electrically amplified guitars had been launched in an attempt to combat the instrument's deficiencies: limited sustaining power and severely limited volume. Charlie Christian was the first guitarist to specialize in the amplified instrument, his expertise reaching a wider audience when he joined Benny Goodman's sextet in 1939. He went on to participate in the famous bebop sessions at Minton's Playhouse, an experience that must have stimulated him to achieve new levels of fluency and rhythmic momentum through the seemingly endless melodic lines for which he was celebrated. Christian's innovations were taken still further by Wes Montgomery, whose career peaked in a series of recordings for Riverside around 1960. The impact of Montgomery's revolutionary left- and right-hand techniques continues to be felt in the melodic style of contemporary guitarists Pat Metheny (• p. 199) and Lee Ritenour.

The merging of jazz and rock styles in the late 1960s allowed the electric guitar and electric bass guitar to come into their own (• p. 127), but in the meantime the ACOUSTIC or semi-acoustic instrument continued to feature as a member of the rhythm section in both small and large ensembles. Fine rhythm-section playing was typified by Al Casey, stalwart guitarist of the popular COMBO Fats Waller and His Rhythm (• p. 105). The work of Barney Kessel and Herb Ellis in the 1950s showed how the instrument could move between accompanying and solo functions with ease, and both players successfully combined elements of the bop and SWING styles.

In the 1960s, Joe Pass began to experiment with more complex textures, exploiting a phenomenal technical facility that enabled him to play melodic IMPROVISATIONS, supporting harmonies and independent bass lines simultaneously. His unaccompanied playing was, as a result, amongst the richest and most satisfying of all guitarists, and his exquisite duets with Ella Fitzgerald showed him to be a consummate and sensitive accompanist.

World Events

February–March
British army in Libya and Ethiopia

April
German campaign in North Africa

6 April
Germany invades Yugoslavia

22 June
Germany invades Russia

12 July
Anglo-Soviet agreement, Moscow

7 December
Japanese bomb Pearl Harbor, Hawaii

8 December
USA and UK declare war on Japan

11 December
USA declares war on Germany and Italy

- Orson Welles directs and stars in *Citizen Kane*

Below Charlie Christian's singular talent on electric guitar helped shape the distinctive style of bop melodic improvisations on all instruments.

1942

INDUSTRIAL ACTION

The premature deaths of guitarist Charlie Christian and bass player Jimmy Blanton deprive jazz of two blossoming talents in a year blighted by the onset of strike action by the major American musicians' union.

Jazz Events

14 January
Fats Waller (• p. 105) appears at Carnegie Hall (• p. 91), but his performance is adversely affected by alcohol.

2 March
Charlie Christian dies at the age of twenty-five, New York.

April
Twenty-three-year-old Leonard Bernstein appears as jazz pianist at the Fox and Hounds, Boston, with vocalist Eric Stein. The following year, Bernstein works on Tin Pan Alley (under the pseudonym Leonard Amber), producing published transcriptions of improvised solos by figures such as Coleman Hawkins and Earl Hines.
• The Nazi-controlled German Dance and Entertainment Orchestra begins work in Berlin.

11 June
Trumpeter Bunk Johnson begins recording in New Orleans, marking the beginning of the revival of pre-SWING jazz styles.

30 July
Duke Ellington's former bass player Jimmy Blanton dies of tuberculosis at the age of twenty-four, Los Angeles. This same summer, Barney Bigard (clarinet) and Ivie Anderson (vocals) leave the Duke Ellington Band.

Above This 1942 radio broadcast in Hollywood, dedicated to US servicemen overseas, features (l. to r.): Dinah Shore, Spike Jones, Count Basie, Bob Burns, Lionel Hampton, and Tommy Dorsey.

Right Ray Nance, who played both trumpet and violin in Duke Ellington's band for more than two decades.

Below The young Leonard Bernstein, who shot to international fame as a conductor in 1943, and later composed numerous works in a symphonic jazz idiom.

VIOLIN

Like the BANJO, the violin had been a popular instrument with slave musicians in the nineteenth century, and was therefore a prominent participant in MINSTREL-SHOW ensembles. Violins (and sometimes cellos) featured in RAGTIME bands such as that led by James Reese Europe (• p. 41), and became staple members of white dance bands in the 1920s. The presence of violins is one superficial reason why the music of Paul Whiteman (• p. 73) sounds less jazzy than that of contemporaneous black bands, which tended to avoid the instrument.

Joe Venuti, who played with both Whiteman and Jean Goldkette, was one of the first violinists to achieve fame as a jazz soloist. On the other side of the Atlantic, Stephane Grappelli nurtured the instrument's capability for generating suave and sophisticated melodies. Both violinists played in celebrated duos alongside equally influential guitarists (• p. 99). Ray Nance's resourceful exploration of the violin's sonorous potential was a distinctive ingredient in Duke Ellington's orchestra from 1940 onward.

The most influential violinist in recent years has been the classically trained French player Jean-Luc Ponty, who brought the instrument up to date by working with electronic techniques compatible with the demands of jazz-rock FUSION. More controversial has been the attempt of saxophonist Ornette Coleman (• p. 150) to originate a bizarre violin technique to supplement his equally self-taught trumpet playing. In the first decade of the present century, violinist Regina Carter outraged classical-music purists by playing on a priceless antique violin owned by Paganini (• p. 234), and won both critical accolades (• p. 252) and a wide audience for her versatile and attractive playing.

1942

Jazz Events

1 August
James Caesar Petrillo's American Federation of Musicians urges its members not to participate in studio recordings for record companies that fail to pay royalties to performers. Industrial action continues until the end of 1944, but V-discs (● p. 109), manufactured for supply to those on active service overseas, are exempted.

October
Glenn Miller (● p. 107) dissolves his band and enlists as a captain in the US Army Air Force, where he forms a new service band.
● Eighteen-year-old singer Sarah Vaughan (● p. 123) wins a talent competition at Harlem's Apollo Theater with her rendition of "Body and Soul."

December
Charlie Parker (● p. 136) joins Earl Hines's band, alongside Dizzy Gillespie (● p. 219).

- Eddie Condon's mixed-race band appears in a CBS television program.
- *Billboard* magazine publishes the first black record chart under the title "Harlem Hit Parade."

Above One of several Royal Air Force bands performs for the benefit of British servicemen in North Africa, *c.* 1942.

Left Glenn Miller in his US Army Air Force uniform. Both Miller and clarinetist Artie Shaw led bands for the US services in the war, Shaw's Navy band performing throughout the Pacific Theater of Operations in 1943 and Miller's visiting Europe in 1944.

STRIKE UP THE BAN

The gradual collapse of big-band jazz in the 1940s was accelerated by several factors, not least the general reaction against extravagance that affected all the arts after the calamities of World War II. The war had also deprived many bands of their leading players through conscription into the armed forces, making it virtually impossible to maintain consistency of personnel. As if the severe wartime shortage of the shellac used in the manufacture of recordings were not problem enough, a series of disastrous strikes by several musicians' unions quickly struck the final nail in the coffin of the big bands.

The most powerful performing-rights organization in the USA during the 1930s was the American Society of Composers, Authors, and Publishers, which collected and distributed royalties earned by its members. Increasing dissent over royalties payable on radio transmissions led to the formation of the rival BMI and the decision by ASCAP to boycott radio broadcasts in 1940. Composers managed by ASCAP, including Duke Ellington, could not broadcast their own music until the dispute was resolved, and many resorted to broadcasting non-copyright tunes until the boycott ceased when a settlement was agreed in the summer of 1941.

Next came more prolonged industrial action against recording companies instigated by the American Federation of Musicians (AFM). Recordings were technically not licensed for broadcast in the 1930s, but the restriction had been widely ignored. In spite of its members' assertions that their livelihoods had actually been improved by the enormous publicity brought by exposure on the airwaves, the AFM's pugnacious leader James Caesar Petrillo insisted on strike action in August 1942. Record companies began to reissue recordings made prior to the strike, but went on to reach agreements with the AFM by the end of 1944. In the meantime, vocalists such as Frank Sinatra and Bing Crosby (who were exempted from strike action) enjoyed a rise to prominence that would culminate in the modern phenomenon of the pop superstar. A renewed recording ban of shorter duration was enforced by the AFM in 1948.

Although it has often been stated that the recording ban was responsible for a dearth of recordings of early bebop – Charlie Parker, for example, did not begin recording in earnest until 1944 – an important consequence was the emergence of independent labels, such as Savoy and Dial, which did much to promote the new music.

Above James Caesar Petrillo (left), pictured here with Canadian musicians' union boss Walter C. Murdoch at a New York opera gala in October 1954.

World Events

January
Japanese campaigns in East Indies, Malaya, and Burma

3 June
Battle of Midway, Pacific Ocean

25 June
"Thousand Bomber" attack on Bremen, Germany

17 August
US bombs Germany

13 September
Germans attack Stalingrad, USSR

23 October
Battle of El Alamein

- Humphrey Bogart and Ingrid Bergman star in *Casablanca*

BLACK, BROWN, AND BEIGE

Duke Ellington embarks on an ambitious series of annual concerts featuring extended symphonic-jazz scores. Fats Waller dies, and Art Tatum inherits his mantle as leading pianist.

Above Duke Ellington in 1943, surrounded by some of his staunchest sidemen (l. to r.): Nance, Stewart, Nanton, Carney, Hodges, and Greer.

Right HMV's long-play reissue of recorded extracts from Ellington's *Black, Brown, and Beige*, coupled with his later *Perfume Suite* (1944).

Jazz Events

23 January
Duke Ellington's fifty-seven-minute work *Black, Brown, and Beige* receives its first performance at Carnegie Hall (• p. 91), New York, and the proceeds are donated to the Russian war-relief fund. It meets with a mixed critical reception, but marks the start of Ellington's annual appearances at this prestigious venue (which cease after 1950). On **11 December** the band, its lineup now expanded to include four trumpets, presents another large-scale work, *New World a-comin'*, at Carnegie Hall.

April
Sarah Vaughan (• p. 123) joins Earl Hines's band as second pianist and singer, and soon after begins work with Billy Eckstine.

May
Gene Krupa serves a short jail sentence for employing a minor in his band, but after his release he plays again with Benny Goodman (• p. 84) in **September**.

August
Ben Webster quits Duke Ellington.

15 December
Fats Waller dies during a rail journey to New York: his body is discovered at Kansas City station. Three days later, his former mentor James P. Johnson records "Blues for Fats."

29 December
Singer Dinah Washington, currently with Lionel Hampton's band, records popular BLUES numbers in New York.

"My father [Fats Waller] had a unique system to reward inventiveness in improvisation. Pop kept two bottles of gin on a table during the rehearsals. One bottle was for himself . . . The other bottle was the 'encourager,' as he called it. When one of the band excelled in an improvisational section, Dad would stop the rehearsal, pour him a healthy shot of gin, and the two of them would toast each other."

Maurice Waller

Left Fats Waller, an infectiously high-spirited entertainer endowed with a prodigious keyboard technique.

Jazz Events

- Art Tatum establishes a piano trio with Tiny Grimes (guitar) and Slam Stewart (bass), following the pioneering example of Nat King Cole.
- Glenn Miller (• p. 107) publishes a textbook guide to arranging music for big bands.
- Django Reinhardt (• p. 75), in panic at the news that the Nazis are sending gypsies to the gas chamber, attempts to reach Switzerland from occupied France. Stopped at the border, he is sent back without punishment by a German officer who is an admirer of jazz.
- In Germany, the Luftwaffe fits some of its Heinkel, Junkers, and Messerschmitt fighter-bombers with a device nicknamed *Schräge Musik* ("slanting music," a slang term for the banned HOT jazz): two machine guns located on top of the aircraft, to be used in oblique attacks from beneath enemy bombers.

THE HARMFUL LITTLE ARMFUL

Fats Waller's death in December 1943, accelerated by his habitual overindulgence, was a worldly exit fully in keeping with his flamboyant lifestyle. His clowning and infectious capers disguised a top-ranking musical genius whose importance lay in two distinct areas: the development of the STRIDE style of piano playing to its limits of virtuosity, and the promotion of jazz as a medium for refined popular entertainment.

Waller's early keyboard training was as a church organist, an experience that enabled him as a teenager to gain employment playing in the cinemas and theaters of New York. (In later life he shocked the musical establishment by playing jazz on the organ of Notre Dame cathedral in Paris.) His skills as a pianist were fostered by James P. Johnson (• p. 46), whose own piano concerto *Yamekraw* Waller performed at Carnegie Hall in 1928. Waller's astonishing keyboard facility and compositional fluency resulted in a steady succession of fine works for solo piano characterized by a combination of dazzling virtuosity and harmonic ingenuity, including *Smashing Thirds*, *Alligator Crawl*, and *Handful of Keys*. Among his admirers was Al Capone, who allegedly had Waller kidnapped at gunpoint in Chicago in the mid-1920s, just to get him to play at the gangster's birthday party.

Waller's incomparable aptitude for songwriting was developed in collaboration with lyricist Andy Razaf. Many of their numerous hits began life in stage shows, including "Ain't Misbehavin,'" popularized by the vocal talents of Louis Armstrong (• p. 57), on whose gravelly tone Waller partly modeled his own singing voice. The peak of Waller's achievements came after 1934 in a series of recordings on the Victor label, made with a versatile COMBO billed as "Fats Waller and His Rhythm." In this context he found full expression for his remarkable comic talents, interpreting his own songs with infectious wit and a strong dose of satire. Among the most celebrated numbers in his vast repertoire was "Honeysuckle Rose," which became an indispensable STANDARD for later jazz musicians, not only in its original form, but as a harmonic skeleton on which other compositions were based.

As a keyboard technician, Waller formed an essential link between the first generation of STRIDE performers and the innovative work of later pianists such as Art Tatum (• p. 125) and Thelonious Monk (• p. 155).

World Events

23 January
British capture Tripoli

31 January
Germans surrender at Stalingrad

28 March
Death of Sergey Rachmaninov

12 May
Germans surrender in Tunisia

16 May
"Dambusters" raid by the RAF

21 June
Michael Tippett imprisoned for conscientious objection, UK

26 July
Mussolini resigns after Allied invasion of Sicily

3 September
Allies land on mainland Italy

13 October
Italy turns against Germany

1944

ALL-AMERICAN ALL-STARS

Pianist Thelonious Monk emerges as a composer of striking originality, as both bebop and swing idioms are pursued side by side. The big-band movement suffers a major loss when Glenn Miller is declared missing, presumed dead.

Above Billie Holiday and Art Tatum at the *Esquire* concert held at New York's Metropolitan Opera House in January 1944.

Jazz Events

18 January
Esquire magazine holds an All-American All-Stars concert at the Metropolitan Opera House, New York, featuring Roy Eldridge, Art Tatum (• p. 125), Coleman Hawkins, Louis Armstrong (• p. 57), Jack Teagarden, Lionel Hampton (• p. 70), Barney Bigard, and Billie Holiday (• p. 131).

April
Trombonist Juan Tizol quits Duke Ellington to play with the Harry James orchestra.

July
Producer Norman Granz initiates the series "Jazz at the Philharmonic" with concerts at the Los Angeles Philharmonic Auditorium. These popular touring JAM SESSIONS last until 1967.

22 August
Trumpeter Cootie Williams makes the first recording of Thelonious Monk's "'Round about Midnight." Monk makes his first recordings, with the Coleman Hawkins Quartet, on **19 October**.

September
Charlie Parker (• p. 136) leaves Billy Eckstine's band, where he has been playing alongside Dizzy Gillespie (• p. 219) since April.
• Eighteen-year-old Miles Davis (• p. 217) arrives in New York to attend the Juilliard School of Music. Inspired by Billy Eckstine's band (which he has recently heard at the Riviera Club in St. Louis), he soon falls in with Parker and Gillespie.

30 September
Lester Young is drafted into the US Army, in the same year he is voted most popular tenor saxophonist by *Down Beat* and appears in the short film *Jammin' the Blues*.

November
RCA Victor and Columbia finally agree to the demands of the American Federation of Musicians (• p. 103) and the recording ban is lifted.

November–December
Pianist Erroll Garner records prolifically in New York, where he occasionally stands in for Art Tatum at the Three Deuces club.

15 December
Glenn Miller, who has become a major in the US Army Air Force, is presumed dead after his aircraft disappears during a flight from London to liberated Paris.

December
Duke Ellington (• p. 63) records extracts from his *Black, Brown, and Beige* (• p. 104) for RCA.

• Pianist Oscar Peterson forms a piano trio along the lines of the famous examples led by his keyboard idols, Nat King Cole and Art Tatum. Cole's trio is voted Best Small COMBO of the year by *Down Beat*, an achievement they repeat in each of the next three years. They also win the similar *Metronome* poll annually from 1945 to 1948.

THE JAZZ IMPRESARIO: NORMAN GRANZ

Norman Granz's jazz empire began to take shape in 1944 with the mounting of his highly successful jam sessions at the Los Angeles Philharmonic Auditorium in aid of charity. Two years later the venue lent its name to Granz's roadshow, "Jazz at the Philharmonic," which took Oscar Peterson (• p. 163), Ella Fitzgerald (• p. 195), Charlie Parker, Dizzy Gillespie, and many other leading figures on worldwide tours. These ultimately resulted in some of the best recordings of live jazz ever issued.

Granz founded his record label Clef in 1946, which became incorporated into a bigger company, Verve, ten years later. A new label, named Pablo after the painter Picasso and adopting a design by the artist as its logo (• p. 188), was founded by Granz in 1973. It continued to promote the work of "Jazz at the Philharmonic" stars, and spawned a related label, Pablo Live, set up in 1977 to preserve live jam sessions (many recorded at the tenth Montreux Jazz Festival held in Switzerland in that same year), which remained Granz's speciality.

GLENN MILLER: WARTIME SERENADE

Trombonist Glenn Miller, the name most inextricably associated with the SWING music of the war years, has remained one of the hardest jazz talents to assess. The popular image of the uniformed bandleader taking his music across the Atlantic to entertain his nation's servicemen must be seen in the wider context of a popularity that propelled his band into an enviable and long-standing position at the top of the US record charts. This success was maintained throughout the war, but sometimes at the expense of musical quality. Several commentators have argued, with reason, that Miller's brand of big-band jazz could be stilted, often failed to swing, and marked the parting of the ways between true jazz and the broader appeal of nascent pop music. Others have admired his cultivation of an immediately recognizable "sound world," based on a distinctive consistency of orchestration. The latter included his trademark techniques of doubling a clarinet melody with massed saxophones an octave lower, and employing four trombones for sonorous chordal backgrounds.

After working as a SIDEMAN for the Dorsey brothers in the mid-1930s, it took Miller several years to establish himself as a leader. In 1939 his second band appeared at New York's Glen Island Casino, where regular broadcasts secured him many young and enthusiastic fans. The same year brought two hit recordings, "In the Mood" and "Moonlight Serenade," the latter stylishly demonstrating the lengths to which the parallel harmonies of the swing style could be taken. Movie appearances by the band in 1941–42 significantly augmented their popular following. Miller's career in the US Army Air Force began in 1942, when he formed a new band to entertain troops both at home and (in 1944) abroad. The band's visit to Britain, where they broadcast for the BBC, was rapturously received and did much to boost Allied morale. In December 1944, while flying ahead of his band to Paris, where they were scheduled to play, his aircraft was lost without trace in bad weather.

27 January
End of Leningrad siege

April–May
Soviet advances in Rumania and the Crimea

6 June
Allied landings on Normandy beaches ("D-Day")

20 July
Unsuccessful assassination attempt on Hitler

25 August
Liberation of Paris

5 September
Liberation of Brussels

11 September
US Army crosses German border

16 December
Ardennes campaign ("Battle of the Bulge")

Left Captain Glenn Miller consults with Marjorie Ochs in June 1943 about the radio show "I Sustain the Wings," mounted at Yale by the US Army Air Force's Technical Command.

RESTLESS PEACE

Jazz becomes polarized between the continuing bebop style, which receives new blood in the shape of the young Miles Davis, and the conservative idiom championed by the revivalist movement.

Above At New York's Town Hall on 16 May 1945, the new bop style was celebrated by Charlie Parker and Dizzy Gillespie, accompanied by Curly Russell (bass) and Harold "Doc" West (drums). The left hand of pianist Al Haig can just be discerned in the background.

Jazz Events

9 January
Dizzy Gillespie (• p. 219) records "Bebop" in New York.

17 January
Sidney Bechet (• p. 43) returns to New Orleans for the first time in twenty-five years and plays with Louis Armstrong (• p. 57) at the Municipal Auditorium.

1 February
Lester Young, still in the US Army, is arrested for possession of marijuana and court-martialed. He spends the next ten months in detention and is then discharged.

24 July
Duke Ellington (• p. 182) records his *Perfume Suite*, performed the previous December at Carnegie Hall.

September
Bunk Johnson performs in New York during the ongoing revival of New Orleans jazz.

October
Charlie Parker (• p. 136) hires nineteen-year-old trumpeter Miles Davis (• p. 217) to replace Dizzy Gillespie at the Three Deuces on West 52nd Street, New York. Davis promptly abandons his studies at the Juilliard School to record with Parker's Ree Boppers.

26 November
Charlie Parker records "Now's the Time" for Savoy in New York in his first session as leader. His ensemble includes Dizzy Gillespie (on piano, under the pseudonym "Hen Gates"), Miles Davis, and Max Roach (drums). In December he plays with Gillespie in Los Angeles, and their quintet becomes the leading light of BEBOP.

31 December
Pianist Mary Lou Williams gives the first performance of her *Zodiac Suite* at New York's Town Hall.

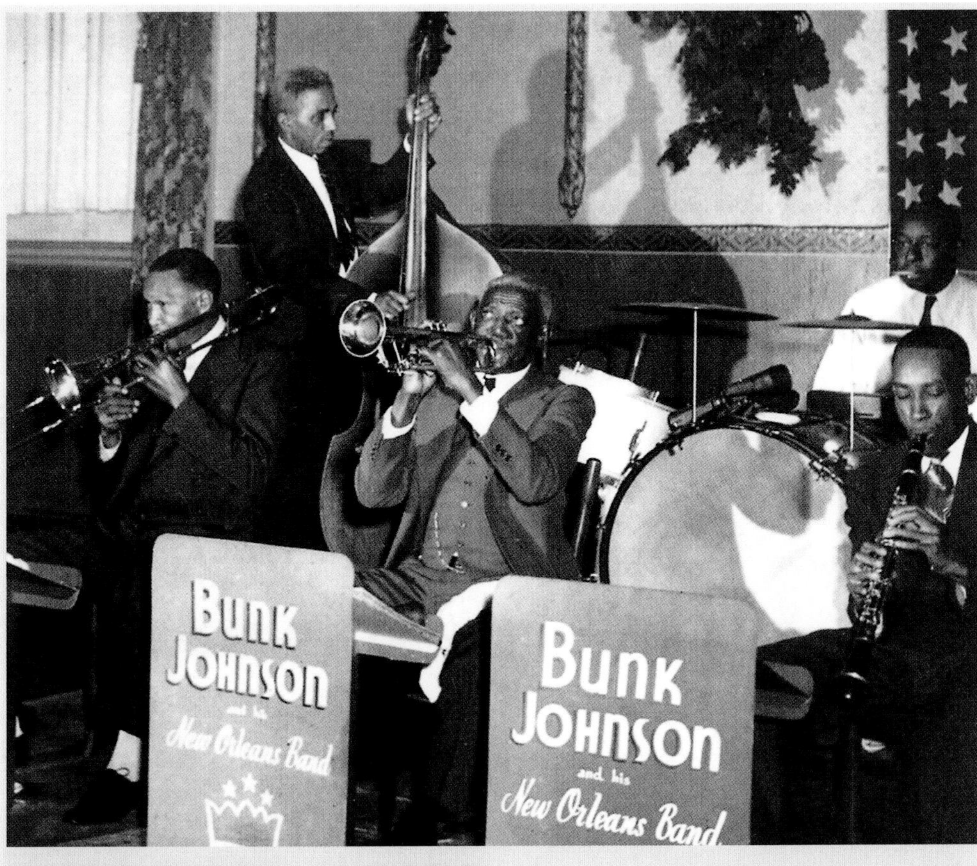

OPERATION V-DISC

The industrial action against record companies enforced by the American Federation of Musicians in 1942–44 (• p. 103) did not extend to recordings made as part of the war effort. Between October 1943 and 1949, more than nine hundred recordings were issued in the "V-disc" series (the "V" denoting "Victory"), exclusively for distribution to personnel of the US Army, Navy, Marine Corps, and Coast Guard. The total number of copies circulated has been estimated at eight million. The AFM had only allowed the project to proceed on the strict understanding that no discs would be made commercially available, and in compliance with this demand Major Howard C. Bronson was appointed to oversee the destruction of the master discs after the war. Copies of the mass-produced discs survived in private ownership, however, and have been reissued in CD compilations so that these historic musical documents might enjoy a renewed circulation.

The V-disc operation was managed by a team of experts who had formerly worked for major record companies, and were thus able to source and reissue recordings made before the imposition of the AFM ban. They also organized ad hoc groups of performers to make new recordings. Material circulated on V-discs included the legendary *Esquire* jazz performances at New York's Metropolitan Opera House in 1944 (• p. 106), for which Lionel Hampton's "Flying Home" was retitled "Flying on a V-Disc." Recordings of broadcasts were also issued, including radio interviews with famous musicians such as Louis Armstrong.

Above Members of Bunk Johnson's revivalist band performing at New York's Stuyvesant Casino in 1945.

Above Although variable in musical quality, wartime V-discs are unique survivors from a period when all other new recordings of jazz were boycotted by industrial action.

World Events

17 January
Warsaw falls to USSR

13 February
Budapest falls to USSR

7 March
Cologne falls to Allies

12 April
Death of President Roosevelt, USA

28 April
Mussolini lynched

30 April
Hitler commits suicide

2 May
Berlin captured by Russian troops

7 May
Total surrender of German forces

6 and 9 August
US atomic bombs dropped on Hiroshima and Nagasaki

14 August
Japan surrenders

15 September
Composer Anton Webern accidentally shot dead by US military policeman, Austria

26 September
Death of Béla Bartók

24 October
United Nations founded

- Benjamin Britten's opera *Peter Grimes*

Opposite The Three Deuces club on West 52nd Street, New York, in the late 1940s, when "The Street" hosted the finest jazz performances in the world. Founded in 1937, the Three Deuces (like many neighboring establishments) became a strip joint in the early 1950s.

Style and Idea: Jazz styles begin to diverge and coexist: bop intensifies into hard bop, "cool" jazz is developed as its refreshing antidote, Latin jazz becomes increasingly popular, and the "third stream" continues the synthetic ideal of symphonic jazz.

1946-

–1958

1946–47

Dizzy Gillespie breaks new ground in the development of Afro-Latin and Afro-Cuban jazz. Stravinsky and Bernstein revitalize symphonic jazz, ragtime is revived, and musicians increasingly succumb to hard drugs.

THE LATIN TINGE

Above Bop pianist Bud Powell, pictured here in 1953, was one of several prominent musicians to receive electric-shock treatment for personal problems.

Jazz Events

1946

28 January
Charlie Parker and Dizzy Gillespie play for Norman Granz's "Jazz at the Philharmonic" in Los Angeles. In the same month, Miles Davis plays with Parker at the Finale Club in Little Tokyo, Los Angeles.

31 January
Django Reinhardt and Stephane Grappelli (• p. 75) are reunited after their wartime separation and record "Echoes of France" in London.

13 February
The first concert performance of Leonard Bernstein's *Three Dance Episodes* (from his musical *On the Town*) takes place in San Francisco. The piece becomes popular as one of the jazziest of jazz-influenced orchestral scores.

16 February
Billie Holiday's concert at New York's Town Hall is promoted as a "jazz *Lieder*" event in an attempt to acquire for jazz the status of concert music, the venue marking a significant contrast to the nightclub scene.

25 March
First performance of Igor Stravinsky's *Ebony Concerto*, a "jazz concerto grosso" written for Woody Herman's First Herd, at Carnegie Hall.

28 March
Miles Davis records with Charlie Parker's septet for Dial in Los Angeles; takes include "Ornithology" and "Night in Tunisia." Davis then rejoins Billy Eckstine's band.

20 July
Trombonist Joe "Tricky Sam" Nanton dies, San Francisco.

29 July
Charlie Parker is arrested on a drug-related arson charge after igniting his hotel bed and walking naked through the streets of Los Angeles. He is committed to Camarillo State Hospital for six months, where he receives electric-shock treatment.

- Arranger Don Redman tours Europe with a band that includes saxophonist Don Byas.
- Dizzy Gillespie forms a big band including John Lewis (future founder of the Modern Jazz Quartet) on piano and Kenny Clarke on drums.
- Pianist Luckey Roberts records RAGTIME numbers for Circle Records. Ragtime is on the verge of a major revival (• p. 116).
- Bud Powell, a leading keyboard exponent of the BEBOP style, is sent by his mother to the Bellevue Hospital in New York, where he receives electric-shock treatment for mental instability.
- Norman Granz founds the Clef record label, which is later incorporated into Verve Records (• p. 107).

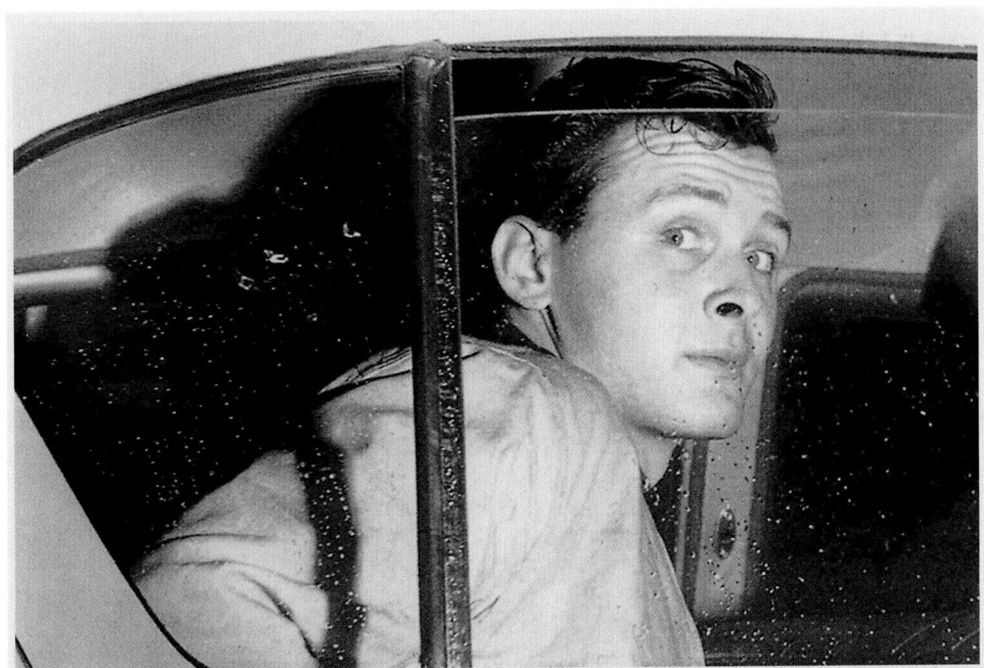

DRUGS

Billie Holiday's narcotics conviction in 1947 was but the tip of a depressing iceberg. Until the rock scene became a major forum for hard drugs in the 1960s, it was jazz that was inevitably associated with substance abuse.

A first resort for musicians had been illicit alcohol during Prohibition, a time when both cocaine and marijuana were also common. Military discipline during World War II was responsible for bringing some musicians' drug habits out into the open, as in the case of conscripted saxophonist Lester Young, who was busted for smoking marijuana (• p. 108). By the time of Charlie Parker's notorious heroin-induced breakdown in the late 1940s, hard drugs had become widely available at very low prices, and their consumption was almost universal among musicians. Some naively thought that if they consumed enough of the stuff, they would end up playing like Parker.

Many, including Billie Holiday (• p. 131), spent a high proportion of their earnings on heroin. Brushes with the law were frequent: Holiday was (with ridiculous insensitivity) arrested again on her hospital deathbed, and COOL trumpeter Chet Baker (• p. 210) served time in an Italian prison in 1960. Both Holiday and Thelonious Monk (• p. 155) lost their New York cabaret cards as a result of drug offenses, which meant they were barred from performing in nightclubs. Holiday's answer was to perform in prestigious venues such as New York's Carnegie Hall and Town Hall, eloquently demonstrating the hypocrisy of the system. (Cabaret cards were eventually abolished in 1967.)

Later musicians who battled against heroin addiction, with varying degrees of success, included John Coltrane and Miles Davis. A full list of players whose deaths were accelerated by their habit would be long and dispiriting, but a glance through the Biographical Index (• pp. 254–61) will graphically illustrate the seriously limited life-expectancy of jazz musicians whose careers peaked in the two decades following the bop revolution.

"Heroin was a major figure in the bop movement, as significant in shaping the music as Parker himself, because one after another it took away most of the leading figures."

James Lincoln Collier, *The Making of Jazz*, 1978

Above A stunned Stan Getz peers from a police car in Seattle after attempting to steal narcotics from a drugstore in 1954 ("It's the craziest thing I've done," he later commented). Having fled from the scene of his crime empty-handed, Getz was apprehended after he telephoned the shop assistant to apologize for his folly.

Right Musical and spiritual soulmates Billie Holiday and Lester Young unwind at Birdland in the late 1940s. Both their careers were affected by drug habits.

World Events

1946

1 February
Hungary becomes Republic

24 February
President Perón assumes power, Argentina

2 June
Italy becomes Republic

25 July
US nuclear tests on Bikini Atoll

August
Mao Tse-Tung revives Chinese Civil War

14 November
Death of Manuel de Falla

15 November
Indonesia gains independence from Holland

- Alfred Hitchcock's movie *Notorious*

JAZZ LATIN STYLE

Jelly Roll Morton identified what he termed the "Latin tinge" in jazz during its very earliest years, when simple rhythmic characteristics of Latin American music were adopted in such surprising contexts as W. C. Handy's *St. Louis Blues* (published in 1914). It was the growing vogue for Latin American dances in the 1930s, however, that resulted in a more prominent presence of Latin rhythms and harmonies in jazz. Elements from Cuban music were promoted in a big-band context by "Machito" (Raúl Grillo), who formed an Afro-Latin band in New York in 1941.

Dizzy Gillespie's strong interest in the music during the same period was reflected in the large number of BEBOP compositions sporting Latin characteristics, including "Night in Tunisia" and "My Little Suede Shoes." In 1947, having experienced Afro-Cuban music at first hand (thanks to his friendship with Machito's onetime musical director, Mario Bauzá), Gillespie formed his own Latinesque big band and cocomposed "Manteca" with Chano Pozo, a conga player he had imported into his RHYTHM SECTION. The same year Gillespie produced "Cubana Be/Cubana Bop," its title suggesting the synthesis of bop and Latin idioms then taking place.

Also active in the development of big-band Latin jazz was the WEST COAST leader Stan Kenton, whose hit track "The Peanut Vendor" (recorded in December 1947) featured an authentic three-man Latin percussion team, including Machito on maracas. The piece became popular once again in the UK during the 1970s after its overexposure in a television advertising campaign for salted peanuts.

In the 1960s and 1970s, Brazilian music stole the initiative from Cuba and began to make a strong impact on jazz, first with the BOSSA NOVA craze – imported by jazz musicians of the stature of saxophonist Stan Getz (• p. 152) – and then with the effective adaptation of Brazilian vocal and percussion techniques as part of the burgeoning jazz-rock scene of the 1970s and 1980s.

Above The "Mambo King," Machito (far right), plays maracas alongside other members of his Afro-Latin band.

Left Painted in 1946 by German artist Max Beckmann (1884–1950), *Begin the Beguine* took its title from the hit version of Cole Porter's song, recorded by Artie Shaw and his band in 1938.

1947

16 January
Mississippi riverboat performer Fate Marable dies, St. Louis.

8 February
Louis Armstrong appears at Carnegie Hall with Billie Holiday.

March
Miles Davis records with Illinois Jacquet's band, New York.

8 May
Davis begins a series of recordings with Charlie Parker, with whom he is playing at the Three Deuces on West 52nd Street, New York.

17 May
Louis Armstrong introduces his new All Stars group at Town Hall, New York.

27 May
Billie Holiday is convicted for possession of heroin, and serves time in the Federal Reformatory for Women at Alderson, West Virginia. She is released on 16 March 1948.

14 August
Miles Davis makes his first recordings as leader. His "All Stars" COMBO includes Charlie Parker, John Lewis (piano), and Max Roach (drums).

29 September
Ella Fitzgerald (• p. 195) and Dizzy Gillespie appear in a sellout concert at Carnegie Hall. The program includes Gillespie's "Cubana Be/Cubana Bop," an example of his flair for Afro-Cuban jazz; he records it in **December**, along with "Manteca."

October–November
Thelonious Monk (• p. 155) records several of his compositions in New York, including "In Walked Bud" and "'Round About Midnight."

October–December
Charlie Parker records numerous tracks for the Dial and Savoy labels in New York and Detroit.

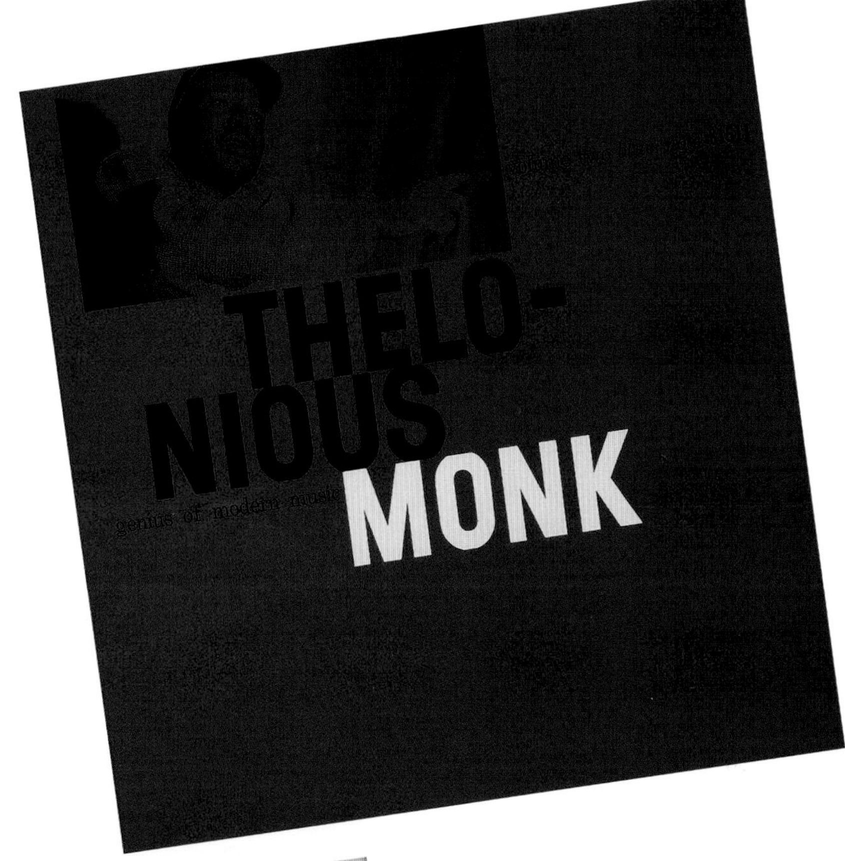

Above RCA Victor's LP reissue of popular tracks recorded by Louis Armstrong in the 1930s and 1940s.

Top Thelonious Monk made his recording debut for Blue Note in the autumn of 1947.

- Woody Herman, Meade Lux Lewis, Louis Armstrong, and Billie Holiday appear in the movie *New Orleans*.
- The Atlantic label is founded by the Turkish entrepreneur Ahmet Ertegun in New York. From 1955, he runs the company with his brother Nesuhi.
- Duke Ellington records as prolifically as ever, and continues his annual series of large-scale works at Carnegie Hall with the premiere of his new *Liberian Suite*. *The Deep South Suite* was heard at the venue in 1946; *The Tattooed Bride* follows in 1948.
- Coleman Hawkins bases his unaccompanied "Picasso" on "Body and Soul" (• p. 95).
- Drummer Art Blakey founds an octet called Jazz Messengers.
- Radio listeners in New York are treated to a contest between the new bebop and old TRAD styles, promoted by Barry Ulanov and Rudi Blesh, respectively. Performers illustrating the bop idiom include Charlie Parker and Dizzy Gillespie.

THELONIOUS MONK: 'ROUND MIDNIGHT

The premier recording of Monk's "'Round Midnight" – or, to give it its full title, "'Round About Midnight" – was made by trumpeter Cootie Williams in August 1944, some three years before the bop pianist entered the studio to record the composition for himself. With vibraphonist Milt Jackson, Dizzy Gillespie recorded a version for septet in Hollywood on 7 February 1946, also before Monk.

Not surprisingly, Monk's own interpretation, preserved in a New York studio in 1947 with a quintet including drummer Art Blakey, is far more innovative than its predecessors. Subtle allusions to the dreamy theme are introduced by alto saxophone, piano, and trumpet in laid-back CALL-AND-RESPONSE before a brief unaccompanied bass link ushers in the full melody. Monk's typically spiky and angular piano technique here contrasts effectively with the sustained backing supplied by the horns, while complex added-note harmonies and sharp offbeat DISSONANCES alternate with filigree cascades up and down the keyboard, many based on the whole-tone SCALE originally introduced into jazz from French impressionist music. Particularly expressive after so much chromaticism is the unexpected shift to a bright major chord in the final cadence of each thematic statement, as is Monk's occasional playing of adjacent notes simultaneously to create stark "wrong note" effects.

"'Round Midnight" quickly became a favored STANDARD, and with Gillespie's "Night in Tunisia" continues to be celebrated as one of the most harmonically inventive bop compositions. Notable among later interpretations is Bill Evans's multilayered OVERDUBBED version in *Conversations with Myself* (1963).

Above Bunk Johnson (left) performs with famous blues singer Huddie "Leadbelly" Ledbetter, a convicted murderer who was pardoned and released from his Louisiana prison when he sang for the governor.

REVIVING RAGTIME

As the 1930s came to a close, interest in the old genres of RAGTIME and New Orleans jazz blossomed. With the onset of the radical innovations of BEBOP in the early 1940s (• p. 97), many conservative listeners and performers began to cultivate an exclusive interest in earlier, historic styles (and were uncharitably dubbed "moldy figs" by more progressive thinkers). Jelly Roll Morton's 1938 retrospective (• p. 90) was soon followed by the foundation of the Blue Note label in 1939, which stimulated Sidney Bechet to make new recordings in the traditional New Orleans style and prompted a popular revival of the BOOGIE-WOOGIE piano music that had been more or less dormant for a decade.

Trumpeter Bunk Johnson, who had known the mythical Buddy Bolden (• p. 25), was brought out of retirement in 1942 to become the leading practitioner of the revivalist movement. Trombonist Kid Ory (• p. 61) was rediscovered in the following year and participated in a series of radio broadcasts hosted by Orson Welles. In 1947, musicians schooled in both bop and traditional idioms competed against one another in a high-profile radio broadcast (• p. 115).

During this same period, books devoted to the historic figures of early jazz appeared. Titles included Frederic Ramsey, Jr. and Charles Edward Smith's *Jazzmen* (1939), W. C. Handy's autobiography (1941), Rudi Blesh and Harriet Janis's *They All Played Ragtime* (1950), and Alan Lomax's *Mister Jelly Roll* (1950).

Above Jazzing in the movies: Billie Holiday and Louis Armstrong in the 1947 film *New Orleans*. At the piano is Charlie Beal, who had recorded with Armstrong in the 1930s.

Right Woody Herman, whose virtuoso band inspired Stravinsky to compose his *Ebony Concerto* in 1945.

World Events

1947

February–March
Crisis in Palestine

20 July
Dutch fight Indonesians in Java

15 August
India and Pakistan gain independence from Britain

31 August
Communists assume power, Hungary

- Arnold Schoenberg composes *A Survivor from Warsaw*
- Tennessee Williams's play *A Streetcar Named Desire*

THE FIRST JAZZ FESTIVAL

French jazz aficionados mount the first major festival, in Nice. Bop earns itself an enthusiastic European following, while Miles Davis's nonet lays the foundation for new stylistic directions in America.

Above Stan Getz at around the time he recorded "Early Autumn" in 1948.

Jazz Events

February
Dizzy Gillespie (• p. 219) brings BEBOP to Europe, appearing at the Nice Jazz Festival. Other participants include Louis Armstrong's All Stars, which Earl Hines (• p. 125) joins this year. Organized by Hugues Panassié and the Hot Club de France, the Nice event is the first international jazz festival.

March
Billie Holiday sings two concerts at Carnegie Hall, and breaks their box-office records on both occasions.

21 June
Columbia introduces microgroove discs made from vinyl, the first "long-playing" records to be marketed.

September
Miles Davis (• p. 217) forms a nonet that appears for two weeks at the Royal Roost on Broadway as a temporary replacement for Count Basie's band (• p. 87).

November
Ben Webster rejoins Duke Ellington's orchestra.

Autumn
Benny Goodman (• p. 84) plays with his newly formed sextet and septet, in which he is reunited with pianist Teddy Wilson.

2 December
Dizzy Gillespie's Cuban drummer, Chano Pozo (• p. 114), is shot dead in Harlem.

15 December
End of second recording ban by the American Federation of Musicians.

30 December
Tenor saxophonist Stan Getz (• p. 152) performs an impressive solo in a recording of "Early Autumn" made by Woody Herman's Second Herd in Los Angeles.

December
Miles Davis quits Charlie Parker and plays at the Onyx Club on West 52nd Street, New York. He has grown increasingly disillusioned with Parker, who earlier this year gets them both fired from the Argyle Show Bar in Chicago when, too stoned to perform, Parker still insists on collecting his fee. A union official orders him from his office at gunpoint.
• British Decca launches a subsidiary label, Capitol, to sell imported recordings made by Capitol in the US (founded in 1942).

- Duke Ellington and his orchestra tour Europe, with only part of the band appearing in London because of British union restrictions on appearances by American musicians (• p. 77).
- Art Blakey visits Africa to study native drumming techniques.

World Events

30 January
Assassination of Gandhi, New Delhi

25 February
Communists gain control of Czechoslovakia

15 May
British abandon Palestine

May
Foundation of State of Israel

24 June
USSR isolates Berlin, leading to massive airlift

29 July
London hosts first Olympic Games since 1936

15 August
Republic of South Korea instituted

- George Orwell's novel *1984*

DRUMS

Jazz drumming originated as a unique synthesis of rhythmic patterns borrowed from military MARCHES and African tribal drumming, the greater complexity of the latter coming increasingly to the fore as the music developed. Primitive drum kits, in which a bass drum was played by a pedal mechanism so that the hands were left free to play cymbals and/or snare drum, were used in RAGTIME and theater orchestras early in the century. The influence of standard marching rhythms (known as the "rudiments") persisted in New Orleans jazz. Although the playing of drummers such as Tony Sbarbaro, of the Original Dixieland Jazz Band (• p. 37), may sound crude and stiff today, the DIXIELAND style added SYNCOPATION and, at the time, must have appeared strikingly novel. As jazz developed into the faster-tempo, dance-oriented Chicago idiom of the 1920s, the drumming became more sophisticated, involving increased use of crisp suspended cymbal strokes as a form of punctuation and developing the "fill" technique (any short rhythmic formula used to fill brief gaps in the musical texture).

The pounding bass-drum playing of early jazz, often comprising one stroke per beat, gradually yielded to a subtler approach. In the late 1920s the invention of the "high-hat" (a pair of horizontally mounted cymbals opened and closed by a foot pedal) allowed rhythmic continuity to be maintained in the background. This RHYTHM was achieved with simple and unwavering SWING patterns played on the high-hat with a single stick, while the pedal opened and closed the cymbal plates on alternate beats. Drummer–bandleaders such as Gene Krupa and Chick Webb began to promote themselves as soloists in the 1930s, although the quality of their solos was distinctly variable and often relied more on a flamboyant visual impact than on imaginative rhythmic creations. Sonny Greer's work in Duke Ellington's orchestra (• p. 63) initiated the fashion for a "jungle" style of drumming, involving ancillary instruments such as gongs, timpani, tom-toms, and cymbals of different sizes.

Above Duke Ellington and Sonny Greer with the latter's impressive array of percussion, pictured at Chicago's Hotel Sherman in 1940. Notable exotica are the orchestral timpani (far right), five Chinese temple blocks (center), tubular bells (rear), and two gongs of different pitches mounted on tall stands for optimal visual impact.

Below A typical modern drum kit, comprising "high-hat" cymbal (front), two suspended cymbals, pedal-operated bass drum (rear), snare drum, and three tom-toms of different sizes.

In tandem with the rapid development of other musical parameters in the 1940s, bop drumming introduced a refreshing liberation from typical rhythms. Although the "swing" figuration often persisted in the background (now transferred to a single "ride" cymbal), the bass drum and snare drum were used to supply unpredictable offbeat accentuation (• p. 97). At the hands of Kenny Clarke and Max Roach, drum solos became more elaborate affairs on a par with those of the melodic instruments. Drum "fills" and accompaniments began closely to mirror and develop fragments of themes emerging in improvised sections, thus ensuring that the drummer became a far more integrated member of the ensemble. These trends were also reflected in the resourceful work of Buddy Rich (who led his own small groups and drummed for bandleader Harry James until 1966), and Roy Haynes (whose collaborators ranged from Charlie Parker to Chick Corea).

Bop drumming reached its apogee in the intricate playing of Art Blakey (• p. 139), who studied African drumming in 1948–49 and developed a sophisticated technique of POLYMETER, in which pulses of different speeds are superimposed. The prodigious Tony Williams, in his work as a teenager with Miles Davis in the early 1960s, showed that Blakey's exhilarating approach could be taken to still higher levels of complexity. The experimentation of the FREE JAZZ movement (• p. 150) led at times to the total abrogation of a regular pulse, but the craze for FUSION (• p. 171) in the 1970s concentrated on the heavy regular BACKBEATS of rock music that had been a feature of some HARD BOP pieces since the late 1950s. Rock also influenced the use of quaver patterns in "straight" (i.e., not SWUNG) rhythm, and an extended kit in which multiple tom-toms and cymbals of graded pitches became commonplace. Electronic drums and the generation of computerized drum techniques have also contributed to the development of modern jazz (• p. 220).

MIGRATION TO FRANCE

The first Festival International de Jazz in Paris seduces American players to the rapidly expanding European jazz scene. Back in the US, new developments in recording technology are set to revolutionize the music industry.

Jazz Events

1 January
To celebrate the lifting of the recording ban imposed by the American Federation of Musicians (• p. 103), RCA records the *Metronome All-Stars* with musicians including Miles Davis (• p. 217), Dizzy Gillespie (• p. 219), Fats Navarro, J. J. Johnson, Kai Winding, Buddy DeFranco, Charlie Parker (• p. 136), Lennie Tristano, and Shelly Manne under arranger/director Pete Rugolo. The union sets a three-hour limit to recording sessions; any work in addition to this is deemed to be overtime.

10 January
45rpm and 33$^1/_3$ rpm discs introduced in the US.

21 January
Miles Davis and Gil Evans record the first of three nonet sessions, eight tracks from which are issued as *Birth of the Cool* on the Capitol label in 1954.

8 April
Premiere of Leonard Bernstein's Second Symphony, *The Age of Anxiety* (based on the poem by W. H. Auden), by the Boston Symphony Orchestra under Serge Koussevitzky. The Boston critic Cyrus Durgin describes the work's exhilarating scherzo ("The Masque") as "a marvellous distillation of the movement of jazz."

May
The Festival International de Jazz, held in Paris, features appearances by Charlie Parker, Dizzy Gillespie, Sidney Bechet, Miles Davis, and Kenny Clarke. The reception they are given is so positive that Bechet and Clarke decide to settle in Europe, while Davis returns to the US thoroughly disillusioned with the American jazz scene.

Above left Charles Delaunay's jazz festival was held in 1949, 1952, and 1954 at the Salle Pleyel, Paris. A second Paris festival ran for four years in the late 1960s; today's event was instituted in 1980.

BIRTH OF THE COOL

The epithet "COOL" in jazz has no precise definition, being used as a loose opposite of HOT and embracing a wide range of styles. The intricate ensemble arrangements by Gil Evans, inspired by Claude Thornhill's orchestra and recorded by Miles Davis's nonet in 1949–50 after the band appeared at the Royal Roost on Broadway, were issued with the prophetic title *Birth of the Cool* in 1954. These influential tracks were later seen to epitomize certain aspects common in all later cool jazz: emotional restraint (achieved partly through an avoidance of expressive playing techniques, such as VIBRATO), and a harmonic and contrapuntal sophistication made possible by more PRE-COMPOSITION and therefore less IMPROVISATION. Although the Davis nonet continued to demonstrate its debt to bop, the subsequent evolution of cool jazz represented a sometimes self-conscious turning away from the highly charged and spontaneously virtuosic atmosphere of the bop style.

Participating in Davis's nonet were saxophonists Gerry Mulligan and Lee Konitz, who went on to spearhead their own WEST COAST "cool school" (• p. 134). The term "cool" has also been applied to the tightly organized music of John Lewis's Modern Jazz Quartet (• p. 129), and to the refined piano styles of George Shearing and Dave Brubeck (• p. 189).

Above Miles Davis's nonet at a Capitol recording session on 21 January 1949. Davis is standing behind saxophonists Gerry Mulligan and Lee Konitz.

Below French and American musicians rehearse for the Festival International de Jazz in May 1949. The lineup includes US tenor saxophonist Don Byas (second from left), whose emigration to France in 1946 was followed by many of his American colleagues, attracted to the energy and freedom of the European jazz scene.

1949

Jazz Events

16 May
Lennie Tristano's recordings *Digression* and *Intuition* constitute an early experiment in free ensemble IMPROVISATION.

7 July
One of the earliest jazz legends, trumpeter Bunk Johnson, dies in Los Angeles.

September
Norman Granz pairs Canadian pianist Oscar Peterson and bassist Ray Brown for a "Jazz at the Philharmonic" concert at Carnegie Hall. The two men later work together in Peterson's two famous piano trios (1951–66).
• Dave Brubeck (• p. 134) records in San Francisco with his piano trio and experimental Jazz Workshop Ensemble octet.

15 December
The nightclub Birdland, named after Charlie Parker (• p. 136), opens on Broadway.

25 December
Charlie Parker appears at Carnegie Hall.

- New Jazz and Prestige record labels founded by Bob Weinstock in New York.
- Stan Kenton and his twenty-piece orchestra play their PROGRESSIVE JAZZ at Carnegie Hall.

Above 15 December 1949: the scene at Birdland, the nightclub named after Charlie Parker, on its opening night. Performing at the venue are (l. to r.): Max Kaminsky (trumpet), Lester Young (tenor saxophone), "Hot Lips" Page (trumpet), Charlie "Yardbird" Parker (alto saxophone), and blind pianist Lennie Tristano.

Right Parker warms up before going on stage at the 1949 Festival International de Jazz in Paris.

SASSY

Sarah Vaughan (nicknamed "Sassy" for her sharp tongue) began a five-year Columbia contract in 1949, cutting over twenty tracks in one year. Seven years before, she won an amateur talent competition at New York's Apollo Theater, which secured her first engagements with pianist Earl Hines (• p. 125) and singer Billy Eckstine. Endowed with one of the richest voices in jazz, Vaughan combined an almost operatic power with a phenomenal variety of color and an unusually wide range: she could instantly switch from deep huskiness to brilliant high notes with ease, and her tone could veer from the lushly romantic to the bitterly ironic within a single phrase.

Although her widespread popularity depended largely on interpretations of sentimental BALLADS, she was a brilliant (if sparing) exponent of SCAT (• p. 61) and knew how to adapt her melodic shapes to the harmonic demands of the bop style (• p. 97). From the 1950s her career followed parallel paths, her recordings divided between commercially oriented popular song (often with saccharine background strings) and more compelling virtuoso interpretations of STANDARDS with some of the finest jazz musicians of the time.

Above and right Sarah Vaughan's beauty and stunning artistry won her an enthusiastic popular following in the 1940s. She is seen here in a studio portrait (above), and during a live performance in the early 1950s.

World Events

18 April
Republic of Eire established

23 May
(West) German Federal Republic established

27 July
Maiden flight of the world's first jet passenger aircraft, the De Havilland Comet

8 September
Death of Richard Strauss

1 October
People's Republic of China founded by Chairman Mao Tse-Tung

7 October
(East) German Democratic Republic established

16 October
End of Civil War in Greece

30 December
Vietnam achieves independence from France

- Movie version of Leonard Bernstein's musical *On the Town* wins two Oscars

PARKER IN SCANDINAVIA

Charlie Parker tours Sweden and Benny Goodman crosses the Atlantic, stimulating a growing appreciation of jazz in northern Europe.

Jazz Events

March
Oscar Peterson (• p. 163) makes his debut recordings in New York. Over the next four decades he becomes one of the most prolific recording artists of all time.

18–19 May
Sarah Vaughan (• p. 123) records in New York with Miles Davis (• p. 217) as SIDEMAN.

June
Charlie Parker (• p. 136) and Thelonious Monk (• p. 155) record together in New York. Their sessions include interpretations of "Bloomdido" and "My Melancholy Baby."

7 July
Trumpeter Fats Navarro dies of tuberculosis at the age of twenty-six, New York.

Summer
Miles Davis, Art Blakey (• p. 139), Dexter Gordon, and Charlie Parker are apprehended at Los Angeles's Burbank Airport for possession of drugs, but they are later acquitted. Thelonious Monk is subsequently arrested for possession and banned from appearing in New York nightclubs for the next six years.

6 November
Benny Goodman (• p. 84) and the NBC Symphony Orchestra give the first performance of Aaron Copland's Clarinet Concerto, New York. This year Goodman also goes on a European tour with trumpeter Roy Eldridge.

November
Charlie Parker tours Sweden.

- Erroll Garner composes his piano solo "Misty" (soon to become a STANDARD) on a flight from San Francisco to Denver, but does not record it until 1954.
- Pianist Ahmad Jamal founds his first trio with Ray Crawford (guitar) and Eddie Calhoun (bass).
- Both the Count Basie (• p. 87) and Dizzy Gillespie orchestras experience financial difficulties and are forced to disband. Basie forms a new small COMBO that includes Clark Terry (trumpet) and Buddy Rich (drums).
- Members of the Willesden Music Makers' Club are taken to court for organizing the illegal entry to, and performances in, the UK of Sidney Bechet in November 1949, and Coleman Hawkins in December 1949. Legislation prompted by the demands of the British Musicians' Union has effectively banned American musicians from appearing in Britain since 1935 (• p. 84), and is not repealed for another four years (• p. 134).
- Two important books are published in New York: Alan Lomax's *Mister Jelly Roll*, based on the memoirs of Jelly Roll Morton (• p. 45), and Rudi Blesh and Harriet Janis's *They All Played Ragtime*.

Above Charlie Parker performing in Sweden in November 1950.

Above right Jelly Roll Morton's colorful memoirs are a vivid, if sometimes unreliable, account of early New Orleans jazz.

PIANISTS

After the untimely death of Fats Waller (• p. 105) in 1943, three performers independently continued to augment the potential of the piano as one of the most versatile of jazz instruments. Their innovations were influential on two younger players who began to establish themselves in the early 1950s – Oscar Peterson and Erroll Garner.

Earl Hines first revealed his talents during early work with Louis Armstrong (• p. 57) in the late 1920s. His TRUMPET STYLE of playing was the first tangible departure from the post-RAGTIME STRIDE idiom, cultivating a right-hand melodic technique more directly comparable to that of FRONT-LINE melody instruments, and using octave doublings to emphasize certain passages. Hines also possessed the crucial ability to make his often florid embellishments seem an essential part of the melody, in contrast to the superficial decorative patterns of so many performers. In his 1951 recording of Waller's "Honeysuckle Rose" with Armstrong's All Stars, for example, he deploys a glittering array of GLISSANDI and trills that wittily merge into various parts of the theme. Hines also deserves credit for furthering the role of the piano as a featured instrument in big-band jazz during his Chicago years (• p. 65).

Nat King Cole, who was strongly influenced by Hines's rhythmic sophistication, created an altogether new jazz medium in the shape of the piano trio. Originally a combination of piano, guitar, and bass (• p. 88), the trio format provided a buoyant backing for Cole's suave singing and explored novel textures such as closely interlocking figurations played simultaneously by piano and guitar. Although Cole was a gifted pianist, his success as a vocalist was destined to sidetrack him from further innovation at the keyboard. His trio disbanded in 1951 as he became increasingly involved in popular broadcasting (he had his own cult television show in 1956). But the trio medium proved to be one of the most enduring ensemble formats in jazz, later acquiring a greater rhythmic drive when Oscar Peterson replaced the guitarist with a drummer in 1958.

Art Tatum, virtually blind from birth, modeled his own trio on the original Cole format in 1943. Endowed with the most prodigious technical facility of any jazz pianist, Tatum was held in awe by his contemporaries, who habitually referred to him as "God." His style was deeply rooted in the stride school, especially its virtuoso manifestation at the hands of Fats Waller. Tatum's left-hand figurations became infinitely more flexible, however, sometimes only hinting at an underlying stride motion. His harmonic vocabulary was the most sophisticated yet seen in jazz, and it allowed him to explore revelatory new approaches to well-worn traditional themes. Rhythmic surprises and complexities of texture both reached a high point in Tatum's work, and his sheer technical perfection made any performance an exciting experience. Unlike Hines, however, his abilities sometimes led him to display his technical accomplishments merely for their own sake.

Left Earl Hines, here sporting the trademark hat and cigar of early jazz pianists, was the first performer to break significantly away from the stride style.

World Events

12 January
Death of George Orwell

3 April
Death of Kurt Weill

8 March
Soviet Union declares its nuclear weaponry

28 June
North Korean forces enter Seoul and provoke Korean War

26 September
Liberation of Seoul by UN troops

24 October
Chinese invade Tibet

2 November
Death of George Bernard Shaw

November–December
Chinese army repels UN forces in Korea

Above Dizzy Gillespie, pictured before his adoption of a trumpet with its bell bent upwards (• p. 219).

MODERN JAZZ

Pianist John Lewis begins work with a group soon to become the influential Modern Jazz Quartet. Meanwhile, Charlie Parker's professionalism deteriorates and the young Miles Davis emerges from his shadow.

Above Lennie Tristano, voted Musician of the Year by *Metronome* in 1947, smoothed out the rhythmic irregularities of bop in his highly intellectual brand of cool jazz.

Jazz Events

17 January
Miles Davis records in New York with Charlie Parker and resumes his GIGS at Birdland.

30 January
Earl Hines (• p. 125) makes a live recording with Louis Armstrong's All Stars at a concert in Pasadena, California, and soon after quits the band.

January
Duke Ellington's *Harlem Suite* is performed at New York's Metropolitan Opera House. Johnny Hodges (alto saxophone) and Sonny Greer (drums) both quit the orchestra in **February**, the latter after twenty-seven years' membership.

March
Cab Calloway draws attention to the growing drug problem in jazz in an article published in *Ebony* magazine.

July
Charlie Parker loses his cabaret card because of involvement with narcotics, and is unable to play in New York nightclubs. On his birthday, **29 August**, he is informed that the American Federation of Musicians is considering investigating his erratic behavior. In spite of the popularity of his performances with string accompaniment, he is in growing financial debt to his agent.

5 October
The Miles Davis All Stars record their first long-playing album for Prestige.

30 October
Blind pianist Lennie Tristano records *Ju-Ju*, an early experiment in OVERDUBBING. This year he forms a jazz conservatory in New York with the help of Lee Konitz (alto saxophone) and Warne Marsh (tenor saxophone).

12 December
Formerly married to vibraphonist Red Norvo (• p. 70), singer Mildred Bailey dies in Poughkeepsie, New York. The couple had been dubbed "Mr and Mrs Swing."

- Pianist Dave Brubeck (• p. 189) forms his first quartet, with alto saxophonist Paul Desmond.
- John Lewis forms a quartet with Milt Jackson (vibraphone), Ray Brown (bass), and Kenny Clarke (drums) under the name Milt Jackson Quartet (• p. 129).
- Trumpeter Chet Baker (• p. 210) is court-martialed for desertion from the US Army due to mental instability.
- Sidney Bechet emigrates to France.
- Eleven-year-old pianist Herbie Hancock (• p. 201) performs a Mozart concerto with the Chicago Symphony Orchestra.
- Alex North composes a jazz-influenced score for Elia Kazan's film *A Streetcar Named Desire*, starring Vivien Leigh and Marlon Brando (• p. 141).

ELECTRIC BASS

In 1951 Leo Fender's musical-instrument company developed its "Precision" four-string electric bass guitar, a highly marketable innovation that borrowed the electrical amplification of six-string guitars, first introduced with the Gibson company's pioneering 1936 model. The Fender Precision Bass was only a guitar by virtue of the horizontal manner in which it was played: it is more accurate to consider the instrument as a direct descendant of the double bass, with which it shares the tuning system for its four strings. On some later models, the "frets" characteristic of the guitar fingerboard (metal strips indicating where the left-hand fingers should be placed) were omitted so that the playing technique was much closer to that of the double bass. Designed to be both louder and more portable than a conventional string bass, the electric version was readily accepted as a practical alternative, capable of injecting new vitality into the lowest layer of the musical texture.

Although it quickly became a staple member of rock bands and has continued to dominate the pop and rock scene, the electric bass was promoted by several prominent jazz musicians during the 1950s. Lionel Hampton's bass player, Monk Montgomery, adopted the instrument almost immediately, but it was not until the boom in jazz-rock FUSION (• p. 171) that the electric bass came into its own in the jazz world. Some players fluctuated (and have continued to fluctuate) between ACOUSTIC and electric bass, while others were trained solely on the electric model from the beginning of their careers. The instrument's penetrating rich tone and considerable power made it an ideal vehicle for conveying the potent RIFF patterns that characterized the bass part in a typical fusion piece, while making an obvious aural reference to the color of rock music and rhythm 'n' blues.

One of the most intriguing coincidences in jazz history is the fact that many prominent masters of the electric bass were born in 1951, the year of its launch. These include Stanley Clarke, who tried out a succession of different instruments before settling on electric bass, with which he made a memorable contribution in the 1970s to the often hard-driving sound of Chick Corea's fusion group Return to Forever (• p. 179). Clarke's exact contemporary Jaco Pastorius provided a solid bass support for Joe Zawinul's rival fusion band Weather Report (• p. 175) at the peak of its popularity in 1976–82, developing techniques of stunning flexibility and inventiveness that included chordal playing, harmonics, and GLISSANDI. (His predecessor in Weather Report was Alphonso Johnson, who was also born in 1951.) Miles Davis's electric bassist, Michael Henderson, was another 1951 arrival, as was Mark Egan, who succeeded his teacher Pastorius in Pat Metheny's group (• p. 199) in 1978.

Since the 1970s, the electric bass and six-string electric guitar have also occasionally been employed by composers of classical music in a not entirely successful attempt to bridge the cultural gap between pop music and the concert hall.

World Events

14 March
UN troops take Seoul, Korean War

May
London's South Bank complex opened during Festival of Britain

11 September
Stravinsky's opera *The Rake's Progress* first performed, Venice

- Film version of George Gershwin's *An American in Paris* wins Oscar for Best Picture
- J. D. Salinger's novel *The Catcher in the Rye*

Left The Fender Precision Bass, seen here with an advertisement for the same company's Broadcaster electric guitar, revolutionized the sound of jazz when it came into widespread use in the 1960s.

WEST COAST TRAVELS EAST

Leonard Bernstein directs a critical investigation into the tension between bop and traditional styles as Duke Ellington celebrates twenty-five years in the music business. The new West Coast "cool" school begins to make its presence felt in New York.

Above Chet Baker (trumpet) and Gerry Mulligan (baritone sax) in action with their popular quartet in September 1952.

Right Members of "Jazz at the Philharmonic" rehearse in Stockholm in March 1952 (l. to r.): Ella Fitzgerald, Oscar Peterson, Roy Eldridge, and Max Roach.

Jazz Events

22 and 28 January
Charlie Parker (• p. 136) records sessions with string backing and Latin repertoire for Mercury (Verve).

24 February
Parker receives an award from *Down Beat* for best alto saxophonist on a New York television program, in which he jams with Dizzy Gillespie (• p. 219).

March
Norman Granz's "Jazz at the Philharmonic" (• p. 107) tours Sweden with Lester Young, Roy Eldridge, and Max Roach. Louis Armstrong also visits Europe this year.

March–April
Dizzy Gillespie records numerous tracks in Paris.

April
Charles Mingus (• p. 190) and Max Roach found the record label Debut, which remains in business until 1957.

May
Charlie Parker plays with Chet Baker in Los Angeles, where he participates in a JAM SESSION for "Jazz at the Philharmonic." This summer, Parker gets himself further in debt with his agent and faces union fines for unprofessional conduct.

9 May
Miles Davis (• p. 217) records for Blue Note, in a year in which he is increasingly afflicted by his drug habit.

Spring
Carnegie Hall mounts a concert devoted to Californian jazz (• p. 134), featuring Chet Baker (• p. 210), Gerry Mulligan, and Paul Desmond. Mulligan and Baker form a new quartet, notable for its exclusion of the piano.

13 June
Leonard Bernstein organizes a Festival of Creative Arts at Brandeis University, near Boston, and hosts a high-powered symposium on jazz that debates the conflict of BEBOP with traditional idioms, illustrated by comparative IMPROVISATIONS on the same STANDARDS. Performers include Miles Davis, John Lewis, and Charles Mingus.

2 September
Gerry Mulligan's quartet records "My Funny Valentine."

14 November
Duke Ellington's 25th Anniversary is celebrated in two concerts at Carnegie Hall, with a prestigious lineup that includes Billie Holiday (• p. 131), Charlie Parker, Dizzy Gillespie, and Stan Getz (• p. 152).

22 December
Milt Jackson and John Lewis rename their group the Modern Jazz Quartet, and record for Prestige with a new bass player, Percy Heath.

29 December
Bandleader and SWING innovator Fletcher Henderson (• p. 71) dies, New York. Large crowds attend his funeral in Harlem.

- Avant-garde American composer John Cage creates his musical collage, in which forty-two jazz records are played simultaneously.

JOHN LEWIS AND MJQ

Miles Davis's nonet of 1949 (• p. 121) fully utilized the many talents of bop pianist John Lewis, a skilled arranger and thoughtful composer. Lewis's keyboard technique was characterized by a sensitive delicacy unusual in the bop idiom that prevailed at the time. After working with Charlie Parker, Illinois Jacquet, and Lester Young, Lewis joined vibraphonist Milt Jackson's quartet in 1951, alongside two fellow SIDEMEN from Dizzy Gillespie's big band – bassist Ray Brown and drummer Kenny Clarke. The group soon gained an enormous popular following, and adopted the name Modern Jazz Quartet in 1952, the year in which Percy Heath succeeded Brown on double bass. Connie Kay replaced Clarke two years later, and the Lewis-Jackson-Heath-Kay combination endured for two memorable decades. When the group finally disbanded in 1974, the breakup proved to be only temporary, and in 1981 the acclaimed quartet reformed for a tour of Japan (• p. 196).

Under Lewis's musical direction, MJQ evolved an intellectually satisfying brand of bop that won many admirers in the concert hall, but was criticized by some jazz purists for an approach that was too COOL and seemed to cater primarily to the tastes of classical-music lovers. Lewis's use of classical methods of composition, most notably the strict COUNTERPOINT of the Baroque era (evident in MJQ's extraordinary soundtrack to the 1957 film *No Sun in Venice* (• p. 141), was symptomatic of his frustration with the simplicity and frequent predictability of bop's musical forms. Bop pieces had invariably followed the same pattern: a statement of the theme (HEAD); a succession of improvised variations; and a further statement of the unadulterated theme by way of conclusion. Lewis composed elaborate structures of thematic complexity and textural variety in which bop improvisation remained an essential ingredient. In doing so, he achieved a satisfying hybrid style. Not surprisingly, only a few of his pieces were adopted by other jazz musicians, although "Django" – a tribute to Django Reinhardt (• p. 75) – continues to be reinterpreted as a favorite standard.

However much the purists continue to lament Lewis's clear nods in the direction of a classically oriented audience, his distinctive music introduced many new listeners to jazz who might not otherwise have been drawn to it. His thorough exploration of a possible synthesis between classical and jazz idioms, much of it concentrated in the production of so-called THIRD-STREAM music, was an important artistic breakthrough that exerted a strong influence on the future course of the music's development.

World Events

6 February
Death of King George VI, UK

26 July
Death of Evita Perón, Argentina

3 October
First British nuclear-weapons test

4 November
Dwight Eisenhower elected President, USA

- Columbia University establishes a studio for electronic music
- Samuel Beckett's play *Waiting for Godot*
- Jackson Pollock's abstract paintings cause controversy

The Modern Jazz Quartet Plays No Sun in Venice
Original Film Score by John Lewis

Above left Vibraphonist Milt Jackson, shown here playing in Woody Herman's band at Birdland in June 1950, teamed up with John Lewis the following year to launch the highly successful Modern Jazz Quartet.

Above Album cover for the Atlantic soundtrack recording of MJQ's score to the movie *No Sun in Venice* (1957), featuring a painting by Turner of the Grand Canal.

REVIVING THE BIG BANDS

Trumpeter Chet Baker becomes the star of West Coast jazz. Count Basie and Benny Goodman are both back at the helm of new big bands after postwar austerity put the large ensemble out of fashion.

Above Lionel Hampton's band made a timely tour to Europe in 1953 when the big-band sound was enjoying a popular revival.

Jazz Events

5 February
Charlie Parker (• p. 136) visits Montreal for a television appearance. He returns to Canada for a concert at Toronto's Massey Hall on **15 May**, alongside Bud Powell, Dizzy Gillespie, Charles Mingus, and Max Roach. Back in Montreal in **October**, he is reported to the American Federation of Musicians for allegedly throwing together an inferior band at the last minute.

9 February
Dizzy Gillespie appears at the Salle Pleyel, Paris, where he makes a live recording.

2 March
Dave Brubeck's quartet (• p. 189) records their album *Jazz at Oberlin* at Oberlin College, part of a series of highly acclaimed appearances at American university campuses.

16 May
Gypsy guitarist and original Hot Club de France musician Django Reinhardt (• p. 75) dies, Fontainebleau, France.

24 June
André Previn, working as a film-music arranger and jazz pianist in Hollywood, records an album of Fats Waller STANDARDS in Los Angeles.

June
Charlie Parker appears at the Hi-Hat Club, Boston.

August
Down Beat introduces its first Critics' Poll, in which Chet Baker (• p. 210) wins the "New Star" award.

21 November
Larry Shields, former clarinetist with the Original Dixieland Jazz Band (• p. 37), dies in Los Angeles.

Autumn–Winter
Miles Davis (• p. 217) plays in Detroit.

2 December
Pianist Mary Lou Williams (• p. 196) records with tenor saxophonist Don Byas in Paris, where Byas has lived since 1946.

12 December
Count Basie's new big band records the long-playing album *Dance Session* in New York.

- Benny Goodman's reformed band goes on tour with Louis Armstrong's All Stars. A serious clash of temperaments between the two leaders precipitates Goodman's nervous breakdown.
- Teddy Wilson tours to England, "Jazz at the Philharmonic" appears in London, and Lionel Hampton's band (• p. 70) visits Europe.
- Valve trombonist Bob Brookmeyer replaces Chet Baker in Gerry Mulligan's WEST COAST quartet (• p. 134).
- The Sydney Jazz Club opens in Australia.

World Events

6 March
Deaths of Josef Stalin and Sergei Prokofiev, USSR; news of the composer's death is suppressed for three days

29 May
Sir Edmund Hillary and Tenzing Norgay reach the summit of Mount Everest

2 June
Coronation of Elizabeth II, UK

- Arthur Miller's play *The Crucible*
- Dylan Thomas's play *Under Milk Wood* (• p. 162)
- Karlheinz Stockhausen's composition *Kontra-Punkte*

LADY DAY

In 1952 and 1953, Billie Holiday gradually returned to the performance circuit after several years of serious disruption to her career caused by drug addiction (• p. 113). "Lady Day" – the nickname was coined by her soulmate, tenor saxophonist Lester Young, whom she in turn dubbed "Pres" (for "President") – never recaptured the superior vocal quality of her youthful performances in the 1930s, but her singing retained its affecting idiosyncrasies. Through a series of European tours and American television appearances she remained a high-profile figure until her final breakdown and death in 1959 (• p. 146). Her sartorial trademarks were a gardenia in her hair (• p. 77) and long white gloves: the gardenia was a holdover from the time when she accidentally burnt her hair with a curling iron immediately before a performance and hid the damage with a flower, while the gloves elegantly covered the telltale needle marks on her arms.

Few would argue against the widely held view that Holiday was the finest jazz vocalist of all time. Self-taught, Holiday sang from instinctive musicality, and her Harlem performances in 1933 quickly attracted the attention of producer John Hammond (• p. 209). Her early success also led to work with Teddy Wilson and Benny Goodman (• p. 84), and she made a dazzling series of recordings with both musicians. Moving on to collaborate with bandleaders of the stature of Count Basie (• p. 87) and Artie Shaw, Holiday became renowned for her uncanny ability to recompose well-known tunes as she went along: a melody would never be sung in its usual form, but would be altered on the spur of the moment to produce memorable variations that were often a considerable improvement on the original.

Holiday's singing voice was, by her own admission, modeled squarely on that of Louis Armstrong (• p. 57), but it exuded a captivating blend of vulnerability and sexuality that has never been equaled. Deft virtuoso showpieces such as "What a Little Moonlight Can Do" (1935) were gradually replaced in her repertoire by more tender BALLADS, and in 1939 she unwittingly gained notoriety with her powerful anti-lynching song "Strange Fruit" (• p. 92). In the later 1940s, she appeared at Carnegie Hall (• p. 118) in triumph after undertaking a drug rehabilitation program, but she was continually dogged by a succession of exploitative husbands, unhappy bisexual affairs, and a self-destructiveness that brought her life to an untimely close.

Above Billie Holiday's instinctive reshaping of familiar melodies made her one of the most spontaneously lyrical of all jazz artists.

FLUTE

In June 1953, tenor saxophonist Frank Wess joined Count Basie's big band. Wess also played the flute, and Basie soon began to promote this instrument as a new element in jazz. The innovation was adopted by various West Coast bands during the 1950s, a movement reflected in Gil Evans's inclusion of flute parts in the orchestral arrangements he undertook for Miles Davis in 1958 (• p. 142). By this time, big-band saxophonists were habitually doubling up as flautists, and Herbie Mann emerged as the foremost soloist on the instrument (winning the *Down Beat* flute poll, a category established in 1956, for thirteen consecutive years). But the most significant exponent of the flute was Eric Dolphy, who supported Ornette Coleman in his exploration of FREE JAZZ in the early 1960s (• p. 150) and went on to work with Charles Mingus.

Later flautists tended to polarize at either the avant-garde or commercial end of the stylistic spectrum. Like Dolphy's, Roland Kirk's flute-playing was subservient to his proficiency on a variety of other wind instruments. However, unlike Dolphy, Kirk played lesser-known varieties of the flute family, including nose flutes and a homemade "black puzzle flute." These produced a sonorous contrast to his unique and bizarre method of playing three different saxophones simultaneously. In another vein, Dave Valentin, who recorded for GRP (• p. 214), is a slick technician whose easygoing melodic style is worlds apart from Kirk and other innovators of the 1960s and 1970s.

EAST AND WEST

Major European tours by American stars coincide with the growing popularity of the "cool school" on the West Coast. Charlie Parker attempts suicide and begins a tragic final decline that leads to his premature death in 1955.

Above Chet Baker with members of his sextet at a recording session in 1954. His West Coast colleagues are tenor saxophonist Jack Montrose (center) and alto saxophonist Herb Geller (right).

Jazz Events

9 January
A concert in Stockholm begins Billie Holiday's first European tour, which includes visits to France, Germany, Switzerland, and England.

18 January
Charlie Parker (• p. 136) plays at the Hi-Hat Club, Boston, and makes the first of several radio broadcasts from the venue with "Symphony Sid" Torin as master of ceremonies.

15 February
In Los Angeles, the Chet Baker Quartet (• p. 210), at the height of its popularity, records STANDARDS including "My Funny Valentine" and "But Not for Me."

February
Miles Davis (• p. 217) returns to New York after spending five months playing in Detroit. He records two albums in New Jersey for the Prestige label: *Walkin'* (**29 April**) and *Miles Davis and the Modern Jazz Giants* (**24 December**), the latter with Thelonious Monk (• p. 155) and Milt Jackson (• p. 129).

March
Count Basie's first European tour takes his band to Copenhagen, Stockholm, Amsterdam, Brussels, and cities in France, Germany, and Switzerland.

April
The Dave Brubeck Quartet (• p. 189) records *Jazz Goes to College* at the Universities of Ohio and Michigan. Brubeck's photograph appears on the cover of *Time* magazine this year.

17 May
Drummer Shelly Manne records his album *West Coast Sound* in Los Angeles.

1 June
Saxophonist Gerry Mulligan (• p. 134) appears at the Paris Jazz Festival.

17 July
The first American jazz festival is organized in Newport, Rhode Island, by George Wein.

Above Count Basie enjoying the adulation of female admirers in Paris on 4 March 1954.

Right Recorded in Los Angeles in August 1955, Stan Getz's album *West Coast Jazz* was a success for Columbia and one of many "cool" recordings issued in the mid-1950s.

JAZZ WEST COAST

1954 was a good year for the WEST COAST style, with Chet Baker and Gerry Mulligan both achieving fame and Dave Brubeck appearing on the cover of *Time* magazine. Based in California, the West Coast school took its initial inspiration from Miles Davis's *Birth of the Cool* (1949), to which baritone saxophonist Gerry Mulligan contributed several arrangements. In 1952 Mulligan formed a quartet in Los Angeles with Chet Baker (trumpet), Bob Whitlock (bass), and Chico Hamilton (drums). The group played jazz that showed a considerable degree of emotional restraint, the overriding characteristic of the COOL school (as it was immediately dubbed). Baker based his playing (without VIBRATO) on that of Davis, and cultivated an understated directness both on his trumpet and in his crooning, seductive singing voice, which, together with his handsome looks, rapidly made him a popular idol. Like most other prominent West Coast players, these musicians were white, and their relaxed idiom became familiar on numerous Hollywood soundtracks.

The most successful cool pianist was undoubtedly the enduringly popular Dave Brubeck, who remained based in California. Brubeck received a thorough grounding in classical music, which left its mark on his jazz compositions in their frequent use of advanced harmonies, elaborate structures, and complex or irregular METERS. The most famous example of the last is the experiment with quintuple time in his quartet's 1959 recording of "Take Five," a catchy and now ubiquitous number written by the group's saxophonist, Paul Desmond, who also recorded with Mulligan in this period.

The cool style was not restricted to the West Coast, however: a number of skilled performers promoted it in New York. East Coast exponents include the expatriate English pianist George Shearing (who was blind from birth), and the versatile saxophonist Stan Getz (• p. 152). The influence of Lester Young inspired Getz to develop a highly melodic style of IMPROVISATION that was so distinctive it earned him the nickname "The Sound." His gift for memorable lyricism was developed through the valuable experience of playing in famous SWING bands, including those led by Benny Goodman (• p. 84), Woody Herman, and Stan Kenton. Kenton's band gained notoriety for promoting a sometimes pretentious PROGRESSIVE JAZZ that was often censured by critics. In the 1950s the group featured an impressive number of future West Coast and cool-school players, including saxophonists Lee Konitz and Art Pepper, and drummer Shelly Manne.

Right Dave Brubeck, seen here in 1957, studied classical techniques with French composer Darius Milhaud (• p. 53), a noted pioneer of symphonic jazz.

Jazz Events

24 August
J. J. Johnson and Kai Winding form a trombone duo and record their launch album, *Jay and Kai*.

August
Charlie Parker, in deteriorating health and depressed by the death of his daughter on 7 March, attempts suicide.

September
Parker is admitted to Bellevue Hospital, New York. After his discharge in **October**, poverty forces him to pawn his saxophone.

31 October
Charles Mingus (• p. 190) makes his first recording with members of his newly founded Jazz Composers' Workshop.

23 December
John Lewis, with the Modern Jazz Quartet, records his composition "Django" in memory of guitarist Django Reinhardt (• p. 75), who died in 1953.

- Anthony Mann's film *The Glenn Miller Story*, starring James Stewart as Miller, dramatizes the late bandleader's life and reconstructs his musical arrangements. Among the participating jazz stars are Louis Armstrong, Gene Krupa, and Barney Bigard. The movie receives Oscar nominations for script and music direction.
- British musicians' union laws restricting the appearance of American performers in the UK are relaxed.
- Gene Krupa and Cozy Cole found a school for jazz drummers.
- Louis Armstrong publishes his autobiography, *Satchmo: My Life in New Orleans*.

World Events

1 March
US tests hydrogen bomb on Bikini Atoll

6 May
Roger Bannister beats the "four-minute mile," Oxford, UK

19 May
Death of American composer Charles Ives

3 July
Rationing ceases in UK

July
End of War in Indochina

30 November
German conductor Wilhelm Furtwängler dies

23 December
French troops sent to Algeria to quell disturbances

- J. R. R. Tolkein's *The Lord of the Rings*
- Bill Haley and the Comets introduce the hit song "Shake, Rattle, and Roll"

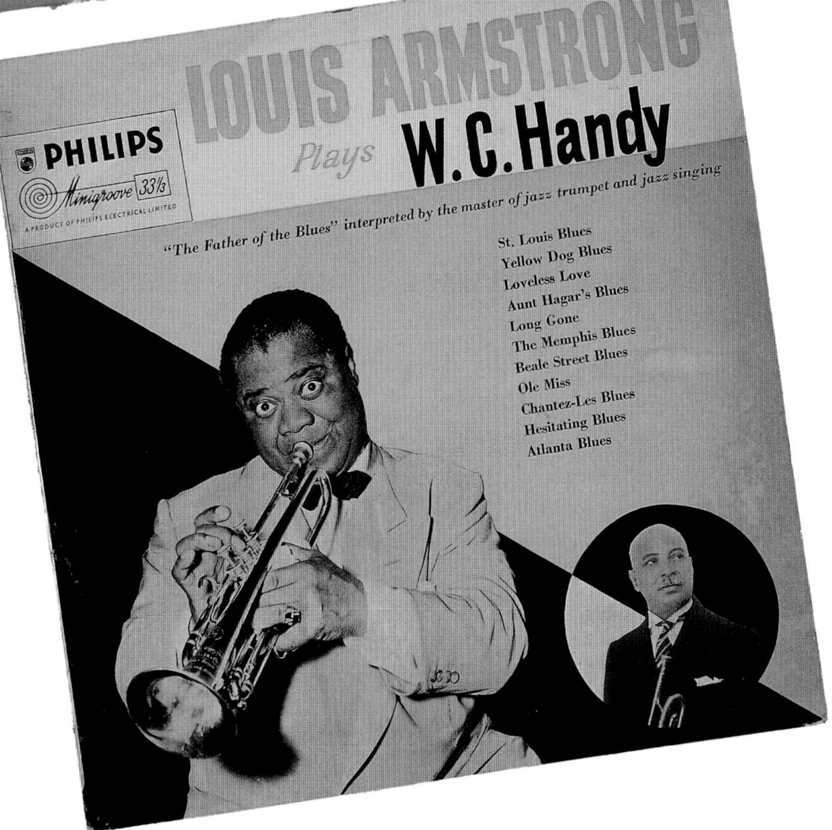

Above The sleeve notes for this 1955 HMV album of original Miller hits inspired by the movie *The Glenn Miller Story* proclaimed: "The Miller music to be heard in the picture is a recreation by a present-day band and, however well done, nothing can match the supremacy of the original."

Right Satchmo's interpretations of standards by W. C. Handy were recorded in June 1954.

STYLE
AND IDEA
1955

Parker's career comes to a tragic end. The jazz scene begins to be dominated by small groups led by Miles Davis, Art Blakey, and Charles Mingus.

DISASTER AT BIRDLAND

Right Charlie Parker in full melodic flight at Birdland in 1950.

BIRD

The year 1955 witnessed the sad final days of one of jazz's most revered and legendary figures, Charlie "Yardbird" Parker. Parker (whose nickname derived from his penchant for fried chicken) began to develop his career in 1939 when he moved from Kansas City to New York. There he sought to escape the clichés of the SWING style by cultivating a novel kind of IMPROVISATION, in which DISSONANT notes were deliberately emphasized. Under the influence of guitarist Charlie Christian (• p. 99), Parker combined this approach with an intelligent use of LICKS to create a new style of playing known as "formulaic improvisation," in which lengthy melodic paragraphs were constructed using a handful of basic note patterns, while subtle dislocated rhythms and angular leaps kept the listener guessing about the music's direction.

From 1942 to 1945 Parker played alongside Dizzy Gillespie (• p. 219) in successful big bands led by Earl Hines (• p. 125) and Billy Eckstine. When Parker and Gillespie joined forces with Kenny Clarke and Thelonious Monk at Minton's Playhouse (• p. 97) in Harlem for a series of JAM SESSIONS, Parker's musical experiments became absorbed into the new bop style as one of its essential ingredients. His music gained more widespread exposure in 1945, both in New York and Los Angeles, but most of the following year was spent in a sanatorium, and his

Above The famous club named after Parker, seen here in 1956, opened on Broadway in December 1949 (• p. 122).

professionalism was continually compromised by escalating drug addiction and alcoholism.

In 1951 he lost his cabaret card, and three years later he attempted suicide (• p. 134). Even when sober, his behavior was pathologically adolescent. Miles Davis described Parker's deterioration toward the end of 1948: "I didn't like whites walking into the club where we were playing just to see Bird act a fool, thinking that he might do something stupid, anything for a laugh . . . It was embarrassing." One musical consequence of Bird's boyish high spirits was his habit of quoting well-known melodies in incongruous musical contexts, as with the sudden intrusion of the jaunty English folk song "Country Gardens" at the conclusion of his 1951 recording of the otherwise lyrical "Lover Man."

In spite of the commercial success of his recordings with saccharine string accompaniment in the period 1947–52, the roots of Parker's innovation remained controversial. He regarded bop as a fundamental departure from the techniques of earlier jazz, although many (including Gillespie) hotly disagreed and preferred to view the new style as a logical continuation of traditional musical values. For all his self-conscious modernism, Parker's compositions were mostly based on the TWELVE-BAR BLUES and tended to use a limited range of harmonies. At his peak in 1947–48, his ensembles provided a bop schooling for several major talents, such as Miles Davis, and no subsequent saxophonist – or, indeed, other instrumentalist – could escape entirely from his colossal influence.

In 1988, serious jazz enthusiast Clint Eastwood directed *Bird*, a moving film portrayal of Parker's final years, using the saxophonist's original recordings as the basis for his soundtrack.

Jazz Events

4–5 March
Charlie Parker plays his last two GIGS at Birdland, with Kenny Dorham, Bud Powell, Charles Mingus (• p. 190), and Art Blakey (• p. 139). The second night is disastrous, largely because of Powell's severe inebriation. As Powell staggers off stage in mid-gig, Mingus tells the audience: "Please don't associate me with any of this. This is not jazz: these people are sick."

12 March
After lying seriously ill for three days in the New York hotel suite of Baroness Pannonica ("Nica") de Koenigswarter, a patroness of jazz musicians, Parker dies while watching Tommy Dorsey's television show. Causes of death are registered as lobar pneumonia and cirrhosis of the liver.

May
A memorial concert for Charlie Parker (lasting four hours) is held at Carnegie Hall (• p. 91).

July
Artists who appear at the second Newport Jazz Festival include Miles Davis (• p. 217), Louis Armstrong (• p. 57), Count Basie (• p. 87), Woody Herman, Dave Brubeck (• p. 189), Gerry Mulligan (• p. 134), and Thelonious Monk (• p. 155).

12 August
Bassist Oscar Pettiford records his *Bohemia after Dark*, making use of the rhythms of Native Americans.

August
Johnny Hodges rejoins Duke Ellington's band after an absence of four years. In this year, Ellington's *Night Creature* is performed at Carnegie Hall with a full symphony orchestra (the broadcasting orchestra, Symphony of the Air).

September
Chet Baker embarks on a seven-month trip to Europe that includes appearances in Iceland and England.

16 October
Leonard Bernstein's television program "The World of Jazz" (ABC) features the conductor singing a BLUES version of iambic-pentameter couplets from Shakespeare's *Macbeth* and declaring that bop is "the real beginning of serious American music." The program includes the first performance of Bernstein's *Prelude, Fugue, and Riffs*, given by Benny Goodman; the score was originally composed for Woody Herman in 1949.

October–November
Miles Davis makes his first recordings with a new quintet including John Coltrane (tenor saxophone), his second choice when Sonny Rollins proves to be unavailable. The RHYTHM SECTION comprises Red Garland (piano), Paul Chambers (bass), and Philly Joe Jones (drums). George Avakian buys Davis out of his Prestige contract, securing him as a Columbia artist who will receive $4,000 for his first recording on the new label.

17 November
James P. Johnson, the "Father of STRIDE Piano," dies, New York.

November
Art Blakey records at the Café Bohemia, New York, with his definitive Jazz Messengers: Horace Silver (piano), Hank Mobley (tenor saxophone), and Kenny Dorham (trumpet). In this year, alto saxophonist Julian "Cannonball" Adderley makes his New York debut at the same venue.

- Pianist Lennie Tristano conducts further experiments in OVERDUBBING on the Atlantic label.
- Charles Mingus founds a "Jazz Workshop" ensemble, for which he composes music communicated to the players by dictation, rather than notation.
- Release of the movie *The Benny Goodman Story*, featuring Steve Allen as Goodman, with appearances by Harry James and Gene Krupa.

World Events

18 April
Death of Albert Einstein

14 May
Warsaw Pact agreed

18 July
Disneyland opens, Los Angeles

12 August
Death of Thomas Mann

- Bill Haley's hit song "Rock Around the Clock"
- Tennessee Williams's play *Cat on a Hot Tin Roof*
- Pierre Boulez's composition *Le Marteau sans maître*

Above An innovator since the 1920s, Earl "Fatha" Hines was still producing fresh-sounding unaccompanied jazz piano in the mid-1950s.

ELLINGTON AT NEWPORT

A thrilling live performance at Newport throws the Duke Ellington orchestra back into the limelight. Hard bop establishes itself in the US as the sound of the day, while British traditionalist Humphrey Lyttelton enters the UK pop charts.

Left Ella Fitzgerald's maturing talents were showcased in the impressive "songbook" recordings preserved by Verve in the 1950s and 1960s.

Jazz Events

30 January
Charles Mingus (• p. 190) records his album *Pithecanthropus Erectus* for Atlantic, breaking new ground in free ensemble IMPROVISATION.

22 June
Sonny Rollins records *Saxophone Colossus*, New York.

26 June
Trumpeter Clifford Brown, who has fronted a quintet with Max Roach for the past two years, is killed in a car crash at the age of twenty-five.

July
Duke Ellington's popularity is spectacularly rekindled by a performance at the Newport Jazz Festival of "Diminuendo and Crescendo in Blue," featuring a searing twenty-seven-CHORUS saxophone solo by Paul Gonsalves. Ellington appears on the cover of *Time* magazine, and the Columbia release of the Newport performance becomes his best-selling record.

11 September
Pianist Art Tatum (• p. 125) and saxophonist Ben Webster record together in Los Angeles for Norman Granz (• p. 107).

September
After anthologizing the works of Cole Porter and Rodgers and Hart, Ella Fitzgerald (• p. 195) continues her "songbook" series for Verve by recording a collection of songs by Duke Ellington in Los Angeles. Irving Berlin is given the same treatment in 1958, George Gershwin (• p. 89) in 1959, Jerome Kern in 1963, and Johnny Mercer in 1964.

October
Miles Davis (• p. 217) completes his Prestige contract by recording four quintet albums: *Workin'*, *Relaxin'*, *Cookin'*, and *Steamin'*. He then leaves for a short tour of Paris, Amsterdam, and Stockholm. John Coltrane (• p. 160) quits the group for a year to seek a cure for his drug addiction: he is temporarily replaced by Sonny Rollins.

5 November
Art Tatum dies, Los Angeles..
• NBC launches its *Nat King Cole Show* on television. Cole is heckled by racists during a live performance in Birmingham, Alabama, this year.

26 November
Tommy Dorsey dies, Greenwich, Connecticut.

November–December
Trumpeter Lee Morgan cuts his first SIDES as leader for the Blue Note and Savoy labels.

12–13 December
Art Blakey records his album *Hard Bop*.

- At the invitation of the US State Department, Dizzy Gillespie (• p. 219) becomes an "ambassador of jazz" and forms a new big band to tour the eastern Mediterranean, the Middle East, Pakistan, and South America.
- Horace Silver leaves Art Blakey's Jazz Messengers.
- Pianist Ahmad Jamal's recording of "On Green Dolphin Street," a theme from a 1947 film starring Lana Turner, exerts a strong influence on Miles Davis (• p. 142).
- Trumpeter Humphrey Lyttelton's "Bad Penny Blues" reaches the top twenty in the UK charts.
- European tours by Louis Armstrong (who also visits Africa), "Jazz at the Philharmonic", and Stan Kenton's orchestra.
- In New York, French author and former jazz violinist André Hodeir publishes his book *Jazz: Its Evolution and Essence*, a revised translation of his *Hommes et problèmes du jazz* (Paris, 1954).
- Billie Holiday (• p. 131) publishes her autobiography *Lady Sings the Blues*, ghostwritten by William Dufty.
- Louis Armstrong appears in the movie *High Society*.

World Events

19 April
Grace Kelly marries Prince Rainier of Monaco

29 June
Marilyn Monroe marries playwright Arthur Miller

July–November
Suez Canal crisis

11 August
Death of Jackson Pollock

14 August
Death of Bertolt Brecht

October
USSR crushes Hungarian rebellion

- Elvis Presley's song "Heartbreak Hotel"
- John Osborne's play *Look Back in Anger*

BOP HARDENS

HARD BOP, a phrase often used to describe a style that emerged from the aftermath of the bop revolution, is one of those terms in jazz that is rarely given a precise definition. In one sense, the powerful rhythmic drive and sometimes aggressive virtuosity of improvisations by the next generation of performers was indeed "hard," and this intensity provided the lingua franca of modern jazz. But in other respects, hard bop represented a move in somewhat different stylistic directions, reflecting a refreshing emphasis on simplified BLUES elements and making clear references to the music of the black church. The latter trend in 1950s and 1960s jazz is otherwise known as SOUL or FUNK, though neither of these labels should be confused with their modern pop equivalents. Of vital importance in disseminating this new music was the Blue Note record label (• p. 167), which flourished throughout both decades, along with the labels Riverside, Prestige, and Atlantic.

Drummer Art Blakey helped spearhead the movement with the foundation of his second "Jazz Messengers" group in 1955. In company with pianist Horace Silver, trumpeter Kenny Dorham, and tenor saxophonist Hank Mobley, Blakey promoted a down-to-earth style, replete with appealing, bluesy melodies and an infectious rhythmic drive. Among the many talents who served their apprenticeship in Blakey's Jazz Messengers over the years were trumpeters Donald Byrd and Lee Morgan, whose hard-bop composition "The Sidewinder" was a hit on his Blue Note album of the same name in 1964. The fluctuating membership of Blakey's long-lasting enterprise later included pianist Keith Jarrett, saxophonist Wayne Shorter, and prodigious young trumpeter Wynton Marsalis. The Messengers were reassembled for a Blue Note promotion in 1985 and for Blakey's seventieth-birthday celebrations in 1989, almost exactly one year before his death.

Right The strong rhythmic drive and melodic appeal of Art Blakey's Jazz Messengers defined the hard-bop sound of the late 1950s.

CINEMA AND THIRD STREAM

Jazz reaches a mass audience through the medium of film, as the "third stream" initiative seeks to unite jazz with elements of classical music.

Above French actress Jeanne Moreau, star of Louis Malle's film *Lift to the Scaffold*, borrows Miles Davis's trumpet during a publicity photoshoot for the movie.

Right Sleeve design for John Coltrane's *Blue Train*, showing the saxophonist in characteristically pensive mood.

Jazz Events

March
Max Roach and Sonny Rollins record *Jazz in 3/4 Time*, an early attempt to break away from the ubiquitous 4/4 METER.

4 April
John Lewis's Modern Jazz Quartet (• p. 129) provide a score to the film *Sait-on jamais* (in English, *No Sun in Venice*), which is recorded by Atlantic. They perform the score live at New York's Town Hall on **12 May**, and during an extensive tour of Europe in the autumn.

14–15 May
Thelonious Monk (• p. 155) records with Art Blakey's Jazz Messengers (• p. 139) for Atlantic in New York.

May
Miles Davis collaborates with arranger Gil Evans on the album *Miles Ahead*.
• Gerry Mulligan tours Sweden.

12 June
Clarinetist and bandleader Jimmy Dorsey dies, New York.

July–August
Charles Mingus (• p. 190) records *Tijuana Moods*, an idiosyncratic and spirited reinterpretation of Latin elements.

19 August
Leonard Bernstein's jazz musical *West Side Story* is staged in Washington, DC. It transfers to New York on **26 September**.

15 September
John Coltrane (• p. 160) records his sextet album *Blue Train* for Blue Note, New York.

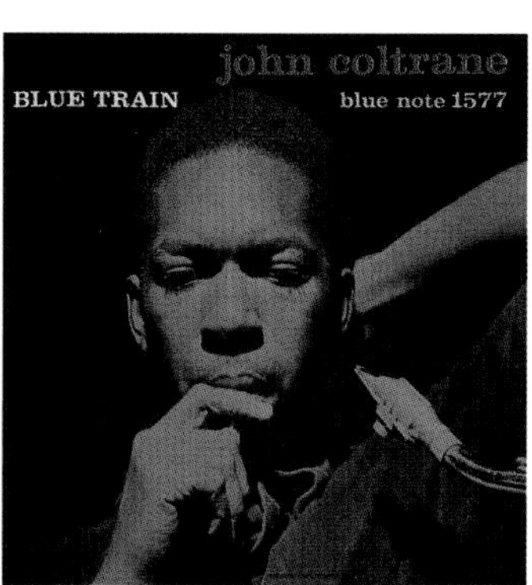

18 September
Louis Armstrong causes controversy by speaking out against President Eisenhower's administration during a prolonged spell of racial violence attendant on an initiative (launched in May) to end segregation in American schools.

4 December
In Paris, Miles Davis records a score to the thriller *L'Ascenseur pour l'échafaud* (*Lift to the Scaffold*); his local quintet includes Pierre Michelot on bass and Kenny Clarke, who emigrated to Europe the previous year, on drums. Back in New York, Davis's lineup includes "Cannonball" Adderley on alto saxophone; John Coltrane rejoins them to form a sextet.

8 December
Billie Holiday performs "Fine and Mellow" in a live television broadcast.

- Brandeis University (• p. 128) commissions THIRD STREAM works from Charles Mingus, Gunther Schuller, George Russell, and Harold Shapero.
- The US State Department continues to promote wide-ranging jazz tours by sending Benny Goodman (• p. 84) to the Far East.
- Former New York waitress Carla Borg marries Canadian pianist Paul Bley, who encourages her to develop her compositional talents.
- Pianist Erroll Garner begins to perform under a pink spotlight.
- Pianist and arranger Toshiko Akiyoshi wins a poll in *Down Beat* and receives her award at Berklee College, Boston, alongside Duke Ellington, who is presented with a "Hall of Fame" award.

JAZZ AT THE MOVIES

By the late 1950s, movie audiences had grown accustomed to the sound of jazz in film soundtracks, numerous cameo appearances on camera by star instrumentalists and singers, and the occasional biopic devoted to the life of an especially celebrated musician. Jazz music in films, however, had been strictly confined to "diegetic" situations: music heard by the film's characters themselves, whether played by a band in full view on the studio set, or issuing from a prop radio or phonograph. All that was changed with Alex North's background score for the 1951 film version of Tennessee Williams's play *A Streetcar Named Desire*. Imbued with a strong jazz flavor, the music helped create a sultry atmosphere, and began a fashion in many later scores for employing jazz to accompany scenes of sleaze or corruption. At the same time, COOL jazz featured more prominently in films as "aural wallpaper," and with so many cool musicians based on the West Coast, this trend produced welcome employment opportunities in Hollywood, though they were mostly reserved for white musicians.

Two unusual and influential jazz film scores were recorded in 1957. Miles Davis found himself in Paris, where he improvised a soundtrack to Louis Malle's thriller *L'Ascenseur pour l'échafaud* (*Lift to the Scaffold*), which in some respects looks forward in style to the MODAL JAZZ he pioneered soon afterward (• p. 147). Meanwhile, John Lewis and his Modern Jazz Quartet provided a score for another French film, Roger Vadim's *Sait-on jamais* (*No Sun in Venice*), which, in its use of sophisticated pre-composed structures and pseudo-Baroque COUNTERPOINT (• p. 129), could hardly have been more contrasted to Davis's instinctive effort. Both musicians went on to produce other notable film scores, Lewis scoring *Odds Against Tomorrow* in 1959, and Davis contributing music to the boxing epic *Jack Johnson* in 1970.

The following chronological list gives a few highlights of the numerous soundtracks created by leading jazz practitioners (and, in the unusual case of Herrmann's *Taxi Driver*, by a non-jazz composer who turned to the idiom late in his distinguished Hollywood career):

Leonard Bernstein: *On the Waterfront* (1954)+
Henry Mancini: *Touch of Evil* (1958)
Chris Barber: *Look Back in Anger* (1959)
Duke Ellington: *Anatomy of a Murder* (1959)
Charles Mingus: *Shadows* (1959)
Duke Ellington: *Paris Blues* (1961)+
John Dankworth: *The Servant* (1963)
Chico Hamilton: *Repulsion* (1965)
Herbie Hancock: *Blow-Up* (1966)
Sonny Rollins: *Alfie* (1966)
Neal Hefti: *The Odd Couple* (1967)
Quincy Jones: *In Cold Blood* (1967)*
Gato Barbieri: *Last Tango in Paris* (1972)
Herbie Hancock: *Death Wish* (1974)
Bernard Herrmann: *Taxi Driver* (1975)+
Oscar Peterson: *The Silent Partner* (1978)
Pat Metheny and Lyle Mays: *The Falcon and the Snowman* (1984)
Herbie Hancock: *Round Midnight* (1986)*
Miles Davis: *Siesta* (1987)
Dave Grusin: *The Fabulous Baker Boys* (1989)
Dave Grusin: *The Firm* (1993)+
Mark Isham: *Afterglow* (1998)
Mark Isham: *The Cooler* (2002)

** Academy Award for Best Original Score*
+ Academy Award Nomination for Best Original Score

World Events

16 January
Death of Arturo Toscanini

20 September
Death of Jean Sibelius

4 October
USSR launches first Sputnik satellite

5 December
Dutch ejected from Indonesia

- Boris Pasternak's novel *Dr. Zhivago* wins Nobel Prize; USSR forbids him to accept
- David Lean's film *Bridge on the River Kwai* wins Oscar for Best Picture

MUSICIANS IN THE MOVIES

Films depicting the lives and work of jazz musicians include:

- *The Fabulous Dorseys* (1947), featuring the Dorsey brothers
- *The Glenn Miller Story* (1954), starring James Stewart
- *The Benny Goodman Story* (1954), starring Steve Allen
- *St. Louis Blues* (1958), starring Nat King Cole as W. C. Handy
- *The Gene Krupa Story* (1959), starring Sal Mineo
- *Lady Sings the Blues* (1972), starring Diana Ross as Billie Holiday
- *Bird* (1988), starring Forest Whitaker as Charlie Parker

Left A beaming Herbie Hancock displays the Oscar he received for his soundtrack to *Round Midnight* in March 1987.

JAZZ MESSENGERS

Art Blakey promotes hard bop in Europe, innovative modal techniques are perfected by Bill Evans and Miles Davis, and a major new festival is established in California.

"I think a movement in jazz is beginning away from the conventional string of chords, and a return to emphasis on melodic, rather than harmonic, variations. There will be fewer chords, but infinite possibilities as to what to do with them."

Miles Davis, December 1958

Right The Harry James Orchestra gained a popular following with its post-Basie swinging big-band sound in the 1950s.

Jazz Events

9 January
Critic Barry Ulanov speaks out against sexism in jazz by publishing an article in *Down Beat* entitled "Women in Jazz: Do They Belong?"

February
Sonny Rollins records his *Freedom Suite* with Oscar Pettiford and Max Roach; the sleeve notes attack continuing racism in America.

28 March
Early BLUES bandleader W. C. Handy (• p. 27) dies, New York. Nat King Cole portrays the "Father of the Blues" in a feature-film tribute entitled *St. Louis Blues*; its cast also includes singers Cab Calloway, Ella Fitzgerald, and Mahalia Jackson.

March
Dave Brubeck's quartet tours Denmark, while Oscar Peterson (• p. 163) appears at the Concertgebouw, Amsterdam.

2–3 April
Miles Davis's sextet (• p. 140) records *Milestones*, which includes an early example of MODAL JAZZ.

26 May
Miles Davis records "On Green Dolphin Street" (• p. 138) with pianist Bill Evans (• p. 157).

July–August
Miles Davis and Gil Evans record large-ensemble arrangements of STANDARDS from George Gershwin's opera *Porgy and Bess* (• p. 85).

30 October
Art Blakey's Jazz Messengers (• p. 139) record *Moanin'* for Blue Note, a defining album in the HARD BOP style.

October
The first annual Monterey Jazz Festival is mounted by Ralph J. Gleason in California.
• Billie Holiday's second tour of Europe takes her to France and Italy, and includes an appearance in a small hall at La Scala opera house, Milan.

November
Art Blakey and his Jazz Messengers appear in Paris a few weeks after Blakey records *Holiday for Skins* for three jazz drummers and seven Latin percussionists.

15 December
Bill Evans records *Everybody Digs Bill Evans*, which includes the influential modal track "Peace Piece."

- Duke Ellington (• p. 182) appears before Queen Elizabeth II at the Leeds Festival during his first trip to England for twenty-five years. He commemorates the occasion the next year by recording *The Queen's Suite* in a limited edition of one disc, which is sent to Buckingham Palace.
- Stan Getz (• p. 152) and Oscar Pettiford emigrate to Europe, both settling in Copenhagen.
- More US State Department tours take Woody Herman to South America, Dave Brubeck to the Middle East and Indian subcontinent, and Jack Teagarden to the Far East.
- Harold "Duke" Dejan forms his Olympia Brass Band in New Orleans, recapturing the flavor of the city's early processional music (• p. 29).
- Antonio Carlos Jobim, director of Odeon Records, launches the BOSSA NOVA craze by recording João Gilberto's "Chega de Saudade."

Below W. C. Handy, who died in 1958 at the age of eighty-four.

World Events

1 January
European Economic Community established

February
Munich air disaster decimates Manchester United soccer team

29 March
Pablo Picasso's mural *The Fall of Icarus* unveiled, UNESCO, Paris

26 August
Death of Ralph Vaughan Williams

- Boeing 707 jet revolutionizes air travel
- Hovercraft invented

THIRD STREAM

The interest in SYMPHONIC JAZZ stimulated by Paul Whiteman's collaborations with Gershwin and others in the 1920s (• p. 55) remained strong throughout the 1930s and 1940s, influencing classical composers and jazz musicians alike. From the desire to unite elements of art-music and jazz emerged various synthetic styles – some laying themselves open to charges of pretentiousness, such as that promoted by Stan Kenton's WEST COAST band, Innovations in Modern Music.

When critic and jazz scholar Gunther Schuller (formerly a French horn player with the orchestra of New York's Metropolitan Opera) invented the term THIRD STREAM while at Brandeis University in 1957, he intended it to signify a wholesome union between high art and jazz. However, many purists in both camps regarded the trend with unwarranted and self-protective cynicism. Schuller produced a series of model third-stream compositions for widely varied instrumental groups (including full orchestra), and he collaborated with the like-minded John Lewis, one of the more successful jazz practitioners to espouse classical compositional techniques. In 1960 Lewis's Modern Jazz Quartet (• p. 129) recorded Schuller's *Concertino* for jazz quartet and orchestra on the Atlantic label. Other musicians who made notable contributions to the third-stream movement were Charles Mingus (• p. 190), Anthony Braxton, and pianist Ran Blake, who broadened the definition to embrace the use of musical material from non-Western cultures.

The barriers between modern classical music and jazz were more spectacularly broken down by the controversial avant-garde performers of the early 1960s (• p. 150), by which time the third stream seemed more in the nature of a luxurious anachronism than a potent musical force. For many listeners, Duke Ellington's achievements many decades before (• p. 63), which combined considerable intellectual sophistication with an uncompromised jazz idiom, seemed a more worthwhile synthesis.

"'Third stream' describes the theoretical merging of two souls into one, those of jazz and European composed music. The unrequited love on both sides for the most incompatible characteristics of the other has resulted in many illicit encounters, and quite a few bastard offspring . . ."

Brian Priestley, 1995

Above left The formidable Gunther Schuller (seen here conducting at London's Barbican Centre in 1991): composer, jazz historian, and music educator.

Opposite Jacob Lawrence's painting *Cabaret* (1962).

The Birth of Modern Jazz: During the 1960s, a drastic upheaval of jazz styles matches the instability equally evident in other art forms. Harmonic innovation and structural freedom causes jazz audiences to dwindle, until Miles Davis introduces a spectacularly successful hybrid jazz-rock style at the end of the decade.

1969

GIANT STEPS

In a year during which jazz is deprived of some of its most enduringly popular talents (Lester Young, Billie Holiday, and Sidney Bechet), its stylistic development strides ahead with the innovations of modal and free jazz.

Above Miles Davis "resisting" arrest in August 1959, an instance of alleged police brutality and racism that gained rapid and widespread publicity.

Jazz Events

14 February
Drummer Baby Dodds dies, Chicago.

28 February
Thelonious Monk (• p. 155) appears at New York's Town Hall.

February
Louis Armstrong (• p. 57) plays at the Nordstrandhallen, Norway.

1 March
Miles Davis records *Kind of Blue*, pioneering the technique of MODAL JAZZ, and creating one of the finest spontaneously improvised albums of all time.

15 March
Tenor saxophonist Lester Young dies, New York.

4 May
Saxophonist John Coltrane (• p. 160) records *Giant Steps* in New York.

14 May
Saxophonist/clarinetist Sidney Bechet dies, Paris.

22 May
Ornette Coleman (• p. 150) records *The Shape of Jazz to Come* in New York.

12 June
Billie Holiday (• p. 131) is arrested in hospital for possession of narcotics; she dies on **17 July** of cirrhosis of the liver with multiple complications.

12 August
Dave Brubeck and his Quartet record *Time Out*, which includes Paul Desmond's hit "Take Five."
• Miles Davis is assaulted by police outside Birdland on Broadway in New York (where his sextet is playing), having been told to move on. Photographs of him, bloodstained and handcuffed to a police officer, appear in the next day's newspapers; he is later cleared of all charges.

Summer
Duke Ellington (• p. 182) composes his first complete film score, for the courtroom drama *Anatomy of a Murder*, starring James Stewart. The film includes a brief cameo appearance by Ellington, who performs a piano duet with Stewart at a restaurant.

October
John Lewis (• p. 129) composes music for the movie *Odds Against Tomorrow* and records it with the Modern Jazz Quartet.

Autumn
Ornette Coleman plays FREE JAZZ at the Five Spot, New York.

- Ronnie Scott opens his jazz club on London's Gerrard Street.
- Gene Krupa's life story is celebrated in the Hollywood biopic *The Gene Krupa Story* (released in Europe as *Drum Crazy*).
- Oscar Peterson (• p. 163) forms a trio with Ray Brown (bass) and Ed Thigpen (drums).
- Trumpeter Chet Baker is arrested in Harlem on a narcotics charge and moves to Europe. He remains there until 1964, as does pianist Bud Powell.
- Wayne Shorter joins Art Blakey's Jazz Messengers.
- Charles Mingus (• p. 190) provides music for John Cassavetes's movie, *Shadows*.

World Events

2 January
Fidel Castro assumes power in Cuba

8 January
Columbia and Princeton Universities receive Rockefeller grant to establish a center for electronic music

3 February
Death of Buddy Holly

18 March
Hawaii joins USA

9 April
Death of Frank Lloyd Wright

26 April
Panama invaded by Cuban forces

22 September
China barred from joining UN

September
First cassette tapes launched in US

14 December
Archbishop Makarios becomes first President of Cyprus

- William Wyler's movie *Ben-Hur* costs $4 million

THE DAVE BRUBECK QUARTET: BLUE RONDO À LA TURK

Brubeck's album *Time Out* (1959) is a fine illustration of two of the pianist's most important characteristics: his debt to classical music and his rhythmic originality. "Blue Rondo à la Turk" acknowledges the classics in its rondo structure (a form in which repetitions of a main theme are interspersed with contrasting episodes) and in its emulation of the pseudo-oriental flavor of Mozart's famous *Turkish Rondo*.

"Blue Rondo" uses an unconventional irregular METER, subdividing the nine beats of each measure into a 2+2+2+3 pattern, instead of the more conventional 3+3+3. Departing from normal jazz textures, Brubeck has all the instruments play this pattern simultaneously to intensify the effect. The opening section builds to a thrilling climax in which percussively dissonant piano chords suggest the influence of twentieth-century classical masters such as Bartók and Stravinsky. Then, in a delicious moment of unpredictability, the music sideslips effortlessly into a bluesy and swinging four-beat tempo. This attempt to establish a conventional jazz idiom is checked three times with brief interruptions by the edgy 2+2+2+3 rondo theme, before the music finally settles into a TWELVE-BAR BLUES.

Alto saxophonist Paul Desmond improvises four twelve-bar CHORUSES with his inimitable polished tone, then Brubeck offers a carefully controlled piano solo: the thicker chordal voicings of its central section (choruses 2 and 3) are symmetrically framed by sparse right-hand melodic work in the two outer sections (choruses 1 and 4). Desmond reenters, as if to embark on another leisurely saxophone solo, but the irregular rondo theme makes three further sudden interruptions and emerges into a recapitulation of the opening section.

CHANGING MODES

Until the late 1950s, all jazz performances were based on preset sequences of CHORDS, referred to by musicians as the CHANGES (i.e., changes of HARMONY). These harmonic sequences might be borrowed from well-known songs, or be newly composed. In either case, a performance would normally begin with a statement of the original theme as a HEAD, and be followed by a series of solo IMPROVISATIONS based on repetitions of the song's underlying harmonies (each solo being termed, rather confusingly, a chorus). A final statement of the head would bring the piece to a close. From the 1920s to the 1940s, the chordal vocabulary of jazz increased in complexity through the importation of more advanced harmonies (mostly borrowed from modern classical music), but the underlying structural principle of the "changes" remained constant.

This process was revised when Miles Davis (• p. 217), John Coltrane, Bill Evans (• p. 157), and others began to base some of their improvisations on SCALES rather than on chords. These were not the overworked major and minor scales familiar in earlier popular or classical music: they were the MODES, which had provided the basis for music during the Middle Ages and the Renaissance, and which had been resurrected by composers such as Debussy (• p. 24) at the turn of the twentieth century. Instead of constructing a sequence of familiar chords, PROGRESSIVE JAZZ musicians now based large stretches of music on the limited pitches of a single MODE. Contrast might be created by switching abruptly to a different mode in a later section of the piece. Famous early examples of this practice are heard in Davis's 1958 album *Milestones*, and in certain tracks of the seminal *Kind of Blue* (1959).

The new modal approach had two important stylistic effects. First, the soloists were able to achieve more flexible melodic improvisations, being freed from the confines of strict harmonic schemes. Second, the essentially "static" nature of modal music (as opposed to the "dynamic" sense of progression created by the tension and relaxation inherent in any good sequence of chords) led to a contemplative mood in which pieces might be protracted to sometimes inordinate length.

Two further techniques emerged from modal jazz during the 1960s. As a compromise between the strict application of modes and more conventional harmonic schemes, pieces might be built up from repetitions of just two different chords (which rapidly became a cliché). Then, with the emergence of jazz-rock FUSION in the late 1960s and early 1970s (• p. 171), long stretches of modal music were animated by successions of RIFFS, often provided by the funky electric bass guitar.

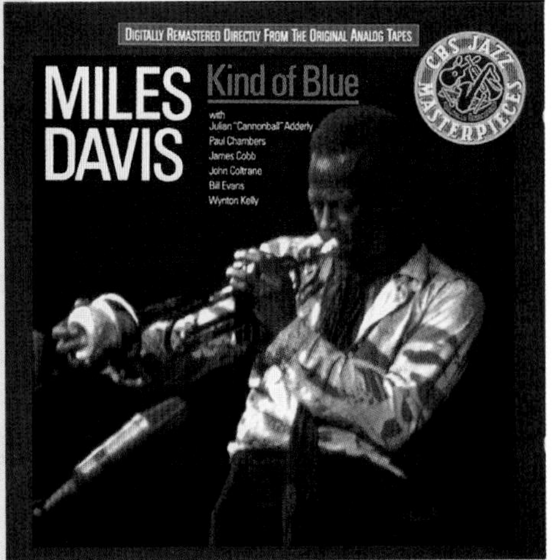

Above CD reissue of *Kind of Blue* (CBS), the 1959 album by Miles Davis's sextet that pioneered modal jazz.

THE FREEDOM PRINCIPLE

European appearances by mainstream American musicians are now commonplace, as a radical new avant-garde "free" jazz begins to assert itself stateside.

Above Gerhard Aspheim (left) and Eovind Salberg perform at Oslo's Metropol Jazzhus, which opened on 9 January 1960.

Right The Metropol quickly established itself as a premier European jazz venue within months of opening.

Jazz Events

9 January
The Metropol Jazzhus opens in Oslo, hosting a performance by Stan Getz (• p. 152) on **1 April**.

January–February
Dave Brubeck's quartet (• p. 189) records selections from Leonard Bernstein's *West Side Story*.

13 February
Ella Fitzgerald (• p. 195) records live on tour in Berlin.

February
John Coltrane (• p. 160) purchases his first soprano saxophone.

10–11 March
Declaring that "flamenco is the Spanish counterpart of our BLUES," Miles Davis completes his album *Sketches of Spain* with Gil Evans and then embarks on a European tour, which includes a visit to London. John Coltrane quits again, and is replaced by Sonny Stitt on the British leg of the trip.

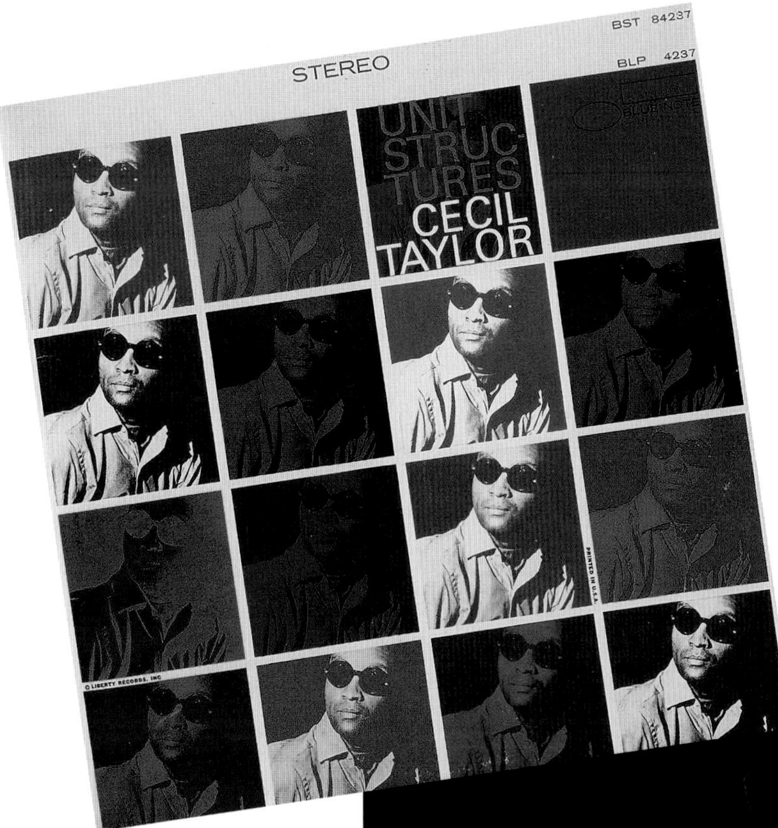

World Events

4 May
Albert Camus killed in a car crash

11 June
Benjamin Britten's opera *A Midsummer Night's Dream* premieres, UK

9 November
John F. Kennedy elected President, USA

- Laser beams demonstrated
- Federico Fellini's film *La Dolce Vita*
- Alfred Hitchcock's film *Psycho*

Above The abstraction of the sleeve design for Cecil Taylor's Blue Note album *Unit Structures* (1966) reflected the esoteric nature of the music Taylor had been producing since the early 1960s.

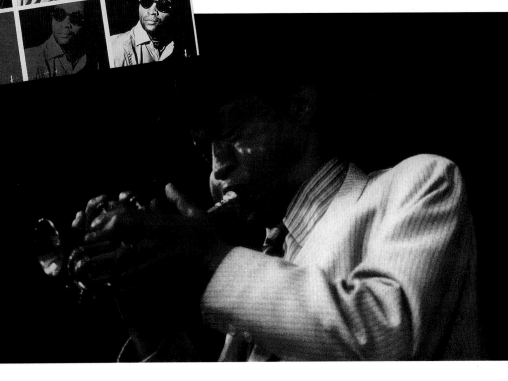

Right Don Cherry, a leading light of the jazz avant-garde, improvises on his notorious "pocket" trumpet.

2 April
Bud Powell appears in Essen, West Germany.

April
The Modern Jazz Quartet (● p. 129) tours Scandinavia, then returns to New York to make an album with orchestral accompaniment in **June**.

June
Crowd disturbances interrupt the Seventh Newport Jazz Festival. Charles Mingus (● p. 190) mounts an alternative event at nearby Cliff Walk Manor Hotel in **July**.

June–July
John Coltrane and Don Cherry collaborate on the album *The Avant-Garde*, under the influence of innovative saxophonist Ornette Coleman (● p. 150).

August–September
Max Roach records his album *We Insist!: Freedom Now Suite*, with a lineup that includes Coleman Hawkins.

8 September
Bassist Oscar Pettiford dies in Copenhagen, two years after his emigration to Europe.

LAND OF THE FREE

Whereas MODAL JAZZ (• p. 147) had been only a mild departure from the harmonic and melodic basis of earlier jazz styles, a movement that began to flourish in the early 1960s represented what many commentators saw as the final abrogation of conventional musical values in the interests of artistic gimmickry. The social context for the iconoclastic FREE JAZZ movement is crucially important, for the trend intensified alongside increasingly heated civil rights protests. The new generation of black musicians was angry, and espoused musical freedom as a potent symbol for the liberation of the black community from oppression. In some respects, the social significance of jazz had come full circle, and returned to its very earliest preoccupations.

The leading light of the 1960s avant-garde was Ornette Coleman, a controversial figure who sometimes played a white plastic alto saxophone. Self-taught, he was ridiculed by many and was branded as an exponent of "anti-jazz," a term also applied by critics such as John Tynan and Leonard Feather to the later work of John Coltrane (• p. 160) and the achievements of newcomer Don Cherry (who played a miniscule "pocket" trumpet). Cherry collaborated with Coleman on *The Shape of Jazz to Come* in 1959, and the new movement was christened with the appearance of their album *Free Jazz* in the following year. This venture, an astonishingly radical extended IMPROVISATION for octet, exerted a palpable influence on Coltrane's *Ascension* (1965), but was otherwise treated with derision in most quarters.

While Coleman disappeared into a self-imposed retirement in 1962, pianist Cecil Taylor continued to develop his own unique brand of "free" (but in essence often highly disciplined) jazz. His 1966 album *Unit Structures* (• p. 149) was characterized by musical textures of such unorthodox complexity that to all intents and purposes it sounded closer to experimental art music than to jazz.

Avant-garde techniques were simultaneously proving to be little more than a minority interest in the field of classical music, and the failure of the free jazz movement to reach a wide audience is not surprising. Many musicians, alienated (some by design) from the jazz mainstream, organized themselves into collectives in the early 1960s to promote their artistic creeds in an environment where commercial success was not an overriding concern. The best known of these was the Chicago-based Association for the Advancement of Creative Musicians, founded in 1965, which three years later spawned the influential Art Ensemble of Chicago. This group, like many other free jazz artists, later found a more receptive audience in Europe, where free jazz thrived in the late 1960s and early 1970s.

Above A civil rights demonstration in April 1960 takes place outside department stores accused of racial discrimination in Little Rock, Arkansas, which had experienced serious race riots three years before.

Top Passengers traveling on a Greyhound bus look on as their vehicle is set ablaze by a racist mob in Anniston, Alabama, in May 1961.

"A whole lot of younger players and critics jumped down my throat after I put down Ornette [Coleman], called me 'old-fashioned' and shit. But I didn't like what they were playing, especially Don Cherry on that little horn he had. It just looked to me like he was playing a lot of notes and looking real serious, and people went for that because people will go for anything they don't understand if it's got enough hype . . . White people are especially like that, particularly when a black person is doing something they don't understand. They don't want to have to admit that a black person could be doing something that they don't know about . . . so they run around talking about how great it is until the next 'new thing' comes along."

Miles Davis, 1989

Right Eric Dolphy, a talented multi-instrumentalist who played bass clarinet on Ornette Coleman's groundbreaking album *Free Jazz*.

Jazz Events

September
Duke Ellington's *Suite Thursday* (inspired by John Steinbeck's novel *Sweet Thursday*) is performed at the Monterey Jazz Festival. This year Ellington spends two months in Paris, where he composes a film score to *Paris Blues*, in which he appears alongside Louis Armstrong and Paul Newman. With Billy Strayhorn, he arranges suites based on Tchaikovsky's ballet *The Nutcracker* and Edvard Grieg's *Peer Gynt*.

12–13 October
Pianist Cecil Taylor and tenor saxophonist Archie Shepp record *The World of Cecil Taylor*.

20 October
Back in the US after an appearance in Antibes in **July**, Charles Mingus and Eric Dolphy record an interpretation of Mingus's "What Love," featuring avant-garde instrumental voice imitations. Recorded during the same sessions, the complex "Fables of Faubus" dramatizes the notorious attempts by the Governor of Arkansas to resist the abolition of segregation.

October
John Coltrane records *My Favorite Things* with his new quartet. The group also records *Coltrane's Sound* and *Coltrane Plays the Blues*.

2 November
Drummer Shelly Manne opens his own club, "Shelly's Manne-Hole," in Los Angeles.

November
Gerry Mulligan (● p. 134) plays in Milan and Berlin. In this year, he makes an acting appearance in the movie *The Subterraneans*, which features a score composed by André Previn.
● Saxophonist Joe Harriott, a Jamaican emigré, records *Free Form* in London.

December
Ornette Coleman records his octet album *Free Jazz*, an extended avant-garde improvisation issued with Jackson Pollock's *White Light* as its cover design.

- Chet Baker is arrested in Italy on a drug charge.
- Stan Tracey becomes house pianist at Ronnie Scott's jazz club in London, a position he holds for the next seven years.
- Sidney Bechet's autobiography, *Treat it Gentle*, is published posthumously.

"If Coltrane 'progressed from' (i.e., was more horrible than) Parker, who but Ornette Coleman has progressed from Coltrane? Where Coltrane had two chords, Coleman has none at all, no pitch, no rhythm, no nothing . . . This is free form. Its drawback is that it all sounds alike . . . in the main the effect is like watching twenty monkeys trying to type the plays of Shakespeare."

Poet and *Daily Telegraph* jazz critic Philip Larkin, 1967

Duke Ellington and Count Basie join forces in the recording studio for the first time. Free jazz is savagely attacked by critics, and Stan Getz's return to the US helps launch a craze for bossa nova.

THE DUKE MEETS THE COUNT

Jazz Events

2 January
Art Blakey takes his Jazz Messengers (• p. 139) to perform in Tokyo. Other musicians who visit Japan this year include Oscar Peterson (• p. 163) and Ella Fitzgerald (• p. 195).

January
Stan Getz leaves Copenhagen and returns to the US.

22 February
Nick LaRocca, onetime leader of the Original Dixieland Jazz Band (• p. 37), dies in New Orleans.

4 March
Dizzy Gillespie appears at Carnegie Hall.

14–22 April
Miles Davis records live at San Francisco's Black Hawk. The resulting albums are spliced together from different takes and are marred by inconsistent speeds.

11 May
Don DeMichael attacks Ornette Coleman's album *This is Our Music* in a savage review

STAN GETZ AND THE BOSSA NOVA

When versatile tenor saxophonist Stan Getz left Denmark and returned to the US in January 1961, he already enjoyed a reputation as one of the finest melodists in jazz. He served a solid SWING-style apprenticeship in the bands of Stan Kenton, Benny Goodman, and Woody Herman in the 1940s, and produced a popular lyrical interpretation of "Early Autumn" in a recording cut in 1948. These achievements led to his first work as a leader in 1949. Thereafter Getz remained refreshingly aloof from current stylistic "schools," although his 1950s work increasingly revealed its debt to the fashionable COOL approach.

Getz's homecoming after his brief European interlude brought him renewed fame when he began to concentrate on the growing fashion for BOSSA NOVA ("new tendency"). This supremely marketable blend of laid-back Brazilian exoticism and sophisticated WEST COAST jazz scored its first success in 1962 when Getz collaborated with guitarist Charlie Byrd in the recording *Jazz Samba* (• p. 154), which won a Grammy award. The biggest bossa nova triumph was recorded by Getz with the husband-and-wife team of Astrud and João Gilberto in 1963. "The Girl from Ipanema" became a major hit when rereleased as a single in the following year, and has been cited as one of the five most-played songs of all time.

Both native Brazilians, the Gilbertos injected considerable authenticity into the style, as did Rio-born pianist Antonio Carlos Jobim. The latter had launched the new craze with his own record company back in 1958, and his song "Desafinado" was featured on the Getz–Byrd *Jazz Samba* release.

Brazilian music continues to exert a strong influence on modern jazz, especially in the seductive melodic style of the more popularly orientated FUSION groups, such as that led by Pat Metheny (• p. 199), and those promoted by the GRP label (• p. 214).

Above Stan Getz pauses for a photo opportunity while boarding a Scandinavian Airlines jet at Copenhagen in 1958, bound for Frankfurt. Getz lived in Denmark between 1958 and 1961.

for *Down Beat*. Coleman's avant-garde quartet (• p. 150) disbands this year.

19 May
Miles Davis and Gil Evans appear at a Carnegie Hall concert for the African Research Foundation, during which Max Roach stages an anti-racist protest.

25 May
John Coltrane (• p. 160) records *Olé Coltrane* with Freddie Hubbard and Eric Dolphy.

May
Thelonious Monk (• p. 155) tours England, France, Switzerland, and Sweden.

6 July
Duke Ellington and Count Basie record *The First Time: The Duke Meets the Count*, featuring music from Ellington's recent score to the movie *Paris Blues* (• p. 151).

• Scott LaFaro, Bill Evans's prodigious bass player, is killed in a car accident at the age of twenty-five in Geneva, New York; a few days earlier, the Bill Evans Trio (• p. 157) had recorded two live albums at the Village Vanguard, Greenwich Village, widely considered to be among the finest of their kind.

September
Saxophonist Eric Dolphy tours Denmark.

23 November
John Tynan, associate editor of *Down Beat*, brands the recent work of John Coltrane and Eric Dolphy as "anti-jazz."

- After riots in the previous year, the Newport Jazz Festival is canceled and subsequently relocates to New York.
- Billie Holiday (• p. 131) is posthumously elected a member of *Down Beat*'s Hall of Fame.
- Philip Larkin begins work as *Daily Telegraph* jazz critic, UK.

World Events

12 April
Yuri Gagarin is first man in space

16 June
Rudolf Nureyev defects from USSR to West

2 July
Death of Ernest Hemingway

17 August
Berlin Wall completed

- Birth-control pill introduced
- Joseph Heller's novel *Catch-22*
- David Lean's film *Lawrence of Arabia* wins Oscar for Best Picture

DOUBLE BASS

Jazz double-bass playing progressed from its primitive function in RAGTIME orchestras and early New Orleans groups, where the instrument merely emphasized the main beats of the prevailing MARCH rhythm, to a more flexible role in the bands of the Swing Era. The familiar WALKING BASS was an essential feature of both swing music and the bop style that succeeded it. Its continued use represented an increase in melodic interest in the lowest part of the music's texture and the new importance of the bass line in maintaining rhythmic momentum.

As bands grew larger, the double bass became less audible. One attempt to combat this problem was the evolution of the "slap" pizzicato, which causes the string to rebound off the instrument's fingerboard with a sharp percussive noise. Ultimately, the inability of the double bass to compete with louder instruments on equal terms was a significant factor behind the rise in popularity of the electric bass guitar in the 1970s (• p. 127), although the introduction of metal strings and electric amplification on the ACOUSTIC instrument partly alleviated the problem.

In spite of its inherent drawbacks, many players retained a preference for the conventional double bass. Both Ray Brown and Charles Mingus (• p. 190) successfully adapted bop IMPROVISATION techniques for it, and by the 1940s it had become a solo voice in its own right. Scott LaFaro, Gary Peacock, and Niels-Henning Ørsted Pedersen (right) revealed the double bass's surprising capability for virtuosity by playing it in the high register with a dexterity more typical of guitarists. Technical flexibility continues to characterize the work of contemporary bass players such as Dave Holland (famed for his speed of execution), Charlie Haden (a SIDEMAN of Ornette Coleman, who later became an important leader in his own right), and Charnett Moffett.

Above Virtuoso Danish bass player Niels-Henning Ørsted Pedersen, staunch sideman to Oscar Peterson in the 1970s and 1980s.

1962

The eccentric Thelonious Monk becomes a household name as his performances receive high critical acclaim. Mainstream American jazz musicians appear in the Soviet Union for the first time, and European jazz benefits from the active presence of Bud Powell and Dexter Gordon.

THROUGH THE IRON CURTAIN

Above Benny Goodman entertains a delighted young audience in Red Square, Moscow, in the summer of 1962.

Right Cootie Williams, who returned to the Ellington fold in 1962.

Jazz Events

February
Stan Getz and Charlie Byrd record "Desafinado" in Washington and start a craze for BOSSA NOVA, on which Getz capitalizes by mounting an ambitious big-band session recorded in **August**.

24 March
Bandleader Jean Goldkette dies, Santa Barbara, California.

28 May
Herbie Hancock (• p. 201) records his first album as leader, *Takin' Off*.

July
Benny Goodman (• p. 84) and pianist Teddy Wilson visit the Soviet Union under the auspices of the US State Department, forming part of the first group of American jazz musicians ever to appear in the country.

August
Count Basie's band tours Sweden.

17 September
Duke Ellington records *Money Jungle* with Max Roach and Charles Mingus (• p. 190), showing his awareness of ongoing stylistic trends in jazz.

26 September
Duke Ellington records with John Coltrane (• p. 160) in New York.

September
Trumpeter Cootie Williams rejoins the Duke Ellington orchestra after an absence of twenty-two years.
• Dexter Gordon tours to London and decides to remain in Europe (he settles in Copenhagen and does not return to the US until 1977). In **November** he appears at Oslo's Metropol Jazzhus, which has already hosted an appearance by Bud Powell on **1 September**. Powell also plays in Stockholm, Copenhagen, and Paris this year.

12 October
Charles Mingus fronts a big band at New York's Town Hall.

October
Tenor saxophonist Archie Shepp, recently departed from Cecil Taylor (• p. 150), records his first album with a new quartet featuring trumpeter Bill Dixon.

23 November
Cecil Taylor records live at the Café Montmartre, Copenhagen.

November
A bossa nova concert is mounted at Carnegie Hall.

15–16 December
Oscar Peterson's trio (• p. 163) record their BLUES-based album *Night Train* in Chicago.

December
Dave Brubeck (• p. 189) on tour in Amsterdam.

• Guitarist Joe Pass, recently discharged from a drug rehabilitation center, names his first recording, *Sounds of Synanon*, after the institution.

World Events

25 May
New Coventry Cathedral consecrated, UK; Benjamin Britten's *War Requiem* is commissioned in celebration

5 August
Death of Marilyn Monroe

6 August
Death of William Faulkner

October
Cuban missile crisis

- Opening of Lincoln Center for the Performing Arts, New York
- Alexander Solzhenitsyn's novel *One Day in the Life of Ivan Denisovich*

THELONIOUS MONK: WRONG NOTES AND SILLY HATS

Thelonious Monk's popularity was at its height in 1962, when he was awarded a high-profile recording contract by Columbia. Perhaps the quintessential bop musician, Monk presented an image of arty bohemian eccentricity with his trademark hats and awkward stage presence. His seemingly clumsy piano playing masked a very real compositional talent; in his way, he was just as influential on younger musicians as Charlie Parker (• p. 136), his sometime collaborator at Minton's Playhouse (• p. 97).

Initially eclipsed by the rapid success of his pupil Bud Powell, Monk made his first recordings with Coleman Hawkins's small ensembles in the closing stages of World War II. Engagements with Dizzy Gillespie (• p. 219) and Duke Ellington's former trumpeter Cootie Williams led to the latter's recording in 1944 of what remains Monk's best-known composition, "'Round Midnight" (• p. 116). A steady series of sessions for Blue Note (1947–52), Prestige (1952–55), and Riverside (1955–61) gradually cemented Monk's reputation as an originator of harmonically daring pieces that showed a flair for idiosyncratic yet catchy melodies. His collaborations in 1957 with Art Blakey (• p. 140) and John Coltrane propelled him into the limelight for the first time, and an appearance with a ten-strong band at New York's Town Hall in 1959 received critical acclaim. He became famous both at home and in Europe, where he had first appeared at the 1954 Paris Jazz Festival and where he toured widely in 1961. Three years later, his international status was confirmed by an appearance on the cover of *Time* magazine and a tour of Japan.

It is often claimed that Monk's distinctive piano style was rooted in the STRIDE idiom, but this tended to show itself only in his rendering of slow BALLADS. At a faster tempo, his playing was often muscular and dominated by a stiff-finger technique that produced percussive sonorities. Unlike most bop performers, he employed a bare minimum of notes, frequently studding his improvised solos with pregnant silences that kept the audience in suspense as to his next move: abrupt cascades based on Debussy's whole-tone SCALE were a favorite device. According to the individual listener's sympathies, his playing could be described as either crudely inept, or replete with emotional significance and a laudable economy of musical material. The most memorable description of his keyboard style has undoubtedly been Philip Larkin's likening it to a "*faux-naif* elephant dance."

Though Monk's playing was controversial, his compositions continue to receive almost universal praise for their originality and memorability. Alongside "Round Midnight," other Monk pieces that have established themselves in the repertoire of STANDARDS include "Straight, No Chaser," "Epistrophy," "Blue Monk," "In Walked Bud," "Rhythm-a-Ning," and "Evidence."

Above left Monk's eccentric image and apparent lack of a fluent keyboard technique belied his serious musical philosophy and significant compositional innovations.

1963-64

Highly varied studio sessions by Bill Evans, John Coltrane, and Charles Mingus break new ground in recording techniques and achieve considerable expressive power.

TECHNOLOGY AND SPIRITUALITY

Left Tony Williams was the youngest and most virtuosic jazz drummer of the decade. He is seen here playing with Miles Davis in London in the late 1960s.

Jazz Events

1963

20 January
Charles Mingus (• p. 190) records *The Black Saint and the Sinner Lady*, one of the finest experiments in extended structure of its time, in which post-Ellington sophistication meets OVERDUBBING techniques and free IMPROVISATION.

January–February
Bill Evans records his solo album *Conversations with Myself*, on which three separate keyboard parts are superimposed by overdubbing.

22 February
Dave Brubeck (• p. 189) appears at Carnegie Hall.

February
Coleman Hawkins appears at the Metropol Jazzhus, Oslo.

May
Dexter Gordon records in Paris.
• Thelonious Monk (• p. 155) makes live recordings in Tokyo.

26 July
Miles Davis appears with seventeen-year-old drummer prodigy Tony Williams in Antibes. Williams now forms part of Davis's new quintet – featuring George Coleman (tenor saxophone), Herbie Hancock (piano), and Ron Carter (bass) – which recorded *Seven Steps to Heaven* in New York in **May**.

6 September
Duke Ellington (• p. 182) embarks on a tour arranged by the US State Department. His itinerary includes Syria, Jordan, Jerusalem, Beirut, Afghanistan, India, Ceylon, Pakistan, Iran, Iraq, Kuwait, Turkey, Cyprus, Egypt, and Greece. The tour is abandoned after the assassination of President John F. Kennedy on **22 November**.

World Events

1963

30 January
Death of Francis Poulenc

28 August
Martin Luther King, Jr. addresses civil rights rally, Washington, DC

31 August
Death of Georges Braque

11 October
Death of Jean Cocteau

22 November
President Kennedy assassinated, Dallas, Texas

• National Theatre opens, London

EVERYBODY DIGS BILL EVANS

Bop piano playing quickly ran itself into a stylistic rut when second-rate pianists found themselves unable to achieve the individuality of Thelonious Monk (• p. 155) or Bud Powell. Mechanical, fragmented improvised melodies in the right hand were invariably supported by spiky and seemingly random chords in the left (a type of accompaniment known as "comping"), and it all sounded much the same.

Bill Evans proved himself to be practically the single-handed savior of modern jazz piano when he emerged from working with Charles Mingus and Miles Davis in the late 1950s to establish himself as a strongly individual talent. His interest in modal techniques was demonstrated by the track "Peace Piece" on his album *Everybody Digs Bill Evans* in 1958, and was intensified the following year by his collaboration with Davis on the seminal project *Kind of Blue* (• p. 146). Modal techniques, stemming ultimately from Evans's awareness of the music of classical French composers such as Debussy (• p. 24) and Satie, became part of an unusually rich harmonic vocabulary that allowed him to escape from the clichés of other bop pianists. Arguably his finest work was recorded in 1959–61 with a trio featuring bassist Scott LaFaro and drummer Paul Motian. This ensemble, which benefited from an outstanding instinctive rapport between the three men, was cruelly curtailed by LaFaro's untimely death (• p. 153).

Evans's most important and influential attribute was his innate lyricism, which added a vein of sensitivity and expressiveness into jazz at a time when it was most in need of it. Unlike some other COOL performers, Evans combined his relaxed musical intimacy with sophisticated compositional and improvisational techniques that never allowed the listener to lapse into complacency. His work was widely emulated in Europe in the 1970s, and had a decisive impact on later American pianists such as Keith Jarrett (• p. 185) and Lyle Mays (• p. 211).

Right This expressive sketch of Bill Evans was drawn by Norwegian jazz critic Randi Hultin.

Left Polygram/Verve reissued Evans's boldly original *Conversations with Myself* on CD in 1984.

OVERDUBBING

Bill Evans's solo album *Conversations with Myself* (1963) was a bold experiment in overdubbing, a technique also known as multi-track recording, which allowed Evans to accompany himself by adding two further tracks to his original take. His compositional skill produced textures of great fluidity, shot through with harmonic resourcefulness and contrapuntal ingenuity. He repeated the experiment with *Further Conversations with Myself* (1967). His was not the first such venture, however: it had been inspired by Lennie Tristano's *Ju-Ju* (recorded in 1951, but released in 1971) and *Requiem* (1955), a radical project in which the master tape was played back at increased speed to create a disconcerting timbre.

All this technological wizardry was made possible by the introduction of magnetic tape, which rapidly supplanted the old electrical recording method (• p. 59) in the late 1940s. In addition to its multi-tracking possibilities (which later extended to the provision of twenty-four individual tracks on a two-inch tape), magnetic tape could be easily cut, spliced, and remixed to create seemingly endless artistic possibilities. Creative overdubbing and editing techniques were pioneered by Charles Mingus, notably in his album *The Black Saint and the Sinner Lady* (also recorded in 1963), and by Miles Davis in collaboration with his Columbia producer, Teo Macero, from 1968 onward.

Jazz Events

1963

November
John Coltrane's "Alabama" is inspired by the fate of four black children killed in a church bombing incident.

Autumn
Sonny Rollins plays in Stuttgart, Germany.

14 December
Dinah Washington dies in Detroit of an accidental drug overdose.

21 December
Lee Morgan records his best-selling HARD-BOP hit *The Sidewinder* for Blue Note.

- Count Basie's band tours to Japan.

1964

15 January
Trombonist and singer Jack Teagarden dies, New Orleans.

12 February
The Miles Davis Quintet performs at New York's Philharmonic Hall. The event spawns the album *My Funny Valentine*, one of the greatest of all live jazz recordings. After the group's appearance in Tokyo in **July**, Wayne Shorter replaces George Coleman as tenor saxophonist. The group attends the Berlin Festival in **September**.

Above Hard-bop trumpeter Lee Morgan, pictured here in London in 1961. He scored a major success with *The Sidewinder* in 1964, but his career was brutally curtailed by a bullet in 1972 (• p. 178).

Below Dinah Washington performs in Los Angeles in 1959, four years before her death. Her vocal artistry straddled the gospel, popular, and jazz styles.

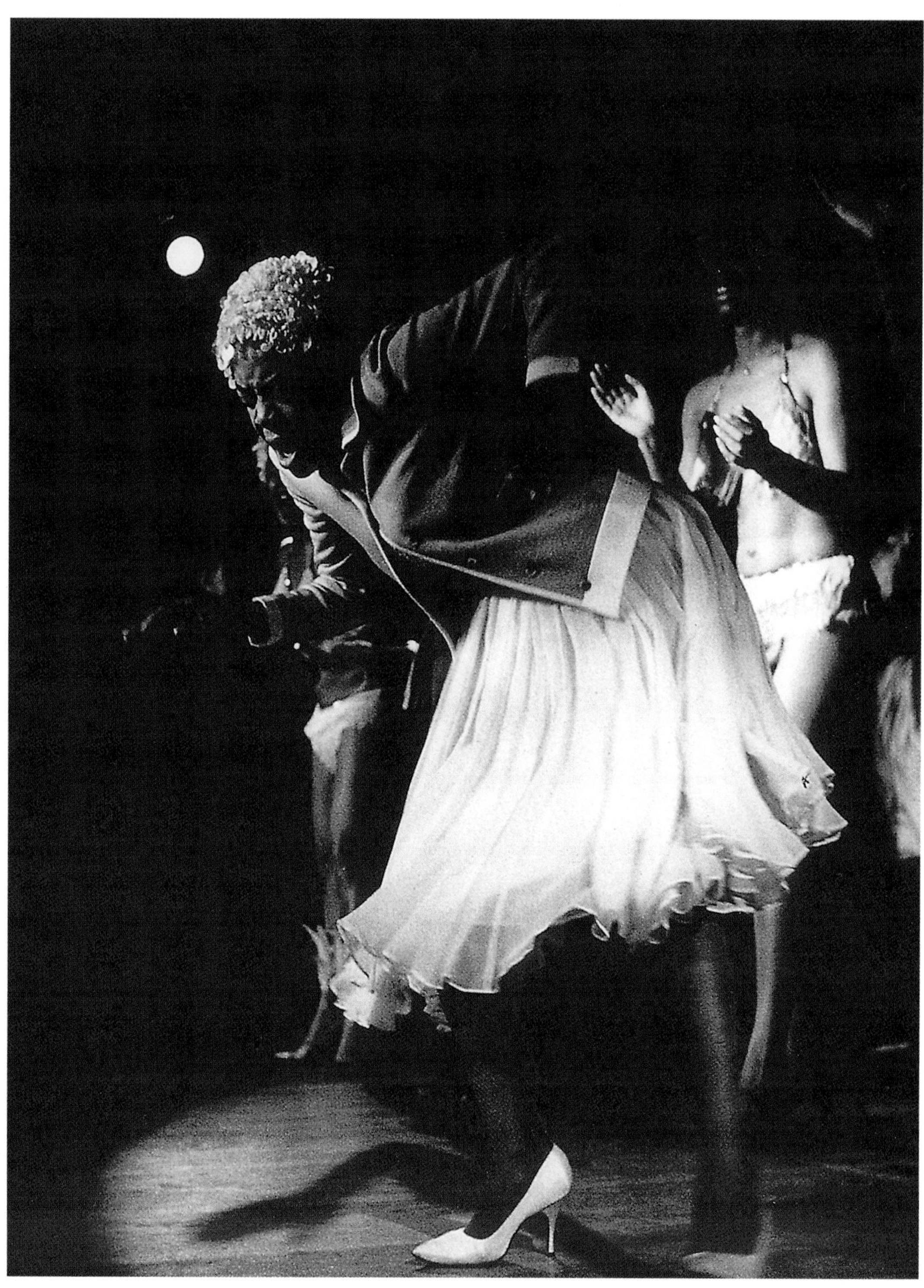

25 February
Saxophonist Eric Dolphy records *Out to Lunch* for Blue Note with a quintet that includes Freddie Hubbard and Tony Williams. Dolphy shows his versatility by playing both bass clarinet and flute.

3 March
Chet Baker (● p. 210) is deported from Germany to the USA.

March
Trumpeter Clark Terry and valve-trombonist Bob Brookmeyer begin a three-year series of recordings together.

April
Charles Mingus and Eric Dolphy perform in Amsterdam, Paris, Wuppertal, and Stuttgart.

7 June
BOOGIE-WOOGIE pianist Meade Lux Lewis is killed in a car accident, Minneapolis.

29 June
Eric Dolphy dies from a heart attack in Berlin during his European tour with Charles Mingus.

A LOVE SUPREME: JOHN COLTRANE

Above The somber sleeve for Coltrane's album *A Love Supreme*, on which the other musicians taking part were not credited – perhaps so as not to dilute the sense that this was a single artist's ultimate spiritual statement.

Top Coltrane in action at the Concertgebouw, Amsterdam, on 2 December 1962.

"Not merely loved, not merely idolized, [Coltrane] came to be revered as a saint, a mystic being whose simple presence on earth, some of his worshippers believed, would set the world straight. One writer, Frank Kofsky, wrote his name in for vice president during the 1964 elections. Another placed him in a pantheon along with Muhammad and Jesus. Yet another, Joachim Berendt, claimed that there emanated from him 'a hymnic power of love' . . . John Coltrane, in sum, was seen – and still is seen by many – not merely as a great jazz musician, but as a spiritual leader on a level with the founders of the world's great religions."

James Lincoln Collier, 1978

Few performers straddled the apparent gulf between HARD BOP and the avant-garde with the conviction of tenor saxophonist John Coltrane. A solid bop apprenticeship with Dizzy Gillespie (• p. 219) in 1949–51 laid the foundations for his improvising technique, but it was not until he joined Miles Davis's famous quintet (• p. 137) in 1955 that his uncompromising musical personality began to assert itself. Unlike Davis, however, Coltrane's IMPROVISATIONS often comprised strings of notes delivered at a frenetic speed that sometimes conflicted with the underlying chords (an approach aptly described by critic Ira Gitler as "sheets of sound").

Coltrane's own quartet – featuring the talents of pianist McCoy Tyner, bassist Jimmy Garrison, and drummer Elvin Jones – was established by 1961 and survived until the year before his death in 1967. By then, Coltrane had begun to associate himself with the FREE JAZZ movement, absorbing Ornette Coleman's experiments into his own octet album *Ascension* (1965), and working with leading innovators such as saxophonists Eric Dolphy and Pharoah Sanders. Sanders and Archie Shepp were primarily responsible for furthering the aggressive tone representative of Coltrane's playing at its most powerful, a sound that became a prominent feature of the avant-garde in the later 1960s.

Coltrane emerged from a drug-related personal crisis in 1957 with a heightened sense of spirituality and a strong religious fervor. His deliverance from self-destruction was celebrated in the 1964 recording *A Love Supreme*, a landmark in the development of the "concept" album, which connected as much with white hippies of the time as it did with black civil rights activists. In the first track, "Acknowledgement," a four-note instrumental motif is reiterated to saturation point and then is explained when the quartet sings it to the four syllables of the album's title. The fourth and final track is an ambitious "Psalm," in which the saxophonist improvises, in a suitably declamatory style, an instrumental interpretation of his own poem of praise and thanksgiving printed in the sleeve notes.

Coltrane had as great an influence on younger tenor saxophonists as Charlie Parker did on subsequent alto players, especially in terms of tone production. The impact of his playing was immediately evident in the 1960s, and it continued without significant interruption to affect the work of musicians such as Michael Brecker, Courtney Pine, and Branford Marsalis.

Jazz Events

June–July
Duke Ellington's first tour to Japan. In **September**, he records selections from the film *Mary Poppins* in Chicago.

June–August
Dexter Gordon makes a series of recordings in Copenhagen.

9 September
Avant-garde tenor saxophonist Albert Ayler (● p. 165) records his album *Ghosts* in Copenhagen.

September
Charles Mingus presents his large-scale *Meditations on Integration* at the Monterey Jazz Festival.

26 October
Horace Silver records *Song for My Father* for Blue Note.

October
Blind multi-instrumentalist Roland Kirk performs at Stockholm's first "Newport in Europe" festival, held in the city's Johanneshov Ice Stadium.

7 November
Pianist Erroll Garner appears at the Concertgebouw, Amsterdam.

30 November
Arranger Don Redman dies, New York.

9 December
John Coltrane records his album *A Love Supreme*, a spiritual statement about his recovery from drug addiction. It sells hundreds of thousands of copies.

- British saxophonist/composer John Dankworth and his wife, singer Cleo Laine, record their album *Shakespeare and All That Jazz*, setting the bard's texts to music that veers between lyricism and playful eccentricity.
- The classic Benny Goodman Quartet (● p. 84) of the 1930s reforms to record *Together Again!* for RCA.
- The Jazz Composers' Guild is formed in New York to promote avant-garde jazz.

World Events

1964

June
Nelson Mandela begins life sentence, South Africa

14 October
Martin Luther King, Jr. receives Nobel Peace Prize

15 October
Death of Cole Porter

- Film musical *My Fair Lady* receives Oscar for Best Picture
- Stanley Kubrick's film *Dr. Strangelove*
- The Beatles appear in the film *A Hard Day's Night*

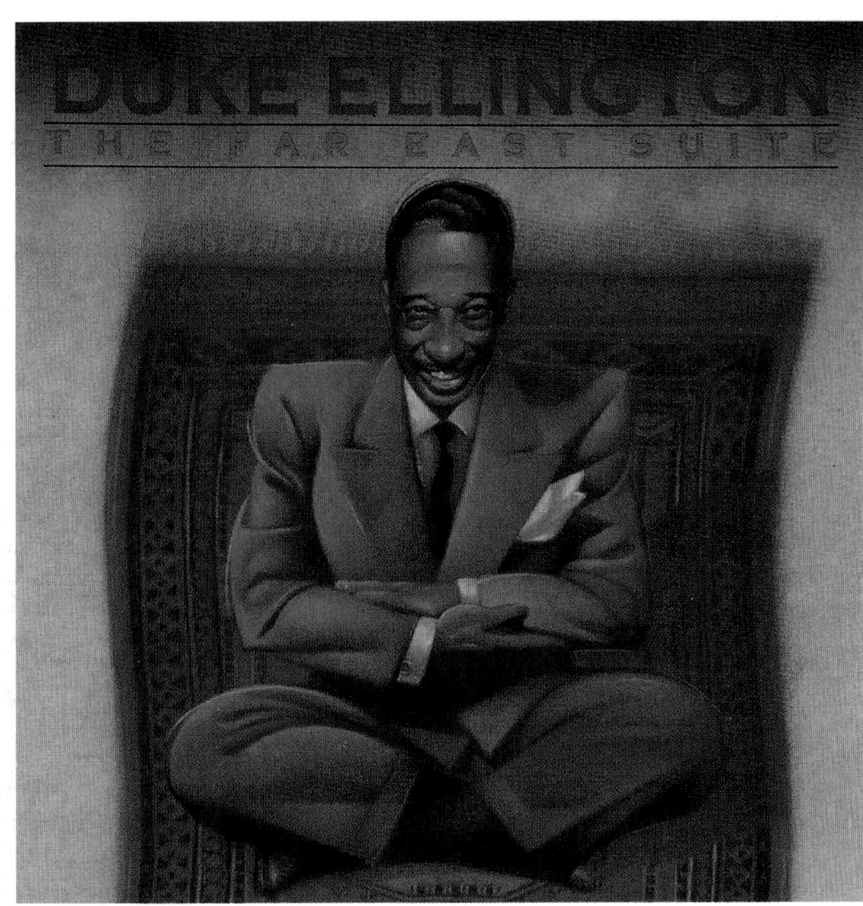

Above Duke Ellington and Billy Strayhorn's *The Far East Suite* (recorded in 1966) was a musical celebration of the band's visits to India and the Middle East in 1963, and to Japan in 1964.

1965

John Coltrane joins the avant-garde with his album *Ascension*, while Duke Ellington's spirituality is revealed in a very different musical idiom. Ben Webster emigrates to Europe, and Wayne Shorter makes his mark with the Miles Davis Quintet.

'TRANE ASCENDANT

Jazz Events

20–22 January
Miles Davis records the album *E.S.P.* in Los Angeles with a quintet featuring Wayne Shorter alongside Herbie Hancock (● p. 201), Ron Carter, and Tony Williams.

January–February
Ben Webster, now settled in Copenhagen, is active in Denmark and Norway.

15 February
Nat King Cole dies of cancer at the age of forty-seven, Santa Monica, California.

17 March
Herbie Hancock records *Maiden Voyage* with his colleagues in Davis's RHYTHM SECTION and trumpeter Freddie Hubbard. The album's title track demonstrates a sophisticated application of modal techniques.

25 March
Stan Tracey's quartet records the suite *Under Milk Wood* in London. The work is inspired by the writings of Welsh poet and playwright Dylan Thomas.

March
Stan Getz (● p. 152) performs in Vancouver, British Columbia.

20 June
A Pittsburgh piano workshop showcases the talents of Mary Lou Williams and Earl Hines (both closely associated with the city), alongside Duke Ellington and Willie "The Lion" Smith.

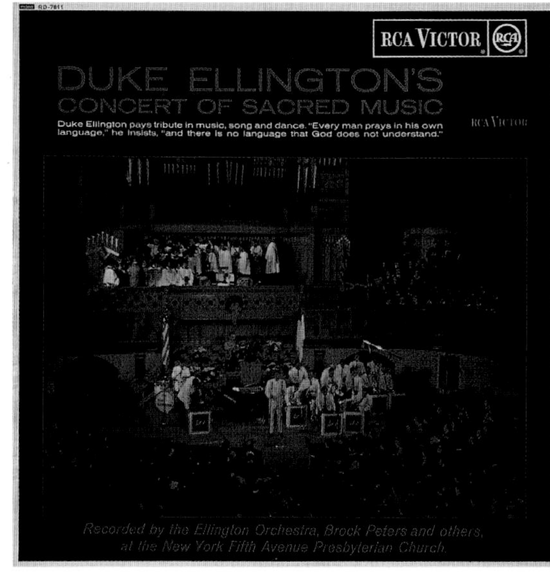

Above This LP release of Duke Ellington's *Concert of Sacred Music* shows the scene at the second performance of the work in New York's Fifth Avenue Presbyterian Church on Boxing Day 1965.

28 June
John Coltrane (● p. 160) records *Ascension*, a bold experiment in collective IMPROVISATION loosely modeled on the spirit of Ornette Coleman's *Free Jazz* (● p. 150). The work is issued in two versions due to Coltrane's indecision about which take he prefers.

July
Fresh from a concert at Newport shared with Archie Shepp, Coltrane travels to Paris and Antibes.

21 August
Thelonious Monk (● p. 155) records live in Montreal, where, four days later, Oscar Peterson also plays.

16 September
Grace Cathedral, San Francisco, hosts the first of Duke Ellington's "Sacred Concerts" under the title *In the Beginning, God*. It is repeated on **26 December** at the Presbyterian Church on Fifth Avenue, New York, and then receives over fifty further performances. The Pulitzer Prize committee declines to accept a proposal to award a citation to Ellington.

September
Albert and Donald Ayler (● p. 165) record *Spirits Rejoice*, featuring Call Cobbs in a rare jazz use of the harpsichord.
● Dizzy Gillespie and Charles Mingus are the stars of this year's Monterey Jazz Festival.

6 November
Pianist Clarence Williams dies, New York.

December
Trumpeter Thad Jones and drummer Mel Lewis found a rehearsal orchestra that blossoms into one of the finest big bands working in a post-Basie idiom.

- Ornette Coleman emerges from two years of retirement to appear at the Village Vanguard, Greenwich Village, and also plays at the Golden Circle in Stockholm.
- Two important organizations are formed to promote the interests of the jazz avant-garde: the Association for the Advancement of Creative Musicians, founded in Chicago by Muhal Richard Abrams; and the Underground Musicians and Artists Association on the West Coast.
- The first annual Ragtime Festival is held in St. Louis, Missouri.
- The Blue Note label (● p. 167) is taken over by Liberty Records this year.

OSCAR PETERSON

Canadian pianist Oscar Peterson, one of the most prolific recording artists of all time, acquired his phenomenal technical fluency after spending ten hours a day practising Chopin's *Études* in his youth. With a solid classical technique behind him, Peterson set about emulating characteristics of the jazz pianists he admired, most notably the dexterity and harmonic ingenuity of Art Tatum and the melodic appeal of Nat King Cole (• p. 125). These features were amalgamated into a distinctive keyboard style that alternated attractive melodies and glittering virtuoso passages, and was distinguished by sensitive and inventive accompanying behind the solo work of other instrumentalists.

Peterson came to prominence in the USA following an appearance at Carnegie Hall in 1949, after which he became a stalwart member of Norman Granz's touring venture "Jazz at the Philharmonic" (• p. 107). His preferred medium was the piano trio, a format he inherited directly from Cole and Tatum, in which the additional instruments were originally a guitar (Herb Ellis) and double bass (Ray Brown). In 1958, he substituted a drummer (Ed Thigpen) for the guitarist to create a group capable of greater rhythmic drive. This innovation prompted the pianist's style to move closer to the prevailing HARD BOP idiom of the day. After a spell devoted to solo concerts in the early 1970s, Peterson formed a new trio, with Danish bassist Niels-Henning Ørsted Pedersen (• p. 153) and British drummer Martin Drew, which became popular in the UK through its studio performances in the BBC television series *Oscar Peterson's Piano Party*.

Peterson played a special Bösendorfer grand piano, which he took on tour with him. The instrument featured additional keys at the bottom of the keyboard that allowed bass lines to be extended below the normal register. When not in use, these extra keys were intended to be hidden by a hinged cover, so as not to distort the pianist's normal perspective. On one memorable occasion at London's Royal Festival Hall when Peterson was sharing a GIG with Count Basie, he left the stage having forgotten to cover up the extra bass notes. When Basie came onstage to play a STRIDE solo on Peterson's unusual piano, he stunned himself (and the audience) by missing every single bass note. Basie was not amused.

World Events

4 January
Death of T. S. Eliot

February–March
Intensified US offensives in Vietnam

18 March
First spacewalk (by Alexei Leonov)

11 August
Thirty-four killed in Los Angeles race riots

27 August
Death of Le Corbusier

- Film musical *The Sound of Music* receives Oscar for Best Picture
- First performance of Charles Ives's Symphony No. 4

Above The Oscar Peterson Trio's celebration of the blues: *Night Train* (Verve, 1962).

Left Peterson's prodigious keyboard technique and musical sensitivity delighted audiences across the globe after he first came to prominence in the 1950s.

1966

The Village Vanguard, in New York's Greenwich Village, cements its reputation as a leading venue by hosting the Jones–Lewis big band. The increasingly international nature of jazz takes John Coltrane and Duke Ellington to Japan, Earl Hines to Russia, and many other American musicians to Europe.

GREENWICH VILLAGE

Above Thelonious Monk's protégé Bud Powell (seen here in Paris in 1960 at the height of his powers) returned to the USA in 1964, whereupon severe mental health problems forced him into retirement – and, soon after, an early grave.

Jazz Events

26 January
Sonny Rollins records themes from his soundtrack to the British movie *Alfie*, starring Michael Caine.

February
Thad Jones and Mel Lewis debut with their new big band at the Village Vanguard, a long-standing GIG that lasts until the 1980s.

April
Duke Ellington attends the World Festival of Negro Arts held at Dakar, Senegal. This year, Ellington also tours Japan and visits France and England, where his *First Sacred Concert* (• p. 162) is performed in Coventry Cathedral. Back home, he receives the President's Gold Medal of Honor from Lyndon Johnson.

19 May
Cecil Taylor (• p. 150) records his complex *Unit Structures* (• p. 149) with an unorthodox ensemble that includes an oboe. His avant-garde style comes closer to the sound of contemporary classical composers than to jazz.

May
Earl Hines (• p. 125) plays in London.

22 July
John Coltrane (• p. 160) records live during a tour of Japan.

31 July
Pianist Bud Powell dies, New York.

July–August
Earl Hines takes his band to the Soviet Union on a US State Department goodwill tour.

4–7 August
An international jazz festival is held in Molde, Norway.

24–25 October
The Miles Davis Quintet (• p. 137) records *Miles Smiles*, the trumpeter's musical style reaching out for more abstraction while retaining powerful rhythmic momentum and strong BLUES elements.

November
Albert Ayler tours Germany and France.

19–21 December
The Duke Ellington orchestra records *The Far East Suite*, celebrating its recent State Department tours to the Middle East (• p. 161).

- Pianist Bill Evans plays in Denmark and at Oslo's Munch Museum.
- Louis Armstrong (• p. 57) appears as "Sweet Daddy Willie Ferguson" in the movie *A Man Called Adam*.

WITCHES, DEVILS, SPIRITS, AND GHOSTS

Saxophonist Albert Ayler had only been recording for four years in 1966, but in that short time he had acquired a reputation as a singular talent among the new wave of avant-garde musicians. Often collaborating with his brother Donald (trumpet), Ayler specialized in small-ensemble work characterized by the absence of a pianist – a feature inherited directly from the music of Ornette Coleman (• p. 150).

Under the influence of Coleman's and Cecil Taylor's radical attitudes to HARMONY, RHYTHM, and texture, Ayler developed a remarkably free approach to IMPROVISATION that was most notable for its abandonment of regular METERS and even of recognizable tempos. As in much avant-garde jazz, Ayler seemed at times not to know when to stop playing (the same failing was openly confessed by Coltrane in his later years), and many of his improvisations lasted well beyond the limits of audience endurance.

Early work in Scandinavia in 1962 was followed by a mixed reception back in the USA, where, as in the case of Coleman, Ayler's provocative music led some critics to claim that he lacked a basic technical competence on his instrument. Coleman had been criticized for showing no apparent awareness of the history of jazz styles, but the Ayler brothers forestalled such criticism by absorbing elements culled directly from revered New Orleans traditions (funeral music, MARCHES, and folk songs). Brief snatches of simple melody would emerge from chaotic group improvisation like a breath of fresh air, only to be swallowed up again in another burst of frenzied and complex musical activity. The foundations for this sometimes bizarre style were laid in a series of idiosyncratic recordings, including two albums from 1964 – *Witches and Devils* and *Spiritual Unity*, the latter featuring Ayler's composition "Ghosts" – and *Spirits Rejoice* in 1965.

In the few years before his untimely death, which occurred in circumstances sufficiently ambiguous to make him a cult figure (• p. 174), Ayler returned to his roots in rhythm 'n' blues and appeared to have jumped back off the avant-garde bandwagon. As with many musicians tempted by the allure of commercially viable genres, he faced accusations of having "sold out." But avant-garde jazz was destined to remain essentially a minority interest, and many of the finest performers who subscribed to its artistic tenets found it necessary to earn their daily bread by other means.

Above The Ayler brothers in New York, 1966: Albert (left) and Donald (right).

World Events

30 July
England wins soccer's World Cup, London

31 July
Race riots in New York, Cleveland, and Chicago

13 August
Cultural Revolution, China

16 September
Samuel Barber's *Antony and Cleopatra* opens new Metropolitan Opera House, New York

12 October
Gunther Schuller's opera *The Visitation*, based on a work by Franz Kafka, is performed, Hamburg

- Truman Capote's novel *In Cold Blood*
- Dolby hi-fi noise-reduction system introduced

Right Trumpeter and bandleader Thad Jones, here assuming the less familiar role of percussionist. In the background is his coleader, drummer Mel Lewis.

ENDS AND BEGINNINGS

In a year that brings the deaths of numerous influential talents, attention turns increasingly toward the burgeoning rock scene.

Above John Coltrane, who died in 1967 after attracting a cult following.

Jazz Events

20 February
Duke Ellington performs his *First Sacred Concert* (• p. 162) at Great St. Mary's Church, Cambridge, UK.

February
John Coltrane (• p. 160) makes his last recordings, *Interstellar Space* and *Expression*.

23 March
BOOGIE-WOOGIE pianist Pete Johnson dies, Buffalo, New York.

March–April
Earl Hines (• p. 125) and Roy Eldridge take a large group on tour to Europe.

27 April
Ben Webster records in London with trumpeter Bill Coleman.

31 May
Billy Strayhorn, Duke Ellington's cocomposer (• p. 182), dies in New York. In **August**, Ellington records Strayhorn's compositions on an album, *And His Mother Called Him Bill*, dedicated to his memory.

May
Saxophonist Charles Lloyd tours the Soviet Union and records live in Tallinn.

May–July
The Miles Davis Quintet records the albums *Sorcerer* and *Nefertiti*. Most of the former and the title track of the latter are composed by Wayne Shorter.

17 July
John Coltrane dies from liver disease, aged forty, in New York.

20–21 July
Dexter Gordon records in Copenhagen.

July
The first Montreux Jazz Festival is mounted in Switzerland at Montreux Casino.
• In a potent sign of changing musical fashions, *Down Beat* announces that it will henceforth devote attention to rock music as well as jazz.

9 August
Bill Evans records *Further Conversations with Myself* (• p. 157).

7 September
Former Duke Ellington trumpeter Rex Stewart dies, Los Angeles.

29 December
Bandleader Paul Whiteman dies, Doylestown, Pennsylvania.

December
The Dave Brubeck Quartet disbands after a quarter of a century together.

- Trumpeter Lester Bowie forms the Art Ensemble of Chicago.
- Mayor John Lindsay abolishes the New York cabaret card, which musicians formerly had to acquire in order to appear at nightclubs. Such a card was refused to Billie Holiday when she applied for it after her prison term (• p. 113), and Thelonious Monk and Charlie Parker (• p. 126) both had their cards confiscated.
- Duke Ellington receives an Honorary Doctorate of Music from Yale University.
- Herbie Hancock (• p. 201) supplies a score for the trendy British film *Blow-Up*, directed by Michelangelo Antonioni and starring David Hemmings and Vanessa Redgrave.
- Frith Street becomes the new location for Ronnie Scott's famous London jazz club, founded in 1959.

BLUE NOTE: ANATOMY OF A RECORD LABEL

In 1967 Alfred Lion retired from his position at the helm of Blue Note, the influential record label he founded in New York twenty-eight years earlier (• p. 95). The label made its name during a revival of interest in early jazz by putting its faith in Sidney Bechet (• p. 43), then a neglected figure, who recorded a quintet version of Gershwin's "Summertime" for Lion in June 1939. The sudden craze for boogie-woogie piano in the wake of John Hammond's Carnegie Hall concert in the previous year prompted Lion to promote the work of Meade Lux Lewis, Albert Ammons, and Pete Johnson – with considerable commercial success. Other major traditionalists who were signed up by Blue Note in the 1940s included DIXIELAND trumpeter "Wild" Bill Davison, pianists James P. Johnson (• p. 46) and Earl Hines, and Cab Calloway's tenor saxophonist, Ike Quebec.

Quebec served as the label's A&R (Artists and Repertoire) man in the late 1940s. He persuaded Lion and his partner, Francis Wolff, to back recordings in the new bop style. This initiative resulted in Thelonious Monk's famous sessions in 1947–52, and those cut by Bud Powell in 1949–51 and Miles Davis in 1952–53. Blue Note's commitment to bop soon led naturally enough to a close involvement with the development of HARD BOP. By that time, the talents of recording engineer Rudy van Gelder, who was also employed by Prestige and Savoy, had earned all three labels a reputation for producing some of the finest mono sounds in the business. Blue Note issued an unrivaled selection of seminal hard-bop and SOUL-jazz recordings in the late 1950s and 1960s, including the best-known albums by drummer Art Blakey (• p. 139), trumpeters Lee Morgan and Freddie Hubbard, and pianist Horace Silver. Important new additions to the Blue Note catalog in the 1960s were Herbie Hancock and Wayne Shorter, both members of Davis's second great quintet, who used the label to establish themselves as leaders in their own right.

Blue Note's importance was by no means confined to the consistently high quality of the music it preserved. The label paid musicians for rehearsals, a policy almost as unusual in the 1950s as it had been for Jelly Roll Morton in the 1920s, which undoubtedly had a beneficial effect on performance standards. And the recordings themselves were issued in striking sleeves (• pp. 149 and 168), designed by Reid Miles and often featuring photographs by Francis Wolff himself. Having been bought by Liberty in 1963 and then by EMI in 1980, Blue Note maintained its commitment to the reissue of its earlier classic recordings, as well as fostering a new generation of traditional players under its subsidiary label Forecast. Michael Cuscuna first set this policy in motion in the mid-1970s and went on to issue much important Blue Note material (including the complete Monk sessions) under the aegis of his Californian company, Mosaic.

"Hot jazz . . . is expression and communication, a musical and social manifestation, and Blue Note records are concerned with identifying its impulse, not its sensational and commercial adornments."

Launch catalog for Blue Note, 1939

World Events

27 January
Apollo space crew killed in launchpad fire, Houston, Texas

6 March
Death of Zoltán Kodály

5 June
Six-Day War, Middle East

29 November
Karlheinz Stockhausen's electronic *Hymnen* performed in Cologne

- First heart-transplant operation
- Mike Nichols receives Best Director Oscar for *The Graduate*, popularizing the songs of Simon and Garfunkel

Below One of a pair of related sleeve designs produced for Blue Note by Andy Warhol in 1958.

BLUE LIGHTS KENNY BURRELL
Louis Smith, Junior Cook, Tina Brooks
Duke Jordan, Bobby Timmons
Sam Jones, Art Blakey
Blue Note 1597 Volume 2
andy Warhol

Herbie Hancock and Chick Corea are the leading lights of modern jazz piano, both having served apprenticeships with Miles Davis. The free jazz movement receives a boost from the impressive work of Anthony Braxton and Carla Bley.

NEW TALENTS

Above CD reissue of Herbie Hancock's *Speak Like a Child*, exemplifying the striking sleeve designs for which Blue Note records were celebrated.

Jazz Events

19 January
First performance of Duke Ellington's *Second Sacred Concert* before an audience of seven thousand at the Cathedral of St. John the Divine, New York. Further performances are mounted in San Francisco, Paris, Stockholm, Barcelona, and Orange, France.

5 February
STRIDE pianist Luckey Roberts dies, New York.

23 February
Vibraphonist Gary Burton appears at Carnegie Hall.

9 and 11 March
Herbie Hancock (• p. 201) records the album *Speak Like a Child* for Blue Note with a sextet that includes Thad Jones and bassist Ron Carter.

6 June
Alto saxophonist Phil Woods records live at the 9th Ljubljana Jazz Festival, Yugoslavia.

15 June
Guitarist Wes Montgomery dies, Indianapolis, Indiana. His album *A Day in the Life*, recorded in 1967, is the year's best-selling jazz LP.

July
Cecil Taylor (• p. 150) records *Praxis* in Italy.

August
Herbie Hancock quits the Miles Davis Quintet.

1 September
Duke Ellington visits South America, performing in Brazil, Argentina, Uruguay, and Chile.

September
Chick Corea (• p. 179) and bassist Dave Holland join Miles Davis to replace Herbie Hancock and Ron Carter in the final recording session for the album *Filles de Kilimanjaro*.

25–26 October
Ronnie Scott records live at his London club.

Autumn
Artists appearing at the Newport Jazz Festival in **June** undertake an extensive tour to Europe and appear at Jazz Expo '68 in London. Musicians involved include Dave Brubeck, Gary Burton, Benny Carter, Dizzy Gillespie, Earl Hines, and Gerry Mulligan.

Above Ronnie Scott's world-famous jazz club on London's Frith Street, premises it has occupied since 1967. A fine tenor saxophonist in his own right, Scott allegedly took his own life in 1996 after suffering from severe depressive illness for many years.

A NORDIC FRONT

The European audience for jazz remained small outside France and England during the Swing Era, although musicians in Scandinavia began to copy American styles as early as the 1930s. Danish violinist Svend Asmussen emulated the work of Joe Venuti (• p. 101) and accompanied Fats Waller when he visited Copenhagen in 1938, while Minneapolis-born violinist Leon Abbey appeared at the city's Hollaenderbyen restaurant the same year. Abbey also played at Saga-Cinema in Oslo and Nojesfaltet amusement park in Stockholm in the late 1930s, and Asmussen took his own brand of jazz to Stockholm's China Theater in 1942.

Sweden became an important center for the emerging European bop movement in 1948, when Dizzy Gillespie's big band toured the country and influenced emerging Swedish saxophonists Lars Gullin and Arne Domnérus. Domnérus participated in the seminal 1949 Paris Jazz Festival (• p. 120), and Gullin distinguished himself in 1954 as the first European musician to head a *Down Beat* poll. Around this time, Gullin began to absorb the new COOL style of Miles Davis and others. When Stan Getz (• p. 152) emigrated to Denmark in 1958, he brought a further influx of cool techniques with him.

In the 1960s, Scandinavian jazz venues became some of the most stimulating nightspots in Europe, hosting performances by high-ranking American musicians, many of them expatriates. The most prominent venues were Oslo's Metropol Jazzhus (opened in 1960) and Stockholm's Golden Circle, where Ornette Coleman (• p. 150) recorded in 1965. The initiative passed to Copenhagen in 1976 with the reopening of the Montmartre Jazzhus (founded in the 1950s), which secured residencies by Dexter Gordon and Thad Jones and fostered the growing European FREE JAZZ movement. International awareness of Danish jazz was fostered by the impressive work of bass player Niels-Henning Ørsted Pedersen (• p. 153), who made his name as a member of Oscar Peterson's trio.

Norwegian jazz grew in importance during the 1970s, thanks largely to the tireless endeavors of critic Randi Hultin, whose energy and enthusiasm attracted a stream of American musicians to Oslo. Native talents included bassist Arild Andersen, who collaborated with free-jazz trumpeter Don Cherry in 1968, and then with saxophonist Jan Garbarek in the early 1970s. Garbarek, a leading name on the ECM label (• p. 177), allied himself to a new synthetic jazz idiom that made considerable use of Scandinavian folk elements. This distinctively northern European jazz style had already been pioneered by Swedish trumpeter Bengt-Arne Wallin in his album *Old Folklore in Swedish Modern* (1962), and by Finnish baritone saxophonist Seppo Paakkunainen and his group, Karelia.

World Events

4 April
Martin Luther King, Jr. assassinated, Memphis, Tennessee

May
Student protests in Paris

21 August
Soviet invasion of Czechoslovakia

10 October
Premiere of Luciano Berio's *Sinfonia*, New York

- Film musical *Oliver!* wins Best Picture Oscar
- London Bridge dismantled and shipped to Arizona

- Saxophonist Anthony Braxton, a member of the Chicago Association for the Advancement of Creative Musicians, now forms his own Creative Construction Company, records a mammoth solo performance in his double album *For Alto Saxophone* and collaborates with other AACM members on *Three Compositions of New Jazz*.
- Chet Baker is mugged by a gang of drug addicts in San Francisco and loses several of his teeth. He is unable to play for two years.
- Flugelhorn player Art Farmer moves to Vienna, where he plays with the Austrian Radio Orchestra.
- The Black Artists' Group is formed in St. Louis along the lines of early avant-garde collectives (• p. 150).
- Carla Bley's Jazz Composers Orchestra Association forms the New Music Distribution Service to disseminate its recordings.
- Saxophonist Joe Harriott (• p. 151) and violinist John Mayer form a double quintet in London to record music that synthesizes elements of jazz and Indian music with a ten-piece ensemble, comprising six jazzmen and four Indian players.
- Gunther Schuller completes his book *Early Jazz*, the first critical and analytical study of the music's origins and development.

Above Autograph manuscript of *Randi's Rag*, a personal tribute to Norwegian jazz critic Randi Hultin composed by stride pianist Eubie Blake (• p. 200) in 1974 at the age of ninety-one.

1969

Spectacularly rescued from dwindling public interest by the arrival of jazz-rock fusion, jazz is now an approved academic pursuit in US universities, and its history is celebrated at the White House.

NEW HORIZONS

Above President Richard Nixon addresses the assembled company at his White House party to celebrate Duke Ellington's seventieth birthday.

Right A late photograph of Coleman Hawkins, a supremely lyrical master of swing-style saxophone, who died in 1969.

Jazz Events

4 January
Bassist Paul Chambers dies from tuberculosis.

18 February
Miles Davis records his album *In a Silent Way* in New York.

29 April
President Nixon holds a seventieth-birthday party for Duke Ellington at the White House, awarding him the Medal of Freedom. Jazz celebrities attending the event include Ellington's mentor Willie "The Lion" Smith, Dave Brubeck, Earl Hines, and Clark Terry.

April
Pianist Herbie Hancock records *The Prisoner* for Blue Note.

19 May
Tenor saxophonist Coleman Hawkins dies.

26 May
Duke Ellington Day is proclaimed in the State of New York.

12 August
The Art Ensemble of Chicago records in Paris, where Don Cherry also appears this year.

19–21 August
Miles Davis records his album *Bitches Brew* (• pp. 172–73) in New York.

September
The University of California at Berkeley stages an international symposium on the work of Duke Ellington.

October
Miles Davis is wounded in a Brooklyn shooting incident.

November
Duke Ellington appears in Manchester and Bristol. This year he also tours Eastern Europe and the West Indies.

- Manfred Eicher founds the record label ECM (Edition of Contemporary Music) in Cologne (• p. 177), which soon establishes an innovative house style synthesizing FREE JAZZ and jazz-rock FUSION.
- Drummer Tony Williams forms Lifetime with John McLaughlin (guitar) and Larry Young (organ).

"Jazz as we know it is dead."

Front cover, *Down Beat*, 5 October 1967

Left Miles Davis at Tanglewood, 18 August 1970. Compare his attire to the conventional dress of his earlier career (• p. 146).

World Events

2 March
Concorde's maiden flight

17 March
Golda Meir becomes Premier of Israel

8 June
US government pledges gradual withdrawal from Vietnam

21 July
First moon landing

15 August
British troops sent to Belfast

1 September
Colonel Gaddafi seizes power in Libya

- Woodstock festival of pop music, US
- Philip Roth, *Portnoy's Complaint*
- Mario Puzo, *The Godfather*

BIRTH OF FUSION

Although the 1960s brought many exciting innovations in jazz, the decade also saw one of its greatest crises as a new generation of young listeners were seduced away by the mass appeal of the blossoming pop and rock industry. Jazz had grown increasingly respectable since the 1940s, and could no longer represent the heady spirit of rebellion it had once championed. Once a music associated with sex, illicit alcohol, and (later) drugs, jazz now seemed almost squeaky clean. (Significantly, rock rapidly succeeded jazz not only as a more popular music, but also as the core of the escalating 1960s drug scene.)

Much worse, or so it seemed at the time, jazz was becoming increasingly characterized by an esoteric intellectualism guaranteed to alienate even its most devoted adherents. The gritty, avant-garde experiments carried out by the likes of Ornette Coleman, Cecil Taylor, and Albert Ayler (• p. 165) could never hope to achieve the global popularity of the catchy numbers The Beatles manufactured with such tuneful ease. Even jazz stars of the magnitude of Miles Davis and John Coltrane found themselves performing to half-empty venues in the mid-1960s.

The solution, which remains controversial among jazz aficionados, was a classic case of "if you can't beat 'em, join 'em." The Columbia label, concerned that Miles Davis's album sales were dwindling, boldly suggested that they cash in on the rock craze. Davis accordingly produced two albums in 1969 that launched a new concept of jazz-rock fusion, *In a Silent Way* and *Bitches Brew*. The latter went on to distinguish itself as one of the best-selling jazz albums of all time, thus vindicating Columbia's policy – at least in commercial terms. The new music unashamedly borrowed two prominent features from rock – a bias toward electronic and amplified sounds (principally electric bass guitar with ELECTRIC PIANO and/or SYNTHESIZERS), and non-swinging rhythmic patterns characterized by emphatic BACKBEATS. The traditional WALKING BASS disappeared, replaced by syncopated bass RIFFS that could be repeated at length. Davis also embraced challenging avant-garde techniques as part of his new fusion soundworld.

Later developments in fusion (and other CROSSOVER ventures) were made by a clutch of talented SIDEMEN who participated in Davis's 1969 recordings. These included keyboard players Chick Corea, Herbie Hancock, and Joe Zawinul, drummer Tony Williams, and British guitarist John McLaughlin.

"Miles hears, and what he hears he paints with. When he sees he hears, eyes are just an aid to hearing if you think of it that way. It's all in there, the beauty, the terror, and the love, the sheer humanity of life in this incredible electric world, which is so full of distortion that it can be beautiful and frightening in the same instant."

Ralph J. Gleason, sleeve note to *Bitches Brew*, 1969

Right Miles Davis's aggressive fusion double album *Bitches Brew*, released by Columbia in 1970, proved to be one of the best-selling and most influential recordings in jazz history.

Innovation and Reaction: Jazz-rock fusion wins itself a vast new audience in the 1970s, but the next decade is one of stylistic indecision. Traditional jazz styles are resurrected, the avant-garde movement acquires a renewed impetus, and European jazz begins to explore novel crossover idioms.

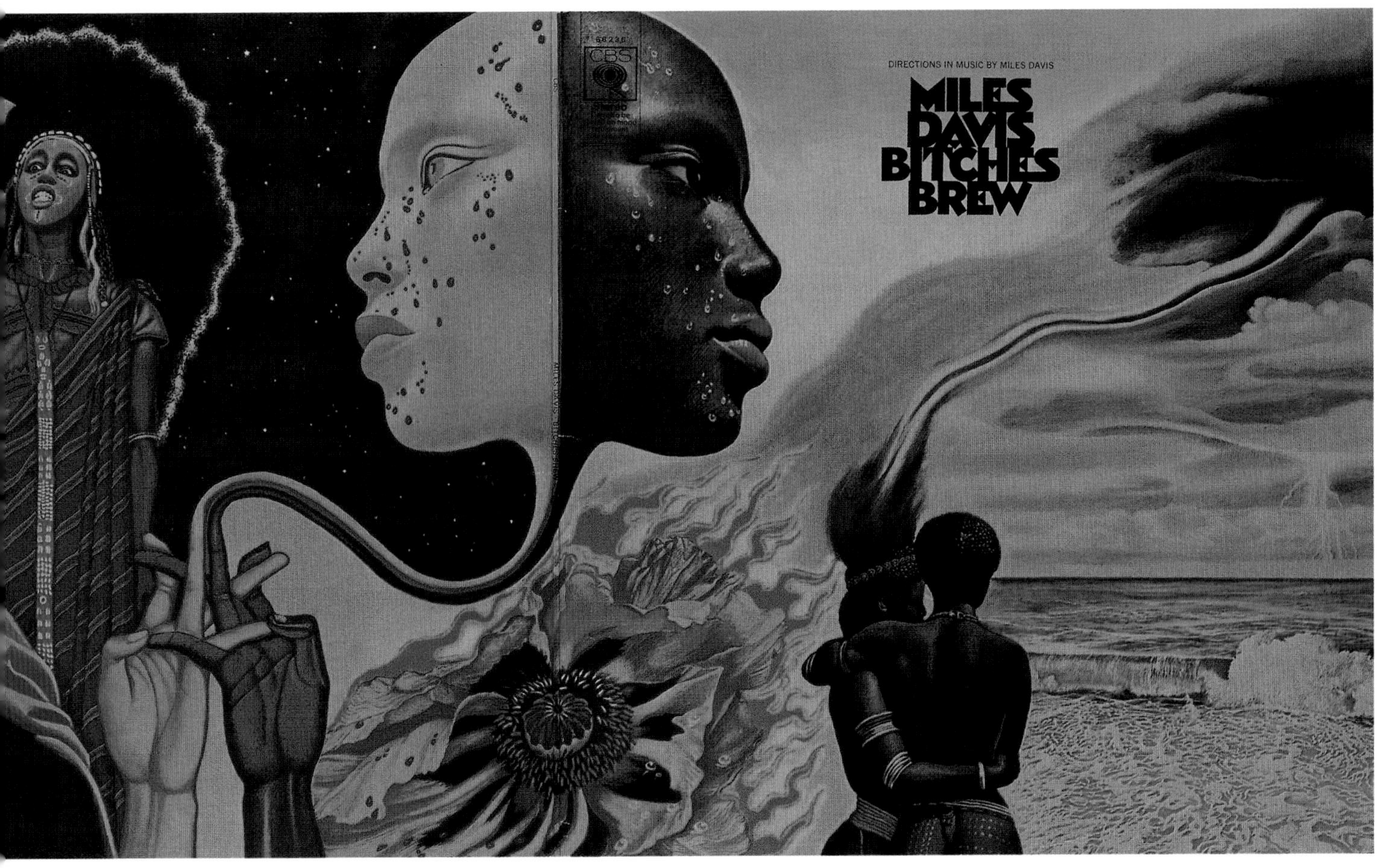
DIRECTIONS IN MUSIC BY MILES DAVIS
MILES
DAVIS
BITCHES
BREW
CBS

-1995

FORECAST UNSETTLED

Keyboard players Joe Zawinul and Chick Corea are poised to take American jazz into a new electronic realm. In the UK, Ian Carr and Tony Oxley continue the surge of creative energy already initiated by John McLaughlin.

Above Albert Ayler, whose body was discovered in a New York waterway in November 1970. Widely misunderstood, his music attempted to unite traditional New Orleans elements with progressive avant-garde techniques.

Jazz Events

January
British trumpeter Ian Carr records his first album, *Electric Rock,* with his jazz-rock group Nucleus in London. They go on to win a major prize at the Montreux Jazz Festival this year, as well as appearing at the festival in Newport.

7 February
British drummer Tony Oxley records *Four Compositions for Sextet* in London.

February–June
The Art Ensemble of Chicago undertakes a series of recording sessions in Paris.

March
Miles Davis (• p. 217) is arrested when a police officer attempting to move him away from a restricted parking zone notices he is carrying brass knuckles for protection. He spends a night in a police cell and is fined for not possessing a vehicle registration.

7 April
Chick Corea's trio records *The Song of Singing* for Blue Note, an eclectic album that includes a satisfying and musical experiment with ATONALITY.

April
Davis's double album *Bitches Brew* (• pp. 172–73) is released. It meets with phenomenal commercial success, and initiates jazz-rock FUSION as the jazz style of the future. Davis begins work on his movie score to the boxing epic *Jack Johnson*.

11 May
Duke Ellington's celebrated alto saxophonist Johnny Hodges dies, New York.

25 June
Duke Ellington's ballet *The River* is performed by the American Ballet Theater at the State Theater, New York.

June
Keith Jarrett (• p. 185) joins Miles Davis's group, playing electric organ.

Summer
Bill Evans (• p. 157) plays at the Kongsberg Jazz Festival, Norway.

23–23 September
Soprano and tenor saxophonist Jan Garbarek records *Afric Pepperbird* in Oslo for ECM (• p. 177). He visits the USA with the aid of a Norwegian government grant this year.

October
Chick Corea and Dave Holland quit Miles Davis, later forming the group Circle with drummer Barry Altschul and saxophonist Anthony Braxton.
• Thelonious Monk (• p. 155) appears in Tokyo.

24 November
Duke Ellington Day is proclaimed in New Mexico.

25 November
Saxophonist Albert Ayler's body is recovered from New York's East River after he had been missing for three weeks. Whether his drowning was self-inflicted or an act of homicide is never established.

November
Charles Mingus and Sun Ra record in Berlin.

- Joshua Rifkin records Scott Joplin's piano RAGS for the Nonesuch label.
- Max Roach refuses to record in the USA as a protest against exploitation of musicians. His protest lasts until 1976.
- Poet and *Daily Telegraph* jazz critic Philip Larkin publishes his collected criticism in London under the title *All What Jazz: A Record Diary, 1961–68.*

WEATHER REPORT

The astonishing speed with which jazz styles were changing as the new decade began was aptly summarized by the name of a new fusion group founded in December 1970: Weather Report. The band was the brainchild of Austrian-born keyboard player Joe Zawinul and saxophonist Wayne Shorter, both of whom had served as SIDEMEN to Miles Davis during his recent stylistic watershed (• p. 171). Weather Report soon became one of the most influential groups in the history of jazz. It survived until 1986, producing on average one album per year on the Columbia label (which began reissuing its work on CD in 1990). During the band's sixteen-year career, its members included some of the most significant younger talents of the fusion boom, notably Jaco Pastorius (electric bass) and drummers Alex Acuña, Steve Gadd, and Peter Erskine.

Like Chick Corea in his work with Return to Forever, Zawinul's fusion style promoted infectious dance rhythms and enticing melodies that were a sharp contrast to the provocative and adventurous approach taken by Davis in *Bitches Brew*. Zawinul's expertise with SYNTHESIZERS resulted in fresh and sophisticated musical textures, and in its first two years the band began to absorb significant rock influences (although Zawinul later objected to the comparison, commenting that rhythm 'n' blues had a more potent impact on his work). The album *Heavy Weather* scored a major success in 1976, realizing phenomenal sales that were only eclipsed by The Manhattan Transfer's subsequent pop vocalization of the album's most famous track, "Birdland."

Among Weather Report's more impressive achievements was the ability to synthesize diverse musical elements into a coherent and immediately recognizable style, presenting its music in a commercially viable format without compromising artistic standards. The striking sleeve designs of their LPs may have been closer to the pop market than to those of mainstream jazz records, but the group could just as happily work in an avant-garde idiom as in a more superficially "popular" style. Snatches of banal yet catchy melodies were disrupted by a skillful application of unpredictable rhythms and unexpected harmonies so that themes always sounded fresh and original, even where the individual ingredients might be clichéd. Subtle and sensitive use of electronic tones, real-life sound effects, and free IMPROVISATION were amalgamated with sometimes strictly pre-composed structures to create music that appealed (like all great music) to both heart and mind.

World Events

2 February
Death of Bertrand Russell

25 February
Death of Mark Rothko

April
Apollo 13 crew stranded in space

30 April
US Army in Cambodia

18 September
Jimi Hendrix dies from drug overdose

4 October
Janis Joplin dies from drug overdose

- Columbia introduces quadrophonic discs
- Glenda Jackson wins Best Actress Oscar for Ken Russell's *Women in Love*

Above Weather Report's best-selling album *Heavy Weather* (1976) spawned a pop hit by The Manhattan Transfer.

Top left Wayne Shorter coled Weather Report with Joe Zawinul, and developed an ethereal tone on soprano saxophone that exerted a major influence on fusion players.

1971

Louis Armstrong dies one month before his seventieth birthday and is internationally mourned. Jazz-rock fusion gathers momentum with the music of Weather Report and the Mahavishnu Orchestra.

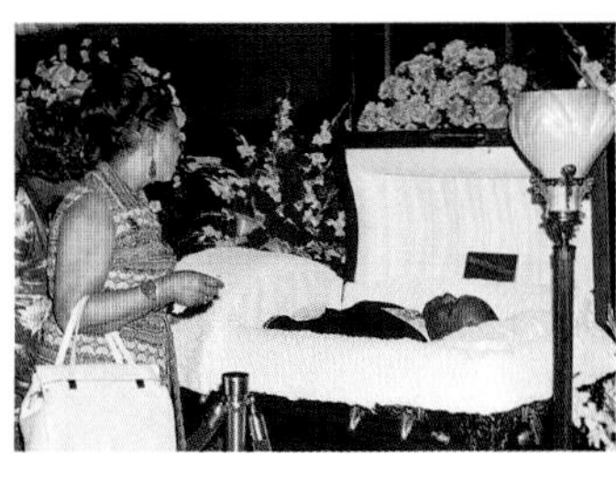

Above Louis Armstrong lying in state in the summer of 1971.

DEATH OF A LEGEND

Jazz Events

January
British tenor saxophonist Tony Coe (the performer of Henry Mancini's famous *Pink Panther* theme) records with compatriot Brian Lemon's piano trio in London.

16–17 February
Joe Zawinul's new FUSION group Weather Report (• p. 175) records *Orange Lady* in New York.

21 February
Circle (• p. 174) tours to Paris, where the quartet's concert is recorded by ECM.

February
Anthony Braxton records in London.

12 April
Pianist Wynton Kelly dies, Toronto.

21–22 April
Chick Corea (• p. 179) records two sets of *Piano Improvisations* in Oslo for ECM.

12 June
Vibraphonist Gary Burton records in Tokyo. This year he also collaborates with Keith Jarrett (• p. 185).

6 July
Louis Armstrong dies, New York. Three weeks later, his first wife, Lil Hardin Armstrong (• p. 48), dies of a heart attack.

July
Miles Davis plays four concerts to a sparse audience in New York, during a difficult year in which he is taken to court for breach of contract, pursued by tax inspectors, and served with an $11,000 bill for repairs to his Lamborghini (one of his several prized sports cars).

14 August
John McLaughlin's newly formed Mahavishnu Orchestra records *The Inner Mounting Flame* in New York.

September
Duke Ellington (• p. 182) visits the Soviet Union for a five-week tour of major cities. On the way home in **October**, his orchestra visits the UK, appearing in Bristol and Birmingham.

November
Thelonious Monk (• p. 155) records extensively in London, where Miles Davis appears at the Royal Festival Hall.

December
Sun Ra's Arkestra is on tour in Cairo.

- Jack DeJohnette and Keith Jarrett quit Miles Davis.
- Charles Mingus (• p. 190) publishes his autobiography, *Beneath the Underdog*.

"[Armstrong's] style of improvisation would seem to have combined the highest reaches of instrumental virtuosity with the most tensely disciplined melodic structure and the most spontaneous emotional expression, all of which in one man you must admit to be pretty rare."
Virgil Thomson, 1981

Above left One year before his death, "Satchmo" was pictured on the steps of his home in Queens, Long Island. His impromptu music-making with black youngsters recalled images of his own humble musical beginnings at the New Orleans Colored Waifs' Home (• p. 28).

ECM AND THE NEW EUROPEAN JAZZ

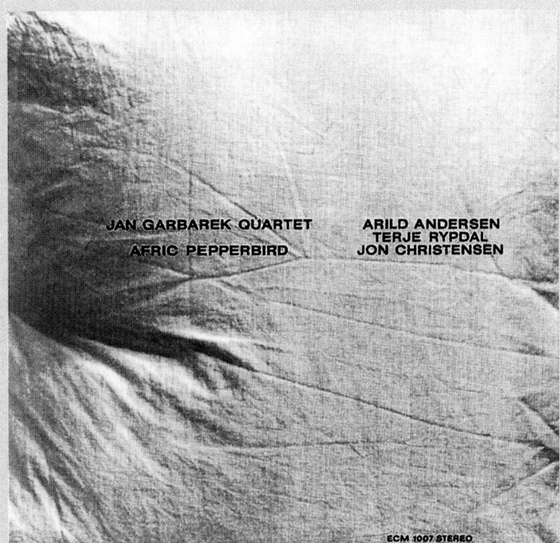

JAN GARBAREK QUARTET
AFRIC PEPPERBIRD
ARILD ANDERSEN
TERJE RYPDAL
JON CHRISTENSEN
ECM 1007 STEREO

Above right Jan Garbarek's album *Afric Pepperbird,* recorded with an all-Norwegian quartet, was the first release on Manfred Eicher's ECM label in 1970.

"Just trying to emulate the great American innovators was not enough. It's true, they lived completely different lives. My thinking was that the blues provided roots for those innovations, but we also have our own blues equivalents, our own folk music. I later discovered many similarities with the American blues, because in fact all folk musics are related. I had a feeling in the '70s that jazz's image had become too cluttered. It was developed to a point where everybody was a soloist, standing side by side, but not necessarily playing together . . . It was too complicated. I wanted some clarity."

Jan Garbarek, in an interview published in 1995 to celebrate his 1993 recording *Twelve Moons* (ECM's 500th issue)

As several leading members of the American avant-garde migrated to Europe in the late 1960s, European musicians grew more confident in developing a new brand of jazz that departed from the hegemony of orthodox American styles. One of the most enduring borne on this new wave of independence was that of the Edition of Contemporary Music, a record label established in Cologne by bassist Manfred Eicher in 1969. Initially linked to the FREE JAZZ movement, ECM seduced many cutting-edge American musicians into its studios during the 1970s, including pianists Keith Jarrett and Chick Corea, vibraphonist Gary Burton, and guitarist Pat Metheny (• p. 199).

The unique house sound cultivated by ECM was the first European jazz style to have had a perceptible influence on the development of American jazz. Beginning with an unlikely but artistically successful amalgamation of free jazz and jazz-rock fusion, ECM went on to encourage ACOUSTIC recordings at a time when electronic techniques prevailed. More important, at least as far as European musicians were concerned, was the label's commitment to an innovative mixture of jazz-rock and folk music, which continued to produce some of the freshest sounds in jazz into the next century.

The linchpin of ECM's jazz-folk ventures was the Norwegian saxophonist Jan Garbarek, who used plaintive and sometimes plangent tones on saxophone to evoke the atmosphere of Scandinavian landscapes in prolonged modal IMPROVISATIONS. Varied and equally striking soundscapes were created by German bassist Eberhard Weber, who, together with his pianist Rainer Brüninghaus, often collaborated on the label with Garbarek in the 1980s. Pat Metheny's early albums with ECM (1975–84) tapped into reminiscences of American country music, and provided a sound basis for his later explorations of free jazz and jazz-rock.

World Events

6 April
Death of Igor Stravinsky

July
Color television relay of US astronauts driving on moon's surface

26 December
US aircraft bomb North Vietnam

- Stanley Kubrick's film *A Clockwork Orange* withdrawn in UK
- Andy Warhol exhibition at Tate Gallery, London

Jazz critic Martin Williams reviews Charles Mingus's autobiography and concludes:

"Beneath the armor of destructive (if thoroughly understandable) self-pity, there is a man who seems compelled to ask the world to hurt and misuse him, and who therefore shows the world his (and its) shadow side. And beneath that man is a being in torment who protests his accomplishments in music and his conflicting heritage as an American mulatto but who seems unable really to believe in them or to take confidence in them or take heart from them, and accept his place as an American musician. The Gods have indeed looked with favor upon those complex and gifted men who, like Ellington, discover, accept, and live out their destinies from the beginning."

THE OLD AND THE NEW

Scott Joplin's opera *Treemonisha* (1911–15) receives a long overdue professional performance, while the frontiers of jazz-rock fusion are broadened by the continuing work of Chick Corea and Joe Zawinul.

Jazz Events

January
Joe Zawinul's Weather Report (• p. 175) records the album *I Sing the Body Electric*.

2–3 February
Chick Corea records his debut album with FUSION group Return to Forever.

4 February
Charles Mingus (• p. 190) appears at the Philharmonic Hall, New York.

19 February
HARD-BOP trumpeter Lee Morgan is shot dead at Slug's jazz club, New York, by his former mistress Helen More.

June
Miles Davis (• p. 217) records *On the Corner.*

17 July
Beginning of Duke Ellington Week in Wisconsin. Ellington tours the Far East this year.

October
Miles Davis is involved in an automobile accident that leaves him with both legs broken.

- Thelonious Monk begins a ten-year period of retirement at the home of jazz patron Baroness Nica de Koenigswarter (• p. 137).
- Saxophonist Ornette Coleman's *Skies of America* for jazz quartet and orchestra is performed by the London Symphony Orchestra.
- Scott Joplin's opera *Treemonisha* (• p. 21) receives its first professional performance at the Memorial Arts Center, Atlanta.
- Billie Holiday's autobiography *Lady Sings the Blues* (ghostwritten by William Dufty in 1956) is made into a film by director Sidney Fury, with Diana Ross starring as Holiday.
- John McLaughlin records *Birds of Fire* and *Love Devotion Surrender* with his Mahavishnu Orchestra.

Above left Chick Corea, who typified the new stylistic versatility of jazz musicians in the 1970s.

Above British-born guitarist John McLaughlin, who moved to New York in 1969 and made a vital contribution to the emerging fusion movement.

World Events

30 January
British troops kill thirteen in Northern Ireland shootings

17 February
UK decides to join European Economic Community

May
Strategic Arms Limitations Treaty (SALT) limits US and Soviet nuclear weapons

28 May
Death of Duke of Windsor (formerly Edward VIII)

5 September
Eleven Israelis murdered by Arab terrorists at Munich Olympics

November
Final US bombing campaign against North Vietnam

• Andrew Lloyd Webber's rock opera *Jesus Christ Superstar*

CHICK COREA AND RETURN TO FOREVER

The stylistic implications of Miles Davis's pioneering fusion album *Bitches Brew* (• pp. 172–73) were later fully explored by two keyboard players featured on that release: Joe Zawinul, who founded Weather Report in 1970, and Chick Corea. Already established as a virtuoso ACOUSTIC pianist with a wide-ranging approach before his encounter with Davis, Corea became renowned in the early 1970s not only as a leading exponent of electronic keyboards, but also as the founder of the fusion group Return to Forever in 1972. The band went through several personnel changes during the rest of the decade, moving from a Latin-tinged flavor in the earlier years to a heavier rock style. Stalwart members included Stanley Clarke (electric bass), Al Di Meola (electric guitar), and Lenny White (drums) – performers whose stunning virtuosity was a perfect match for Corea's own technical dexterity. The group's success coincided with Corea's deep involvement in L. Ron Hubbard's cult of Scientology, which promotes the concept of clearing away the mental constraints that prevent direct communication.

Corea has always been a resourceful composer, and the music he created with Return to Forever was distinguished by an entirely characteristic concern for structural variety. As a result, the band's achievements are some of the most cogent and enduring of the fusion era. Its POLYTONAL harmonies and intricately woven textures reflect an intellectual approach to jazz composition quite unlike Davis's intuitive originality, and its material was sufficiently memorable for several pieces to become STANDARDS in their own right.

Corea played a number of electronic keyboard instruments, including the Fender Rhodes ELECTRIC PIANO (with its distinctive metallic timbre that today sounds dated) and a variety of SYNTHESIZERS (• p. 193). Yet he continued to perform on a conventional acoustic piano and integrated the instrument into an otherwise electronic rock-influenced context. After Return to Forever disbanded in 1980, Corea returned once more to the reputable territory of acoustic jazz in a succession of fine trio and quartet sessions, and appeared alongside performers of the stature of Herbie Hancock (• p. 201) and Gary Burton. In the mid-1980s he recorded classical music and composed a Piano Concerto, but he then inspired a fusion revival with his new Elektric Band (• p. 204), which signed with the popular GRP label (• p. 214).

"What I am striving for is incorporating the discipline and beauty of the symphony orchestra and classical composers – the subtlety and beauty of harmony, melody, and form – with the looseness and rhythmic dancing quality of jazz and more folky musics."

Chick Corea, interviewed in *Down Beat*, 1974

Above left Return to Forever's album *No Mystery* (1975) featured compositions by all members of the group, and tempered their formerly aggressive rock sonorities with the addition of Corea's delicate acoustic piano.

1973–74

Herbie Hancock scores a major fusion success with *Headhunters*. Free jazz expands in Europe, and the deaths of Ben Webster and Duke Ellington mark the end of a mainstream era.

HEADHUNTERS

Above Herbie Hancock's album *Headhunters* included the track "Chameleon," which became a chart hit.

Right Willie "The Lion" Smith playing at the Newport Jazz Festival in 1971, two years before his death. He still sports the trademark hat and cigar of the 1920s stride pianists.

Jazz Events

1973

23 January
Trombonist Kid Ory dies, Honolulu.

January
Bill Evans (• p. 157) performs in Tokyo, where Cecil Taylor and Sarah Vaughan appear later this year.

23 February
Miles Davis is arrested at his home for possessing cocaine and an unlicensed handgun, and is later fined $1,000. In this year, the trumpeter's already wide musical horizons broaden further through a growing interest in the avant-garde music of Karlheinz Stockhausen.

18 April
STRIDE pianist Willie "The Lion" Smith dies, New York.

Summer
Gil Evans, moving on from his earlier post-Ellington style of pre-composed band music (• p. 120), joins the electronic bandwagon with his album *Svengali*.

20 September
Tenor saxophonist Ben Webster dies in Amsterdam, two weeks after appearing at his last GIG.

16 October
Drummer Gene Krupa dies, Yonkers, New York.

24 October
Duke Ellington's *Third Sacred Concert* ("The Majesty of God") is performed at Westminster Abbey, London. His autobiography, *Music is My Mistress*, is published this year.

27–28 November
Jan Garbarek records his version of Jim Pepper's *Witchi-Tai-To* in Oslo for ECM (• p. 177).

31 December
John McLaughlin's first Mahavishnu Orchestra disbands after recording the album *Between Nothingness and Eternity*.

December
In Los Angeles, Joe Pass records his solo-guitar album *Virtuoso*, the first disc to be issued by the new Pablo label established by Norman Granz (• p. 107).
• German bassist Eberhard Weber records his album *The Colours of Chloë* for ECM, with a group featuring pianist Rainer Brüninghaus.

- Herbie Hancock (• p. 201) records his jazz-rock album *Headhunters* in San Francisco with multi-instrumentalist Bennie Maupin, bassist Paul Jackson, drummer Harvey Mason, and percussionist Bill Summers. Achieving widespread popularity through the use of down-to-earth funky elements, it immediately breaks all sales records for jazz.
- The comedy thriller *The Sting*, starring Robert Redford and Paul Newman, is a smash hit at the box office, and promotes wider public awareness of the RAGTIME music of Scott Joplin by using the composer's piano rags in its soundtrack. The movie's score is arranged by Marvin Hamlisch and Gunther Schuller, who goes on to reconstruct ragtime arrangements from *The Red Back Book* (1915), which he performs with the New England Conservatory Ragtime Ensemble.
- Dizzy Gillespie (• p. 219) arranges a comeback appearance for Chet Baker (• p. 210) after a temporary retirement.

JOPLIN TRIUMPHANT

By the end of the 1960s, the ancient ragtime art of Scott Joplin (• p. 21) seemed a world away from the social and stylistic preoccupations of contemporary jazz. In one of the most astounding turnarounds in the history of music, ragtime found itself propelled back into the limelight during the early 1970s, and even entered the pop charts.

Three factors created this entirely unpredictable situation. One influence was Joplin's opera *Treemonisha*, which had its first professional performance in 1972 (• p. 178) and won its composer a posthumous Pulitzer Prize when recorded four years later. A second ragtime-related success was the Oscar-winning movie *The Sting,* which made an overnight hit of Joplin's ragtime two-step *The Entertainer* in 1973. Lastly, pianist Joshua Rifkin began a series of "authentic" recordings of ragtime pieces, reconstructing the restrained, unadorned manner of presentation Joplin had ceaselessly championed. By treating the music with a musicological respect normally reserved for the work of classical composers, Rifkin's performances seemed to bestow on Joplin's legacy that aura of classicism for which America's first great black composer had always yearned.

Right Made famous once again in the 1970s by the movie *The Sting* (above), Joplin's *The Entertainer* was in fact an anachronism in this context: the film was set in the 1930s when old-fashioned ragtime had sunk into virtual oblivion.

World Events

1973

1 January
UK becomes full member of European Economic Community

27 January
End of Vietnam War

26 March
Death of Noël Coward

8 April
Death of Pablo Picasso

May
Watergate scandal, USA

28 September
Death of W. H. Auden

20 October
Sydney Opera House opens

- Peter Schaffer's play *Equus*

THE ELLINGTON PHENOMENON

Duke Ellington's death in 1974 at the age of seventy-five robbed the jazz world of arguably its greatest talent. Ellington was universally praised for creating memorable pieces in which complex techniques assimilated from classical music were inextricably fused with spontaneous jazz elements. In doing so he bridged the gap between nightclub and concert hall, and has been regarded by many commentators as the finest American composer of all.

After departing from the Cotton Club (• p. 63), Ellington's band continued to flourish, thanks to its outstanding and unusually stable membership. In the 1930s, Ellington began to experiment with extended pieces and was the first jazz composer to attempt to break away from the structural limitations imposed by 78rpm discs (which could only accommodate a little over three minutes of music on each side). "Reminiscing in Tempo" (1935), for example, occupied all four sides of two discs, and his large-scale "Diminuendo and Crescendo in Blue" sounded so avant-garde in 1937 that it only became popular nearly twenty years later (• p. 138).

His inspiration never flagging, Ellington created a steady stream of popular compositions showcasing the talents of valve-trombonist Juan Tizol, trumpeter Cootie Williams, saxophonists Ben Webster and Harry Carney, and (from 1939) the highly skilled arranger Billy Strayhorn. Strayhorn composed numerous pieces for the Ellington band, including its signature tune "Take the 'A' Train" (1941), and was as important as its leader to its continuing success story until his death in 1967.

Ellington's ambitious extended jazz works had meanwhile crystallized in a series of performances at Carnegie Hall, commencing with *Black, Brown, and Beige* in 1943 (• p. 104), which met with a mixed critical reception. Avoiding direct confrontation with the manifold artistic and technical difficulties involved in composing successful extended structures, his later large-scale ventures were invariably couched in the form of the suite (a succession of individual movements linked by common subject matter or similar musical material), for which the new medium of the long-playing disc was ideally suited. Among the most notable examples to have originated in live performances were the three "Sacred Concerts" (1965, 1968, and 1973), and the *Far East Suite* (1966), inspired by Ellington's worldwide travels to exotic countries on behalf of the US State Department (• p. 161).

In 1973 Ellington published his autobiography, *Music is My Mistress*. His book touchingly reminisces about the individual players whose talents and loyalty did much to secure the band its consistent success. It also reveals two preoccupations that greatly affected Ellington's character, his religious fervor and his obsession with middle-class respectability, which resulted in a sometimes embarrassing deference to authority figures, notably the British monarchy (• p. 142). Yet these attributes may have been partly responsible for the refreshingly clean image of the Ellington orchestra, which survived the heroin-drenched bop era with its reputation intact, while still responding artistically to the important stylistic developments introduced at the time.

After Ellington's death, the leadership of the band passed to his son Mercer, an accomplished trumpeter in his own right who composed the band's hit tune "Things Ain't What They Used to Be" in 1941. He took the orchestra to Europe in 1975 and 1977, and recorded spirited performances on various labels in the 1980s, including GRP (• p. 214). While not quite catching the unique sound quality of the legendary Ellingtonians of previous decades, digital technology has nonetheless imbued the Duke's perennial masterpieces with renewed vitality.

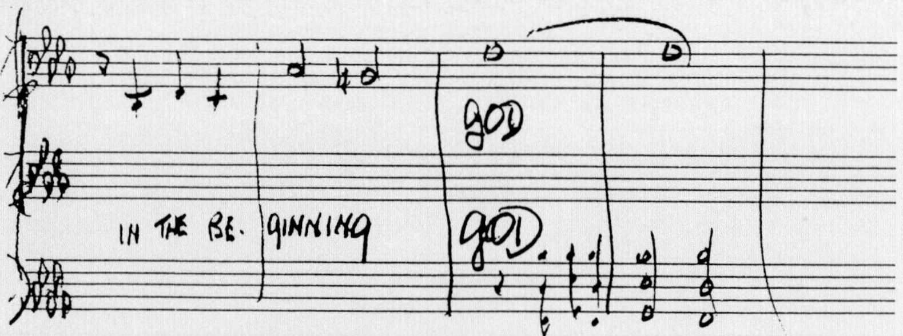

"In music, as you develop a theme or musical idea, there are many points at which direction must be decided, and any time I was in the throes of debate with myself, harmonically or melodically, I would turn to Billy Strayhorn. We would talk, and the whole world would come into focus . . . He was not, as he was often referred to by many, my alter ego. Billy Strayhorn was my right arm, my left arm, all the eyes in the back of my head, my brainwaves in his head, and his in mine."

Duke Ellington, 1973

Above The principal theme of Ellington's *First Sacred Concert*, in the hand of its composer.

Far left The elder statesman of jazz: Duke Ellington toward the end of his distinguished career.

Jazz Events

1974

February
Soprano saxophonist Steve Lacy performs in Paris, appearing later in the year in Italy and the Netherlands.

March
Thad Jones and Mel Lewis take their big band (• p. 162) to Tokyo.

April
The Akiyoshi–Tabackin big band records in Los Angeles. Formed in Hollywood the previous year by pianist Toshiko Akiyoshi and her second husband, saxophonist Lew Tabackin, the group forges a reputation for sophisticated arrangements and vivid instrumental colorings.
• Jan Garbarek and Keith Jarrett (• p. 185) record together in Norway.

14 May
Paul Gonsalves (• p. 138) dies, London.

24 May
Duke Ellington dies, New York.

29 May
Anthony Braxton performs in Denmark, in a busy year in which he also visits London and Toronto.

May
John McLaughlin reforms an eleven-strong Mahavishnu Orchestra.

4 July
Stephane Grappelli (• p. 75) and Earl Hines (• p. 125) perform together in London.

August
Herbie Hancock records the soundtrack to Michael Winner's violent movie *Death Wish*, starring Charles Bronson.

Summer
Chick Corea and Return to Forever (• p. 179) record their FUSION album, *Where Have I Known You Before?*

8 October
Baritone saxophonist Harry Carney dies, New York.

October
Dutch saxophonist Willem Breuker records with his unorthodox Kollektief orchestra; he is soon regarded as one of the leading lights of the European avant-garde.

25 November
The Modern Jazz Quartet (• p. 129) gives a final concert at New York's Lincoln Center before disbanding after over twenty years together, as Milt Jackson decides to pursue his own career. The group reforms in 1981 (• p. 196).

November
Oscar Peterson (• p. 163) visits the Soviet Union.

8 December
Jazz critic Hugues Panassié (• p. 80) dies, Montauban, France.

- Count Basie (• p. 87) and his band make an amusing cameo appearance in Mel Brooks's comedy Western, *Blazing Saddles*.
- German author Ekkehard Jost publishes his book *Free Jazz* in Graz.

World Events

1974

13 February
Alexander Solzhenitsyn exiled by USSR

20 July
Turkish forces invade Cyprus

8 August
President Nixon resigns, USA

- David Hockney's paintings exhibited in Paris
- Tom Stoppard's play *Travesties*
- Sidney Lumet's film *Murder on the Orient Express*

Above Willem Breuker, whose eclectic musical style cultivated a bizarre mix of elements drawn from folk traditions and avant-garde free jazz.

DAVIS BOWS OUT

Miles Davis's poor health forces him into retirement, while the fusion boom he initiated continues to flourish. Scott Joplin's posthumous reputation is strengthened by triumphant stagings of his opera in the US.

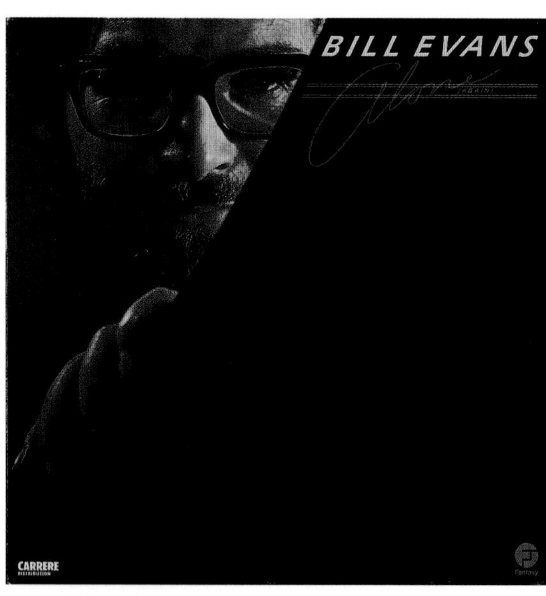

Above A master of sophisticated keyboard textures and musical sensitivity, Bill Evans continued to demonstrate the virtues of acoustic jazz piano in the midst of a rock-tinged decade.

Jazz Events

24 January
Keith Jarrett makes a recording of a solo concert in Cologne for ECM (right).

January
Tenor saxophonist Michael Brecker and his trumpeter brother Randy record together in New York.
• Chick Corea and Return to Forever (• p. 179) record *No Mystery*.

February
Miles Davis (• p. 217) appears in Japan, in spite of increasing ill health.

23 May
Scott Joplin's opera *Treemonisha* (• p. 21) is staged in Houston under the direction of Gunther Schuller. According to *The New York Times,* "Nobody applauded, they just yelled. Some even lost control and dashed onto the stage to join in." The work is equally successful when it opens on Broadway.

June
Paul Desmond and Dave Brubeck (• p. 186) join forces on board the *SS Rotterdam,* recording for BBC television.

Spring
French violinist Jean-Luc Ponty quits John McLaughlin's Mahavishnu Orchestra over a royalty dispute.

June–July
The Montreux Jazz Festival continues to flourish as a center for excellence in jazz, hosting performances by Bill Evans, Dizzy Gillespie, Milt Jackson, Joe Pass, Oscar Peterson, Archie Shepp, and Japanese saxophonist Sadao Watanabe.

July
Miles Davis plays at the Newport Jazz Festival and, following a performance in Central Park in **August**, decides to retire. He contracts pneumonia and has a hip operation in **December**, and does not play in public for five years.

8 August
Saxophonist Julian "Cannonball" Adderley dies, aged forty-six, in Gary, Indiana.

September
Eberhard Weber's group Colours records his richly textured album *Yellow Fields* for ECM.

December
Bill Evans records his solo album *Alone (Again)* on the West Coast.
• Guitarist Pat Metheny (• p. 199) records his first album *Bright Size Life* for ECM, supported by bassist Jaco Pastorius and drummer Bob Moses.

- Fourteen-year-old trumpet virtuoso Wynton Marsalis (• p. 197) performs Haydn's Trumpet Concerto with the New Orleans Symphony Orchestra.
- Alfred Hitchcock's former composer, Bernard Herrmann, writes a moody jazz score for Martin Scorsese's *Taxi Driver,* starring Robert De Niro. The theme is performed on the soundtrack by alto saxophonist Ronny Lang.

JARRETT IN COLOGNE

The ECM label (• p. 177) received a major boost in 1975 when its recording of pianist Keith Jarrett's live solo concert in Cologne became a best-seller; it has now sold well over three million copies. The success of his first ECM album, *Facing You* (1971), spawned an eighteen-concert tour of Europe in 1973. As a result of that achievement, Jarrett began a series of solo concerts in which he improvised colossal and richly varied extended pieces that demonstrated his absorption of jazz, classical, rock, and country influences. Recordings of these performances at Bremen and Lausanne were released by ECM on a triple-LP set that was singled out as the best issue of 1974 by both *Down Beat* and *The New York Times*.

Jarrett's decision to concentrate on ACOUSTIC piano performances in the midst of the FUSION boom's obsession with electronics may, in retrospect, be viewed as one of the most tenacious and significant musical gestures of the decade. In dividing his time between work in Europe and the USA, he also typified the increasingly global nature of modern jazz. Since making his name in the 1970s, Jarrett has devoted his considerable energies to several clearly defined areas of activity: recordings of classical music (notably works by Johann Sebastian Bach in 1988 and Shostakovich in 1992); the composition of sometimes large-scale pieces for the concert hall; further extended solo IMPROVISATIONS on the Cologne model (in Germany in 1981, Paris in 1988, and London and Vienna in 1991); and a reexploration of jazz STANDARDS with a trio featuring Gary Peacock (bass) and Jack DeJohnette (drums). His output extended to collaborations with Jan Garbarek (• p. 192), whose preoccupations with economy of musical material and haunting tones were well in accord with Jarrett's own thinking.

An unfortunate characteristic of Jarrett's performances is his tendency to sing along as he plays. With some pianists, notably Oscar Peterson (• p. 163), this habit can be infectiously high-spirited. But in the case of Jarrett, his wheedling and strained voice sometimes constitutes a serious distraction from the sensitive and musical nature of his keyboard playing, as in his trio's otherwise fine tribute to Miles Davis, *Bye Bye Blackbird* (ECM, 1991).

"There was once a joke that in the year 2045 someone brought out a 'Best of Keith Jarrett' set in the currently fashionable laser-hologram/ virtual-reality format. It consisted of eighty-seven LHVR diskettes. (There was an audiophile vinyl option, but you needed your own truck to take it home.)"

Richard Cook and Brian Morton, 1994

Left Keith Jarrett relaxes in the New York studios of Atlantic Records in 1971 under the watchful eye of his producer, George Avakian.

World Events

21 May
Barbara Hepworth killed in house fire, Cornwall, UK

17 April
Khmer Rouge takes control in Cambodia

April
North Vietnam invades South Vietnam; Saigon evacuated by US

- Steven Spielberg's blockbuster *Jaws*

CONSOLIDATION

In the wake of the fusion boom of the early 1970s, performers explore varied new musical directions and some return to earlier styles for inspiration.

Above Paul Desmond (left) and Dave Brubeck, whose popular quartet celebrated its twenty-fifth anniversary in 1976.

Jazz Events

1976

28 January
Ray Nance, former violinist and trumpeter with Duke Ellington (• p. 101), dies in New York.

10 March
Dave Brubeck celebrates the twenty-fifth anniversary of the formation of his quartet in a Michigan reunion with Paul Desmond (alto saxophone), Gene Wright (bass), and Joe Morello (drums).

June
The Newport Jazz Festival hosts what is destined to be the last public performance by Thelonious Monk (• p. 155). Also at the Festival, Herbie Hancock (• p. 201) records live on **29 June** with his group VSOP.

25 July
Paul Bley appears in Japan and records live. Other artists visiting Japan this year include Keith Jarrett, Duke Jordan, Johnny Griffin, Milt Jackson, Hank Jones, and Jim Hall.

July
John McLaughlin disbands his second Mahavishnu Orchestra.

August–September
Charles Mingus on tour in Europe.

9 September
The Thad Jones–Mel Lewis big band plays in Munich.

Above Born in Manchuria, pianist Toshiko Akiyoshi made her name in Japan in the early 1950s during the postwar boom in the Japanese jazz scene. After moving to the USA, she was active on both the West and East Coasts.

JAPAN

Jazz was initially slow to develop in Japan, a country that, until the Meiji Restoration of 1868, had been all but impervious to foreign cultural influences. Some early Western performers had spread the music to limited regions of Southeast Asia during the Swing Era, but with the outbreak of World War II the Japanese authorities banned jazz completely with a totalitarian censorship directly analogous to the prohibitions in Nazi Germany (• p. 81) and the Soviet Union (• p. 207). After the cessation of global hostilities in 1945, however, a surge in imported American influences resulted in a sudden boom in indigenous Japanese jazz and a growing enthusiasm for the bop style.

By the early 1950s, the Hot Club of Japan (founded in 1946) had begun to flourish, and the climate was ripe for American performers to undertake high-profile tours to locations in Tokyo and Osaka. Many such visits were sponsored by Norman Granz's "Jazz at the Philharmonic" (• p. 107) from 1953 onwards, and tours by artists of the stature of Miles Davis, John Coltrane, and Art Blakey had become commonplace in the mid-1960s. By the 1970s, Japanese jazz had acquired an exciting international flavor, and the nation's capital frequently provided a meeting place for the finest performers in the world. In the 1980s and 1990s, enterprising Japanese record companies embarked on substantial programs of reissuing classic American recordings, which stimulated the growth of similar efforts in Europe and the United States.

Many Japanese performers forged impressive reputations for themselves in the West, but none more successfully than pianist Toshiko Akiyoshi. A protégée of Oscar Peterson, Akiyoshi emigrated to the US in 1956 to study at Berklee College of Music in Boston. She worked with Charles Mingus in the early 1960s, and by the early 1970s had become internationally renowned as one of the finest and most sophisticated big-band arrangers in the business. Saxophonist Sadao Watanabe, who assumed the leadership of Akiyoshi's quartet when she emigrated and who duly followed her to Berklee in 1962, also achieved world acclaim, and he is equally at home in post-bop and jazz-rock FUSION idioms. The latter at first proved to be more successful in Japan than FREE JAZZ, which was pursued more actively by expatriate Japanese performers working in Europe, but today Japan has a flourishing free-jazz scene.

World Events

1976

20 July
Viking space probe transmits pictures from Mars

25 July
Philip Glass's minimalist opera *Einstein on the Beach* premieres in Avignon, France

2 November
Jimmy Carter becomes the first Southerner to be elected US President since the Civil War

4 December
Death of Benjamin Britten

- National Theatre opens, London
- Alex Haley's novel *Roots*
- US bicentennial celebrations

Jazz Events

15 September
Montmartre Jazzhus opens in Copenhagen (• p. 169).

October
Lee Konitz records with a nonet that continues to reflect the influence of the COOL sound originally pioneered by Miles Davis and Gil Evans (• p. 121). This year Konitz makes two visits to London and an appearance in Rome.

December
Ornette Coleman plays in Paris. The saxophonist's comeback is further celebrated this month with the album *Dancing in Your Time,* revealing an absorption of FUSION influences in the use of electric guitars by his new group, Prime Time.

- Weather Report records their best-selling Columbia albums, *Black Market* and *Heavy Weather* (• p. 175).
- Scott Joplin receives a posthumous Pulitzer Prize as his opera *Treemonisha* is recorded for the first time.

Jazz Events

1977

2 January
Pianist Erroll Garner dies, Los Angeles.

February
Guitarist Pat Metheny records his ACOUSTIC album *Watercolors* for ECM with Lyle Mays (piano), Eberhard Weber (bass), and Danny Gottlieb (drums).

30 May
Alto saxophonist Paul Desmond dies, New York.

July
Count Basie's band, Dave Brubeck's new quartet and Dizzy Gillespie appear at the Montreux Jazz Festival. Many performances at the Festival are recorded live on Norman Granz's new label, Pablo.

Summer
Charles Mingus again tours Europe, but the trip is blighted by his deteriorating health.

September
The Monterey Jazz Festival celebrates its twentieth anniversary in California.

October
Vibraphonist Lionel Hampton and baritone saxophonist Gerry Mulligan record together in New York.

November
Sarah Vaughan records *I Love Brazil* in Rio de Janeiro.

Autumn
Pianist Earl Hines makes a series of comeback recordings in Chicago and New Orleans.

5 December
Multi-instrumentalist Roland Kirk dies, Bloomington, Indiana.

- Foundation of the eclectic World Saxophone Quartet by Hamiet Bluiett, Julius Hemphill, Oliver Lake, and David Murray.
- Tenor saxophonist Scott Hamilton, aged twenty-three, records his debut album for Concord. The disc's title, *Scott Hamilton Is a Good Wind Who is Blowing Us No Ill,* borrows a phrase coined by critic Leonard Feather. Hamilton soon becomes a leading revivalist.
- Soprano saxophonist Steve Lacy is active in Italy, France, Switzerland, and Germany.
- Drummer Kenny Clarke returns to the US from Europe, where he has lived for twenty-one years.
- Martin Scorsese directs *New York, New York,* starring Robert De Niro as a saxophonist. His mimed playing is coached by tenor player Georgie Auld, a former SIDEMAN with Artie Shaw, Benny Goodman, and Count Basie.

Above Roland Kirk (seen here in New York in 1967), who died in 1977. The ostensible gimmickry of his simultaneous playing on multiple instruments belied his genuine musicality and the high regard for mainstream jazz styles invariably revealed by his performances.

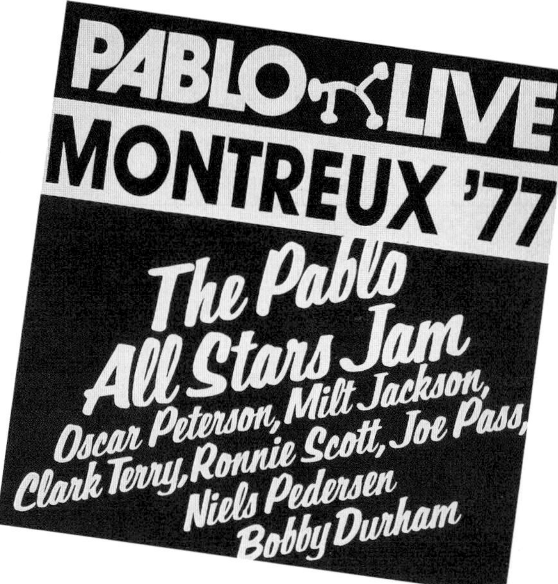

Right One of the live recordings from the 1977 Montreux Jazz Festival issued on the Pablo label, with its distinctive Picasso logo at top center.

DAVE BRUBECK'S SILVER JUBILEE

In 1976 Dave Brubeck's famous quartet reunited to celebrate twenty-five years since its inception. The event drew attention once more to the Californian pianist's stature as one of the most popular and influential of the first generation of COOL performers. Unlike those other pioneers of cool, Miles Davis (• p. 121) and John Lewis (• p. 129), Brubeck had not served his musical apprenticeship in the bop style. His training was primarily in classical music, and included lessons from expatriate French composer Darius Milhaud, who espoused the cause of SYMPHONIC JAZZ in the 1920s (• p. 53). This classical stance allowed Brubeck to avoid the clichés of 1950s bop from the outset, and he went on to create jazz compositions that were highly original in both texture and structure. His music appealed to the listeners' intellect as much as their emotions without sacrificing melodic appeal, and became widely known during a series of much-publicized tours of American university campuses in the mid-1950s.

Brubeck's early work is best represented by his perennially popular album *Time Out* (1959), which featured the hit track "Take Five," written by his alto saxophonist Paul Desmond (• p. 186). This famous tune is cast entirely in bars containing five beats, an irregular METER much used in modern classical music but here making its jazz debut. Other tracks on the disc offered more complex attempts to break away from the 4/4 time ubiquitous in jazz, including "Blue Rondo à la Turk," which subdivided nine beats into the irregular pattern 2+2+2+3 (• p. 147).

Brubeck's definitive quartet disbanded in 1967 when Desmond quit and Brubeck himself decided to concentrate on the creation of concert works. His variously constituted jazz COMBOS in the 1970s sometimes featured the talents of his three sons (proficient on keyboards, trombone/bass guitar, and drums), and critics formerly opposed to the apparent lack of SWING in his early playing began to discern a greater sense of lyrical freedom as a new decade began and he appeared at the Newport and Concord Jazz Festivals (in 1980 and 1982, respectively).

WEATHER REPORT: BLACK MARKET

The title track of Weather Report's album *Black Market* (1976) is a perfect illustration of the mixture of commercial appeal and sophistication so typical of early FUSION music. It also celebrates the African-American heritage of the style, which the group's leader Joe Zawinul claimed to be of far greater significance than the white rock music that lent its name to jazz-rock.

The piece begins with the recorded sound of animated chatter in an ethnic marketplace, an atmosphere that is heightened when the instruments enter with a persistent use of a pentatonic (i.e., five-note) SCALE. (Pentatonicism is common in many ethnic musics, and African pentatonicism may well have been responsible for the development of BLUE NOTES in early jazz.) The exuberant bass RIFF and Zawinul's cheerfully meandering SYNTHESIZER melody both adhere rigidly to the scale, a technique clearly influenced by Miles Davis's earlier modal experiments. A restatement of the theme is reinforced by the addition of a driving rock beat from Alex Acuña: in all, no fewer than three drummers are used on the track.

Just as the hypnotically revolving five-note patterns seem in danger of outstaying their welcome, the music launches into a passage of vibrant, complex harmonies enlivened by the unpredictable yet catchy SYNCOPATIONS typical of the style. As the rock accompaniment increases in intensity, Wayne Shorter plays a hard-edged soprano saxophone solo. Then, as the volume decreases, the bass-riff patterns gradually begin to suggest the pentatonic music of the opening. Yet the main theme fails to return, and the music merges into sound effects (thunderclaps and explosions suggestive of a fireworks display) as the piece fades away.

World Events

1977

27 March
World's worst aviation disaster kills 582, Tenerife, Canary Islands

12 August
Test flight of US space shuttle

16 August
Elvis Presley dies (or does he . . .?)

- Pompidou Centre opens, Paris
- George Lucas's movie blockbuster *Star Wars*

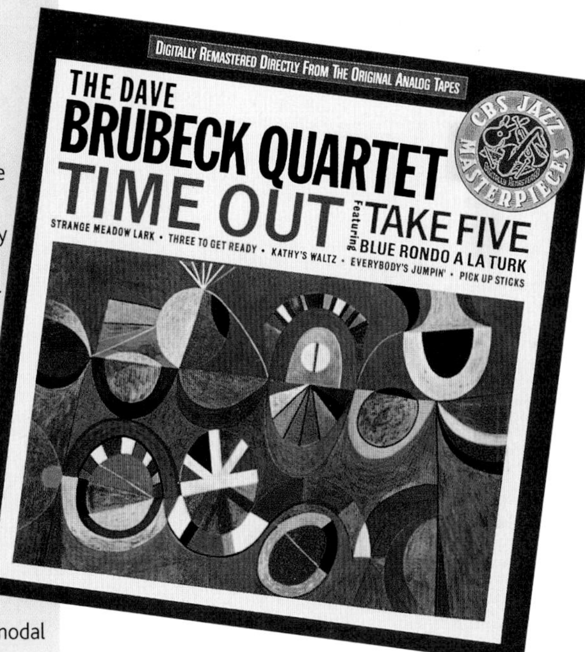

Above CD reissue of Brubeck's *Time Out,* one of the most tuneful examples of 1950s cool jazz and rhythmically innovative recordings of its time.

MINGUS AND HIS DYNASTY

Charles Mingus made his last important recordings in 1977, bringing to a close a career marked by innovation, controversy, and the grueling demands he constantly imposed on his distinguished SIDEMEN. Although his exploration of advanced double-bass technique was itself notable (• p. 153), Mingus will be best remembered for the seriousness of his intellectual attitude to jazz. Such an approach paid dividends in the creation of intelligent and often challenging structures within a richly varied musical language. At times, he flirted with the avant-garde by verging on the brink of ATONALITY and total rhythmic freedom.

Highlights of his work in the 1950s include his colorful interpretation of Hispanic elements in *Tijuana Moods* (1957), an early example of the imaginative use of tape-editing to reduce the duration of the tracks. The project was in part a cathartic experience intended to dispel one of the bassist's habitual dark moods. "All the music in this album," Mingus wrote, "was written during a very blue period of my life. I was minus a wife, and in flight to forget her with an unexpected dream in Tijuana … After finding myself with the sting of tequila, salt, and lime in my mouth and burning my nostrils, I decided to benefit musically from this experience and set out to compose and recreate what I felt and saw around me. It included a strip tease ['Ysabel's Table Dance'] in one of the many local night clubs."

Less entertaining, if more prophetic musically, was the previous year's album *Pithecanthropus Erectus,* with its passages of free IMPROVISATION boldly foreshadowing the work of Ornette Coleman (• p. 150) and modal techniques looking ahead to Miles Davis (• p. 147). But many critics single out *The Black Saint and The Sinner Lady* (1963) as Mingus's most important work, not merely as an unusually early example of OVERDUBBING, but also for his conception of the album as one continuous piece of music (the release was segmented into separate tracks at the behest of the nervous record company). Along with conquering technological limitations, here Mingus achieved a balance between spontaneity and orderly PRE-COMPOSITION only equaled in the work of Duke Ellington.

Mingus's importance in jazz history lies in his serious promotion of the work of other like-minded musicians through his own record label, Debut (founded in 1952), in his collaboration with the Jazz Composers' Workshop (which he formed in 1953), and in setting up a new festival at Newport during the official festival's crisis period (• p. 149). After his death in 1979, Mingus's artistic legacy was promoted in performances by his widow's band, Mingus Dynasty (• p. 192) and, since 1991, by the Mingus Big Band in New York.

For critic Martin Williams's thoughts on the significance of Mingus's utterly depressing 1971 fantasy-autobiography, *Beneath the Underdog,* see • p. 177.

"I am a good composer with great possibilities, and I made an easy success through jazz, but it wasn't really success – jazz has too many strangling qualities for a composer . . . If music lovers knew the wealth of talent being wasted in the name of jazz they'd storm the managers' and bookers' offices and tell them they refuse to settle for the crap they're getting! How many jazz musicians would stay in the clubs if they could even make a living playing in parks and simple places without the big buildup that's now an absolute necessity for survival? Tote that Down Beat, win that poll, hope I get a mention before I'm too old! . . . If I want it right, Nat, guess I'll have to leave jazz – that word leaves room for too much fooling."

Charles Mingus to Nat Hentoff

Above Charles Mingus was equally important as a virtuoso bassist and provocative composer.

Jazz Events

1978

March
The Ganelin Trio (• p. 207) records *Strictly for Our Friends* in Moscow.

5 April
Violinist Stephane Grappelli plays at New York's Carnegie Hall.

May
The Art Ensemble of Chicago records in Germany.

18 June
President Jimmy Carter hosts a jazz concert at the White House in honor of Charles Mingus. Participants include Stan Getz (• p. 152), Dizzy Gillespie (• p. 219), Dexter Gordon, and Max Roach.

Above Blind pianist Lennie Tristano, who died in 1978, pictured playing at New York's Keynote in 1946 at around the time of his early collaboration with bop stars Charlie Parker and Dizzy Gillespie.

11 August
Tenor saxophonist David Murray appears in London. Other American artists visiting the English capital this year include Phil Woods (**March**), Oscar Peterson (**October**), and Joe Pass (**November**).

14 August
Violinist Joe Venuti dies, Seattle, Washington.

23 September
Dexter Gordon plays at Carnegie Hall.

September
Tenor saxophonist Johnny Griffin, who has lived in Europe since 1963, makes a rare US appearance at the Monterey Festival. He goes on to record in Berkeley with trumpeter Nat Adderley, brother of saxophonist Julian "Cannonball" Adderley.
• Don Cherry records *Codona* for ECM (• p. 177) with Collin Walcott (sitar and tablā) and Naná Vasconcelos (percussion). The album, inspired by Indian music, is a landmark in the CROSSOVER between jazz and ethnic music soon to be a strong feature of the 1980s (• p. 205).

October
Chick Corea (• p. 179) and Gary Burton record *Duet* in Oregon, while Herbie Hancock (• p. 201) plays a series of concerts in Tokyo.

18 November
Pianist Lennie Tristano dies, New York.

28–29 December
Chet Baker (• p. 210) records in Paris.

- Drummer Peter Erskine joins Weather Report.
- The Cuban group Irakere promote Afro-Cuban jazz at the Newport and Montreux Jazz Festivals.
- Gil Evans appears at the Royal Festival Hall, London.
- Keyboard player Bob James scores a popular success with his FUSION theme to the American television comedy *Taxi*.

Below A marching band parades on the White House lawn (top) and President Jimmy Carter joins in the festivities (bottom) at a party held in 1978 to celebrate the achievements of Charles Mingus.

World Events

1978

17 March
György Ligeti's opera *Le Grand Macabre* staged, Stockholm

April
Revolution in Afghanistan

1 May
Death of Aram Khachaturian

- Hit film musical *Grease*
- Michael Cimino's movie *The Deer Hunter* wins five Oscars

1979

Influential composer and virtuoso bassist Charles Mingus dies, aged fifty-six. Other leading performers join forces in small groups, some of which celebrate his work.

THE MINGUS LEGACY

Above right Stan Kenton, whose controversial "progressive jazz" had been one of the few big-band styles to flourish after World War II.

Below Norwegian saxophonist Jan Garbarek (• p. 177), who recorded with Keith Jarrett in 1979.

Jazz Events

5 January
Charles Mingus (• p. 190) dies, Cuernavaca, Mexico.

8 February
In an interview published in *Down Beat,* Joe Zawinul argues that the music of his seminal FUSION group Weather Report (• p. 175) is based more on (black) rhythm 'n' blues than on (white) rock music.

March
Drummer Jack DeJohnette collaborates with tenor saxophonist David Murray on the ECM album *Special Edition,* which becomes the name of a succession of small ensembles led by DeJohnette.

May
Keith Jarrett (• p. 185) and Jan Garbarek record *Nude Ants* at the Village Vanguard, New York, for ECM.

9–10 July
Mingus Dynasty, formed by Susan Graham Ungaro Mingus in memory of her late husband, records *Chair in the Sky.*

25 August
Bandleader Stan Kenton (• p. 134) dies, Los Angeles.

August
Don Cherry (trumpet), Dewey Redman (tenor saxophone), Charlie Haden (bass), and Billy Higgins (drums) give a renewed boost to the FREE JAZZ movement with their album *Old and New Dreams.*

• The Concord Jazz Festival features performances by Dave Brubeck (• p. 189), Ray Brown, and Charlie Byrd .

September
Clarinetist Woody Herman takes part in the Monterey Jazz Festival.

17 October
British trombonist Chris Barber records *Come Friday* in Germany.

28 October
Chick Corea (• p. 179) and Gary Burton perform together in Zurich.

11 November
Milt Jackson and Sonny Stitt record together in Milan.

26 November
Pianist Bill Evans (• p. 157) makes his last major recordings, in Paris.

- Pianist Horace Silver records his final album for Blue Note, *Silver 'n' Strings,* ending a twenty-eight-year association with the label.
- Thad Jones quits drummer Mel Lewis, with whom he has led a superior big band for fourteen years (• p. 162), and moves to Denmark. The band continues to perform under Lewis's sole leadership.
- The Manhattan Transfer's *Extensions* makes a pop hit of Joe Zawinul's "Birdland" (• p. 175).
- Dizzy Gillespie (• p. 219) and Al Fraser publish their book *To Be or Not to Bop.* Also published this year is William Gottlieb's *The Golden Age of Jazz,* a photographic collection of artists from the SWING and bop eras.

ELECTRIFYING JAZZ

The importation of electrically amplified and electronically generated sonorities in the 1970s revolutionized the sound of jazz. Initially inspired by the desire to cash in on the commercial success of rock music, the use of electronic technology later produced artistically satisfying creative results. In the case of the guitar, available in amplified versions since the late 1930s, the stylistic progression was a relatively smooth affair; this was equally true of the electric bass guitar (• p. 127), which first came into its own with the fusion boom.

The earliest electric keyboard instrument to gain widespread acceptance in jazz was the electric organ, popularized (in its original Hammond model) by Fats Waller in the late 1930s before Jimmy Smith expanded the instrument's stylistic horizons in the 1950s and promoted its association with BLUES-based idioms. The organ remained popular until the early 1970s, when it was quickly supplanted by advancing technology. First came the ELECTRIC PIANO, which, as with the electric bass guitar, had originally been developed in the 1950s in an attempt to combat the ACOUSTIC instrument's perceived deficiencies in both volume and portability. The most popular variety by far proved to be the Fender Rhodes model, launched in 1965, which produced a bright, metallic sound characteristic of innumerable albums recorded in the 1970s. The most influential exponents were Chick Corea, Joe Zawinul (• p. 175), and Herbie Hancock (• p. 201), but part of the credit for its promotion must go to Miles Davis, who prompted all three keyboard players to explore the instrument's potential while working on his epoch-making early fusion albums in 1968–69 (• p. 171).

More radical in both technology and creative potential was the SYNTHESIZER. A source of experimentation by avant-garde classical musicians in the 1960s, it was favored because it offered seemingly limitless possibilities for unusual timbres. The first generation of synthesizers lacked today's digital technology, producing "source" sounds that were then modified by a variety of processing devices. Until the mid-1970s, only a single melodic line could be played, and the performance style was inevitably influenced by that used on the electric guitar. Paul Bley and Sun Ra were early advocates of the Moog synthesizer, which became available in a compact portable version (the "Minimoog") in 1970.

Zawinul, Hancock, and Corea progressed from the electric piano to working with synthesizers after leaving Miles Davis and founding their own fusion bands in the early 1970s. The Oberheim company's development in 1974 of a device that could play more than one note at a time provided a timely stimulus to further experimentation, and resulted in the appearance of the "Polymoog" and a rash of comparable instruments manufactured by other companies. The advent of digital technology permitted players to use complex SAMPLING and SEQUENCING techniques, while introducing an impressive capacity for storing prearranged timbres. This new versatility culminated in the computerized and phenomenally capable Synclavier, used by Lyle Mays to create a stunning range of atmospheric effects in his work with Pat Metheny in the 1980s (• p. 211).

The keyboard is not the only mechanism capable of controlling a synthesizer, and alternative technologies evolved to allow guitarists, drummers, and even wind players to access the astonishing soundscapes made possible by this versatile invention. Both Akai and Yamaha launched so-called "electronic wind instruments" in 1987, and in the same year saxophonist Michael Brecker featured the Akai model on his debut album.

World Events

24 February
Alban Berg's opera *Lulu* receives its first complete performance in Paris, forty-four years after the composer's death

4 May
Margaret Thatcher becomes UK's first female Prime Minister

- Peter Shaffer's play *Amadeus*
- Francis Ford Coppola's movie *Apocalypse Now*
- *Kramer vs. Kramer* wins five Oscars

Above Sonny Stitt, seen here in conversation with fellow saxophonist Red Holloway in London in 1980, developed Charlie Parker's style of improvisation to an unsurpassed degree of perfection.

As the new decade begins, performers once more polarize between classicism and post-fusion modernism.

COMPLEMENTARY PATHWAYS

Above Bill Evans, the most influential jazz pianist of the early 1960s, appearing at Ronnie Scott's London club in August 1980 shortly before his death.

Jazz Events

29 May
Pat Metheny (• p. 199) records *80/81* with saxophonists Michael Brecker and Dewey Redman, bassist Charlie Haden, and drummer Jack DeJohnette.

27 June
Clarinetist Barney Bigard dies, Culver City, California.

June
SOUL-jazz saxophonist Grover Washington, Jr. records his album *Winelight*, including the hit song "Just the Two of Us." The disc wins two Grammy awards.
• Miles Davis (• p. 217) records *The Man with the Horn*, marking his return to the recording studio after five years of retirement.

July
Eighteen-year-old trumpeter Wynton Marsalis (• p. 197) records at the Montreux Jazz Festival with Art Blakey's Jazz Messengers (• p. 139). Meanwhile, Oscar Peterson and Freddie Hubbard top the bill at Holland's North Sea Jazz Festival in The Hague.

Summer
The Art Ensemble of Chicago is active in Germany and Italy.

15 September
Pianist Bill Evans (• p. 157) dies, aged fifty-one, in New York. The date provides the title for a haunting memorial track on the Pat Metheny/ Lyle Mays album *As Falls Wichita, So Falls Wichita Falls* (ECM).

October–November
A new annual jazz festival is launched in Paris, with main events broadcast by Radio France.

15–16 November
The Ganelin Trio (• p. 207) records in Leningrad.

December
Vibraphonist Mike Mainieri and tenor saxophonist Michael Brecker form the FUSION group Steps, which records in Tokyo.

- Guitarist Bill Frisell begins working with drummer Paul Motian, formerly a SIDEMAN with Bill Evans.
- The newly formed Savoy Sultans (who borrow their name from a Swing Era band) popularize a modern brand of SWING at the Newport Jazz Festival and Kool Festival, the latter held in Waterloo Village, New Jersey.
- Danish guitarist Pierre Dørge forms his New Jungle Orchestra, which goes on to explore novel syntheses between traditional jazz, Ellingtonian "jungle" music, and various ethnic musical traditions (• p. 205).
- "Wild" Bill Davison brings his own variety of the old Chicago style to Carnegie Hall.
- Trumpeter Doc Cheatham, aged seventy-five, promotes traditional jazz in a regular Sunday GIG at Greenwich Village's Sweet Basil club.

World Events

22 February
Death of Oskar Kokoschka

August
US film stars go on strike

4 November
Ronald Reagan elected President, USA

8 December
John Lennon murdered, New York

- Umberto Eco's novel *The Name of the Rose*

ELLA FITZGERALD: FIRST LADY OF JAZZ

Ella Fitzgerald, who received a Grammy award in 1980 at the age of sixty-two, had long been one of the most popular vocalists in jazz. While some listeners regretted the considerable refinement of her vocal technique, which could never match the raw emotional resonances of an artist such as Billie Holiday (• p. 131), many found that Fitzgerald's comforting sense of self-assurance and vocal agility combined to produce one of the most infectiously spirited sounds in all jazz.

Fitzgerald first came to public attention in the 1930s when, while still a teenager, she was hired by drummer Chick Webb – a charismatic hunchback – to front his band at the Savoy Ballroom. On Webb's death in 1939, she assumed the leadership of the band (• p. 92), now famous for her interpretation of "A-Tisket, A-Tasket" recorded in the previous year. After the war, she was widely promoted by Norman Granz as part of his "Jazz at the Philharmonic" operation (• p. 107), and it was to Granz's label Verve that she defected from Decca in 1956. She recorded prolifically, and under the patronage of Verve she interpreted huge quantities of STANDARDS in Granz's ambitious "songbook" series, made between 1956 and 1964 (• p. 138) and later available as an eighteen-CD boxed set. As in the case of Sarah Vaughan, her recorded output reached a far wider audience than much mainstream jazz of the 1950s and 1960s. Since the rise of Frank Sinatra and others during the musicians' strikes of the early 1940s (• p. 103), singers have generally been welcomed more readily by the masses than instrumentalists.

Perhaps the finest SCAT singer (• p. 61) of all time, Fitzgerald delighted audiences with her textless IMPROVISATIONS on numbers such as Gershwin's "Lady Be Good" and Billy Strayhorn's "Take the 'A' Train." Her ability to imitate the pyrotechnics of bop instrumentalists also allowed her to work with virtuoso performers in the context of small ensembles. She recorded classic performances alongside bassist Ray Brown (her husband from 1948 until 1952), Louis Armstrong (• p. 57), Oscar Peterson (• p. 163), Joe Pass, and countless others. She was no stranger to big bands, either, collaborating memorably with Duke Ellington (• p. 63) in the late 1950s, and with Count Basie's band (• p. 87) in 1990.

Fitzgerald continued to perform well into her old age, but increasingly succumbed to the ravages of a heart condition and diabetes; complications from the latter resulted in the tragic amputation of both legs below the knee, which put her permanently into a wheelchair. She died on 14 June 1996 at the age of seventy-eight.

Right Ella Fitzgerald in 1955.

JAPAN MOVES CENTER STAGE

As Miles Davis emerges from temporary retirement, he tours Japan in a year in which the country also hosts inspired performances by the reunited Modern Jazz Quartet, Wynton Marsalis, and Herbie Hancock.

Jazz Events

29 January
Drummer Cozy Cole dies, Columbus, Ohio.

28 May
Pianist Mary Lou Williams dies, Durham, North Carolina.

5 July
Miles Davis (● p. 217) appears at Avery Fisher Hall, New York, during the Newport Jazz Festival. The event marks his return to the live-performance circuit after a prolonged retirement caused by ill health.

September–October
Miles Davis tours Japan with a group that includes Bill Evans (soprano saxophone) and Marcus Miller (bass). He earns $700,000 for eight appearances.

October
The Modern Jazz Quartet is reformed for a reunion concert in Tokyo as part of the Monterey Jazz Festival's tour to Japan; its members have spent seven years apart. The event is commemorated by their recording *Reunion at Budohkhan*.

- Wynton Marsalis leaves Art Blakey's Jazz Messengers and tours Japan with Miles Davis's former RHYTHM SECTION: Herbie Hancock (piano), Ron Carter (bass), and Tony Williams (drums). He records with them for CBS and is signed up to record an album, *Wynton Marsalis,* as leader on the same label.
- Martial Solal composes his Concerto for Jazz Trio and Orchestra.
- Alto saxophonist David Sanborn records his album *Voyeur*, combining FUSION with popular FUNK. The track "All I Need is You," composed by bassist Marcus Miller, wins a Grammy award.

Left Pianist Mary Lou Williams, who died in 1981 at the age of seventy-one. Her *Zodiac Suite* was performed by the New York Philharmonic in 1946, but she is best remembered as an exceedingly versatile pianist and accomplished swing-band arranger.

World Events

12 April
First US space-shuttle mission

April
Race riots in Brixton, London

29 July
Wedding of the Prince of Wales and Lady Diana Spencer

6 October
Assassination of President Sadat of Egypt

13 December
Poland declares martial law to quash the trade union, Solidarity

- Assassination attempts on US President Reagan and Pope John Paul II.

Left A child prodigy and cultural icon, Wynton Marsalis has combined careers in classical music and jazz with equal success.

WYNTON MARSALIS

In 1981, at the age of nineteen, Wynton Marsalis entered the record books by becoming the first performer to sign recording contracts for both classical music and jazz simultaneously. Born in New Orleans in 1961, he had followed in the footsteps of his illustrious predecessors by playing in a marching band (at the age of eight), before acquiring a formidable instrumental technique that allowed him to play Haydn's Trumpet Concerto with the New Orleans Philharmonic Orchestra when he was only fourteen. His two careers developed in parallel through classical studies at New York's renowned Juilliard School and through membership of Art Blakey's equally renowned Jazz Messengers (• p. 139), which he joined in 1980. Four years later he again made history as the first artist to receive Grammy awards for both classical and jazz recordings.

Marsalis's rapid rise to prominence in the jazz world came when he joined the members of Miles Davis's formidable rhythm section – Herbie Hancock (• p. 201) on piano, Ron Carter on bass, and Tony Williams on drums – to play at the Newport Jazz Festival and tour Japan in 1981. The group also recorded for CBS with Hancock as leader. In 1983 Wynton's older brother Branford joined the group as tenor saxophonist and, under the name VSOP II, the quintet's debt to Davis's style of the 1960s became patently obvious. In the mid-1980s Marsalis formed his own quartet, and its performances of STANDARDS were soon hailed as the finest of the decade. From 1988 onward he devoted his attention to projects reclaiming the heritage of early jazz, whether the New Orleans style or the masterpieces of Duke Ellington. In the 1990s he made a name for himself as a fluent lecturer and music educator, skillfully presenting a series of television programs for children (*Marsalis on Music*), which were given worldwide exposure.

Marsalis entered jazz at a time when it was seriously in need of a new, younger audience to sustain its development. His youthful, fresh image and precocious talents (backed up by marketing on the part of CBS/Sony, rivaled only by their earlier promotion of Miles Davis) made him appear to be its timely savior. Outspoken against what he saw as the artistic sellout of fusion, Marsalis promoted the performance of live ACOUSTIC jazz firmly rooted in traditional musical values. As with many of jazz's most capable technicians, however, his consummate facility sometimes encouraged him to stray into mere virtuosity for virtuosity's sake, and his exhortations on his definition of "real" (i.e., historically aware) jazz and its superiority to jazz-rock hybrid styles led to a temperamental clash with his idol Miles Davis, who in 1986 refused to allow him to play with his band in Vancouver. "I was never jealous of him," Miles said, but added, "the more famous he became the more he started saying things – nasty, disrespectful things – about me, things I've never said about musicians who influenced me and who I had great respect for."

"I really liked Wynton when I first met him. He's still a nice young man, only confused. I knew he could play the hell out of classical music, and had great technical skills on the trumpet . . . But you need more than that to play great jazz music, you need feelings and an understanding of life that you can only get from living, from experience."

Miles Davis,
The Autobiography (1989)

Jazz Events

17 February
Thelonious Monk (● p. 155) dies, Weehawken, New Jersey. Entirely by coincidence, the new group Sphere (its name borrowed from Monk's middle name, and established to promote his music) is scheduled to record its first album, *Four in One*, on the same day.

20–21 February
Oscar Peterson's trio (● p. 163) performs in Japan with guitarist Joe Pass and records a live Pablo double album, *Freedom Song*, partly inspired by the prolonged incarceration of Nelson Mandela in South Africa.

23 March
Sonny Greer, founder-drummer of the Ellington orchestra (● p. 119), dies in New York.

March
Bassist Eberhard Weber records *Later That Evening* for ECM, with an ensemble including guitarist Bill Frisell and pianist Lyle Mays.
● Pianist Monty Alexander, a performer strongly influenced by Oscar Peterson, tours Japan and performs in Osaka and Tokyo. His trio features former Peterson SIDEMEN, bassist Ray Brown and guitarist Herb Ellis.

April
Milt Jackson (● p. 129) makes several appearances at Ronnie Scott's London club, concentrating on STANDARDS by Thelonious Monk.

April–May
Electric guitarist John Scofield joins Miles Davis (● p. 217) on his European tour.

15 June
Alto saxophonist Art Pepper dies, Panorama, California.

June
Vibraphonist Lionel Hampton (● p. 70) plays in Tokyo.

23 July
Charlie Parker's disciple, alto saxophonist Sonny Stitt, dies one month after recording his final sessions in New York.

- Trumpeter Shorty Rogers tours the UK with the National Youth Jazz Orchestra.
- Benny Goodman (● p. 84) reforms his original quartet with Teddy Wilson (piano) and Lionel Hampton (vibraphone). The deceased Gene Krupa is replaced by drummer Panama Francis.
- Chick Corea (● p. 179) records Mozart's Concerto for Two Pianos.
- Wynton Marsalis (● p. 197) leaves Art Blakey's Jazz Messengers (● p. 139).
- Bassist Jaco Pastorius leaves Weather Report to start his own band.

AFTER MONK

Thelonious Monk's death inspires a rash of memorial tributes, and his compositions remain a core part of the standards repertoire.

Above Playing at London's Camden Jazz Week in 1980, Eberhard Weber demonstrates his solid-bodied bass, which combines features of both acoustic and electric instruments.

PAT METHENY AND THE NEW VERSATILITY

Guitarist Pat Metheny will be remembered as one of the most artistically resourceful and commercially successful artists who came to prominence in the 1980s. His career has achieved a workable (and very rare) balance between a mass popular appeal – more typical of a rock musician than a jazz performer, and capable of filling a football stadium at a live GIG – and a consistent devotion to musical innovation that has led him to collaborate with notable figures from the avant-garde. Predictably, this diversity has not always found favor from purist critics, some finding certain of his FUSION albums (a term he dislikes) too easygoing in their tunefulness, while a seminal experimental album – such as his collaboration with Ornette Coleman, *Song X* (• p. 204) – has been viewed as a compromise merely because some of the session's most radical takes were not included in the original release.

Born near Kansas City, Missouri (• p. 64), Metheny played with vibraphonist Gary Burton at the age of twenty, having already displayed his prodigious talents by teaching at Miami University and Boston's Berklee College of Music while still a teenager. In 1976 he began working with pianist Lyle Mays, whose style was deeply rooted in the idioms of Keith Jarrett (• p. 185) andBill Evans (• p. 157) and whose talents as cocomposer injected considerable harmonic and structural sophistication into the work of the resulting Pat Metheny Group, which recorded its first album in 1978. Subsequent recordings for the German ECM label (• p. 177) showed Metheny to have absorbed the influence of American country music, which imparted melodic freshness to a style of guitar playing already reflecting the work of Wes Montgomery (• p. 99).

Like Joe Zawinul with Weather Report (• p. 175), Metheny found he could successfully package limited avant-garde experimentation in the context of popular fusion albums. His best-selling *Offramp* (released in 1982) sported an aggressive title track, in an ATONAL idiom of extreme textural and rhythmic unpredictability, alongside highly melodic compositions more akin to easy listening than self-conscious modernism. When his group switched to the Geffen label in 1985, its style grew notably lighter and began to betray the overt influence of Brazilian music by insistently including a (sometimes wordless) vocal line.

Lyle Mays went on to produce three albums as leader (• p. 211), the first in 1986, and continues to collaborate with Metheny after a fruitful association of more than three decades.

GUITAR SYNTHESIZER

Metheny's album *Offramp* featured striking effects created by a guitar SYNTHESIZER, used to control the powerful digital Synclavier operated by Lyle Mays's keyboard. Guitar synthesizers were launched by the Roland instrument company in 1977, and have been adopted by performers such as John McLaughlin, Al Di Meola, Bill Frisell, and Lee Ritenour. Inspired by the unlimited range of sonorities possible on the keyboard synthesizers that entered jazz in the early 1970s (• p. 193), the guitar synthesizer adapted the technology to the playing technique of a stringed instrument. Three basic categories of sound are at the performer's disposal: electronic imitations of conventional instruments, pure electronic effects, and complex timbres created by the processing of material sampled from a live source.

Above The Pat Metheny Group performs at Bracknell, Berkshire, in 1980 (l. to r.): Lyle Mays (keyboards), Pat Metheny (guitar), Mark Egan (electric bass), and Danny Gottlieb (drums).

World Events

2 April
Argentina invades the Falkland Islands

1 May
British offensive to retake the Falklands begins

14 June
Argentine troops surrender to British forces

20 December
Death of Arthur Rubinstein

• Oscar winners this year include Richard Attenborough's *Gandhi* (eight awards) and Steven Spielberg's blockbuster *E.T.* (four awards)

PRODIGIES

The dazzling talents of Wynton Marsalis and Tommy Smith suggest that jazz is being redefined by, and for, a much younger generation.

Above Veteran pianist Eubie Blake indulges in a little domestic music-making on a late visit to Norway.

Jazz Events

1983

January
Pianist Keith Jarrett (• p. 185) makes his first recordings of STANDARDS with a trio featuring Gary Peacock (bass) and Jack DeJohnette (drums).

12 February
STRIDE pianist Eubie Blake dies in New York, five days after his 100th birthday. Having eaten a fried breakfast every day of his adult life, as well as being a smoker and drinker, he said when interviewed shortly before his death, "If I'd known I was going to live this long, I'd have taken better care of myself."

9–10 March
Anthony Braxton records his album *Four Compositions (Quartet) 1983* in Milan. Its title, like many of Braxton's creations, betrays the influence of avant-garde visual art.

22 April
Pianist Earl Hines (• p. 125) dies, aged seventy-nine, in Oakland, California.

May
Miles Davis (• p. 217) tours Japan.

8–10 June
Lee Konitz collaborates with German trombonist Albert Mangelsdorff (• p. 61) on the album *The Art of the Duo,* recorded at Villingen.

June
Davis releases his album *Star People,* featuring saxophonist Bill Evans, guitarist John Scofield, and bassist Marcus Miller.

5 July
Trumpeter Harry James dies, aged sixty-seven, in Las Vegas.

26–27 July
British trumpeter Humphrey Lyttelton performs in Toronto. This year, he establishes his own record label under the name Calligraph.

August
British saxophone prodigy, sixteen-year-old Tommy Smith, makes his recording debut and goes on to join the Whizz Kids Band, organized by Gary Burton at Berklee College of Music, Boston.

October
Bassist Dave Holland collaborates with Canadian trumpeter Kenny Wheeler on the ECM album *Jumpin' In*.
• The first of an annual series of Floating Jazz Festivals is held on the SS *Norway*, which departs from Miami on a musical cruise.

November
Radio City Music Hall, New York, presents a tribute to Miles Davis ("An American Musical Legend"), hosted by comedian Bill Cosby (• p. 216). Davis also receives an honorary degree from Fisk University in Nashville, Tennessee.

December
Pablo Records preserves Count Basie's last big-band performances on the live album *Fancy Pants*.
• Swing Era clarinetist and bandleader Artie Shaw emerges from retirement to play with Dick Johnson's band at the Glen Island Casino, once made famous by the music of Glenn Miller (• p. 107).

- Wynton Marsalis makes musical history as the first artist to win simultaneous Grammy awards for a jazz album (*Think of One*, recorded in collaboration with his saxophonist brother Branford) and a classical recording (Haydn's Trumpet Concerto).
- Toshiko Akiyoshi and Lew Tabackin form their second big band.
- Ornette Coleman's *Skies of America* (• p. 178) is revived this year, and later performed in Verona, Italy (1987), and London (1988).
- Herbie Hancock's synthesized dance hit "Rockit," from the album *Future Shock*, reaches number one in the pop charts.
- Scott Joplin (• p. 21) appears on a US postage stamp.

HERBIE HANCOCK, MEGASTAR

Herbie Hancock's brand of electronic FUNK captivated listeners of pop music with such consummate ease in 1983 it scarcely seemed possible that two decades before he had been one of the most challenging musicians working in the jazz mainstream. An earlier indication of his commercial viability came ten years before with the phenomenal sales of his album *Headhunters*, and in his fluctuation between popular FUSION hits and less marketable ACOUSTIC jazz, Hancock's later career has been typical of many jazz musicians of his generation. He frankly admitted, however, that his increasing attraction to the popular marketplace arose from the realization that his jazz work could scarcely rival the awe-inspiring talents of geniuses such as Charlie Parker, John Coltrane, or Miles Davis.

Like Wynton Marsalis (• p. 197), Hancock was a child prodigy who first revealed his skills to the world in the context of classical music. Trumpeter Donald Byrd (• p. 12) enticed him to move to New York from his home city of Chicago, and he recorded his first album, *Takin' Off,* in 1962. This disc, which includes the original version of his later hit "Watermelon Man," marked the beginning of a long and fruitful association with the Blue Note label (• p. 167), for which he went on to serve as house pianist. A year later he fell in with Miles Davis and, together with bassist Ron Carter and drummer Tony Williams, formed the renowned RHYTHM SECTION for the trumpeter's second quintet. Meanwhile, his own career as leader blossomed with the appearance of his Blue Note albums *Empyrean Isles* (1964) and *Maiden Voyage* (1965). The former contains his popular composition "Cantaloupe Island," a SAMPLE from which formed the basis for the 1993 hit "Cantaloop," by the jazz-pop group Us3.

On quitting Davis in 1968, Hancock began work with REED-player Bennie Maupin in the context of a sextet, and began to concentrate on electronic keyboards (• p. 193), a sign of the times. In 1973, Hancock restructured the group as a quartet and issued *Headhunters*, with its hit opening track, "Chameleon," also released as a best-selling pop single. After his music became more pop-oriented in the later 1970s, he returned to orthodox jazz by reuniting his former Davis SIDEMEN to create the group VSOP with trumpeter Freddie Hubbard, who had figured prominently on his earlier Blue Note albums. This group provided invaluable experience for Wynton Marsalis at the start of his career. Another former Blue Note associate, tenor saxophonist Dexter Gordon, made a moving acting appearance in the film *'Round Midnight* (• p. 206), for which Hancock composed (and performed on screen) an Oscar-winning soundtrack in 1987. Hancock's album *The New Standard* (1996) continued to reassess pop material by reworking songs by the rock group Nirvana, Peter Gabriel, and The Beatles.

World Events

1983

25 February
Death of Tennessee Williams

8 March
Death of William Walton

29 July
Death of Luis Buñuel

October
US troops invade Grenada

- First compact discs marketed
- *Terms of Endearment* wins Oscar for Best Picture

Above Herbie Hancock in 1986, showing how in live performances funk-oriented keyboard players liked to drape their instrument around the neck in the fashion of a guitar.

Left Hancock accepts his Grammy for "Best Rhythm and Blues Instrumental," won by his hit track "Rockit" in 1984.

NEW JAZZ IN BRITAIN

Jazz had become such an international commodity by the 1980s that it might seem misleading to consider the work of musicians active in a single European country (as if nationalism ever had any meaning in jazz outside the nation in which it was born). But in Britain, the desolate years during which American musicians were banned from appearing in the country (• p. 84) had the regrettable consequence of ensuring that British jazz remained behind the times. Both traditional jazz and bop grew steadily in stature in the 1950s before a new, younger generation of musicians finally placed the UK firmly on the global jazz map in the midst of the growing stylistic indeterminacy of the post-FUSION 1980s.

The lead was taken by tenor saxophonists Courtney Pine and Andy Sheppard. Pine, who made his recording debut in 1986 (• p. 206) and whose playing revealed the influence of Sonny Rollins and John Coltrane (• p. 160), tirelessly sought to encourage black musicians in Britain to espouse the cause of jazz through his Abibi Jazz Arts organization. In the process, he admitted overtly West Indian musical characteristics into his style and successfully reached out to a large audience. After years of relative obscurity spent in Paris, Sheppard entered the record catalogs one year after Pine, and progressed from a similar post-Coltrane background to achieve soundscapes more reminiscent of Jan Garbarek's distinctively European work with ECM (• p. 177). Both players were a potent inspiration to emerging young talents up and down the country.

In the sphere of jazz composition, the rise to prominence of keyboard player Django Bates and his group Loose Tubes set new and formidable standards at around the same time.

Above Saxophonist Courtney Pine, an unflagging campaigner for the wider recognition of jazz in the UK.

Entering the recording studio in 1984 and causing a sensation at Ronnie Scott's in the following year (• p. 204), Loose Tubes offered a breathtaking fare of highly sophisticated arrangements, taking on board any stylistic material that caught their fancy. Such was the quality of their work that they were later promoted by producer Teo Macero, who had masterminded the recording of much of Miles Davis's music on the Columbia label. Bates also channeled his energies into work for the groups Human Chain, Earthworks, and Delightful Precipice, the latter producing exciting music to accompany performances by the Snapdragon circus company in the early 1990s.

Jazz Events

1984

27 February
Bandleader and keyboard player Sun Ra, aged seventy, visits Athens to perform at the Praxis 84 festival. This year he is also voted a member of *Down Beat*'s prestigious Hall of Fame.

March
The Soviet Union's Ganelin Trio (• p. 207) appear at London's Bloomsbury Theatre as part of their UK tour. Their collective artistry is demonstrated with an eccentric theatrical presentation recalling the avant-garde jazz of the 1960s.

23 April
Juan Tizol, composer of Duke Ellington's hit "Caravan," dies, aged eighty-four, in Inglewood, California.

26 April
Count Basie dies in Hollywood, at the age of seventy-nine. His autobiography, *Good Morning Blues*, is published posthumously.

April
Guitarist John Abercrombie records *Night* for ECM with tenor saxophonist Michael Brecker and drummer Jack DeJohnette.

May
Wynton Marsalis records *Hot House Flowers*, with a lineup that includes brother Branford on saxophone and Ron Carter on bass.

Spring
Saxophonist Lee Konitz is on tour in Scotland and the north of England.

July
Steve Gadd, virtuoso of the modern drum kit (• p. 220), records his album *Gaddabout*.

August
Gil Evans's band records live at the Sweet Basil club, Greenwich Village, where they have been resident for the past year.

26 September
Drummer Shelly Manne dies, aged sixty-four, Los Angeles.

Above The Dirty Dozen Brass Band appearing at the 14th JVC Grande Parade du Jazz in Nice, France, in 1987.

World Events

1984

22 August
First black franchise granted, South Africa

31 October
Indira Gandhi assassinated

6 November
Ronald Reagan elected to second term as US President

- Academy Award-winning films include *A Passage to India*, *The Killing Fields*, and *Amadeus* (Best Picture)

December
Miles Davis visits Denmark to receive a Sonning Foundation award (• p. 204). This year, he records *You're Under Arrest*, a pop-oriented album featuring singer Sting and guitarists John McLaughlin and John Scofield: the highlight of the disc is a reinterpretation of Michael Jackson's "Human Nature." This recording is his final release on the Columbia label after a twenty-nine-year association; he begins recording on the Warner label in 1986 (• p. 206). Warner pays him a seven-figure sum merely to sign up, but Davis declines to negotiate his publication rights and, as a result, his own compositions are not featured on subsequent recordings.

- Trumpeters Malachi Thompson and Lester Bowie form the group Brass Fantasy.
- The early New Orleans style is reassessed from a modern perspective in the debut recording of the Dirty Dozen Brass Band's *My Feet Can't Fail Me Now*.
- Francis Ford Coppola's movie *The Cotton Club* reconstructs the atmosphere of the famous Harlem venue in 1928 (• p. 63).

Left A former sideman of Fletcher Henderson in the 1940s, Sonny Blount assumed the name Sun Ra and went on to dazzle audiences with his heady blend of music-theater, free jazz, and popular styles.

Above Don Cherry, the archetypal "world musician," who mastered instruments from numerous ethnic traditions and promoted a brand of crossover jazz he liked to term "primal music."

"For jazz musicians to assume that they had any reason or any right to start playing with musicians of other cultures implied a new self-confidence on the part of the jazz community, and could probably only have happened thanks to the 1960s climate of the civil rights movement."

Brian Priestley, 1995

Jazz Events

1985

26 January
Drummer Kenny Clarke dies at the age of seventy-one, near Paris.

January
Jack DeJohnette temporarily abandons his drum kit in favor of the keyboard to record *The Piano Album* for Landmark.

10 February
Thad Jones returns to the US from Copenhagen to assume leadership of the Count Basie band.

22 February
The relaunch of Blue Note (• p. 167) is celebrated by a concert at New York's Town Hall. Participants include Art Blakey (• p. 139), Ron Carter, Herbie Hancock (• p. 201), Freddie Hubbard, Cecil Taylor, Grover Washington, Jr., and Tony Williams.

25 February
Art Blakey visits London to play at Ronnie Scott's club.

February
Miles Davis (• p. 217) visits Denmark to record *Aura*, written in his honor by fellow trumpeter Palle Mikkelborg when Davis received his Sonning Award.

May
Loose Tubes appears at Ronnie Scott's. This twenty-one-piece British band, led by twenty-five-year-old keyboard player Django Bates, astonishes audiences with its heady mixture of vibrant musical idioms and irrepressible energy (• p. 202).
• Bassist Marc Johnson records *Bass Desires* for ECM, supported by guitarists Bill Frisell and John Scofield, and drummer Peter Erskine.

July
Sonny Rollins records an album of live solo saxophone IMPROVISATIONS at New York's Museum of Modern Art.

30 August
Drummer Philly Joe Jones dies, aged sixty-two, Philadelphia. He is affectionately remembered for his "Philly lick," the distinctive use of a rim-shot on the final beat of a bar, best known from its appearance on Miles Davis's 1958 album *Milestones*.

15 September
Trumpeter Cootie Williams dies, aged seventy-four, New York.

12–14 December
Guitarist Pat Metheny (• p. 199) explores avant-garde territory by collaborating with Ornette Coleman (• p. 150), Charlie Haden, and Jack DeJohnette on the Geffen album *Song X*, to which Coleman contributes a characteristically idiosyncratic violin solo.

December
Twenty-two-year-old singing star Cassandra Wilson records *Point of View* with saxophonist Steve Coleman.
• Weather Report (• p. 175) records its final album, *This is This!*

- Chick Corea captivates a new youthful audience with his Elektric Band (• p. 215). Although denounced by purists, the group initiates a revival of interest in jazz-rock FUSION. After releasing an album featuring guitarist Scott Henderson, its membership stabilizes: Chick Corea (keyboards), Eric Marienthal (saxophones), Frank Gambale (guitar), John Patitucci (bass), and Dave Weckl (drums).
- Saxophonist Branford Marsalis tours with pop singer Sting, who has recorded the jazzy album *The Dream of the Blue Turtles*.
- Benny Goodman (• p. 84), now seventy-six, fronts an orchestra founded by Loren Schoenberg to revive classics of the SWING-band repertoire.
- Drummer Mel Lewis celebrates twenty years of regular performances at the Village Vanguard, Greenwich Village.
- Dave Grusin (keyboards) and Lee Ritenour (guitar) record their album *Harlequin* on Grusin's own GRP label (• p. 214).

ETHNIC CROSSOVERS

The barriers between jazz and classical music had been broken down as early as the 1920s (• p. 55), and by the 1980s the concept of THIRD STREAM music that synthesized the best of both worlds had become commonplace. New CROSSOVER ventures in the 1970s looked to more distant horizons by appropriating the musical traditions of exotic cultures, borrowing freely from ethnic music to create a musical potpourri entirely in keeping with the concept of the Global Village.

The most consistent champion of this approach was trumpeter Don Cherry, who participated in the avant-garde jazz of the early 1960s (• p. 150) at a time when John Coltrane (• p. 160) was demonstrating an interest in Indian ragas and Eric Dolphy's sights were also turning toward world music. In 1978, Cherry collaborated with Collin Walcott and Naná Vasconcelos in the first of a trilogy of recordings for ECM entitled *Codona*, in which Walcott played two Indian instruments – the sitar (a plucked stringed instrument) and the tablā (two small hand-beaten drums). Walcott's first important sitar recording was made in 1969 when he played on Tony Scott's album *Homage to Lord Krishna*, and the ethnic crossover movement proceeded to flourish alongside the phenomenal growth of jazz-rock fusion. The tablā player Zakir Hussain was the linchpin of John McLaughlin's group Shakti (1973–77), in which the guitarist played a special instrument based on an Indian prototype.

Since 1980, the Danish bandleader Pierre Dørge and his New Jungle Orchestra have successfully combined features borrowed from Eastern European, African, and Japanese traditional music in a style rooted in the post-Ellington band tradition. Influences from the Indian subcontinent remained prominent: saxophonist Jan Garbarek recorded his album *Ragas and Sagas* with Pakistani musicians in 1990 (• p. 214).

Today, cross-cultural borrowings in all music (whether classical or jazz) are close to becoming de rigueur. In jazz circles, at any rate, they enjoy a continuing justification in the realization that pan-cultural artistic synthesis directly reflects the tension between African and European music that gave birth to jazz a century ago.

World Events

1985

13 July
Bob Geldof's charity concert Live Aid reaches a global audience

1 September
Wreck of the *Titanic* located

2 December
Death of poet and jazz critic Philip Larkin

7 December
Death of Robert Graves

- Kurt Vonnegut's novel *Galapagos*
- *Out of Africa* wins Oscar for Best Picture

Above The virtuoso British band Loose Tubes, which took London by storm in the mid-1980s.

ENVOI TO THE LAST OF THE GREAT LEADERS

An era closes with the passing of Benny Goodman, Teddy Wilson, Thad Jones, Woody Herman, and Gil Evans.

Left An aging Benny Goodman conveys his thanks after receiving a Grammy Lifetime Achievement award at a ceremony held in Los Angeles on 25 February 1986, less than four months before his death.

Jazz Events

1986

January
Saxophonists Gerry Mulligan (● p. 134) and Scott Hamilton (● p. 188) record together in New York.

April
The World Saxophone Quartet's *Plays Duke Ellington* shows that the Duke's masterpieces are as vibrant as ever twelve years after his death.

6 June
Chet Baker (● p. 210) plays at Ronnie Scott's, London.

13 June
Benny Goodman dies, aged seventy-seven, New York.

June
Debut of Gary Giddins's American Jazz Orchestra at the Cooper Union, New York.

31 July
Pianist Teddy Wilson dies, aged seventy-three, New Britain, Connecticut.

July
Woody Herman's fiftieth-anniversary concert is staged at the Hollywood Bowl; another West Coast celebration is mounted in San Francisco.

July–August
Saxophonist Courtney Pine (● p. 202) makes his recording debut with *Journey to the Urge Within*. His sextet features up-and-coming talents Julian Joseph (piano) and Martin Taylor (guitar).

20 August
Thad Jones dies, aged sixty-three, Copenhagen. His former position at the helm of the Count Basie band is now held by saxophonist Frank Foster.

September
Wynton Marsalis (● p. 197) cements his growing reputation as a performer of jazz STANDARDS with his album *Standard Time*.

November
Alto saxophonist Benny Carter joins forces with Oscar Peterson (● p. 163) in Los Angeles.

December
Alto saxophonist Frank Morgan emerges from obscurity and reestablishes his reputation with a GIG at the Village Vanguard, New York.

- Miles Davis (● p. 217) begins his Warner contract with the album *Tutu*, named after Desmond Tutu and inspired by the persisting racial tensions in South Africa. This year Davis takes a cameo role as a drug-dealing pimp in the television series *Miami Vice*.
- Bertrand Tavernier's film *'Round Midnight*, with a score by Herbie Hancock (● p. 201), stars tenor saxophonist Dexter Gordon as a composite character amalgamated from incidents in the lives of Lester Young and Bud Powell.
- Keyboard player Bob James and saxophonist David Sanborn collaborate on the album *Double Vision* with Marcus Miller (bass) and Steve Gadd (drums).
- Keyboard player Lyle Mays (● p. 211) records his eponymous debut album for Geffen with a group including Bill Frisell (guitar), Alex Acuña (drums), and Naná Vasconcelos (percussion).
- Chick Corea (● p. 179) composes a Piano Concerto.

GLASNOST: THE JAZZ RESURGENCE IN THE USSR

The appearance of the first jazz recordings in 1917 inauspiciously coincided with the Russian Revolution, and for a decade afterward the new music was welcomed in the Soviet Union under the watchful patronage of Lenin. Leopold Teplitsky was officially encouraged to travel abroad in search of American arrangements to bring back to the fledgling USSR. Classical composer Dmitri Shostakovich, who produced a witty orchestral arrangement of "Tea for Two" in 1928, went on to compose two suites for jazz band, but the conservative style of his later works demonstrates how the iron hand of Stalin had by the early 1930s tightened its grip on Soviet culture. American HOT jazz was now as much out of favor as it was in Nazi Germany, and was gradually replaced in official circles by innocuous dance music deemed more suitable for consumption by the masses. Genuine jazz was branded by the Russian political newspaper *Pravda* as the music of the "fat bourgeoisie," and described by Stalinist author Maxim Gorky in savage terms that suggested it was still inextricably linked with the decadent and sexually depraved demimonde that had allegedly created it. Posters soon began to appear declaring, "Today you play jazz, tomorrow you will betray your country."

Under Stalin's reign of terror, Teplitsky and other prominent Soviet musicians were sent into exile and the jazz scene remained barren until the leader's death in 1953. While cultural restrictions remained severe under the succeeding regime, the influence of bop nevertheless belatedly began to assert itself behind the iron curtain. American musicians began to visit the USSR in 1962, opening Soviet ears to broader musical experiences. Notable American performers who toured there included Benny Goodman and Teddy Wilson in 1962, Earl Hines in 1966, Charles Lloyd in 1967, Duke Ellington in 1971, Oscar Peterson in 1974, and Dave Brubeck in 1987–88. Meanwhile, as in the sphere of classical music, a growing number of Soviet musicians defected to the West in search of wider artistic horizons.

The most remarkable aspect of Soviet jazz was undoubtedly the sudden flowering of the avant-garde during the 1970s. In terms of its political symbolism, this movement exactly paralleled the emergence of FREE JAZZ in the US in the early 1960s by representing the performers' need for civil, as well as artistic liberation. The best known of the Soviet free-jazz groups was the influential piano trio led by Vyacheslav Ganelin, which began recording in the USSR in 1976 after an acclaimed tour to Poland (a vital center for the new Eastern-bloc jazz since the foundation of the Sopot Festival in 1956). Ganelin's highly eclectic group synthesized elements borrowed from bop, Chicago free jazz, and the eccentric multi-instrumental effects developed by Roland Kirk (• p. 188), and presented its music in a vividly theatrical atmosphere. Recordings made by them in East Germany in 1977–82 were smuggled to the West. The more congenial climate prevailing in the Soviet Union in the 1980s allowed the trio to visit London in 1984 and the USA in 1986, when they astonished audiences at the JVC Jazz Festival in New York. Ganelin thereupon decided to defect, and settled in Israel in 1987.

World Events

1986

28 January
Space shuttle *Challenger* explodes on launch

15 April
US bombs Libya from British airbase

26 April
Nuclear disaster at Chernobyl, USSR

31 August
Death of Henry Moore

- Oliver Stone's film *Platoon*, based on the war in Vietnam, wins Best Picture at the Academy Awards

Above left Soviet pianist Vyacheslav Ganelin, who formed the boldly innovative Ganelin Trio in 1971 with Vladimir Chekasin (reeds) and Vladimir Tarasov (drums).

Jazz Events

1987

22–24 February
The Danish Radio Big Band tours Scotland and northern England.

February
Eighty-year-old Benny Carter is honored with a major retrospective presented by the American Jazz Orchestra at New York's Cooper Union.

March
Dave Brubeck visits the Soviet Union.

March–April
The Pat Metheny Group achieves further commercial success when they record their album *Still Life (Talking)* for the Geffen label.

2 April
Drummer Buddy Rich dies, aged sixty-nine, Los Angeles.

May
Doc Cheatham (• p. 195) visits Sweden to present a musical tribute to Billie Holiday.

10 July
Record producer John Hammond dies, New York.

17 July
The twentieth anniversary of the death of John Coltrane (• p. 160) is commemorated by several albums, including *Blues for Coltrane* (Pharoah Sanders and McCoy Tyner) and *Homage to John Coltrane* (Dave Liebman).

21 July
Saxophonist Andy Sheppard (• p. 202) makes his first album as leader in London, his style strongly influenced by John Coltrane.

August
Loose Tubes (• p. 204) appear at the Royal Albert Hall, London, as part of the BBC Promenade Concerts.

14–15 September
Charlie Haden (bass) records *Etudes* with trio partners Geri Allen (piano) and Paul Motian (drums).

21 September
Bassist Jaco Pastorius dies, aged thirty-five, after he is beaten up during a nightclub brawl, Fort Lauderdale.

8 October
Bob Wilber's big band presents their reenactment of Benny Goodman's 1938 Carnegie Hall concert at London's Royal Festival Hall.

29 October
Woody Herman dies, aged seventy-four, in Los Angeles.

November
Alto saxophonist Phil Woods, who this year signs his quintet up with the Concord label, tours Japan and records *Bop Stew* and *Bouquet* in Tokyo.

- Tenor saxophonist Michael Brecker records his eponymous first album as leader for the Impulse label.
- A big band is formed to celebrate Dizzy Gillespie's seventieth birthday and embarks on a world tour.
- Ornette Coleman is reunited with SIDEMEN Don Cherry (trumpet), Charlie Haden (bass), and Billy Higgins (drums).

Far left Ella Fitzgerald receiving the National Medal of Arts from President Reagan at the White House in June 1987 (bottom), and singing live a few days later (top).

Opposite The Diaghilev of Jazz: entrepreneur John Hammond, *c.* 1939.

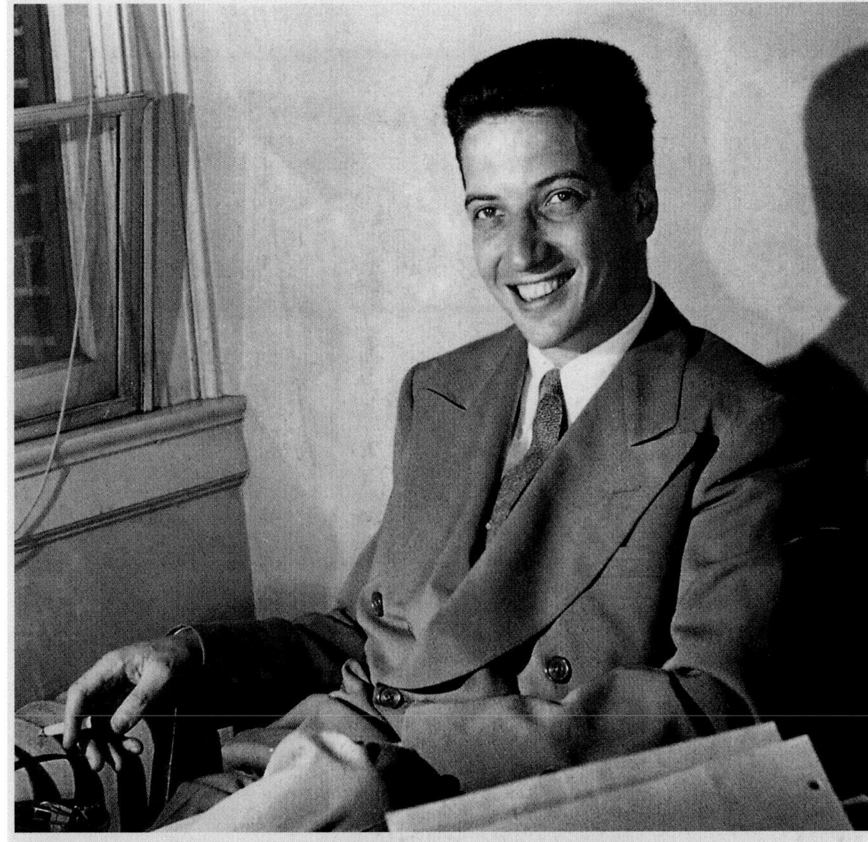

JOHN HAMMOND: TALENT SPOTTER EXTRAORDINAIRE

Progress in the arts is, very occasionally, shaped by the talents of entrepreneurs with a keen eye for both quality and commercial mileage. A prominent example from early in the twentieth century was the great impresario Serge Diaghilev, who nurtured the talents of composers such as Debussy, Ravel, and Stravinsky by commissioning them to write works for his famous Ballets Russes. The strongest candidate for the appellation "the Diaghilev of jazz" is undoubtedly John Hammond, who died in 1987 after a lifetime devoted to the pursuit and promotion of the finest performing talent he could unearth.

Hammond's career as a record producer began in the early 1930s, when his samplings of Harlem musical life drew his attention to bandleaders such as Fletcher Henderson (• p. 71) and Teddy Wilson. Benny Goodman (• p. 84), Hammond's brother-in-law, was able to get his new band off to a flying start in 1934 thanks largely to Hammond's energetic assistance. The following year, Hammond organized Goodman's first appearance as a classical clarinetist, and he later initiated the fruitful partnership between Goodman and bop guitarist Charlie Christian. In 1935 Hammond also made the major discovery of the phenomenal young singer Billie Holiday (• p. 131). It was Hammond's interest in Count Basie's band (• p. 87) that resulted in their relocation from Kansas City to New York and their subsequent rise to fame.

Hammond's association with the Brunswick record company was followed by a move to Columbia in 1939. Around that time he also organized influential jazz concerts at Carnegie Hall (• p. 91) that initiated, among other things, the revival of interest in BOOGIE-WOOGIE piano later exploited by Blue Note records. In later years, Hammond's outlook broadened to encompass the work of rock musicians, including Bruce Springsteen, and folk singers such as Bob Dylan.

World Events

1987

22 February
Death of Andy Warhol

17 August
Hitler's deputy, Rudolf Hess, commits suicide in a Berlin prison

16 October
UK devastated by freak hurricane

19 October
Stock market crashes, New York

- Van Gogh's *Irises* sells for a record $45 million at auction

"Goodman watched Charlie approach the bandstand, looked around the room until he spotted me, and zapped me with the famous Goodman 'ray.' But before the opening night audience there was nothing he could do but go along [with Hammond's proposal that he try Christian out] . . . He chose 'Rose Room,' a standard familiar to Goodman audiences, though one he assumed Charlie would not know. This would be Benny's revenge for my interference.

"I am reasonably certain Christian had never heard 'Rose Room' before, because it was a West Coast song not in the repertoire of most black bands. No matter. Charlie had ears like antennae . . . Benny would play a chorus or two, Lionel [Hampton] would answer him, and their talent would inspire Charlie to greater improvisations of his own. Before long the crowd was screaming with amazement. 'Rose Room' continued for more than three-quarters of an hour and Goodman received an ovation unlike any even he had had before."

John Hammond describing how he introduced Charlie Christian to Benny Goodman at the Victor Hugo Restaurant, Beverly Hills, in 1939

THE RISE AND FALL OF CHET BAKER

Few faces can have displayed the ravaging effects of a lifetime's personal problems as graphically as that of Chet Baker, who died in 1988. The trumpeter's boyish good looks helped shoot him to prominence in the 1950s as the first popular idol of the COOL school (• p. 132). His laid-back image and adolescent sex appeal were immortalized in a series of photographs taken by William Claxton, which set the tone for the decade and have remained influential in pop-music marketing strategies to this day. But when he died at the age of fifty-eight, Baker's craggy wrinkles told a very different story.

From the outset, Baker's trumpet and flugelhorn playing displayed the marked influence of Miles Davis's mature technique (notably in its studied lack of VIBRATO), and never really escaped from Davis's shadow. It was rather his crooning voice, coupled with a skillfully promoted commercial image, that did most to win him popular success. Baker's work is best represented by recordings made with Gerry Mulligan (• p. 134) and Charlie Parker (• p. 128) in 1952–53, and in the work of his own quartet (1953–56), which adopted the pianoless format he had favored during his collaboration with Mulligan. Although Baker's recorded output was vast, few albums have proved themselves to be truly memorable. He will perhaps be most vividly remembered for his laconic treatment of "My Funny Valentine," which typified the understated approach of mainstream cool artists.

Baker's never-ending drug problems became public knowledge in the 1960s, thanks to a series of widely reported encounters with the law while traveling abroad (including a spell in an Italian jail) and occasional deportations. His affliction did not improve on returning to the USA, and in 1968 he was beaten up in a drug-related incident in San Francisco, in which he lost most of his teeth. This savage mugging effectively brought his American career to an end, although he managed to return to the European circuit in the mid-1970s and continued to play and record until his unexplained death.

Above left Chet Baker, pinup of cool-jazz fans in the US during the 1950s, was constantly afflicted by drug problems and spent much of his later career in Europe.

Jazz Events

1988

1 January
Miles Davis performs alongside pop star Prince in Minneapolis.

16 January
Loren Schoenberg and Bob Wilber present a concert at Carnegie Hall celebrating the fiftieth anniversary of Benny Goodman's first appearance there, and reconstructing the original program.

16 February
Charles Delaunay, pioneer of jazz discography (• p. 86), dies near Paris.

February
Singer Cassandra Wilson records *Blue Skies*.

20 March
Composer-arranger Gil Evans dies, aged seventy-five, Cuernavaca, Mexico. His orchestra undertakes a memorial tour of Italy in **July**.

13 May
Former cool idol Chet Baker is killed when he falls from his Amsterdam hotel window in mysterious circumstances. The trumpeter's life soon becomes the subject of a documentary, *Let's Get Lost*, filmed by fashion photographer Bruce Weber.

June
At the age of seventy-one, Ella Fitzgerald (• p. 195) sings at Carnegie Hall.

18–19 August
Alto saxophonist John Zorn records *Spy vs. Spy: The Music of Ornette Coleman*.

17 October
Pianist Keith Jarrett (• p. 185) gives a solo concert in Paris. He is nominated for a Grammy award for his recording of the first book of Johann Sebastian Bach's *48 Preludes and Fugues* this year.

27 October
Wynton Marsalis continues his systematic reassessment of the heritage of early jazz by recording the album *The Majesty of the Blues*.

- Lyle Mays issues his second album, *Street Dreams*. Musicians participating in this eclectic FUSION project include guitarist Bill Frisell and drummers Peter Erskine and Steve Gadd (• p. 221).
- Verve issues *Echoes of Ellington*, a fusion album featuring the talents of trumpeter Randy Brecker and saxophonists Tom Scott and Bill Evans.
- Avant-garde pianist Cecil Taylor tours with British drummer Tony Oxley.
- Dave Brubeck makes a return visit to the USSR.
- Joe Zawinul forms the Zawinul Syndicate with guitarist Scott Henderson.
- Brothers Dave and Don Grusin record their keyboard extravaganza *Sticks and Stones* for GRP.
- Clint Eastwood directs the biopic *Bird*, dramatizing the final years of Charlie Parker's life and using Parker's original recordings as the basis for its soundtrack.
- *The New Grove Dictionary of Jazz* is published in two volumes by Macmillan under the editorship of Barry Kernfeld. Originally priced at £200 in the UK, a single-volume reprint in 1994 is marketed for just £25 and (not surprisingly) achieves phenomenal sales.

World Events

1988

26 January
Climax of Australia's bicentennial celebrations

11 November
George Bush elected President, USA

6 December
Death of Roy Orbison

22 December
Pan-Am jumbo jet explodes over Lockerbie, Scotland

Above Lyle Mays's fusion album *Street Dreams* (1988).

Right One of the finest electronic keyboard technicians in jazz, Mays's acoustic piano playing combined the ongoing influence of Bill Evans with more adventurous textures exploiting the full range of the instrument.

MESSENGERS RETROSPECTIVE

Art Blakey's Jazz Messengers, a group that nurtured several generations of exciting performers, are reunited just one year before the great drummer's death.

Above Art Blakey, high priest of hard bop, who died in 1990.

TRIBUTES TO ART BLAKEY

"Blakey had developed a fiercely individual style that was simultaneously volcanic and severe. Blakey was amongst the least superfluously 'busy' drummers in jazz. His rhythmic sense was so sharp, and his foot and wrist control so precise, that he needed do little more than 'keep time' to create an atmosphere of tremendous power. His accompanying figures, sparsely used, came at the right moments to support the soloist with sudden bursts of energy. Likewise, Blakey's solos were usually structured around a few melodic motifs played against each other contrapuntally as he built to a climax. Musical coherence was never sacrificed to technical flash."

David H. Rosenthal, 1992

"Throughout the 1980s the roster of young talent that passed through Blakey's unique finishing school [the Jazz Messengers] continued unabated . . . It is significant that many young musicians either came to the attention of the jazz world through Blakey's auspices or at least enhanced their reputation as a result of their tenure with him, most going on to shape the sound of mainstream bop on graduating from his ensemble – just as he intended."

Stuart Nicholson, 1990

Jazz Events

1989

26 February
Trumpeter Roy Eldridge dies, aged seventy-eight, Valley Stream, New York.

March
Ralph Sutton and Jay McShann celebrate the origins of jazz keyboard-playing in their album, *Last of the Whorehouse Piano Players*.

9 May
Already suffering from AIDS, trumpeter Woody Shaw, aged forty-five, dies from injuries sustained three months earlier when his left arm was severed by a subway train shortly after he left a GIG at the Village Vanguard.

June
Dizzy Gillespie (• p. 219) plays in a concert televised by the BBC from London's Royal Festival Hall. This year he undertakes a punishing schedule, performing over three hundred gigs in nearly thirty countries; home appearances are made in one hundred US cities across thirty-two states.

August
A tribute to Jelly Roll Morton (• p. 45) is mounted at Alice Tully Hall, New York, by Wynton Marsalis and Dr. Michael White's New Orleans band.

October
A seventieth-birthday celebration for drummer Art Blakey (• p. 139) is held in Leverkusen, West Germany, at which he is reunited with former Jazz Messengers stars Freddie Hubbard (trumpet) and Benny Golson (tenor saxophone).

November
Phil Woods's protégé, saxophonist Richie Cole, tours the Soviet Union.

Left Roy "Little Jazz" Eldridge, a vital link between swing and bop.

December
Drummer Max Roach appears with Cecil Taylor at New York's Town Hall. Roach also makes his first tour to the UK this year, fronting his own quartet.

- Nineteen-year-old trumpeter Roy Hargrove (• p. 223) records *Diamond in the Rough*.
- Alto saxophonist John Zorn records *Naked City* for Nonesuch. Prone to the use of eccentric sound effects (e.g., duck calls) that suggest the influence of Roland Kirk (• p. 188), Zorn makes his name as an important postmodernist capable of both popular appeal and musical freedom.
- Keith Jarrett's trio records STANDARDS live in Oslo for ECM.
- Charles Mingus's large-scale work *Epitaph*, completed and edited by Gunther Schuller, receives a posthumous first performance. The second volume of Schuller's definitive analytical history of jazz (• p. 169) is published this year under the title *The Swing Era*.
- Quincy Jones assembles a vast array of contemporary talent for his album *Back on the Block*, a heady mixture of bop and popular styles, including rap.

World Events

1989

23 January
Death of Salvador Dalí

February
Salman Rushdie sentenced to death in Iran for his allegedly blasphemous novel *The Satanic Verses*

4 June
Tiananmen Square massacre, Beijing, China

19 October
Earthquake in San Francisco

10 November
Berlin Wall comes down

Jazz Events

1990

3 February
Drummer Mel Lewis dies, aged sixty, New York.

18 March
Pianist Ellis Marsalis, father of Wynton (• p. 197) and Branford, records a trio album with bassist Bob Hurst and drummer Jeff Watts.

3 April
Vocalist Sarah Vaughan (• p. 123) dies, aged sixty-six, Los Angeles.

25 April
Saxophonist Dexter Gordon dies, aged sixty-seven, Philadelphia.

4 May
Thirty-three-year-old guitarist Emily Remler, former wife of Jamaican pianist Monty Alexander, dies of a heart attack during a tour of Australia.

May
Jan Garbarek (• p. 177) records *Ragas and Sagas* for ECM with Pakistani musicians, including singer Ustad Fateh Ali Khan.

Jan Garbarek / Ustad Fateh Ali Khan & Musicians from Pakistan
ECM
Ragas and Sagas

Above Jan Garbarek's *Ragas and Sagas* (1990) reflected a growing fashion for world-music crossover styles (• p. 205).

Above right Equally at home in popular fusion and hard-driving bop styles, pianist Dave Grusin originated a stream of impressive Hollywood film scores.

DAVE GRUSIN AND GRP

In 1989, the motion picture *The Fabulous Baker Boys* made an unlikely singing star of actress Michelle Pfeiffer, with a stunning jazz soundtrack composed and performed by Dave Grusin – and skillfully mimed on-screen by the keyboard-playing Baker brothers, played by Jeff and Lloyd Bridges.

A highly experienced composer of major Hollywood scores (including *Tootsie* in 1982, the Oscar-winning soundtrack to *The Milagro Beanfleld War* in 1988, and *Havana* in 1990), Grusin's international exposure in the cinema threatened to overshadow his talents as a performing artist and recording entrepreneur. Over sixty years after the demise of the silent-movie pianists, Grusin showed how simple music for a solo ACOUSTIC piano could provide an admirably flexible commentary to the on-screen action with his score for the Tom Cruise thriller *The Firm* (1993).

Grusin majored in piano at the University of Colorado, where he played with Art Pepper (alto saxophone), Johnny Smith (guitar), and Anita O'Day (vocal), before moving to New York in 1959 to study at the Manhattan School of Music. While serving as musical director for singer Andy Williams (until 1966), he recorded with the Benny Goodman Quintet and in a bop piano trio and quintet (the latter featuring the talents of Thad Jones and Frank Foster). In the early 1970s he recorded with Sarah Vaughan, while acting as arranger to Quincy Jones and Carmen McRae.

In the early 1980s, his record company GRP (Grusin-Rosen Productions, which he cofounded with Larry Rosen) established itself as a stylish purveyor of an easygoing brand of jazz-rock FUSION, which, although never greatly favored by the critics, achieved a popular following through unashamed melodic appeal. Grusin's own albums on this label include fine interpretations of STANDARDS by George Gershwin (1991), Duke Ellington (1993), and Henry Mancini (1997), and a virtuoso electronic duo session with brother and fellow keyboard-player Don Grusin (• p. 211).

Other artists who augmented the GRP catalog include Chick Corea's Elektric Band, guitarist Lee Ritenour, flautist Dave Valentin, singer Diane Schuur, the Duke Ellington Orchestra, and pianist David Benoit. Of these, it was perhaps Corea's energetic young band that was most successful in avoiding the pitfalls of overt commercialization by striving toward adventurous musical horizons.

July
Saxophonist Pharoah Sanders tours London.

August
Jan Garbarek records his album *I Take Up the Runes* in Oslo for ECM.

4 October
Violinist Stephane Grappelli (• p. 75), aged eighty-two, performs in Tokyo.

14 October
Leonard Bernstein dies, aged seventy-two, New York.

16 October
Art Blakey dies, aged seventy-one, New York.

- John McLaughlin records his *Mediterranean Concerto* with the London Symphony Orchestra under conductor Michael Tilson Thomas.
- Photographer Herman Léonard publishes his book *The Eye of Jazz*.
- Milt Hinton publishes his autobiography, *Bass Line*.
- Miles Davis (• p. 217) brings out his best-selling and racy life story, *Miles: The Autobiography* (coauthored with Quincy Troupe).
- Spike Lee's movie *Mo' Better Blues*, with a musical score by his father Bill Lee (double bass), features Denzel Washington as a jazz trumpeter.

World Events

1990

11 February
Nelson Mandela freed, South Africa

2 August
Iraq invades Kuwait

15 October
Mikhail Gorbachev awarded Nobel Peace Prize

- A. S. Byatt's novel *Possession*

Above Chick Corea at the piano in 1989.

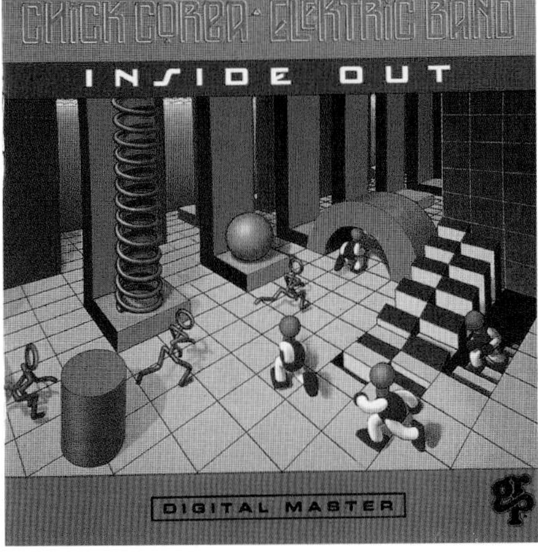

Right Chick Corea's Elektric Band helped revive the fortunes of fusion in the 1980s, and showcased the talents of drummer Dave Weckl (• p. 220).

DOWN BEAT'S CRITICS' POLL: RESULTS HIGHLIGHTS

August 1990

Jazz Artist of the Year Benny Carter (alto saxophone)
Jazz Album of the Year Cecil Taylor, *In Berlin*
Composer Henry Threadgill
Arranger Toshiko Akiyoshi
Acoustic Group Phil Woods Quintet
Electric Group Ornette Coleman's Prime Time
Big Band Sun Ra's Arkestra
Acoustic Guitar Jim Hall
Electric Guitar Bill Frisell
Trumpet Lester Bowie
Acoustic Piano Cecil Taylor; Geri Allen (Talent Deserving Wider Recognition)
Soprano Saxophone Steve Lacy
Alto Saxophone Phil Woods
Tenor Saxophone Sonny Rollins
Baritone Saxophone Hamiet Bluiett; John Surman (Talent Deserving Wider Recognition)
Female Vocalist Betty Carter; Cassandra Wilson (Talent Deserving Wider Recognition)

FAREWELL, PRINCE OF DARKNESS

Miles Davis, arguably the most influential artist in the history of jazz, leaves the stage for the last time.

Above Miles Davis and Gil Evans rehearse for a concert at New York's Carnegie Hall in 1961.

Jazz Events

January
Pat Metheny fights a copyright battle over the unauthorized use of his composition "Last Train Home," from the album *Still Life (Talking)* (• p. 208) in a television advertisement in Miami, Florida.

April
Pianist McCoy Tyner records *New York Reunion* with former quartet SIDEMEN Joe Henderson (tenor saxophone), Ron Carter (bass), and Al Foster (drums).

6 June
Saxophonist Stan Getz (• p. 152) dies, Malibu, California.

June
Lionel Hampton (• p. 70), aged eighty-two, records live with his Golden Men at the Blue Note club, New York, for Telarc. Lead trumpeter for the session is Clark Terry.
• Ornette Coleman (• p. 150) participates in the JVC Jazz Festival at Carnegie Hall.
• Foundation of the Smithsonian Institution's Jazz Masterworks Orchestra, directed by David Baker (University of Indiana) and Gunther Schuller. The band's activities are linked to a series of publications (the Jazz Masterworks Edition), and both ventures are supported by a grant in excess of $330,000 from Congressional funds.

Spring
The Koger Foundation donates $1 million to endow a series of courses in Great American Jazz at the University of North Florida.

July
Miles Davis appears at the Montreux Jazz Festival with Quincy Jones and resurrects his early work with arranger Gil Evans (• p. 120).
• Keith Jarrett (• p. 185) gives one of his increasingly rare solo concerts at London's Royal Festival Hall.

Summer
Chicago's Hot House launches the annual Women of the New Jazz festival, featuring pianist Geri Allen and singer Sheila Jordan.

September
Bill Cosby receives a Lifetime Achievement award from *Down Beat*. A drummer himself, the comedian is the popular host of the Playboy Jazz Festival, held at the Hollywood Bowl annually since 1979.

28 September
Miles Davis dies at the age of sixty-five, Santa Monica, California.

October
The first Akbank International Jazz Festival is held in Istanbul.

- Alto saxophonist David Sanborn, a popular FUSION artist, records *Another Hand* with a distinguished lineup including Bill Frisell, Charlie Haden, Marcus Miller, and Jack DeJohnette.
- The eightieth birthday of Cuban trumpeter Mario Bauzá (• p. 114) inspires a resurgence of interest in "Cubop" in New York.

World Events

16 January
Gulf War begins

25 February
Warsaw Pact collapses

21 May
Rajiv Gandhi assassinated

November
Singer Freddie Mercury dies from AIDS

21 December
Downfall of Soviet Union

Left Miles Davis at New York's JVC Jazz Festival in June 1987.

MILES DAVIS: DEATH OF A LEGEND

On 8 July 1991, a visibly frail Miles Davis took the stage at the Montreux Jazz Festival, backed by a fifty-piece orchestra under the direction of Quincy Jones, and played a tribute to his onetime collaborator, Gil Evans. Two days later, the sixty-five-year-old trumpeter was in Paris to receive the title Commander of Arts and Letters from the Ministry of Culture and play a reunion GIG with former sidemen Wayne Shorter and Dave Holland. On 19 July he visited London for the last time and appeared at the Royal Festival Hall. A little over two months later, in California, the combination of pneumonia and a stroke took his life.

Davis probably accomplished more in his forty-seven-year career – an unusually long period of sustained activity for a jazz musician – than any other performer. As fellow trumpeter Ian Carr put it, "His creativity and his influence as both player and conceptualist were sustained for more than four decades, an example which introduced the idea of permanent conceptual development into the jazz life. That is why he has been an inspirational figure for successive generations of musicians since the 1940s."

Born in East St. Louis, Davis moved to New York in 1944 to take up a place at the prestigious Juilliard School. He quickly grew disillusioned with the school's stifling environment, however, and preferred to gain practical jazz experience by seeking out Dizzy Gillespie and Charlie Parker on West 52nd Street and in Harlem. Davis later explained, "We was all trying to get our master's degrees and Ph.D.s from Minton's University of Bebop under the tutelage of Professors Bird and Diz."

By the close of 1945 he had begun recording with Parker, and was serving a thorough apprenticeship in the bop style. Somewhat limited in playing technique, Davis was unable to compete with Gillespie's pyrotechnics (• p. 219), and in 1948 first asserted his stylistic individuality by forming with Gil Evans the celebrated nonet that initiated the COOL school (• p. 120). Although he continued to work with Evans in large-ensemble ventures, Davis spent much of the 1950s and 1960s developing a refined form of HARD BOP while experimenting with novel modal techniques (• p. 147). Davis's canny initiation of the jazz-rock FUSION movement in 1968–69 was sudden, unpredictable, and hugely successful (• p. 170), and earned him an international status akin to that of a high-profile pop star. Not surprisingly, perhaps, he later collaborated with pop singers, such as Sting and Prince.

Davis's personal and health problems, coupled with an inability to sustain development of his own stylistic innovations, meant that his work in the 1970s and 1980s did not match up to the quality of performances by younger talents, many of whom had been nurtured in his own bands years before. His distinctive manner of trumpet playing was widely imitated, but not to everyone's taste. The poet and highly conservative jazz critic Philip Larkin, jazz reviewer for the *Daily Telegraph* in the 1960s, wrote of the trumpeter's "new inhumanity," and declared that Davis had "several manners: the dead muzzled slow stuff, the sour yelping fast stuff, and the sonorous theatrical arranged stuff, and I disliked them all."

DIVERSITY

Jazz moves into its tenth decade confronted with a richly varied but utterly unpredictable future.

Top Tenor saxophonist Joe Henderson, who won major critical and popular acclaim in 1993.

Above A participant in Miles Davis's early fusion projects in 1969–71, formidable drummer Jack DeJohnette is also proficient as a pianist.

Jazz Events

1992

13 April
Widely respected jazz critic Martin Williams dies, aged sixty-seven, in Washington, DC.

23 April
Pianist Lyle Mays (• p. 211) records an ACOUSTIC trio album, *Fictionary*, with Marc Johnson (bass) and Jack DeJohnette (drums).

August
Miles Davis's last studio album, the rap-based *Doo-Bop* (featuring Easy Mo Bee), and Wynton Marsalis's *Blue Interlude* both receive a grudging 4½ out of five stars in *Down Beat* reviews.

November
The San Francisco Jazz Festival stages a pianists' tribute to the work of Jelly Roll Morton (• p. 45), featuring Wynton Marsalis's pianist Marcus Roberts. Morton's life is further celebrated this year in the Broadway musical *Jelly's Last Jam*.

December
Julius Hemphill's sextet recording *Fat Man and the Hard Blues* (July 1991) receives the maximum five stars in a *Down Beat* review.

- Keith Jarrett (• p. 185) records Dmitri Shostakovich's *Preludes and Fugues*.
- Bob Belden's recording of his jazz reinterpretation of themes from Puccini's *Turandot* (the opera having been popularized by its global exposure in television coverage of soccer's World Cup in 1990) is released only in Japan because of copyright restrictions imposed by Puccini's estate.
- In a sign of the increasing use of ethnic music in a jazz context, the Montreux Jazz Festival renames itself the Montreux Jazz and World Music Festival.

1993

6 January
Dizzy Gillespie dies, aged seventy-five, in Englewood, New Jersey.

30 May
Bandleader Sun Ra dies, aged seventy-nine, in Birmingham, Alabama.

25 July
The Concord Jazz Festival celebrates its silver jubilee in California.

August
In *Down Beat*'s annual Critics' Poll, Joe Henderson's *So Near, So Far (Musings for Miles)* is named Best Album. He goes on to win three awards in its Readers' Poll in **December**.

December
Milt Jackson (• p. 129) receives a special award from *Down Beat* for winning the vibraphone category of its Critics' Poll ten years in succession.
• Cassandra Wilson's first Blue Note album, *Blue Light 'Til Dawn*, receives five stars in *Down Beat*.

- Dave Grusin records an album of Duke Ellington STANDARDS under the title *Homage to Duke* (GRP).
- Pianist Horace Silver records *It's Got to Be Funky* for Columbia.
- Canadian pianist Oscar Peterson (• p. 163) wins a $50,000 prize awarded in memory of his compatriot, classical pianist Glenn Gould. Twenty-nine-year-old pianist Benny Green receives $10,000 and the title "Glenn Gould Protégé in Music."
- Chick Corea's dynamic Elektric Band is refused permission to perform at Baden-Würtemberg, Germany, because of the pianist's membership in the controversial Church of Scientology.
- Jan Garbarek (• p. 177) scores both commercial success and critical acclaim with his unique album *Officium* (ECM), a CROSSOVER venture synthesizing jazz and medieval vocal music. Latin motets performed by the Hilliard Ensemble provide the backdrop for haunting saxophone IMPROVISATIONS.

DIZZY GILLESPIE: ANTICS AND TRIBUTES

"When Pee Wee Marquette finished announcing an attraction at Birdland, he usually walked off the bandstand leaving the microphone at the height he had adjusted it for himself, about three feet from the floor.

"One night, Pee Wee announced, 'And now, ladies and gentlemen, Birdland proudly presents, DIZZY GILLESPIE!' and walked away from the microphone. Out came Dizzy on his knees to accept the applause and announce the first tune. The microphone needed no adjustment."

Bill Crow, 1990

"I wanted to play high and fast like Dizzy just to prove to myself that I could do it. A lot of cats used to be putting me down back in the bebop days, because their ears could only pick up what Dizzy was doing. That's what they thought playing the trumpet was all about. And when somebody like me came along, trying something different, he ran the risk of being put down."

Miles Davis, 1989

"Gillespie was one of the few of the early beboppers who did not destroy himself. He ran his career with intelligence, and even when later movements in music seemed to make bop obsolete, he continued to work, emerging in the 1970s as something as close to an elder statesman as the music has ever seen. Like [Coleman] Hawkins, he kept his standards and continued to play his own way, despite shifts of taste."

James Lincoln Collier, 1978

One of Dizzy Gillespie's distinctive trumpets, on which the bells were bent sharply upwards, was sold by a London auction house in 1996. Gillespie himself described how the unusual modification came about on the night of 6 January 1953:

"The truth is that the shape of my horn was an accident . . . When I got back to the club [Snookie's, on West 45th Street, New York], Stump 'n' Stumpy had been fooling around on the bandstand, and one had pushed the other, and he'd fallen back on to my horn. Instead of the horn just falling, the bell bent. When I got back, the bell was sticking up in the air. Illinois Jacquet had left. He said, 'I'm not going to be here when that man comes back and sees his horn sticking up at that angle.'

"When I came back, it was my wife's birthday and I didn't want to be a drag. I put the horn to my mouth and started playing it. Well, when the bell went back, it made a smaller hole because of the dent . . . The sound had changed, and it could be played softly, very softly, not blarey . . . I contacted the Martin Company, and I had Lorraine, who's also an artist, draw me a trumpet at a forty-five degree angle . . . They made me a trumpet and I've been playing one like that ever since."

Right Dizzy Gillespie shows off his two physical hallmarks: bulging cheeks containing enough air to produce a seemingly endless succession of brilliant notes, and his upward-thrusting trumpet bell.

World Events

1992

12 April
EuroDisney opens, Paris

April–May
Race riots in Los Angeles

3 November
Bill Clinton elected President, USA

9 December
Prince and Princess of Wales separate, UK

- Civil War intensifies in former Yugoslavia

MODERN DRUMMERS

Above Steve Gadd at Nice, France, in 1988.

One of the most significant developments affecting the course of jazz during the FUSION craze was the shift to a rock-influenced style of drumming. The SWING rhythms of earlier jazz were increasingly replaced in the late 1960s by "straight" rhythmic patterns that were often hard-driving and included emphatic BACKBEATS. At the same time, and in sharp contrast, avant-garde drummers concentrated on dissolving all sense of rhythmic pulse in an attempt to break away from conventional attitudes to METER.

As the first wave of experimentation abated and performers began to look back once again to earlier jazz styles for inspiration, jazz drumming readmitted traditional techniques alongside these new approaches. Since the 1980s, drummers have had at their disposal a phenomenal array of rhythmic resources, and the tension between "straight" rock patterns, "SWUNG" jazz rhythms and metrical freedom has been maintained with generally impressive creative results. The succession of drummers who performed with Weather Report (• p. 175) – Alphonse Mouzon, Alex Acuña, Peter Erskine, and Omar Hakim – exemplified varied but equally impressive syntheses of the available techniques. Versatile artists such as Barry Altschul and Steve Gadd developed their own distinctive idioms, with Gadd's "linear" style of playing employing a wide range of percussive timbres with unusual economy and clarity. Weather Report was also typical of its time in featuring an additional performer playing exotic percussion instruments that were often heavily influenced by Brazilian music. The Brazilian virtuoso Naná Vasconcelos brought an extra dimension to the fusion sound with his colorful work with the Pat Metheny Group in the 1980s, and in his CROSSOVER ventures with Don Cherry (• p. 204) and others.

Another product of the 1970s was the electronic drum pad, which produces synthesized drum sounds when struck. Models manufactured by Moog (• p. 193) and Simmons may be used exclusively, or rigged up alongside a conventional drum kit as an ancillary resource. Among the first exponents of the device were Tony Williams, who was Miles Davis's prodigious drummer, and Billy Cobham, who cemented his reputation with his exhilarating drumming for John McLaughlin's Mahavishnu Orchestra. Superb electronic drumming was demonstrated in Chick Corea's Elektric Band by Dave Weckl, who indulged in a drum battle with Steve Gadd on his 1990 album, *Master Plan*.

Once popular but now regarded with suspicion in jazz circles, the so-called drum machine seemed in danger of supplanting live drummers altogether during the 1970s. Fully automated and capable of a rigorous metrical precision beyond even the best human performer, the drum machine has remained an ideal tool in a disco environment, but has proved to be too inflexible for the spontaneous creative context of the best jazz.

World Events

1993

15 October
Nelson Mandela and F. W. de Klerk win Nobel Peace Prize

- Death of Frank Zappa. Steven Spielberg's movie *Schindler's List* receives Oscar for Best Picture, while his film *Jurassic Park* nets $500 million at the box office.

1994

26 April
First multiracial election, South Africa

1 May
Formula One driver Ayrton Senna killed in motor race

- Increasing NATO involvement in former Yugoslavia
- Edvard Munch's painting *The Scream* stolen from Oslo's National Gallery

Above Dave Weckl, who made his name while still in his twenties as the virtuosic timekeeper of Chick Corea's Elektric Band.

Jazz Events

1994

April
The Verve record label celebrates its fiftieth birthday in New York.

23 May
Guitarist Joe Pass dies, Brunswick, New Jersey.

27 May
Trumpeter Red Rodney, formerly a close associate of Charlie Parker, dies in Boynton Beach, Florida.

6 June
The New York Times says of Keith Jarrett's live recordings at the Blue Note, Greenwich Village, "Every new note sounds like a discovery." This year, Jarrett records Baroque music by Handel.

28 July
Singer Cleo Laine and saxophonist John Dankworth perform at the opening night of the first Hawaii International Jazz Festival.

July
Down Beat publishes a special issue to commemorate its sixtieth anniversary.

August
Pianist Maria Schneider receives 4½ stars from *Down Beat* for her album, *Evanescence*.

22 September
Critic Leonard Feather dies, Encino, California.

- Pianist Geri Allen records her trio album *Twenty-One* for Blue Note with Ron Carter and Tony William, former SIDEMEN for Miles Davis and Herbie Hancock.
- A jazz-rap "summit" meeting is mounted in New York by Max Roach, Donald Byrd, and rap artist Q-Tip.
- Classical violinist Itzhak Perlman records a jazz album, *Side by Side*, for Telarc with Oscar Peterson.

December

Trumpeter Roy Hargrove, aged twenty-six, finally ousts Wynton Marsalis from first place in the *Down Beat* Readers' Poll (although Marsalis still tops the Critics' Poll).

- Ornette Coleman's group Prime Time makes a major comeback with their album *Tone Dialing*, issued by the saxophonist's own Harmolodic label (a subsidiary of Verve). Other albums recorded this year include John Scofield's *Groove Elation* (Blue Note) and Chick Corea's quartet disc *Time Warp*.
- Director Robert Altman films *Kansas City*, which includes a reconstruction of a typical 1930s JAM SESSION.
- The Thelonious Monk Institute and Universal Studios, Florida, plan Jazz-Fest USA, set for April 1996, to showcase the best young talent emerging from American colleges.

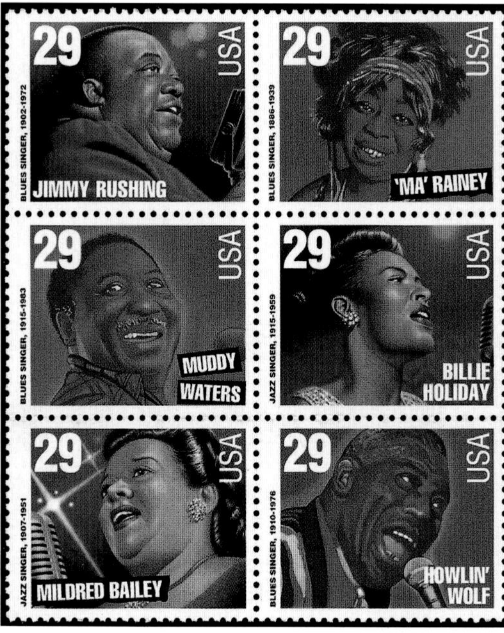

Jazz Events

1995

June

Jan Garbarek records *Visible World* in Oslo for ECM.

September

Maria Schneider is the featured composer at the 38th Monterey Jazz Festival.

October

The Arts Council publishes a review of the state of jazz in England. It concludes that underfunding and underexposure of the work of native jazz musicians has resulted in "insufficient opportunity in this country for [their] important contribution to world music to be fully recognized."

Above A set of six images of jazz and blues singers appeared as US postage stamps in 1994.

Right Free-jazz pioneer Ornette Coleman, seen here (second from right) with his quartet in a famous rehearsal photograph from 1971, made a timely comeback in the mid-1990s.

Above Roy Hargrove, who topped the *Down Beat* Readers' Poll for Best Trumpeter of 1995.

World Events

1995

17 January
Earthquake in Kobe, Japan

23 January
Former football star O. J. Simpson's murder trial in Los Angeles receives global television coverage

February
Civil unrest in Chechnya, former Soviet Union

DOWN BEAT'S CRITICS' POLL RESULTS

August 1995

Hall of Fame Julius Hemphill (alto saxophone)
Jazz Artist of the Year Joe Lovano (saxophones)
Jazz Album of the Year Joe Lovano and Gunther Schuller, *Rush Hour* (Blue Note)
Reissue of the Year *The Complete Bud Powell* (Verve)
Composer Henry Threadgill
Arranger Toshiko Akiyoshi
Acoustic Group Charlie Haden's Quartet West
Electric Group John Scofield
Acoustic Guitar John McLaughlin
Electric Guitar John Scofield
Violin Stephane Grappelli
Acoustic Bass Charlie Haden
Trumpet Wynton Marsalis
Trombone J. J. Johnson
Keyboards Herbie Hancock
Soprano Saxophone Steve Lacy
Alto Saxophone Jackie McLean
Tenor Saxophone Sonny Rollins
Baritone Saxophone Gerry Mulligan
Drums Elvin Jones
Male Vocalist Joe Williams
Female Vocalist Betty Carter

The Readers' Poll results, published in December 1995, were strikingly similar. Notable exceptions were:

Hall of Fame J. J. Johnson
Trumpet Roy Hargrove
Alto Saxophone Phil Woods
Female Vocalist Cassandra Wilson

"Though a premature autopsy of jazz arrives every few years, either because of the deaths of giants or because the business of the music seems down for the count, jazz maintains a startling vitality in New York. This is made possible by the authority of the enduring masters, and by a growing body of young players . . . When the elder statesmen of blues and swing are on the bandstand, one can hear nuances continuing to develop within their styles – the styles of musicians whose experience stretches back to the sixties, the fifties, the forties, the thirties, even (if you're talking about Doc Cheatham) to the twenties and the teens . . . They convey the music's meaning through their gestures, their speech patterns, their anecdotes, their humor and camaraderie, their elegance, their grasp of romantic frailty . . .

"Playing alongside them is the growing flock of younger musicians, who use the misdeeds of their predecessors as invaluable admonishments, and who cherish the timeless triumphs of the jazz idiom with an unprecedented depth of scholarship so tightly focused on the processes of art that it doesn't shrivel into the academic . . . By ignoring the dictates of the mass media, they have become the truest rebels in American music, choosing an intricate and difficult discipline that demands courage, patience, and a willingness to cultivate one of the most fertile traditions this century has produced."

Stanley Crouch, "New York is Jazz," in *The New Yorker*, 26 August–2 September 1996

WOMEN IN JAZZ

Women In Jazz honors the legacy of female jazz pioneers, but musicians mourn the loss of the First Lady of Jazz, Ella Fitzgerald.

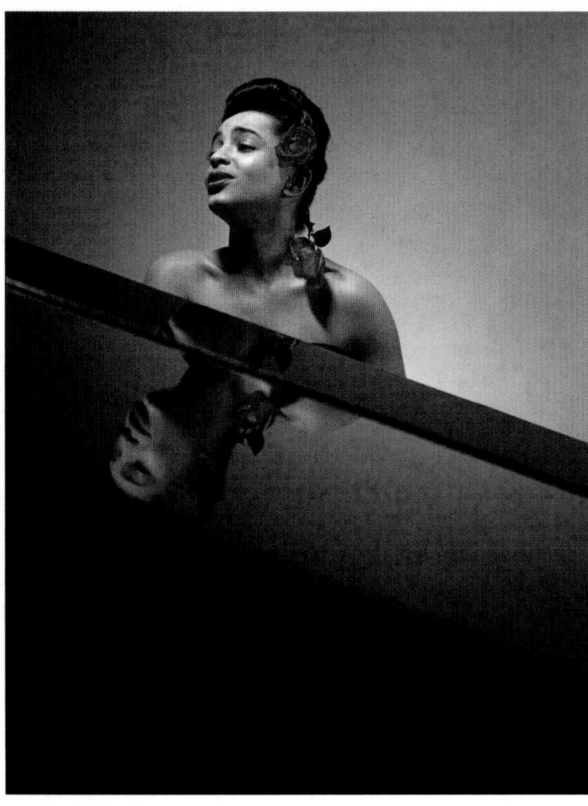

Above Mary Lou Williams at the Café Society, New York, in 1944.

Jazz Events

1996

19 January
Baritone saxophonist Gerry Mulligan (• p. 134) dies, aged sixty-eight, in Connecticut.

January
The Australian Jazz Convention celebrates the conclusion of its fiftieth-anniversary event, begun the previous month in Melbourne. One of the longest-running jazz festivals in the world, the Convention continues to mount a program of trad jazz in a different Australian city each year.

29 April
The inaugural Mary Lou Williams Women in Jazz festival, founded by Dr. Billy Taylor, opens at the Kennedy Center, Washington, DC.

15 June
Singer Ella Fitzgerald (• p. 195) dies, aged seventy-nine, Beverly Hills, California.

June
Pianist Uri Caine and his ensemble record idiosyncratic jazz and klezmer interpretations of music by Gustav Mahler for the album *Primal Light*.

1 July
Jazz at Lincoln Center is named as a constituent organization of the world-renowned New York City arts center, thereby gaining its own artistic and financial independence. It continues to celebrate the great canon of mainstream US ACOUSTIC jazz under the creative leadership of Wynton Marsalis (• p. 197).

12 October
Argentine composer and pianist Lalo Schifrin premieres (with the Quad Cities Symphony Orchestra in Moline, Illinois) his *Rhapsody for Bix*, commissioned by the Bix Beiderbecke Memorial Society as part of the sesquicentennial celebrations in Beiderbecke's native state of Iowa.

17 October
Eastwood After Hours at Carnegie Hall, New York, celebrates the many and varied uses of jazz in films directed by Clint Eastwood. Alongside Eastwood himself, participants include James Carter, Roy Hargrove, Charles McPherson, Jay McShann, and James Moody, with Lennie Niehaus arranging a big-band compendium of the best-known jazz themes from Eastwood's films.

- More than eighty hours of previously unknown recordings of live GIGS, 1966–80, by pianist Bill Evans (• p. 157) are discovered at the Village Vanguard, Greenwich Village, New York.
- Saxophonist John Purcell joins the World Saxophone Quartet, taking the seat formerly occupied by Julius Hemphill.
- Robert Altman's movie *Kansas City* recreates the atmosphere of the famous city in the 1930s, with its action centering on a fictional jazz venue (the Hey Hey Club).

CROSSOVERS AND FUSIONS

Uri Caine's first album of provocative jazz arrangements of the music of Gustav Mahler, recorded in 1996, caused controversy the following year when it received a coveted Mahler award (sharply dividing the judges' opinion in the process), and prompted a demonstration from offended admirers of the Austrian composer's music at a live performance at the Töblach Festival. The protest was a reminder of how narrow-mindedly some jazz and classical-music aficionados still viewed the exciting territory in which different musical traditions can be made to intersect – essentially the same problem that blighted Jelly Roll Morton's RAGTIME versions of Verdi's operatic arias and Duke Ellington's arrangements of famous pieces by Grieg and Tchaikovsky (• p. 151). Purists had always been offended by CROSSOVERS with classical music – even the apparently democratic meldings of the two traditions promoted by the THIRD STREAM movement in the 1950s and 1960s (• p. 143) had upset some die-hard jazz fans – but the bolder FUSIONS with which adventurous jazz musicians experimented in the wake of the initial 1970s boom in jazz-rock finally alienated those for whom electronics, rock, pop, classical composition, and non-US musical cultures had no place in "authentic" jazz.

While initiatives such as ECM's ever-growing catalog continued to encourage innovative blends of jazz, folk, classical, avant-garde, and ethnic music, and harmonic explorations that sometimes owed little or nothing to the blues, in the USA fresh yet distinctively nationalistic sounds were cultivated by bringing together country and jazz idioms. This was most noticeable in the "jazz-grass" (new acoustic music) of BANJO-ist Béla Fleck and mandolinist David Grisman. Fleck in particular broadened his outlook to explore jazz-rock and electronics, and in 2005 celebrated the roots of US folk and jazz traditions (and the universality of the pentatonic SCALE) by traveling to Africa to play with native musicians. But country elements had also been more subtly absorbed by eclectic fusion bands, including the Pat Metheny Group (• p. 199), sometimes in intriguing juxtapositions influenced by such different traditions as Brazilian and Indian music, and they remained deeply embedded in the aesthetics of acoustic players such as bassist Charlie Haden (who, like Metheny, hailed from the Midwest) and guitarist Bill Frisell.

New life was breathed into some of the groundbreaking fusion ventures of the 1970s when the original participants reformed their groups decades later: John McLaughlin's Indian-jazz outfit Shakti (• p. 205) was reconstituted as Remember Shakti in the late 1990s and toured widely in the mid-2000s, for example, and Chick Corea's Return to Forever (• p. 179) were reunited in 2008 and 2011. Herbie Hancock's FUNK-oriented Headhunters came together again in 1998 (• p. 226) and were further revived in 2005. Alongside these ongoing reminders of the rich legacy of the first generation of fusion experimenters, newer crossovers embraced contemporary African-American and Caribbean pop, comfortably absorbing (as had Hancock) aspects of DJ culture and hip hop. In the UK, the saxophonist and rapper Soweto Kinch (who took his music to New York in 2005) was notable for combining jazz with hip hop in concept albums that documented life in inner-city Birmingham, and at the time of writing is garnering a wide popular following.

World Events

1996

January–August
Continuation of hostilities against Chechen rebels, Russia

12 January
Janet Jackson signs record-beating $80 million contract with Virgin Records

9 April
Jonathan Larson's show *Rent* receives Pulitzer Prize

- High-definition television standardized
- Deaths of Jonathan Larson and Toru Takemitsu

Above Soweto Kinch, a pioneering melder of jazz and hip hop.

Left Béla Fleck performs with tablā player Zakir Hussain and bassist Edgar Meyer in Louisville, Kentucky, October 2009.

COLEMAN HONORED

Once regarded as a leading perpetrator of "anti-jazz," free-jazz saxophonist Ornette Coleman is now lauded as "Jazz Artist of the Year."

Above Ornette Coleman, Jazz Artist of the Year.

Jazz Events

1997

9 January
Lionel Hampton receives a National Medal of Arts from President Clinton at the age of eighty-eight. Hampton's New York apartment burns down a few days before the ceremony, and afterwards he composes "Fire in the Sky" to mark the misfortune.

January
The US Post Office issues a set of stamps commemorating the achievements of big-band leaders Count Basie, the Dorsey brothers, Benny Goodman, and Glenn Miller.

23 February
Drummer Tony Williams dies suddenly, aged fifty-one, as the result of a heart attack during routine surgery. A memorial service is held in San Francisco on **28 February**; his pallbearers are Max Roach, Herbie Hancock, Wayne Shorter, Ginger Baker, Ron Carter, Bobby Hutcherson, Stanley Clarke, and Wallace Roney.

2 June
Trumpeter Adolphus "Doc" Cheatham (• p. 195) dies in Washington, DC, eleven days before his ninety-second birthday.

June
Singer Cleo Laine is appointed Dame Commander of the British Empire in the Queen's Birthday Honours List, the first jazz musician to receive the title.

November
Betty Carter tops the list of performers at the Beijing International Jazz Festival, which has grown steadily in significance over the past five years. Still frowned upon by the Communist authorities, jazz now enjoys enormous popularity with Chinese listeners from all backgrounds.

1 December
Violinist Stephane Grappelli (• p. 75) dies, aged eighty-nine, in Paris.

- Recordings are issued by Verve and Extraplatte to celebrate the twentieth anniversary of the Vienna Arts Orchestra and the creative work of its director, the composer Mathias Rüegg.
- The New Orleans Center for Creative Arts establishes a new arts center, located on the outskirts of the historic French Quarter.
- Wynton Marsalis (• p. 197) revives his three-hour big-band oratorio *Blood on the Fields* for a major international tour. The work wins a Pulitzer Prize, the first to be awarded to a jazz musician. First heard in 1994, it tells the story of slavery and is the culmination of a concert-jazz tradition stretching back to Duke Ellington's *Black, Brown, and Beige* in 1943 (• p. 104).
- Dave Grusin (• p. 214) and friends celebrate the fortieth anniversary of Leonard Bernstein's *West Side Story* with a new album of jazz interpretations of the show's memorable tunes. Made for Grusin's new (and short-lived) N2K label, the album is the first audio recording to be issued in DVD format, as well as on CD.

1998

January
The International Association of Jazz Educators celebrates its 25th annual conference with a major program of events in New York, involving approximately 7,500 participants from more than thirty countries.

June
The Playboy Jazz Festival celebrates its twentieth anniversary at the Hollywood Bowl, Los Angeles.

June–July
Phil Collins leads his big band from the drums in a twenty-nine-GIG tour of the US and Europe, with a repertoire that includes jazz versions of songs by Genesis.

August
Down Beat's 46th Annual Critics' Poll votes Ornette Coleman "Jazz Artist of the Year."

26 September
Singer Betty Carter dies, aged sixty-nine, in New York.

Autumn
Dave Brubeck (• p. 189) makes a fortieth-anniversary tour of the UK, including appearances at London, Cardiff, and Northampton.

- Jazz Online and Jazz Alley TV launch an online Jazz Video Showcase, broadcasting weekly music video on the Internet.
- Herbie Hancock reforms Headhunters and presents their work on his new record label, Hancock Records, under the aegis of Verve.
- An initiative to relocate Charlie Parker's body from Independence, Missouri, to Kansas City's new Jazz and Negro League Baseball museums, with the remains to be housed in a 17-foot-high bronze statue of the musician, does not materialize. A new space, the Parker Plaza, and statue are unveiled on 27 March 1999, without Parker's physical presence.

JAZZ AND POP

In 1998 Phil Collins – leading light of the rock group Genesis in the 1970s – led his own jazz big band from the drums on a major tour, playing instrumental versions of the group's hits and surprising his pop fans by not singing. He declared: "I'm trying to bring jazz to a bigger audience. I'm not trying to make money off it ... I will do this 'til I drop now." Collins's initiative was in a sense the opposite of the kind of "sell-out" to pop trends for which jazz greats such as Louis Armstrong (• p. 57) and Miles Davis (• p. 217) had been lambasted by their critics – seemingly oblivious to the fact that, in order to both survive and flourish, jazz and its derivative styles need to be consumed (both aesthetically and commercially) by a wide and diverse audience. The spectacular success of Benny Goodman's and other bands during the Swing Era (• p. 71) was the last time in its history that jazz and internationally exportable popular music had been one and the same, but in the modern era some jazz musicians – and especially vocalists who straddled the worlds of jazz and pop – demonstrated a healthy attitude toward the stylistic and demographic CROSSOVERS that have always been at the heart of the music, steering jazz back toward a popular market in the face of predictably sour critical backlash.

In its reliance on STANDARDS as a basis for IMPROVISATION, jazz has always been indebted to a large repertoire of popular songs, and this tradition was even espoused by the early boppers in spite of their ostensibly anti-commercial stance. While many of today's jazz musicians refuse to extend their thematic boundaries to include modern pop tunes, continuing to rework time and again the familiar nostalgic melodies of yesteryear, others have embraced up-to-date pop melodies as a vital enhancement of the jazz experience and its contemporary relevance. For performers and arrangers such as Don Braden, Gary Burton, Fareed Haque, Brad Mehldau, Pat Metheny (• p. 199), Wallace Roney, and Jacky Terrasson, the ability to absorb and transform post-Beatles pop and film/television material into workable jazz idioms has required both a compositional mentality and a determination to synthesize diverse styles – attributes that not all jazz musicians possess.

A vital figure in the symbiosis of jazz and pop was Herbie Hancock, the first accomplished jazz musician to win spectacular success in the pop world. In the wake of Hancock's *Rockit* (1983) came a growing interest in using samples from classic jazz albums in pop, and, conversely, an increasing level of experimentation with DJ techniques on the part of jazz musicians (Hancock himself included a turntablist in the lineup of his Future2Future touring band in 2001). While the FUSION of jazz, hip hop, and rap in the USA during the 1990s seemed a satisfying update of African-American cultural experiences, long regarded as the lifeblood of authentic jazz, in London jazz-aficionado DJs were largely responsible for launching the Acid Jazz phenomenon, which transformed pop-jazz SAMPLING into a dance craze. As the acid-jazz trend took hold in the US, it diversified through live performances in a thriving club scene and reinforced jazz's former strengths as a music capable of both danceable grooves and instrumental virtuosity and sophistication. At the same time, groups such as Buckshot LeFonque, Incognito, Jamiroquai, and Us3 brought elements of jazz to a wide and grateful pop audience.

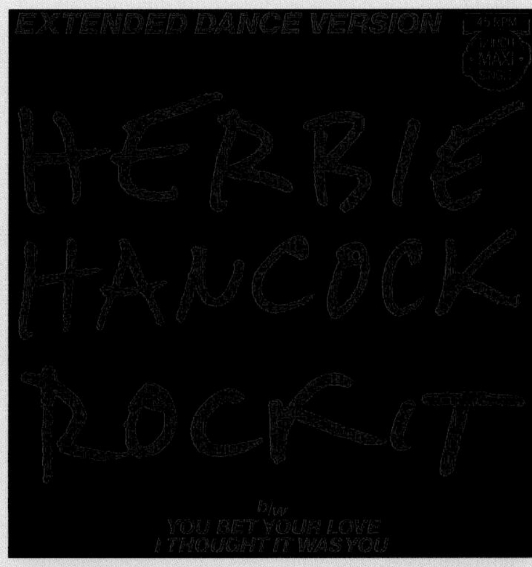

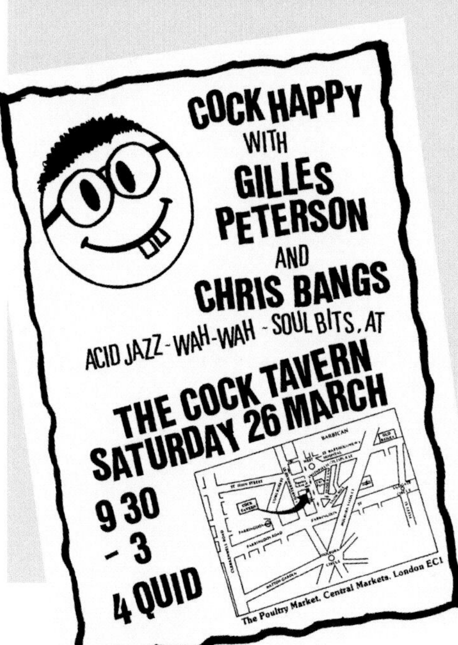

World Events

1998

21 January
News of President Clinton's affair with Monica Lewinksy breaks in US press

27 March
Manufacture of Viagra drug approved by the USFDA

3 May
Eleven countries sign up to new Euro currency

- Serbian aggression in Kosovo
- Deaths of Akira Kurosawa, Frank Sinatra, and Michael Tippett

1997

30 June
UK transfers sovereignty of Hong Kong to China

5 July
Dolly the cloned sheep born

31 August
Diana, Princess of Wales killed in car crash, Paris

- *Titanic* most expensive film to date
- J. K. Rowling's novel *Harry Potter and the Philosopher's Stone*

Above 12-inch vinyl disc of the maxi-single version of Herbie Hancock's dance hit, "Rockit."

Left Trendsetting DJs Gilles Peterson and Chris Bangs spearheaded Acid Jazz at gigs such as this London event in 1988, the first of its kind.

The jazz world marks the centenary of Duke Ellington, born on 29 April 1899.

ELLINGTON'S CENTURY

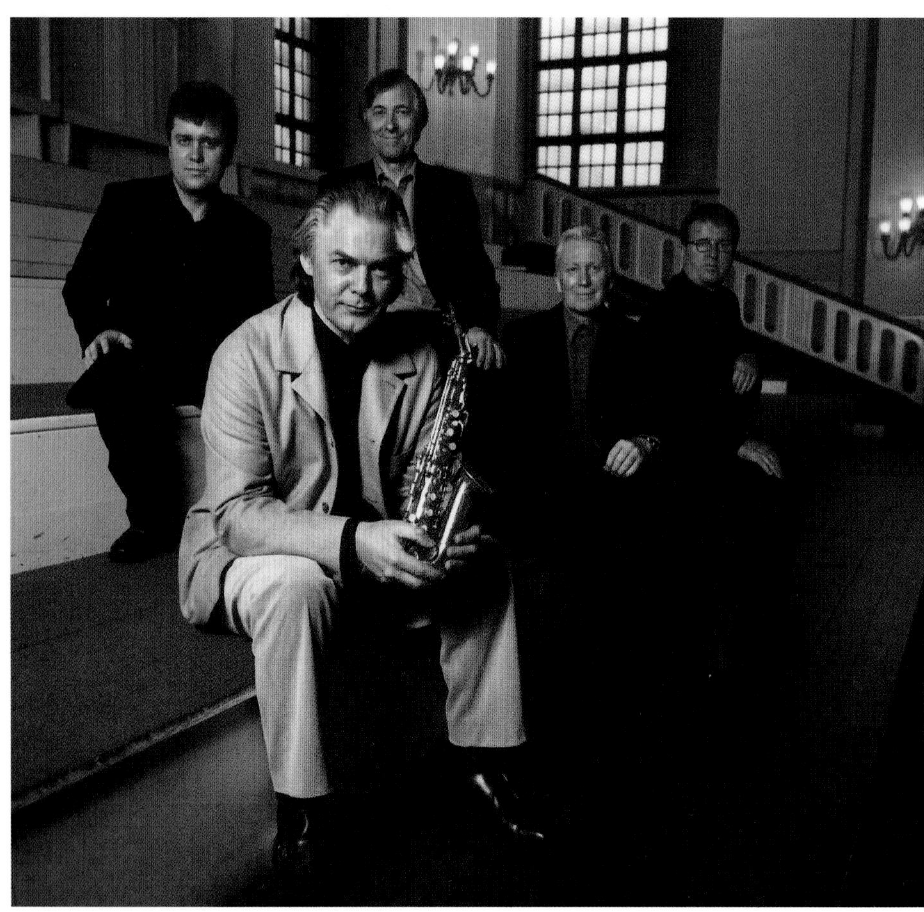

Above Jan Garbarek and the Hilliard Ensemble.

Jazz Events

4–5 February
Ellington centenary concerts at the Kennedy Center, Washington, DC, with the Smithsonian Jazz Masterworks Orchestra under David Baker, and keyboard contributions from Billy Taylor.

5 February
The *Down Beat* Jazz Hall of Fame opens at Universal Studios' CityWalk in Orlando, Florida. The "CityJazz" venue was designed with the assistance of the Thelonious Monk Institute of Jazz, and includes both exhibition and performance spaces.

24 February
Grammy awards for jazz this year include recordings by the Count Basie Orchestra, Gary Burton, Chick Corea (• p. 179), Herbie Hancock (• p. 201), Shirley Horne, Pat Metheny Group (• p. 199), and Arturo Sandoval.

19 March
Jan Garbarek (• p. 177) and the Hilliard Ensemble perform music from their new ECM album *Mnemosyne* at St. Ignatius Loyola Church, New York, mixing musical elements from Native America, Peru, and ancient Greece, along with a hymn from the Russian Orthodox Church. *Down Beat*'s Howard Mandel concludes his review: "Of course, few blue notes intruded on the ancient themes ... But during the concert, I became convinced of its powerful statement: Artists steeped in jazz belong to a worldwide congregation that, since time immemorial, has worshipped the eternal with song."

April–May
Blue Note's young artists tour twenty US cities to celebrate the sixtieth anniversary of the founding of the seminal record label by Alfred Lion and Frank Wolff in 1939 (• p. 95).

9 October
Vibraphonist Milt Jackson (• p. 129) dies, aged seventy-six, New York.

Jazz Events

8 November
Trumpeter Lester Bowie dies, aged fifty-eight, New York.

Autumn
Willem Breuker's Kollektief makes a twenty-fifth anniversary tour of twelve US cities. Also in this year, Kevin Whitehead publishes his book *New Dutch Swing*, a detailed examination of the flourishing avant-garde jazz scene in Amsterdam. The music is summarized by the formula "Jazz + Classical Music + Absurdism."

- The Verve Music Group is formed by the merger of Verve with the GRP Recording Co.
- The Library of Congress sets up a website featuring approximately 1,600 images taken by legendary jazz photographer William Gottlieb.

World Events

1999

24 March
NATO launches air strikes against Belgrade

17 August
Powerful earthquake hits Izmit, in western Turkey

30 August
Indonesian government crushes independence-seeking East Timor

- Death of Stanley Kubrick

Above An evocative portrait of West 52nd Street, New York, taken in 1948 by photographer William Gottlieb, whose work was enshrined in a Library of Congress website in 1999.

Opposite Japanese keyboard virtuoso and composer Hiromi, as she appears in artwork for her album *Place to Be* (Telarc, 2009).

Millennium Blues: The new epoch brings terrorist atrocities, natural disasters, and economic catastrophe, but jazz's musical riches continue to remind the world that the blues from which the music evolved a century ago was as much about resilience as oppression.

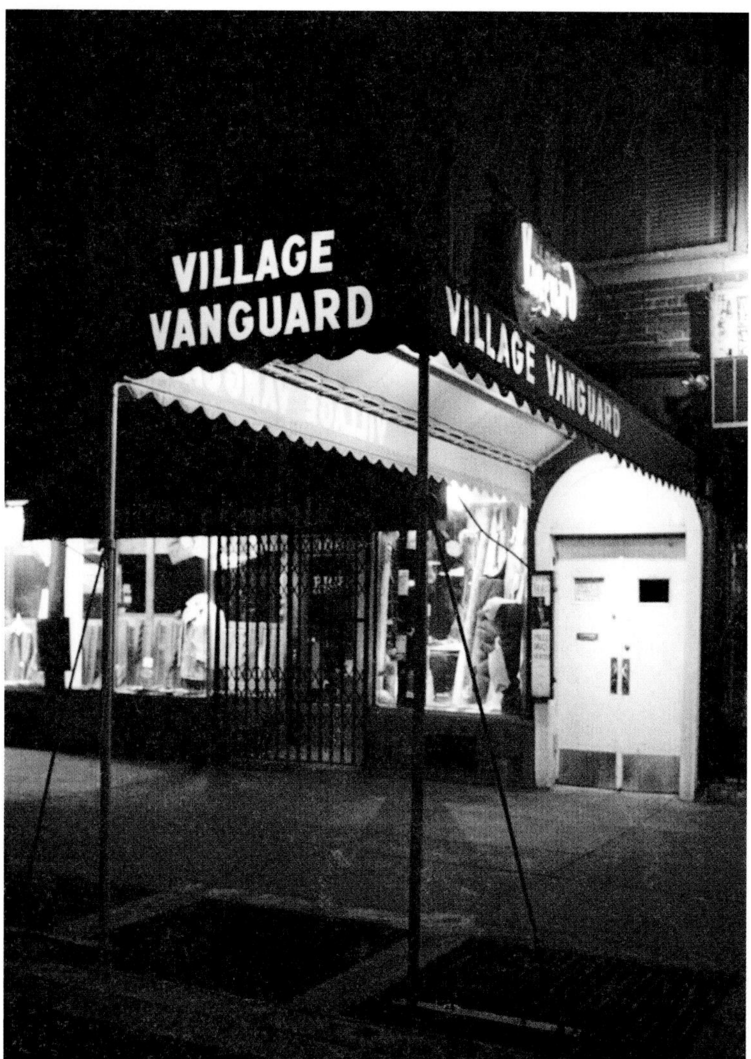

JAZZ IN AMERICA

US schoolchildren and TV viewers are encouraged to revere jazz as a national treasure, while major jazz events continue to flourish in Europe, Africa, and Asia.

Above New York's famous jazz venue in Greenwich Village, which celebrated its sixty-fifth anniversary in 2000, seen here in 1967.

Jazz Events

2000

2 January
Wayne Shorter joins forces with the Detroit Symphony Orchestra in a "Millennium Jazz Celebration," which includes the premier performances of his compositions *Capricorn II* and *Syzygy*.
• Trumpeter Nat Adderley dies, aged sixty-nine, in Lakeland, Florida.

14 February
The Village Vanguard marks its sixty-fifth birthday week with performances by trumpeter Roy Hargrove.

February
In Black History Month, the Thelonious Monk Institute of Jazz launches "Jazz in America," an initiative aiming to ensure that jazz appreciation is included in all fifth, eighth, and eleventh grade classrooms in the US public school system by the year 2003.

17 March
Jazz critic Randi Hultin dies, aged seventy-four, in Oslo.

March
The St. John Will-I-Am Coltrane African Orthodox Church in San Francisco, founded in 1971 with the late John Coltrane (• p 160) as its patron saint, appeals for help in finding a new home following the termination of its storefront lease.

March–April
South African jazz asserts its international importance with the inaugural North Sea Jazz Festival, held at Cape Town's Good Hope Centre.

World Events

2000

25 July
Concorde crashes in Paris

5 October
Protestors storm Yugoslav parliament; Milosevic deposed

November
Close-fought US presidential election involves several recounts

- Stephen King's *Riding the Bullet* is first e-book
- Deaths of actors John Gielgud, Alec Guinness, and Walter Matthau

Above Bassist Ron Carter (right) teaches the young Ben Williams at a masterclass mounted by the Thelonious Monk Institute of Jazz, 1995–96. Williams went on to win the Institute's bass competition in 2009.

Top Chick Corea leads a masterclass for public school students in Washington, DC, an event organized by the Monk Institute in 2002.

March–May
The UMO Jazz Orchestra, based in Helsinki, Finland, gives concerts to celebrate its twenty-fifth anniversary.

April
Danish percussionist Marilyn Mazur becomes the first woman to win Denmark's prestigious Jazzpar prize.

4 June
A "Piano Playhouse" at Tokyo's Yupooto Hall opens the History of Nippon Jazz series, in celebration of promoter Takao Ishizuka's forty years in the music business. The series features an impressive roster of Japanese jazz talents.

June
Down Beat publishes "A Jazz Musician's Guide to Internet Success (Jazz Musicians Use the Internet to Take Control of their Careers in the Information Age)."

Above Wayne Shorter performs with his quartet at the BMW Jazz Festival in São Paulo.

Jazz Events

2001

January
Ken Burns's monumental documentary series on the history of jazz first airs on television. Comprising ten episodes lasting some nineteen hours in total, the venture significantly stimulates sales of jazz recordings in the US (not least the twenty-eight discs specially issued by the Verve Music Group to tie in with the series), but provokes considerable controversy among commentators across the globe on account of what many perceive as the series' almost total neglect of modern jazz and fusion styles.

4 February
Trombonist J. J. Johnson commits suicide, aged seventy-seven, in Indianapolis, Indiana, following a period of ill health.

13 February
South African piano prodigy Moses Molelekwa is found dead in Johannesburg. Aged twenty-seven, the musician is discovered hanging next to the body of his wife and manager Florence Mtoba, who had reportedly been strangled.

7 March
The University of Kentucky holds a "Jazz Spectacular" on the exact date that, fifty years before, the university had banned a jazz performance on the grounds that such music had "no part in the university program ... the university faculty does not believe it is a fit subject for study."

29 March
Pianist and composer John Lewis (• p. 129) dies, aged eighty, New York.

3 May
Drummer Billy Higgins dies, aged sixty-four, in Inglewood, California.

18–20 May
Inaugural International Jazz Festival is held in Singapore.

26 May
A twelve-hour concert, featuring (among others) Herbie Hancock (• p. 201), Wayne Shorter, and Ahmad Jamal, forms the focal point of the St. Louis region's "Miles 2001," celebrating what would have been Miles Davis's seventy-fifth birthday year.

31 July
Inaugural BBC Jazz Awards at the Queen Elizabeth Hall, London. Producer Terry Carter declares, "European jazz is beginning to set the world's agenda. And through its broadcasting, BBC Radio is at the forefront of the movement."

Autumn
Saxophonist Joe Lovano begins his appointment as the first Gary Burton Chair of Jazz Performance at Berklee College of Music, Boston.

December
Regina Carter plays jazz on Paganini's $40-million antique violin in Genoa, Italy, subsequently recording on the instrument for the album *Paganini: After a Dream*.

- Portugal showcases many jazz events during Porto's year as European Capital of Culture.

Left Regina Carter playing Paganini's revered Guarneri violin at the Italian Cultural Institute in New York.

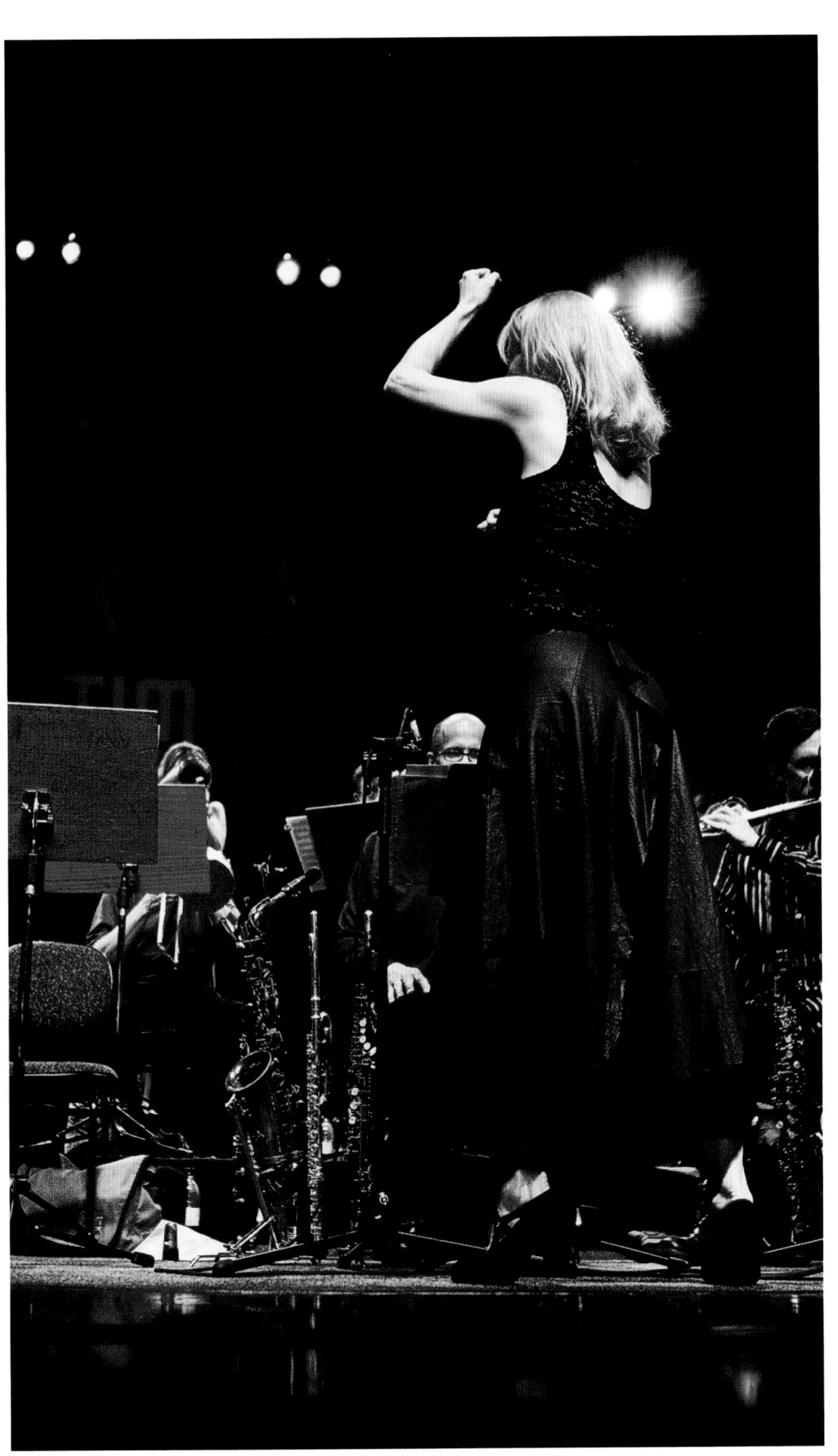

World Events

2001

23 July
International climate accord, Bonn, Germany

11 September
Terrorist attacks on the World Trade Center, New York, and the Pentagon, Virginia

7 October
Allied bombing of Taliban begins, Afghanistan

23 October
Irish Republican Army disarms

- Deaths of George Harrison, Jack Lemmon, and Isaac Stern

"After September 11, I couldn't listen to music for a week. I couldn't play either. I finally dared to play one note and it sounded insignificant. That made me rethink why I was originally attracted to music, which was something like water flowing through me. When music connects, it's the most powerful thing on earth."

Maria Schneider, composer, pianist, and bandleader

Left Maria Schneider directs her orchestra during a performance at São Paulo in 2006.

APPRECIATING JAZZ

As an annual "Jazz Appreciation Month" is launched in America, popular jazz singers reach out to the biggest global audience the music has ever seen.

Above Hiromi Uehara, who recorded her debut album in 2002.

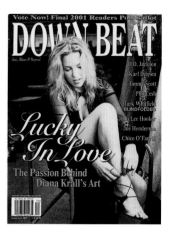

Above right Diana Krall's controversial appearance on the front cover of *Down Beat* in September 2001.

Jazz Events

21 January
Singer Peggy Lee dies, aged eighty-one, in Los Angeles.

5 February
Rossiya Hall, Moscow, hosts a Triumph of Jazz Festival, organized by Russian saxophonist Igor Butman and featuring Randy Brecker, Gary Burton, Billy Cobham, and Joe Lovano.

9 March
Singer-pianist Diana Krall plays in Seattle, Washington, at the start of a forty-city tour highlighting music from her best-selling album, *The Look of Love*.

24 April
Tenor saxophonist George Coleman, recipient of the year's Concertgebouw Jazz Award, appears with the famous Dutch orchestra in Amsterdam.

April
Jazz Appreciation Month is launched by the Smithsonian National Museum of American History. Curator John Edward Hasse declares, "Every April, I'd love to see the country riff, swing, boogie, and bop to the syncopated strains of jazz. Jazz is a great national treasure, arguably our greatest cultural export to the rest of the world."

2 July
Bassist Ray Brown dies, aged seventy-four, in Indianapolis, Indiana.

21 August
The Carnegie Hall Jazz Band gives its final concert at the Hollywood Bowl, prior to disbanding a decade after its foundation.

31 August
Vibraphonist Lionel Hampton (• p. 70) dies, aged ninety-four, New York.

Summer
After thirty-three years spent in Paris, saxophonist Steve Lacy returns to the USA to teach at the New England Conservatory in Boston.

September
Prodigious Japanese pianist and composer Hiromi Uehara, twenty-three years of age and still a student at Boston's Berklee College, records her debut album *Another Mind* for Telarc. Hiromi later says, "Rock fans call it rock, fusion fans call it fusion, jazz fans call it jazz. I don't have a preference. Everything is music."

13 November
Pianist Sir Roland Hanna dies, aged seventy, in Hackensack, New Jersey.

5 December
Saxophonist Bob Berg is killed in a motoring accident in East Hampton, New York, aged fifty-one.

SINGERS ASCENDANT

When the veteran singer Peggy Lee died in 2002, the blend of easygoing popular vocals and big-band backing for which she had become famous in her work with Benny Goodman (• p. 84) during the Swing Era was enjoying a notable renaissance, as contemporary singers cannily tapped the undiminished commercial potential of classic tunes and infectious SWING.

In the 1990s Harry Connick, Jr.'s successes had shown how the appeal of the old-time crooners with whom he was often compared had to some extent continued unabated, but now other male singers cashed in on the Sinatra sound, with Take That star Robbie Williams even dueting with the disembodied voice of Ol' Blue Eyes on the album *Swing When You're Winning* (2001). This best-selling project also included snappy big-band arrangements of STANDARDS by Duke Ellington (• p. 182), Nat King Cole (• p. 125), and George Gershwin (• p. 89). In the UK, the prodigiously young singer-pianist Jamie Cullum also modeled his singing on Sinatra, but championed a wide repertoire including music by Jimi Hendrix and original compositions; Cullum's platinum-selling album *Twentysomething* (2003) quickly made him the best-selling performer in British jazz history. Also notable was Canadian vocalist Michael Bublé, another contemporary crooner who modeled his singing and stage persona on Sinatra, with comparisons having also been made with Bobby Darin and Tony Bennett.

Female vocalists enjoyed even greater success than their male counterparts. Phenomenal album sales were achieved by the Canadian singer-pianist Diana Krall and US singer Norah Jones, whose *Come Away With Me* (2002) sold over seventeen million copies in just two years. As with certain male artists, these singers were constantly in danger of being criticized solely on the basis of an inveterate mistrust of commercial success, or else of being dismissed for merely flirting with the surface of jazz, primarily because of alleged limitations in improvising skills or emotional superficiality. Like Cullum, however, Krall showed herself to be an accomplished hard-bop pianist, as well as possessing a hauntingly sultry alto voice. She moved from a repertoire predominantly comprised of standards to embrace striking original compositions, notably those cocomposed with her husband, Elvis Costello.

In Scandinavia, although a far more localized phenomenon, Norwegian singer Silje Nergaard's albums rocketed to the top of her country's pop charts in the early 2000s, and other female singers, such as Jeanette Lindstrom and Cecilie Nordby, also reached large European audiences. In the UK, the work of the COOL-influenced Claire Martin in the 1990s was followed by the notable impact of Clare Teal's first Sony album, which sold well in 2004 in the wake of Cullum's spectacular homegrown success. Meanwhile, American singer Cassandra Wilson cemented her reputation as a powerful artist (initially inspired by the M-Base collective's aspirations toward "growth through creativity"), who compellingly reinvented jazz singing within its blues-rooted and improvisational traditions, and possessed uniquely expressive vocal timbres that were worthy of comparison with the greatest female singers in earlier jazz.

Left George Coleman onstage at the North Sea Jazz Festival at The Hague, Netherlands, in July 2000.

Above right Robbie Williams's jazz album *Swing When You're Winning* (Capitol, 2001).

World Events

2002

22 February
Ceasefire in Sri Lanka ends nearly two decades of civil war

20 May
East Timor gains independence from Indonesia

12 October
Terrorist bomb explodes in Bali resort

- Death of Billy Wilder
- Eminem, *8 Mile*

A WORLD TREASURE

The US Government passes a law declaring jazz to be one of the country's greatest cultural exports.

Above Voted the UK's "Rising Star" of jazz in 2003, the year in which he also signs a million-pound recording contract, Jamie Cullum is pictured here performing in Spain in July 2011.

Jazz Events

January
Sales of singer Norah Jones's album *Come Away with Me* pass the six million mark, making this the best-selling Blue Note album to date.

April–June
Flushing Town Hall, New York, hosts the Smithsonian's bilingual touring exhibition *Latin Jazz: La Combinación Perfecta*, which opened in Washington, DC, the previous autumn. It is the first time Latin jazz has been celebrated in this way.

15 May
Toronto's Massey Hall marks the fiftieth anniversary of a landmark BEBOP concert given by Charlie Parker, Dizzy Gillespie, Bud Powell, Charles Mingus, and Max Roach in 1953 (• p. 130). Performers in 2003 include Herbie Hancock, Roy Hargrove, Kenny Garrett, Dave Holland, and Roy Haynes.

20 May
Verve releases trumpeter Roy Hargrove's punningly entitled album *Hard Groove*, recorded by his FUNK band RH Factor, with artists representing R&B, nu-soul, and hip hop.

May
Keith Jarrett's piano trio (• p. 185), featuring Gary Peacock (bass) and Jack DeJohnette (drums), celebrates its twentieth anniversary with an appearance in Stockholm, where Jarrett also receives the Royal Swedish Academy of Music's Polar Music Prize.

1 July
Flautist Herbie Mann dies, aged seventy-three, Santa Fe, New Mexico.

12 July
Saxophonist and trumpeter Benny Carter dies, aged ninety-five, Los Angeles.

World Events

2003

1 February
Space shuttle *Columbia* disintegrates on reentry

19 March
Second Gulf War begins, Iraq

13 December
Capture of Saddam Hussein

- Crackdown on illegal music downloads
- iTunes launched
- Deaths of Luciano Berio, Johnny Cash, and Bob Hope

Jazz Events

15 July
The Smithsonian Facilities Authorization Act is passed by the House of Representatives and duly becomes US Public Law 108-72, declaring that jazz is "one of the greatest cultural exports of the United States" and urging "musicians, schools, colleges, libraries, concert halls, museums, radio and television stations, and other organizations" to "develop programs to explore, perpetuate, and honor jazz as a national and world treasure."

29 July
At the BBC Jazz Awards, held at Queen Elizabeth Hall, London, the Esbjörn Svensson Trio are voted Best International Artists, and pianist-singer Jamie Cullum is named Rising Star.

July
Two major European jazz festivals celebrate landmark anniversaries: the Copenhagen Jazz Festival is twenty-five this year, and Italy's Umbria Jazz is thirty.

4–6 September
Inaugural Panama Jazz Festival.

17 October
Toshiko Akiyoshi's orchestra plays a farewell concert at Carnegie Hall, New York, on its thirtieth anniversary, the pianist having decided to concentrate on small-COMBO work and composition.

Above Swedish pianist Esbjörn Svensson, another prizewinner in 2003, is seen in action at the Gent Jazz festival, held in Belgium in July 2007.

2004

In the year of the Coleman Hawkins centenary, bandleader Artie Shaw dies six years short of his own hundredth birthday.

FAREWELL ARTIE

Above Veteran bandleader Artie Shaw, who died in 2004 – exactly fifty years after he decided to retire from playing the clarinet.

Jazz Events

March
Avant-garde pianist Cecil Taylor celebrates the month of his seventy-fifth birthday with a GIG at New York's Iridium Club, fronting his Orchestra Humane Ubuntu.

23 April–2 May
The Jazz and Heritage Festival in New Orleans showcases the music of South Africa, marking ten years since the demise of apartheid.

4 June
Saxophonist Steve Lacy dies, aged sixty-nine, Boston.

22 June
Steven Spielberg's film *The Terminal* is released, starring Tom Hanks as an East European immigrant determined to track down saxophonist Benny Golson in order to complete a collection of autographs of musicians shown in Art Kane's famous 1958 photograph, "A Great Day in Harlem."

30 June–11 July
The Montreal International Jazz Festival celebrates its twenty-fifth anniversary, showcasing native talents Oliver Jones, Diana Krall, and Oscar Peterson (• p. 163).

11–15 August
The Newport Jazz Festival marks its fiftieth year. This famous Rhode Island event also celebrates its half-century with a fifty-city tour of the US.

28 September–2 October
New York's Blue Note club holds a saxophone summit to commemorate the centenary of the birth of Coleman Hawkins. The venue also announces its new policy to make on-the-spot CD recordings of its live gigs for audiences to keep.

18 October
Frederick P. Rose Hall opens at Columbus Circle, Manhattan. It is the new permanent home of jazz at Lincoln Center, and is described by *The New York Times* as "a sparkling addition to the city's landscape."

30 December
Clarinetist and bandleader Artie Shaw dies, aged ninety-four, in Thousand Oaks, California.

- Launch of ArtistShare, a web-based initiative that allows composers and musicians to trade directly with their fan base and to retain ownership rights on their music. The first artists represented are guitarist Jim Hall, composer Maria Schneider (• p. 235), and pianist Rachel Z.
- Diana Krall and her cocomposer husband Elvis Costello release their acclaimed Verve album, *The Girl in the Other Room*.

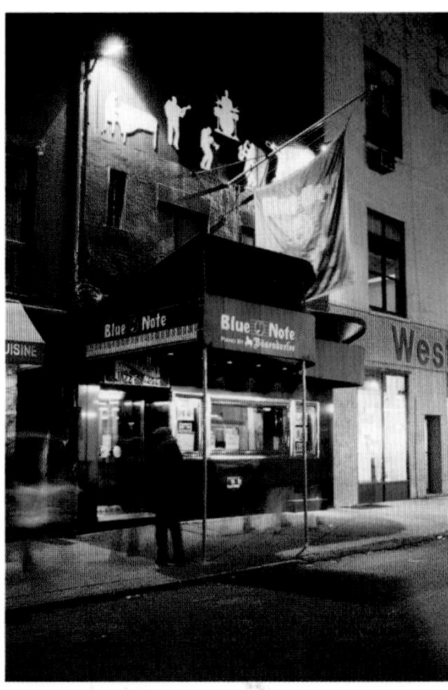

World Events

2004

11 March
Terrorist attacks in Madrid

August
Olympic Games return to Athens

26 December
Massive tsunami devastates areas of Southeast Asia

- Michael Moore, *Fahrenheit 9/11*
- Deaths of Elmer Bernstein, Ray Charles, Jerry Goldsmith, and Ronald Reagan

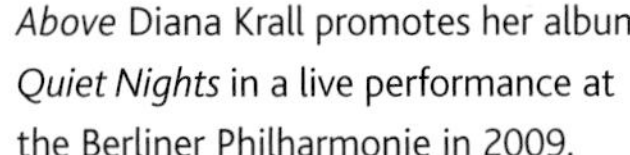

Above Diana Krall promotes her album *Quiet Nights* in a live performance at the Berliner Philharmonie in 2009.

Above right The Blue Note Club, New York, pictured in the 1990s.

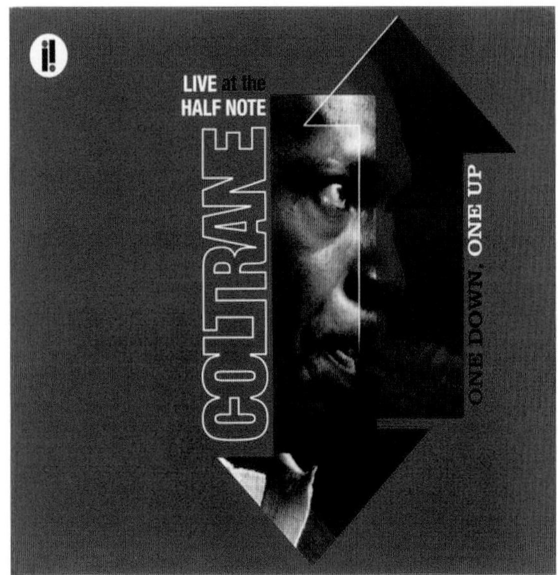

THE WAY UP

As jazz's African origins and legendary players continue to inspire a younger generation, Pat Metheny's creativity once again challenges traditional conceptions.

Jazz Events

January–March
BANJO-ist Béla Fleck travels to Africa to discover "the greatest acoustic music on earth," and records extensively with native musicians. The results are preserved in a television documentary and CD, *Thrown Down Your Heart*.

14–20 February
New York's Village Vanguard club celebrates its seventieth anniversary.

12 March–26 June
San Francisco's SFJazz spring season marks the eightieth birthday of Roy Haynes and features a seven-concert "Coltrane Project," including the saxophonist's son Ravi, who releases his own sax album, *Flux*, this year.

15 May
As part of a world tour, the Pat Metheny Group (● p. 199) performs *The Way Up* at the Konserthus in Oslo, the city where they made many of their early recordings for ECM. The new work, a seventy-minute continuous composition released as an album the previous year, is the pinnacle of the group's creative aspirations to date.

8 June
Herbie Hancock (● p. 201) launches a new-generation Headhunters band in St. Louis.

8–10 July
In its thirtieth anniversary year, the North Sea Jazz Festival bids farewell to The Hague prior to its relocation to Rotterdam in 2006.

September
Blue Note releases a recording of a performance given by the Thelonious Monk Quartet and John Coltrane (● p. 160) at Carnegie Hall in 1957, recently discovered in the Library of Congress. Also this year, Impulse! releases *Coltrane: Live at the Half Note* following the discovery of forgotten 1965 tapes in the collection of Coltrane's widow, Alice. Another recording of a landmark concert, Dizzy Gillespie and Charlie Parker's GIG at New York's Town Hall on 22 June 1945, is also released for the first time on CD.

Autumn
Across the USA, jazz musicians mount benefit concerts for the survivors of Hurricane Katrina, which devastated New Orleans at the end of August. The city's famous son, Wynton Marsalis, comments, "When you take New Orleans from America, our soul equation goes down. Our city will come back, but it will take the entire country."

- British author Stuart Nicholson publishes *Is Jazz Dead? (Or Has it Moved to a New Address)*. *Der Spiegel* reports that Nicholson's book "caused outcries with his allegation that jazz is more advanced in Europe than in the USA ... which for American ears sounds like 'The Russians are coming.'"
- Maria Schneider's *Concert in the Garden* becomes the first Grammy-winning album to be sold entirely via the Internet.

Above Coltrane fans delight at the first release of long-lost recordings made by the saxophonist in 1965.

Right Béla Fleck (left), who visits Africa in 2005 to play with local musicians, jams in Manchester, Tennessee, with Malian kora player Toumani Diabaté during the Bonnaroo Festival, 2009.

Below The Vienna Art Orchestra performs at Zurich's Kaufleuten Saal in 1997.

MODERN BIG BANDS

After the big band's unforgettable role providing the lifeblood of heady dance-oriented entertainment in the Swing Era (• p. 71), and its widespread international popularity in the golden age of radio broadcasting, the fortunes of this type of ensemble had dipped significantly in the era of austerity that followed World War II. Nevertheless, two bandleaders in particular went on to demonstrate the wide range of musical possibilities offered by the big-band format, as they continued to front loyal and closely knit groups throughout the 1950s and 1960s. Count Basie (• p. 87) updated his band's music, which was always rooted in the BLUES, with a canny absorption of the hard-driving blues RIFFS common in popular genres such as rhythm 'n' blues and rock 'n' roll. Duke Ellington (• p. 182), in contrast, exploited both Billy Strayhorn's and his own compositional talents by producing sophisticated and largely pre-composed music that proved well suited to packaging in LP recordings and concert performances in classical and sacred venues.

From 1966 onwards, Basie's protégé Thad Jones and drummer Mel Lewis (• p. 162) combined the best of both these aesthetic worlds in their band's catchy and virtuosic performances. Based at the Village Vanguard in New York, the ensemble still flourishes (as of 2012) as the Vanguard Jazz Orchestra. If the ongoing Jones–Lewis tradition embodies the best of the Basie legacy, the influence of Duke Ellington's and arranger Gil Evans's refined musical structures continues to be strongly felt in the beautifully crafted and Grammy award-winning music of the Maria Schneider Orchestra, also based in New York and notable not only for its resourceful structures and distinctive timbres, but also for its cultural and historical significance as the first big band to disseminate its music entirely through the medium of the Internet (• p. 242). Few would doubt that New York has long been the epicenter of the world's finest big-band output, boasting as it does a large collection of repertory bands and rehearsal orchestras. Strong links with long-established jazz traditions remain central to Wynton Marsalis's work with the world-famous Lincoln Center Jazz Orchestra, which has included large-scale compositions in the SYMPHONIC JAZZ vein established by Ellington's *Black, Brown, and Beige* at Carnegie Hall in 1943 (• p. 104). The city is also renowned for its rich array of Latin, avant-garde, and all-women bands, and for the highly regarded Mingus Big Band, led by the bassist's widow, Sue, and characterized by the collective IMPROVISATION and infectious energy for which Mingus's distinctive music remains celebrated.

Elsewhere, the work of Matthias Rüegg's refreshingly idiosyncratic Vienna Art Orchestra (1977–2010) reflected its leader's firm belief that combining elements of folk traditions and classical music has always been at the heart of jazz, and the band's reinterpretations of music by composers such as Ellington, Satie, and Strauss influenced many more recently established groups. The VAO's sad demise was caused by the contemporary European financial crisis, and serves as a reminder that in the modern age the kind of sustained investment that makes the flourishing Lincoln Center enterprise viable is regrettably rare, especially outside America. But significant commercial success has attended an ongoing initiative, adopted by many popular singers and their record labels, of fronting big bands in Sinatra-style renderings of classic songs (• p. 237).

World Events

2005

7 July
Terrorist attacks in London

15 August
Israel evacuates Gaza Strip

29 August
Hurricane Katrina hits New Orleans

15 December
Democratic parliamentary elections, Iraq

- Deaths of Saul Bellow and Arthur Miller

REBUILDING THE CRADLE

Jazz and its related musics remain the undiminished lifeblood of New Orleans as the city is rebuilt in the aftermath of Hurricane Katrina.

Above John Dankworth performing with his wife Cleo Laine at the 2008 BBC Jazz Awards, at which they were joint recipients of a Gold Award.

Jazz Events

28 January
Wayne Shorter and his quartet receive a standing ovation at the conclusion of their concert with the Los Angeles Philharmonic at the Walt Disney Concert Hall.

January
John Dankworth receives a knighthood in the New Year Honours List. He is the first jazz musician to receive the honor, and until his death in 2010 continues to celebrate his unique musical and personal partnership with his wife, Cleo Laine, who received the equivalent women's honor in 1997.

13 March
In New York, Miles Davis (● p. 217) is posthumously inducted into the Rock and Roll Hall of Fame, along with Black Sabbath, Blondie, Lynyrd Skynyrd, and the Sex Pistols. The event's host, record producer Ahmet Ertegun, comments, "It's important to point out that there's a gray area where jazz and rock 'n' roll overlap."

23 April
Wynton Marsalis (● p. 197) premiers his fourteen-movement *Congo Square* at the famous eponymous location in New Orleans with the Lincoln Center Jazz Orchestra and African drummers and dancers from Ghana. On the same day, legendary jazz photographer William Gottlieb dies, aged eighty-nine, in Great Neck, New York.

29 May
As New Orleans continues to rebuild itself after Hurricane Katrina, Allen Toussaint and Elvis Costello release their album *The River in Reverse* (Verve Forecast). Toussaint had lost both his home and recording studio when New Orleans was devastated, and music on the album marks the first major recording session to take place in the city since the natural disaster.

2006

Below Herbie Hancock inducts the late Miles Davis into the Rock and Roll Hall of Fame at the Waldorf Astoria Hotel, New York, in March 2006.

19–22 June
Inaugural Jerusalem Jazz Festival, Israel.

1 July
Chick Corea (• p. 179) gives the premiere of his Piano Concerto No. 2 at the Vienna State Opera. Commissioned to commemorate Mozart's 250th birthday, the hour-long work comprises six movements, each devoted to one of the world's continents.

23 August
Canadian trumpeter Maynard Ferguson dies, aged seventy-eight, in Ojai, California.

1 September
Saxophonist Dewey Redman dies, aged seventy-five, Brooklyn, New York.

October
Polish trumpeter Tomasz Stanko tours twelve cities in North America with his quartet.

7 December
Bandleader Jay McShann dies, aged ninety, Kansas City, Missouri.

World Events

2006

4 February
Danish newspaper publishes controversial cartoons of Muhammad

19 September
Thai Army stages coup d'état, Bangkok

30 December
Execution of Saddam Hussein

- Growing international fears over nuclear arms in North Korea and Iran
- Deaths of Malcolm Arnold, James Brown, and György Ligeti

2007

Musicians mourn the passing of Donald Ayler, Michael Brecker, Alice Coltrane, Oscar Peterson, Max Roach, and Joe Zawinul.

LOSSES

Above Michael Brecker (1949–2007), a musical and personal inspiration to an entire generation of jazz musicians, playing at Holland's North Sea Jazz Festival in July 2004.

Far right Keith Jarrett celebrating the twenty-fifth birthday of his piano trio in New Jersey during their 2008 anniversary tour.

Jazz Events

12 January
Pianist Alice Coltrane dies, aged sixty-nine, Los Angeles.

13 January
Tenor saxophonist Michael Brecker dies, aged fifty-seven, New York. He has been ill with myelodysplastic syndrome and leukemia for some time, and advertisements in the jazz press have been pleading for assistance to make a bone-marrow transplant possible. Going onstage later the same day with his Liberation Music Orchestra at the New York Hilton, bassist Charlie Haden (who worked closely with both Brecker and Alice Coltrane) tells the audience, "This is going to be real hard."

11 February
Ornette Coleman (• p. 150) receives a Lifetime Achievement award at the 49th Annual Grammy Awards in Los Angeles.

22 May
Michael Brecker's final album, *Pilgrimage*, is released on the Heads Up label. Pat Metheny (• p. 199), who appears on the album alongside Herbie Hancock, Brad Mehldau, Jack DeJohnette, and John Patitucci, remembers: "What happened in the studio during those few days in August [2006] is impossible to describe. It's one of the most amazing, powerful, unbelievable things that I, and all who were there, have ever experienced or will ever see."

8 June
A Carnegie Hall concert in honor of Oscar Peterson, who has Parkinson's disease, takes place without his presence – but with his photograph placed on stage. The pianist dies, aged eighty-two, in Mississauga, Ontario, on **23 December** this year.

10 July
Keith Jarrett's verbal abuse of an audience in Perugia, Italy, results in his being banned from future appearances at the Umbria Jazz Festival. A public letter of apology from the pianist subsequently appears in the Italian press.

16 August
Drummer Max Roach dies, aged eighty-three, New York.

11 September
Keyboard player Joe Zawinul dies, aged seventy-five, Vienna, Austria.

21–23 September
50th Monterey Jazz Festival, California.

21 October
Trumpeter Donald Ayler dies, aged sixty-five, Northfield, Ohio.

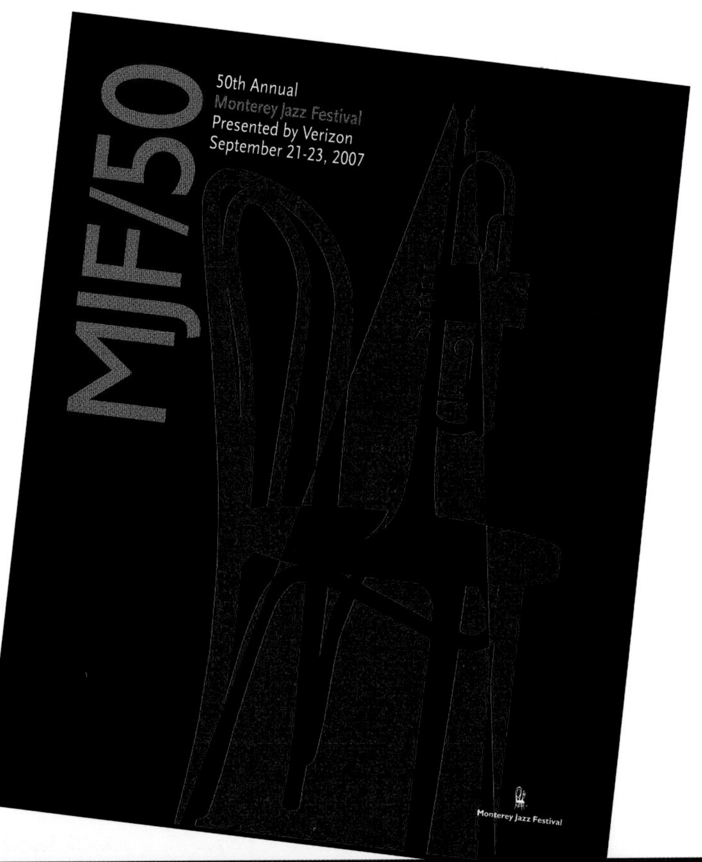

World Events

2007

1 January
Bulgaria and Romania join European Union

26 March
Northern Ireland political accord

26 September
Civil protests in Burma quelled with violence

24 December
Nepalese government announces plans to abolish the country's 240-year-old monarchy

- Deaths of Ingmar Bergman, Norman Mailer, and Karlheinz Stockhausen

Above and top The Monterey Jazz Festival marked its half-century with performances from Ornette Coleman, Dave Brubeck, Sonny Rollins, and a host of younger jazz stars.

2008

A legendary fusion band is reborn in a year that also sees renewed interest in the creative links between jazz and film music.

RETURNING TO FOREVER

Above Brad Mehldau, a highly versatile pianist who is equally at home in solo concerts and sophisticated ensemble work.

Jazz Events

10 February
Herbie Hancock wins a Grammy for his album *River: The Joni Letters*, the first jazz recording to win the Album of the Year award since 1964.

February
The Smithsonian Jazz Masterworks Orchestra performs in Egypt.

19 March
Jazz at Lincoln Center celebrates pianist Marian McPartland's ninetieth birthday. Her own trio performs music from her recent CD, *Twilight World*.

4 April
Bassist Greg Cohen and his quintet perform jazz interpretations of the film music of Bernard Herrmann alongside the Chicago Symphony Orchestra.

18 April
The International Association of Jazz Educators files for bankruptcy after forty years of sterling work in support of the music. Past president David Baker declares, "None of us can afford to let this happen."

25 April
Trumpeter and broadcaster Humphrey Lyttelton dies, aged eighty-six, London.

April–September
New York's Museum of Modern Art showcases the links between jazz and postwar cinema with a major exhibition and performances by artists including the Tomasz Stańko Quartet and Martial Solal, interpreting music from both European and US movies.

29 May
Chick Corea reunites Return to Forever (• p. 179) at the Paramount Theatre, Austin, Texas, twenty-five years after the seminal FUSION group disbanded. On **21 October**, Corea begins a five-month tour with John McLaughlin and the Five Peace Band.

14 June
Pianist Esbjörn Svensson dies in a diving accident in Sweden, aged forty-four.

23 September
Bassist Charlie Haden celebrates his country roots by releasing the album *Rambling Boy*, recorded with his family ensemble and many guest musicians.

29 December
Trumpeter Freddie Hubbard dies, aged seventy, Sherman Oaks, California.

- Electronics giant JVC announces that it will no longer sponsor the international jazz festivals that flourished under its patronage for nearly a quarter of a century since the company first collaborated with legendary US festival promoter George Wein in 1984. Among the best-known JVC-sponsored festivals were those held in Chicago, Concord, Los Angeles, Miami, New York, Newport, the Netherlands, Paris, and Warsaw.
- The two-disc recording project *Miles from India* brings together US and Indian musicians in a celebration of the music of Miles Davis (• p. 217), the project masterminded by saxophonist Bob Belden.

Above Esbjörn Svensson, performing at the Barbican, London, in November 2006.

World Events

2008

19 February
Fidel Castro retires from presidency of Cuba, after nearly half a century in power

May–June
Controversial elections in Zimbabwe

4 November
Barack Obama elected first African-American president of the US

26 November
Terrorist attacks in Mumbai, India

- Deaths of Isaac Hayes, Yves Saint Laurent, and Aleksandr Solzhenitsyn

RENAISSANCE OF THE PIANO TRIO

Swedish pianist Esbjörn Svensson's untimely death in a diving accident in 2008 robbed the jazz world of one of the many inventive young pianists whose work helped keep the venerable COMBO of the piano trio alive and flourishing in the modern era. Associated with an easygoing popular-song repertoire when founded by Nat King Cole in the late 1930s (• p. 125), and acquiring a virtuosic HARD-BOP dynamism in the hands of Oscar Peterson (• p. 163) and others in the second half of the twentieth century, the format had remained an ideal vehicle for the reinterpretation of STANDARDS in both SWING and BEBOP styles. One of the longest-established and most highly acclaimed standards-based groups was that led by Keith Jarrett (• p. 185), whose many inventive trio recordings since the 1980s have inspired others to take a fresh look at sometimes well-worn melodic material. Interviewed in 1996 about the value of playing standards in the modern age, Jarrett described the repertoire as "like a living organism that you can't divorce yourself from," and stressed that three players seemed the optimal number for the kind of spontaneous musical flexibility to which his group aspired.

The most exciting trio developments as the last century came to a close were a palpable increase in the quantity of original compositions for trio (in preference to familiar standards), a far wider range of stylistic elements than ever before (now embracing pop, country, rock, folk, fusion, classical, and minimalist ideas), and innovative keyboard voicings that left bop clichés far behind. Many younger pianists were initially indebted to the influence of the advanced harmonic, rhythmic, and textural thinking of Bill Evans (• p. 157), and impressive talents such as Brad Mehldau and Hiromi Uehara went even further than Evans in showing themselves capable of giving their left and right hands a striking rhythmic and harmonic independence from each other at times. After his first *Art of the Trio* recording in 1997, Mehldau established a reputation as a formidable improviser in both trio and solo concerts, while the effervescent Hiromi's captivating stage routines (sometimes including electronics) incorporated virtuosic fingerwork that rivaled that of her mentor, Oscar Peterson.

The "Nordic sound" of Svensson's E.S.T., Bobo Stenson's trio (also from Sweden), and Norway's Tord Gustavsen Trio in the 1990s and 2000s may initially have seemed part and parcel of the sometimes emotionally neutral and limpidly textured soundscapes characteristic of the pioneering European label ECM (• p. 177), also responsible for Jarrett's standards albums, but as Scandinavian trios blossomed they also came to encompass a truly international range of stylistic references, with Svensson's group in particular often delighting in energetic American-inspired rhythmic grooves alongside more contemplative atmospheres. Among the most interesting European trios that emerged in their wake were Norway's The Country and the Anders Aarum Trio, the Swiss triumvirate led by Colin Vallon, and the Polish pianist Marcin Wasilewski and his RHYTHM SECTION, best known for their quartet work with trumpeter Tomasz Stańko. Svensson spoke for many European musicians when he declared in 2004, "I don't see much creativity in jazz at the moment, so it's not where I get inspiration. I find a lot of it boring and not creative at all, with many bands just repeating what has already been done."

In the USA, pianist Ethan Iverson's The Bad Plus trio debuted in 1990 and quickly broke the conventional mold, offering an energetic and irreverent mixture of pop, rock, avant-garde tendencies, and original tunes, in the process creating an idiom that was "about as badass as highbrow gets," in the memorable assessment of *Rolling Stone* magazine. As with some European groups, Iverson's musical philosophy balanced a creative engagement with recognizable jazz idioms against a certain dissatisfaction with the sterility of post-bop formulaic improvising in what had become an utterly predictable head/solo/head structure.

As the USA salutes its first African-American president, and youthful jazz echoes in the White House, the music continues to flourish and diversify across the globe with undimmed vitality.

HENCEFORWARD . . .

Above The indefatigable Pat Metheny realised a lifelong ambition when he fronted his own mechanical one-man band in the "Orchestrion" project, seen here in full swing at Coutances in January 2010 during the French leg of its world tour.

Jazz Events

2009

7 January
Blue Note pianist Bill Charlap and saxophonist Ravi Coltrane embark with their septet on a major North American tour to mark the iconic record label's seventieth anniversary.

January
Jazz events mark the presidential inauguration of Barack Obama in Washington, DC, with musicians including Wynton Marsalis and Cassandra Wilson, and featuring "Let Freedom Swing," a musical tribute to Martin Luther King, Jr. (whose birthday on **15 January** is marked by a federal holiday).

14 February
Drummer Louis Bellson dies, aged eighty-four, Los Angeles.

25 February
Trumpeter, author, and broadcaster Ian Carr dies, aged seventy-five, London.

15 June
First Lady Michelle Obama welcomes US students to the White House Music Series jazz workshops, held in the building's East Wing.

16 June
Saxophonist Charlie Mariano dies, aged eighty-six, in Cologne.

June–July
Fiftieth anniversary of the Ljubljana Jazz Festival.

1–12 July
The Montreal Jazz Festival celebrates its thirtieth anniversary. Owing to the global economic slump, General Motors is unwilling to act as principal sponsor for future events.

27 July
Theorist and composer George Russell dies, aged eighty-six, Boston.

30 October
Ronnie Scott's jazz club in Soho, London, celebrates its fiftieth birthday.

October
Pat Metheny records *Orchestrion*, an album for one-man "orchestrionics," in which ACOUSTIC percussion and mechanical instruments are triggered by the soloist with the help of solenoids and pneumatics.

24 November
Columbia/Legacy releases a seventy-CD set of Miles Davis's complete recordings for the label.

- Prestige Records celebrates its sixtieth anniversary.
- ECM marks forty years in the recording industry.
- The Apollo Theater, New York, and *Down Beat* magazine both celebrate their seventy-fifth birthdays.

World Events

2009

15 January
Stricken airliner lands safely on Hudson River, New York

7 February
Catastrophic bushfires in Australia

April
Fears of swine-flu epidemic

9 October
Barack Obama wins Nobel Peace Prize

- Deaths of Lukas Foss and Michael Jackson

Above and top A gig takes place at Place des Arts during the 30th Montreal International Jazz Festival in July 2009.

Temperature Check

DOWN BEAT'S POLLS: RESULTS HIGHLIGHTS

	Critics (August)	**Readers** (September)
Hall of Fame:	Muhal Richard Abrams	Chick Corea
Artist of the Year:	Joe Lovano	Chick Corea
Jazz Group:	Joe Lovano Us Five	Dave Brubeck Quartet
Big Band:	Maria Schneider Orchestra	Maria Schneider Orchestra
Trumpet:	Dave Douglas	Wynton Marsalis
Trombone:	Roswell Rudd	Robin Eubanks
Soprano saxophone:	Wayne Shorter	Wayne Shorter
Alto saxophone:	Lee Konitz	Kenny Garrett
Tenor saxophone:	Joe Lovano	Sonny Rollins
Baritone saxophone:	Gary Smulyan	James Carter
Clarinet:	Don Byron	Anat Cohen
Flute:	Nicole Mitchell and	Hubert Laws
	Lew Tabackin	
Piano:	Keith Jarrett	Herbie Hancock
Electric keyboard:	Uri Caine	Chick Corea
Guitar:	Bill Frisell	Pat Metheny
Acoustic bass:	Christian McBride	Christian McBride
Electric bass:	Steve Swallow	Christian McBride
Drums:	Roy Haynes	Jack DeJohnette
Vibraphone:	Gary Burton	----
Violin:	Regina Carter	Regina Carter
Male vocal:	Kurt Elling	Bobby McFerrin
Female vocal:	Cassandra Wilson	Diana Krall
Composer:	Maria Schneider	Maria Schneider
Producer:	Manfred Eicher	----
Record label:	ECM	Blue Note

IN MEMORIAM ...

13 January	Drummer Ed Thigpen, aged seventy-nine, Copenhagen.
6 February	Saxophonist and composer John Dankworth, aged eighty-two, London.
28 March	Guitarist Herb Ellis, aged eighty-eight, Los Angeles.
23 July	Bandleader and composer Willem Breuker, aged sixty-five, Amsterdam.
29 July	Drummer Martin Drew, aged sixty-six, London.
9 December	Saxophonist James Moody, aged eighty-five, San Diego, California.
28 December	Pianist Billy Taylor, aged eighty-nine, New York.

TREME

In April 2010 HBO aired the first episode of its new television series *Treme*, created by the team previously responsible for the critically acclaimed urban drama *The Wire*. Set in one of the oldest neighborhoods in New Orleans, *Treme* celebrates the resilience of the local inhabitants as they rebuild their lives in the aftermath of Hurricane Katrina, which devastated the historic city in August 2005. Central to this theme is the undiminished musical culture of the region, especially the tradition of marching bands from which early jazz was born more than a hundred years before. The soundtrack from the series, performed by a wide range of jazz, BLUES, and brass-band musicians from both Louisiana and across the USA, serves as a potent reminder of the musical riches and expressiveness of the free Creole and African-American population who first nurtured the extraordinary phenomenon of jazz in its legendary urban cradle.

Above right HBO's television series starred Wendell Pierce (third from left) as fictional New Orleans trombonist, Antoine Batiste.

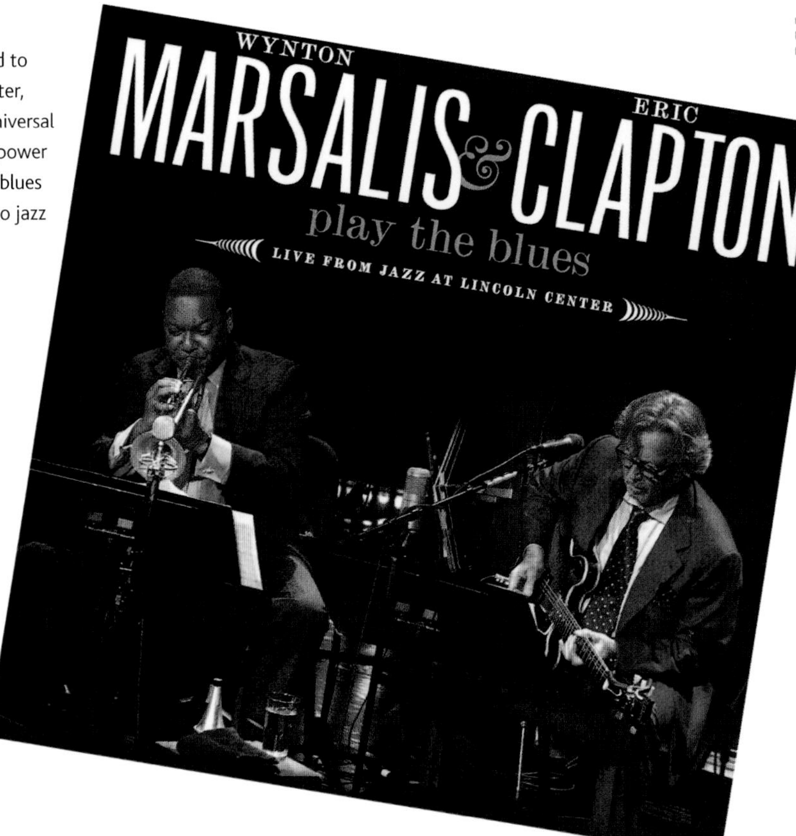

Right This musical summit meeting in 2011, convened to raise funds for Lincoln Center, celebrated the diversity, universal appeal, and undiminished power of music derived from the blues traditions that gave birth to jazz more than a century ago.

World Events

2010

12 January
Earthquake in Haiti

April
Largest oil spillage in history lasts for nearly ninety days, Gulf of Mexico

5 May
Picasso's *Nude, Green Leaves and Bust* sells for over $105 million, New York

May
First UK coalition government since World War II

- Worst global economic crisis since the Great Depression
- Deaths of Claude Chabrol, Henryk Górecki, Lena Horne, and J. D. Salinger

BIOGRAPHICAL INDEX OF MUSICIANS

Muhal Richard Abrams
b. 19 September 1930, Chicago, Illinois
Piano, composer. Leading light of Chicago free jazz in the early 1960s and founder of the Association for the Advancement of Creative Music.

Julian "Cannonball" Adderley
b. 15 September 1928, Tampa, Florida
d. 8 August 1975, Gary, Indiana
Alto and soprano saxophones. Brother of Nat Adderley. Virtuoso bop performer schooled in the tradition of Charlie Parker.

Nat Adderley
b. 25 November 1931, Tampa, Florida
d. 2 January 2000, Lakeland, Florida
Trumpet. Brother of Julian "Cannonball" Adderley, with whom he served as a sideman for twenty years (1955–75).

Toshiko Akiyoshi
b. 12 December 1929, Liaoyang, China
Piano, composer, arranger. Akiyoshi's sophisticated arrangements continued the tradition of big-band composition formulated by Duke Ellington and Gil Evans. Married fellow arranger Lew Tabackin in 1970.

Monty Alexander
b. 6 June 1944, Kingston, Jamaica
Piano. Versatile keyboard technician inspired by the style of Oscar Peterson. He was married to guitarist Emily Remler.

Geri Allen
b. 12 June 1957, Pontiac, Michigan
Piano. Keyboard player and jazz educator.

Barry Altschul
b. 6 January 1943, New York, New York
Drums. Eclectic performer equally proficient in bop and free-jazz idioms.

Albert Ammons
b. 23 September 1907, Chicago, Illinois
d. 2 December 1949, Chicago, Illinois
Piano. Preeminent boogie-woogie pianist in Chicago during the 1930s and 1940s.

Arild Andersen
b. 27 October 1945, Lillestrøm, Norway
Acoustic and electric bass, composer. Sideman of Jan Garbarek in the late 1960s, and voted best European bass player in 1975.

Lil Armstrong (née Hardin)
b. 3 February 1898, Memphis, Tennessee
d. 27 August 1971, Chicago, Illinois
Piano. Married to Louis Armstrong (1924–38), alongside whom she served in King Oliver's Creole Jazz Band.

Louis "Satchmo" Armstrong
b. 4 August 1901, New Orleans, Louisiana
d. 6 July 1971, Queens, New York
Cornet, trumpet, vocals. The first virtuoso improviser in the history of jazz, he laid the foundations from which all mainstream jazz styles developed. He later reached a wide audience as a popular singer. Married to Lil Hardin (1924–38).

Georgie Auld
b. 19 May 1919, Toronto, Ontario
d. 8 January 1990, Palm Springs, California
Saxophone, clarinet. Sideman of Artie Shaw and Benny Goodman who tutored Robert De Niro's mimed playing in the film *New York, New York.*

Albert Ayler
b. 13 July 1936, Cleveland Heights, Ohio
d. 25 November 1970, New York, New York
Saxophones, composer. Inimitable free-jazz performer, inspired by the traditional popular music of pre-jazz New Orleans. Brother of Donald Ayler.

Donald Ayler
b. 5 October 1942, Cleveland Heights, Ohio
d. 21 October 2007, Northfield, Ohio
Trumpet. Brother of Albert Ayler.

Mildred Bailey
b. 27 February 1907, Tekoa, Washington
d. 12 December 1951, Poughkeepsie, New York
Vocals. Singer with Paul Whiteman's orchestra (1929–33); married to Red Norvo (1933–43).

Chet Baker
b. 23 December 1929, Yale, Oklahoma
d. 13 May 1988, Amsterdam, Netherlands
Trumpet, flugelhorn, vocals. Archetypal "cool" performer, whose boyish good looks shot him to prominence in the 1950s.

Chris Barber
b. 17 April 1930, Welwyn Garden City, UK
Trombone, composer. Leading British bandleader with a solid reputation in continental Europe.

William "Count" Basie
b. 21 August 1904, Red Bank, New Jersey
d. 26 April 1984, Hollywood, Florida
Piano, organ, composer, bandleader. Originator of a brand of Kansas City jazz that became the hottest big-band sound of the 1930s and 1940s.

Django Bates
b. 2 October 1960, Beckenham, UK
Keyboards, tenor horn, composer. Wild compositional talent whose work with Loose Tubes in the 1980s exhibited dazzling eclecticism.

Mario Bauzá
b. 28 April 1911, Havana, Cuba
d. 11 July 1993, New York, New York
Trumpet, alto saxophone, composer, arranger. Classically trained performer whose Afro-Cuban collaborators included Dizzy Gillespie.

Sidney Bechet
b. 14 May 1897, New Orleans, Louisiana
d. 14 May 1959, Paris, France
Clarinet, soprano saxophone. Wayward talent of old New Orleans, popular in his adoptive France during the 1950s.

Leon "Bix" Beiderbecke
b. 10 March 1903, Davenport, Iowa
d. 6 August 1931, Queens, New York
Cornet, piano, composer. The first white jazz performer widely admired by black musicians.

Bunny Berigan
b. 2 November 1908, Hilbert, Wisconsin
d. 2 June 1942, New York, New York
Trumpet, vocals. Sideman of the Dorsey brothers, who absorbed the influences of Louis Armstrong and Bix Beiderbecke.

Leonard Bernstein
b. 25 August 1918, Lawrence, Massachusetts
d. 14 October 1990, New York, New York
Composer, conductor. Equally at home in classical and jazz idioms, he came to global prominence as the composer of *West Side Story* in 1957.

Barney Bigard
b. 3 March 1906, New Orleans, Louisiana
d. 27 June 1980, Culver City, California
Clarinet, tenor saxophone. Sideman of Duke Ellington and Louis Armstrong.

Bernard "Acker" Bilk
b. 28 January 1929, Pensford, UK
Clarinet, bandleader. Prominent exponent of British traditional jazz in the 1960s and 1970s.

Eubie Blake
b. 7 February 1883, Baltimore, Maryland
d. 12 February 1983, Brooklyn, New York
Piano. His ragtime and stride playing spanned a century of jazz history.

Art Blakey
b. 11 October 1919, Pittsburgh, Pennsylvania
d. 16 October 1990, New York, New York
Drums. Hard-bop performer whose Jazz Messengers provided an apprenticeship for numerous young performers.

Carla Bley (née Borg)
b. 11 May 1936, Oakland, California
Keyboards, composer. Original compositional talent who made her name with a distinctive brand of free jazz. Married Paul Bley in 1957.

Paul Bley
b. 10 November 1932, Montreal, Quebec
Keyboards, composer. A protégé of Charles Mingus, he later founded the record company Improvising Artists. Married Carla Bley in 1957.

Hamiet Bluiett
b. 16 September 1940, Lovejoy, Illinois
Baritone saxophone. Founder member of the World Saxophone Quartet in 1977.

Charles "Buddy" Bolden
b. 6 September 1877, New Orleans, Louisiana
d. 4 November 1931, Jackson, Louisiana
Cornet. Legendary pioneer of New Orleans jazz, who never recorded.

George Botsford
b. 24 February 1874, Sioux Falls, South Dakota
d. 11 February 1949, New York, New York
Ragtime composer. His best-known composition is *Black and White Rag.*

Lester Bowie
b. 11 October 1941, Frederick, Maryland
d. 8 November 1999, New York, New York
Trumpet, flugelhorn, composer. Member of the Art Ensemble of Chicago, famous for his theatrical manner of performance.

Anthony Braxton
b. 4 June 1945, Chicago, Illinois
Saxophones, clarinets, flute, composer. Controversial free-jazz artist who has appealed more to avant-garde intellectuals than to a wide audience.

Michael Brecker
b. 29 March 1949, Philadelphia, Pennsylvania
d. 13 January 2007, New York, New York
Tenor and soprano saxophones, electronic wind instrument. Versatile fusion artist. Brother of Randy Brecker.

Randy Brecker
b. 27 November 1945, Cheltenham, Pennsylvania
Trumpet. Brother of Michael Brecker, with whom he formed the Brecker Brothers in 1974.

Willem Breuker
b. 4 November 1944, Amsterdam, Netherlands
d. 23 July 2010, Amsterdam, Netherlands
Saxophones, composer, bandleader. Dutch free-jazz guru, founder of the Instant Composers' Pool (1968) and Kollectief (1974).

Bob Brookmeyer
b. 19 December 1929, Kansas City, Missouri
d. 15 December 2011, New London, New Hampshire
Trombone. West Coast artist specializing in the neglected valve trombone.

Clifford Brown
b. 30 October 1930, Wilmington, Delaware
d. 26 June 1956, Bedford, Pennsylvania
Trumpet. Bop performer and close associate of Max Roach.

Ray Brown
b. 13 October 1926, Pittsburgh, Pennsylvania
d. 2 July 2002, Indianapolis, Indiana
Double bass. Mainstream artist, especially associated with Oscar Peterson. Married to Ella Fitzgerald (1948–52).

Dave Brubeck
b. 6 December 1920, Concord, California
d. 5 December 2012, Norwalk, Connecticut
Piano, composer. West Coast performer, studied composition with Darius Milhaud. His rhythmically sophisticated music, achieved in collaboration with Paul Desmond, was enormously popular in the late 1950s and 1960s.

Gary Burton
b. 23 January 1943, Anderson, Indiana
Vibraphone, composer. Revolutionized vibraphone technique in the late 1960s, and has since made a name as an influential music educator.

Don Byas
b. 21 October 1912, Muskogee, Oklahoma
d. 24 August 1972, Amsterdam, Netherlands
Tenor saxophone. One of several bop performers who emigrated to Europe, settling in Paris in 1946.

Donald Byrd
b. 9 December 1932, Detroit, Michigan
d. 4 February 2013, Delaware
Trumpet, flugelhorn, composer. Soul-jazz artist prominent in the Blue Note catalog.

Uri Caine
b. 8 June 1956, Philadelphia, Pennsylvania
Piano, composer. Eclectic performer noted for jazz-klezmer and jazz-classical crossovers.

George "Red" Callender
b. 6 March 1918, Haynesville, Virginia
d. 8 March 1992, Saugus, California
Double bass, tuba. Popular on the West Coast in the 1940s, he was mentor to Charles Mingus.

Cabell "Cab" Calloway
b. 25 December 1907, Rochester, New York
d. 18 November 1994, Hockessin, Delaware

Vocals, bandleader. Charismatic leader whose band succeeded Duke Ellington's at the Cotton Club in the early 1930s.

Harry Carney
b. 1 April 1910, Boston, Massachusetts
d. 8 October 1974, New York, New York
Baritone saxophone. Stalwart sideman of Duke Ellington (1927–74).

Ian Carr
b. 21 April 1933, Dumfries, UK
d. 25 February 2009, London, UK
Trumpet, flugelhorn, writer. Founder of the fusion group Nucleus in 1969, and biographer of Miles Davis and Keith Jarrett.

Benny Carter
b. 8 August 1907, Harlem, New York
d. 12 July 2003, Los Angeles, California
Alto saxophone, trumpet. Mainstream swing artist, prominent in Europe in the late 1930s and again in the 1970s.

Betty Carter
b. 16 May 1929, Flint, Michigan
d. 26 September 1998, New York, New York
Vocals. A protégée of Lionel Hampton in the late 1940s, she continued to top popularity polls in the US.

Regina Carter
b. 6 August 1966, Detroit, Michigan
Violin. A member of the String Trio of New York in the 1990s, she later made headlines by performing jazz on Paganini's violin.

Ron Carter
b. 4 May 1937, Ferndale, Michigan
Acoustic and electric bass. Sideman to Miles Davis and Herbie Hancock in the 1960s, he has been a leader since 1976.

Al Casey
b. 15 September 1915, Louisville, Kentucky
d. 11 September 2005, New York, New York
Guitar. Member of Fats Waller's Rhythm (1934–42).

"Big" Sid Catlett
b. 17 January 1910, Evansville, Indiana
d. 25 March 1951, Chicago, Illinois
Drums. Sideman to Benny Goodman, Louis Armstrong and early bop performers.

Paul Chambers
b. 22 April 1935, Pittsburgh, Pennsylvania
d. 4 January 1969, New York, New York
Double bass. Member of the Miles Davis Quintet (1955–63).

Adolphus "Doc" Cheatham
b. 13 June 1905, Nashville, Tennessee
d. 2 June 1997, Washington, DC
Trumpet. Traditionalist equally at home in New Orleans and Latin styles.

Don Cherry
b. 18 November 1936, Oklahoma City, Oklahoma
d. 19 October 1995, Málaga, Spain
Trumpet, piano, ethnic instruments. Pioneer of world music, he first made his name with Ornette Coleman in the late 1950s.

Charlie Christian
b. 29 July 1916, Bonham, Texas
d. 2 March 1942, Staten Island, New York
Electric guitar. Innovative improviser who influenced the emerging bop style.

Kenny Clarke
b. 9 January 1914, Pittsburgh, Pennsylvania
d. 26 January 1985, Montreuil, France
Drums. After developing bop-drumming techniques in the 1940s, he emigrated to France in 1956.

Stanley Clarke
b. 30 June 1951, Philadelphia, Pennsylvania
Acoustic and electric bass. Founder member of Chick Corea's fusion band, Return to Forever.

Tony Coe
b. 29 November 1934, Canterbury, UK
Saxophones. Sideman to John Dankworth and Stan Tracey, he was the tenor soloist on Henry Mancini's popular *Pink Panther* theme.

Nat King Cole
b. 17 March 1919, Montgomery, Alabama
d. 15 February 1965, Santa Monica, California
Vocals, piano. Originator of the piano-trio format and popular singing star on US television in the 1950s.

George Coleman
b. 8 March 1935, Memphis, Tennessee
Tenor and alto saxophones. Member of the Miles Davis Quintet (1963–64).

Ornette Coleman
b. 9 March 1930, Fort Worth, Texas
Alto and tenor saxophones, trumpet, violin, composer. Controversial pioneer of free jazz in the early 1960s.

Alice Coltrane
b. 27 August 1937, Detroit, Michigan
d. 12 January 2007, Los Angeles, California
Piano. Wife of John Coltrane (1965–67), and leader of many combos in her own right.

John Coltrane
b. 23 September 1926, Hamlet, North Carolina
d. 17 July 1967, Huntington, New York
Saxophones, composer. Enormously influential on subsequent tenor saxophonists, Coltrane became a cultural icon in the 1960s through his spirituality and experiments with free jazz and Asian music.

Ravi Coltrane
b. 6 August 1965, Huntington, New York
Saxophones. Son of John and Alice Coltrane, who made his recording debut (with Elvin Jones) in 1991.

Eddie Condon
b. 16 November 1905, Goodland, Indiana
d. 4 August 1973, New York, New York
Guitar, bandleader. Popular on US television after a groundbreaking broadcast from New York's Town Hall in 1942.

Will Marion Cook
b. 27 January 1869, Washington, DC
d. 19 July 1944, New York, New York
Composer, conductor. His Southern Syncopated Orchestra took Sidney Bechet to Europe in 1919.

Aaron Copland
b. 14 November 1900, Brooklyn, New York
d. 2 December 1990, North Tarrytown, New York
Composer. Foremost US classical composer of the twentieth century, who evolved a nationalistic symphonic-jazz idiom in the 1920s.

Chick Corea
b. 12 June 1941, Chelsea, Massachusetts
Keyboards, composer. Sideman to Miles Davis in the early fusion era, his own fusion bands have included Return to Forever and the Elektric Band. Also a fine acoustic player in styles ranging from hard bop to free jazz.

Jamie Cullum
b. 20 August 1979, Rochford, UK
Piano and vocals. Rising star of popular jazz singing in the UK in the early 2000s.

Eddie Daniels
b. 19 October 1941, New York, New York
Clarinet, tenor saxophone, flute. His work with Thad Jones and Mel Lewis (1966–72) led to solo prominence on the GRP label in the 1980s.

John Dankworth
b. 20 September 1927, Woodford, UK
d. 6 February 2010, London, UK
Alto saxophone, composer, bandleader. Early promoter of bop in the UK in the late 1940s and early 1950s, he later headed a popular big band. Married Cleo Laine in 1958; their son Alec (b. 1960) is a bass player.

Miles Davis
b. 26 May 1926, Alton, Illinois
d. 28 September 1991, Santa Monica, California
Trumpet, flugelhorn, composer. Widely considered to be the most influential figure in jazz history, his early bop playing led to a number of seminal stylistic developments: "cool" jazz, orchestral jazz (with Gil Evans), modal jazz, and jazz-rock fusion.

Claude Debussy
b. 22 August 1862, St. Germain-en-Laye, France
d. 25 March 1918, Paris, France
Composer. As an antidote to the French Impressionist musical style he had himself founded, he became the first European classical composer to engage with ragtime.

Jack DeJohnette
b. 9 August 1942, Chicago, Illinois
Drums, piano. Member of the early Miles Davis fusion bands (1969–71), he has drummed for Keith Jarrett's trio since 1983.

Paul Desmond
b. 25 November 1924, San Francisco, California
d. 30 May 1977, New York, New York
Alto saxophone, composer. Member of the Dave Brubeck Quartet (1951–67), who composed "Take Five" in 1959.

Al Di Meola
b. 22 July 1954, Jersey City, New Jersey
Acoustic and electric guitar. Member of Chick Corea's Return to Forever (1974–76), subsequently leader of the Al Di Meola Project.

Johnny Dodds
b. 12 April 1892, Waveland, Mississippi
d. 8 August 1940, Chicago, Illinois
Clarinet, alto saxophone. Leading clarinetist of early New Orleans jazz, he worked with King Oliver and Louis Armstrong. Brother of Baby Dodds.

Warren "Baby" Dodds
b. 24 December 1898, New Orleans, Louisiana
d. 14 February 1959, Chicago, Illinois
Drums. Brother of Johnny Dodds, with whom he played in King Oliver's Creole Jazz Band.

Eric Dolphy
b. 20 June 1928, Los Angeles, California
d. 29 June 1964, Berlin, Germany
Alto saxophone, flute, clarinet, and bass clarinet. Sideman to Charles Mingus and John Coltrane in the early 1960s.

Arne Domnérus
b. 20 December 1924, Stockholm, Sweden
d. 2 September 2008, Stockholm, Sweden
Alto saxophone. Preeminent Swedish performer who made his name in the 1940s.

Pierre Dørge
b. 28 February 1946, Copenhagen, Denmark
Guitar, composer, bandleader. Founder of the New Jungle Orchestra in 1980, he has absorbed elements borrowed from a wide variety of styles and ethnic traditions.

Kenny Dorham
b. 30 August 1924, Fairfield, Texas
d. 5 December 1972, New York, New York
Trumpet. Bop performer who succeeded Miles Davis as sideman to Charlie Parker in 1948 and then created the Jazz Messengers with Art Blakey.

Jimmy Dorsey
b. 29 February 1904, Shenandoah, Pennsylvania
d. 12 June 1957, New York, New York
Clarinet, alto saxophone. Brother of Tommy Dorsey, with whom he coled the Dorsey Brothers Orchestra in 1934–35 and 1953–56.

Tommy Dorsey
b. 19 November 1905, Shenandoah, Pennsylvania
d. 26 November 1956, Greenwich, Connecticut
Trombone. Brother of Jimmy Dorsey.

Honoré Dutrey
b. *c.* 1894, New Orleans, Louisiana
d. 21 July 1935, Chicago, Illinois
Trombone. Member of King Oliver's Creole Jazz Band.

Billy Eckstine
b. 8 July 1914, Pittsburgh, Pennsylvania
d. 8 March 1993, Pittsburgh, Pennsylvania
Vocals, trumpet, bandleader. His 1940s big band employed emerging bop talents such as Dizzy Gillespie, Charlie Parker, and Miles Davis.

Roy "Little Jazz" Eldridge
b. 30 January 1911, Pittsburgh, Pennsylvania
d. 26 February 1989, Valley Stream, New York
Trumpet, flugelhorn. Leading trumpeter of the late 1930s, whose style remained conservative after the bop revolution.

Edward Kennedy "Duke" Ellington
b. 29 April 1899, Washington, DC
d. 24 May 1974, New York, New York
Piano, composer, bandleader. Creator of numerous masterpieces, many in collaboration with Billy Strayhorn, infusing jazz with the intellectual appeal of classical music. His orchestra found fame at the Cotton Club (1927–31) and in Europe, appeared annually at Carnegie Hall (1943–48), and later specialized in extended works.

Peter Erskine
b. 5 June 1954, Somers Point, New Jersey
Drums. Member of Weather Report (1978–82), much in demand as a session player.

James Reese Europe
b. 22 February 1881, Mobile, Alabama
d. 9 May 1919, Boston, Massachusetts
Bandleader. Promoter of orchestrated ragtime, which he took to Europe in 1918.

Bill Evans
b. 16 August 1929, Plainfield, New Jersey
d. 15 September 1980, Fort Lee, New Jersey
Piano, composer. The most respected keyboard player in modern jazz, whose harmonic daring and rhythmic subtlety influenced many emerging talents in the 1960s.

Bill Evans
b. 9 February 1958, Clarendon Hills, Illinois
Saxophones. Sideman to Miles Davis (1980–84) and a member of John McLaughlin's Mahavishnu Orchestra.

Gil Evans
b. 13 May 1912, Toronto, Ontario
d. 20 April 1988, Cuernavaca, Mexico
Composer, arranger. His collaborations with Miles Davis established the "cool" style and later broke new ground in the blending of pre-composed orchestral music with jazz improvisation.

Herschel Evans
b. 9 March 1909, Denton, Texas
d. 9 February 1939, New York, New York
Tenor saxophone. Member of Count Basie's band (1936–39).

Leonard Feather
b. 13 September 1914, London, UK
d. 22 September 1994, Sherman Oaks, California
Piano, writer. British critic and historian who worked (as both composer and producer) with numerous major talents in the US.

Ella Fitzgerald
b. 25 April 1917, Newport News, Virginia
d. 15 June 1996, Beverly Hills, California
Vocals. Rising to prominence with the Chick Webb Band in the late 1930s, she became renowned as a superb scat singer and versatile interpreter of a phenomenally extensive repertoire of standards. Married to Ray Brown (1948–52).

Béla Fleck
b. 10 July 1958, New York, New York
Banjo. Pioneer of jazz-bluegrass fusion who has collaborated with many jazz musicians, notably Chick Corea and Marcus Roberts.

Frank Foster
b. 23 September 1928, Cincinnati, Ohio
d. 26 July 2011, Chesapeake, Virginia
Tenor saxophone. Member of Count Basie's band in the 1950s, and its leader from 1986.

Bill Frisell
b. 18 March 1951, Baltimore, Maryland
Acoustic and electric guitar. House guitarist for ECM in the 1980s, working with Jan Garbarek, Eberhard Weber, and Charlie Haden, then active in New York and Seattle.

Steve Gadd
b. 9 April 1945, Irondequoit, New York
Drums. Leading jazz-rock drummer who, since working with Chick Corea in the 1970s, has been much in demand as a session player.

Vyacheslav Ganelin
b. 17 December 1944, Kraskovo, Soviet Union
Piano. Founder of the Ganelin Trio in 1971, and largely responsible for bringing Soviet free jazz to an international audience.

Jan Garbarek
b. 4 March 1947, Mysen, Norway
Tenor and soprano saxophones. One of the most distinctive players in European jazz, he absorbed folk and rock influences and boosted sales of the ECM label.

Erroll Garner
b. 15 June 1923, Pittsburgh, Pennsylvania
d. 2 January 1977, Los Angeles, California
Piano. Composer of "Misty," he became a popular trio pianist after deputizing for Art Tatum in the mid-1940s.

Jimmy Garrison
b. 3 March 1934, Miami, Florida
d. 7 April 1976, New York, New York
Double bass. Sideman to John Coltrane in the 1960s.

George Gershwin
b. 26 September 1898, Brooklyn, New York
d. 11 July 1937, Hollywood, California
Composer, piano. He laid the foundations for the symphonic jazz of the 1920s with *Rhapsody in Blue,* and in 1935 produced the "American folk opera" *Porgy and Bess.* Songs from the latter and from his numerous Broadway musicals are a staple part of the standards repertoire.

Stan Getz
b. 2 February 1927, Philadelphia, Pennsylvania
d. 6 June 1991, Malibu, California
Tenor saxophone. Versatile performer who spearheaded the bossa nova craze in the 1960s, and straddled West and East Coast styles.

Astrud Gilberto
b. 30 March 1940, Salvador, Brazil
Vocals. Catapulted to stardom with "The Girl from Ipanema" in 1963, she collaborated with Stan Getz in popularizing bossa nova. Married to João Gilberto.

João Gilberto
b. 10 June 1931, Juaseiro, Brazil
Vocals, guitar. Pioneer of the bossa nova style in Brazil in the late 1950s alongside Antônio Carlos Jobim. Married to Astrud Gilberto.

John Birks "Dizzy" Gillespie
b. 21 October 1917, Cheraw, South Carolina
d. 6 January 1993, Englewood, New Jersey
Trumpet, composer. Leading trumpeter of the emerging bop style in the early 1940s, famed for his onstage antics, penetrating sound, and unique instrument (with its bell bent sharply upwards). His later career took him on worldwide concert tours for the US State Department.

Jean Goldkette
b. 18 March 1893, Valenciennes, France
d. 24 March 1962, Santa Barbara, California
Piano, bandleader. Popular dance-band director of the 1920s and 1930s, who engaged Bix Beiderbecke as soloist.

Paul Gonsalves
b. 12 July 1920, Brockton, Massachusetts
d. 15 May 1974, London, UK
Tenor saxophone. Sideman to Duke Ellington (1950–74), best remembered for his powerful solo for Ellington's orchestra during its appearance at the Newport Festival in 1956.

Benny Goodman
b. 30 May 1909, Chicago, Illinois
d. 13 June 1986, New York, New York
Clarinet, bandleader. The first jazz musician to be equally at home in the world of classical music, he became a household name in 1935 and was dubbed the "King of Swing." In collaboration with Fletcher Henderson, his work defined the big-band sound of the swing era, and his band became the first jazz outfit to appear at Carnegie Hall (1938).

Dexter Gordon
b. 27 February 1923, Los Angeles, California
d. 25 April 1990, Philadelphia, Pennsylvania
Tenor saxophone. Bop performer who moved to Europe in 1962. Best known for his starring role in the film *'Round Midnight* (1986).

Norman Granz
b. 6 August 1918, Los Angeles, California
d. 22 November 2001, Geneva, Switzerland
Record producer. Founder of the Jazz at the Philharmonic tours, and the Clef, Verve, and Pablo record labels.

Stephane Grappelli
b. 26 January 1908, Paris, France
d. 1 December 1997, Paris, France
Violin. With Django Reinhardt, he formed the backbone of the Quintette du Hot Club de France in the 1930s.

Sonny Greer
b. 13 December 1895, Long Branch, New Jersey
d. 23 March 1982, New York, New York
Drums. Stalwart sideman of Duke Ellington (1920–51), who added many exotic percussion instruments to the standard drum kit.

Dave Grusin
b. 26 June 1934, Littleton, Colorado
Keyboards, composer, record producer. Founded the GRP record label with Larry Rosen, and was active as a versatile performer and composer of numerous Hollywood film scores.

Charlie Haden
b. 6 August 1937, Shenandoah, Iowa
Double bass. Sideman to Ornette Coleman (1958–60) and founder in 1969 of the Liberation Music Orchestra, which he reformed in 1982.

Adelaide Hall
b. 20 October 1901, Brooklyn, New York
d. 7 November 1993, London, UK
Vocals. She provided the haunting, wordless vocal line in Duke Ellington's "Creole Love Call" (1927).

Scott Hamilton
b. 12 September 1954, Providence, Rhode Island
Tenor saxophone. Mainstream artist promoted by the Concord label. He served as sideman for Benny Goodman and Woody Herman.

John Hammond
b. 15 December 1910, New York, New York
d. 10 July 1987, New York, New York
Record producer. In the 1930s he promoted the work of Benny Goodman, Count Basie, Fletcher Henderson and Billie Holiday, and mounted the famous Carnegie Hall jazz concerts of 1938 and 1939.

Lionel Hampton
b. 20 April 1908, Louisville, Kentucky
d. 31 August 2002, New York, New York
Vibraphone, drums, bandleader. Member of the Benny Goodman Quartet in the 1930s, and later responsible for heading the longest surviving big band in the history of jazz.

Herbie Hancock
b. 12 April 1940, Chicago, Illinois
Keyboards, composer. Sideman to Miles Davis (1963–68) and house pianist to Blue Note records in the 1960s, he scored major successes in the pop charts with the fusion album *Headhunters* (1973) and single "Rockit" (1983).

W. C. Handy
b. 16 November 1873, Florence, Alabama
d. 28 March 1958, Harlem, New York
Cornet, bandleader, composer. Widely known as the "Father of the Blues," he published the first printed blues arrangement in 1912.

Roy Hargrove
b. 16 October 1969, Waco, Texas
Trumpet, composer. Since his debut album in 1990, he has earned a reputation as a fine exponent of a modern brand of bop.

John Harle
b. 20 September 1956, Newcastle, UK
Soprano and alto saxophone, composer. British artist, equally at home in jazz and modern classical styles.

Ben Harney
b. 6 March 1872, Louisville, Kentucky
d. 2 March 1938, Philadelphia, Pennsylvania
Ragtime song composer. His "You've Been a Good Old Wagon" (1895) was the first published ragtime song.

Coleman Hawkins
b. 21 November 1904, St. Joseph, Missouri
d. 16 May 1969, New York, New York
Tenor saxophone. After a decade in Fletcher Henderson's band (1924–34), his reputation as a soloist capable of lyrical improvisations was cemented with "Body and Soul" in 1939.

Roy Haynes
b. 13 March 1925, Boston, Massachusetts
Drums. Bop drummer whose collaborators included Charlie Parker, Sarah Vaughan, Miles Davis, Thelonious Monk, Lee Konitz, Stan Getz, John Coltrane, Chick Corea, and Pat Metheny.

Percy Heath
b. 30 April 1923, Wilmington, North Carolina
d. 28 April 2005, Southampton, New York
Double bass. Founder member of John Lewis's Modern Jazz Quartet.

Neal Hefti
b. 29 October 1922, Hastings, Nebraska
d. 11 October 2008, Toluca Lake, California
Composer, arranger. Arranger for the Count Basie band in the 1950s, he composed the music for the movie *The Odd Couple* in 1968.

Julius Hemphill
b. 24 January 1938, Fort Worth, Texas
d. 2 April 1995, New York, New York
Alto saxophone. Founder member of the World Saxophone Quartet, with whom he played from 1977 until 1990.

Fletcher Henderson
b. 18 December 1897, Cuthbert, Georgia
d. 28 December 1952, New York, New York

Piano, arranger, bandleader. Originator of the swing-band style of the late 1920s and 1930s. His arrangements were bought in 1934 by Benny Goodman's band, for which he served as staff arranger in 1939–41.

Joe Henderson
b. 24 April 1937, Lima, Ohio
d. 30 June 2001, San Francisco, California
Tenor saxophone, composer. Sideman to Blue Note artists Horace Silver and Freddie Hubbard in the 1960s, he continued to top popularity polls in the US.

Woody Herman
b. 16 May 1913, Milwaukee, Wisconsin
d. 29 October 1987, West Hollywood, California
Clarinet, bandleader. His various bands, called "Herman's Herds," created a polished swing music and inspired Stravinsky to compose his *Ebony Concerto* in 1945.

Earl "Fatha" Hines
b. 28 December 1903, Duquesne, Pennsylvania
d. 23 April 1983, Oakland, California
Piano, bandleader. The first keyboard player to break away from the stride idiom, Hines developed the more melodic and versatile "trumpet style" after working with Louis Armstrong in the 1920s. His big band later became a popular fixture at Chicago's Grand Terrace (1928–40).

Hiromi (Hiromi Uehara)
b. 26 March 1979, Hamamatsu, Japan
Piano, composer. Eclectic pianist renowned for her energetic live performances in both acoustic trio and electric-group formats.

Johnny "Rabbit" Hodges
b. 25 July 1906, Cambridge, Massachusetts
d. 11 May 1970, New York, New York
Alto saxophone. Endowed with a distinctively suave saxophone tone, his sensual playing is heard to best advantage in his work with Duke Ellington's orchestra (1928–51 and 1955–70).

Billie Holiday
b. 7 April 1915, Philadelphia, Pennsylvania
d. 17 July 1959, New York, New York
Vocals. Closely associated with Teddy Wilson and Lester Young, she made her name in the 1930s and is widely regarded as the finest jazz singer of all time; a self-taught artist who instinctively reshaped banal popular songs into memorable and highly expressive melodies.

Dave Holland
b. 1 October 1946, Wolverhampton, UK
Acoustic and electric bass. Sideman to Miles Davis (1968–70) and member of Chick Corea's group Circle (1970–72). More recently, he has worked with Kenny Wheeler and Pat Metheny.

Freddie Hubbard
b. 7 April 1938, Indianapolis, Indiana
d. 29 December 2008, Sherman Oaks, California
Trumpet, flugelhorn, composer. After working with Ornette Coleman on *Free Jazz* (1960), he was a member of Art Blakey's Jazz Messengers until 1964 and remained active on the Blue Note label with various groups.

Dick Hyman
b. 8 March 1927, New York, New York
Piano. A versatile artist embracing many styles in his early career, he has been well known since the 1970s as an advocate of the traditional jazz of New Orleans and the Harlem stride pianists.

Abdullah Ibrahim (Dollar Brand)
b. 9 October 1934, Cape Town, South Africa
Piano, composer. Unable to promote jazz freely in his native South Africa, he moved to Switzerland in 1962 where he was discovered by Duke Ellington.

Milt Jackson
b. 1 January 1923, Detroit, Michigan
d. 9 October 1999, New York, New York
Vibraphone. Leading bop vibraphonist and cofounder (with John Lewis) of the Modern Jazz Quartet in 1952.

Tony Jackson
b. 5 June 1876, New Orleans, Louisiana
d. 20 April 1921, Chicago, Illinois
Ragtime pianist, composer. Mentor of Jelly Roll Morton.

Illinois Jacquet
b. 31 October 1922, Broussard, Louisiana
d. 22 July 2004, Queens, New York
Tenor saxophone. Sideman of Lionel Hampton, Cab Calloway, and Count Basie in the 1940s, he later toured with Jazz at the Philharmonic.

Ahmad Jamal
b. 2 July 1930, Pittsburgh, Pennsylvania
Piano. His piano-trio work influenced Miles Davis during the 1950s.

Bob James
b. 25 December 1939, Marshall, Missouri
Keyboards, composer. Fusion artist and composer of the signature tune to the US television comedy series *Taxi.*

Harry James
b. 15 March 1916, Albany, Georgia
d. 5 July 1983, Las Vegas, Nevada
Trumpet, bandleader. Principal trumpeter with Benny Goodman's band (1937–39), and later a popular big-band leader in his own right.

Keith Jarrett
b. 8 May 1945, Allentown, Pennsylvania
Piano, composer. Sideman to Miles Davis (1970–71), he soon abandoned electronic keyboards and became famous for his large-scale solo improvisations at European venues. He has recorded a sizeable quantity of classical music, and regularly interprets standards with his trio partners Gary Peacock and Jack DeJohnette.

Antônio Carlos Jobim
b. 25 January 1927, Rio de Janeiro, Brazil
d. 8 December 1994, New York, New York
Guitar, piano, composer. Cofounder (with João Gilberto) of the bossa nova style in the late 1950s, he appeared at Carnegie Hall with Dizzy Gillespie in 1962.

Bunk Johnson
b. 27 December 1879, New Orleans, Louisiana
d. 7 July 1949, New Iberia, Louisiana
Trumpet. Sideman to the legendary Buddy Bolden, he came to prominence in the revival of New Orleans jazz in the 1940s.

James P. Johnson
b. 1 February 1894, New Brunswick, New Jersey
d. 17 November 1955, Queens, New York
Piano, composer. Preeminent stride artist and teacher of Fats Waller. He composed the hit song "Charleston" in 1923.

J. J. Johnson
b. 22 January 1924, Indianapolis, Indiana
d. 4 February 2001, Indianapolis, Indiana
Trombone. Leading bop trombonist and sometime sideman to Miles Davis and Sonny Stitt. He founded a quintet with fellow trombonist Kai Winding in the 1950s.

Pete Johnson
b. 25 March 1904, Kansas City, Missouri
d. 23 March 1967, Buffalo, New York
Piano. Boogie-woogie performer, sometime duet partner of Albert Ammons.

Elvin Jones
b. 9 September 1927, Pontiac, Michigan
d. 18 May 2004, Englewood, New Jersey
Drums. Brother of bandleader Thad Jones. He worked with John Coltrane during the 1960s, playing in a bop style heavily influenced by Max Roach and Kenny Clarke.

Philly Joe Jones
b. 15 July 1923, Philadelphia, Pennsylvania
d. 30 August 1985, Philadelphia, Pennsylvania
Drums. Sideman to Miles Davis throughout the 1950s.

Quincy Jones
b. 14 March 1933, Chicago, Illinois
Composer, arranger. After early work with Lionel Hampton (1951–53), he arranged for Count Basie and then became active as a record producer. He founded his own label, Qwest, in 1980, and has worked with such high-profile popular artists as Frank Sinatra, Michael Jackson, and Aretha Franklin.

Thad Jones
b. 28 March 1923, Pontiac, Michigan
d. 21 August 1986, Copenhagen, Denmark
Trumpet, flugelhorn, bandleader. Brother of Elvin Jones. With Mel Lewis, he coled a virtuoso big band at New York's Village Vanguard (1965–78), before emigrating to Copenhagen. He returned to the US briefly in the mid-1980s to lead Count Basie's band.

Scott Joplin
b. 1867, Texarkana, Texas
d. 1 April 1917, New York, New York
Ragtime composer and pianist. The most successful ragtime composer, who attempted to transform the popular genre into an art form. His achievements only came to be fully recognized during a 1970s revival of his work.

Julian Joseph
b. 11 May 1966, London, UK
Piano, composer. After work with Branford Marsalis in 1986, he made his debut album as leader in 1991.

Wynton Kelly
b. 2 December 1931, Jamaica
d. 12 April 1971, Toronto, Ontario
Piano. Sideman to Miles Davis (1959–63), he left to set up his own trio with Paul Chambers and Billy Cobb.

Stan Kenton
b. 15 December 1911, Wichita, Kansas
d. 25 August 1979, Los Angeles, California
Composer, piano, bandleader. Originator of a style of West Coast "progressive jazz" in the late 1940s, borrowing elements from Latin American music and modern classical techniques.

Freddie Keppard
b. 27 February 1889, New Orleans, Louisiana
d. 15 July 1933, Chicago, Illinois
Cornet. A first-generation jazz musician whose playing represented the transition from Buddy Bolden to the style of Louis Armstrong.

Barney Kessel
b. 17 October 1923, Muskogee, Oklahoma
d. 6 May 2004, San Diego, California
Guitar. Session performer who worked with Oscar Peterson's piano trio in the early 1950s.

Soweto Kinch
b. 10 July 1978, London, UK
Alto saxophone, rapper. Creator of an original blend of jazz and hip hop, including concept albums inspired by inner-city Birmingham.

Rahsaan Roland Kirk
b. 7 August 1935, Columbus, Ohio
d. 5 December 1977, Bloomington, Indiana
Saxophones, flute, whistles. Eccentric talent who developed a manner of playing three wind instruments simultaneously, but transcended this ostensible gimmickry to produce music that reflects the values of conventional jazz.

Lee Konitz
b. 13 October 1927, Chicago, Illinois
Saxophones. Leading performer of the West Coast "cool" school, closely associated with the work of Stan Kenton and Lennie Tristano in the 1950s.

Diana Krall
b. 16 November 1964, Nanaimo, British Columbia
Piano, vocals. Phenomenally popular jazz artist, famous for her rich contralto voice.

Gene Krupa
b. 15 January 1909, Chicago, Illinois
d. 16 October 1973, Yonkers, New York
Drums, bandleader. Charismatic sideman to Benny Goodman (1934–38), later a leader in his own right.

Steve Lacy
b. 23 July 1934, New York
d. 4 June 2004, Boston, Massachusetts
Soprano saxophone, composer. Eclectic artist who worked with Cecil Taylor, Gil Evans, and Thelonious Monk between 1955 and 1964, taking free jazz to Italy and France in the late 1960s.

Scott LaFaro
b. 3 April 1936, Newark, New Jersey
d. 6 July 1961, Geneva, New York
Double bass. Enormously influential player whose tragically short career peaked in the Bill Evans Trio (1959–61).

Cleo Laine
b. 28 October 1927, Southall, UK
Vocals. Married to John Dankworth (1958–2010), she has embraced all styles from classical to pop.

Joseph Lamb
b. 6 December 1887, Montclair, New Jersey
d. 3 September 1960, Brooklyn, New York
Ragtime composer. With Scott Joplin and

James Scott, he was one of the team of leading ragtime composers published by John Stark.

Brian Lemon
b. 11 February 1937, Nottingham, UK
Piano. Having made his name during the 1960s and 1970s by accompanying visiting US stars such as Ben Webster, Milt Jackson, and Benny Goodman, he went on to lead his own trio.

John Lewis
b. 3 May 1920, La Grange, Illinois
d. 29 March 2001, New York, New York
Piano, composer. Active as a bop pianist in the 1940s, he participated in Miles Davis's *Birth of the Cool* sessions in 1949. With the establishment of the Modern Jazz Quartet in the early 1950s, he gained a global reputation as a composer of refined musical structures reflecting strong classical influences.

Meade "Lux" Lewis
b. 4 September 1905, Chicago, Illinois
d. 7 June 1964, Minneapolis, Minnesota
Piano. Popular boogie-woogie artist who composed "Honky Tonk Train Blues."

Mel Lewis
b. 10 May 1929, Buffalo, New York
d. 2 February 1990, New York, New York
Drums, bandleader. Coleader, with Thad Jones, of the successful big band based at New York's Village Vanguard from 1965 until 1978, when he assumed sole leadership.

Charles Lloyd
b. 15 March 1938, Memphis, Tennessee
Saxophones, flute. After working with Julian "Cannonball" Adderley and Keith Jarrett in the 1960s, he became one of the more popular free-jazz artists.

Joe Lovano
b. 29 December 1952, Cleveland, Ohio
Saxophones. Sideman to Woody Herman in the late 1970s, and a prominent leader on the Blue Note label in the 1990s.

Jimmie Lunceford
b. 6 June 1902, Fulton, Mississippi
d. 12 July 1947, Seaside, Oregon
Bandleader. His band made its reputation at New York's Cotton Club in the mid-1930s.

Humphrey Lyttelton
b. 23 May 1921, Eton, UK
d. 25 April 2008, London, UK
Trumpet, writer. A popular broadcaster on British radio, he took part in the Dixieland revival of the late 1940s and became a champion of traditional jazz.

Howard McGhee
b. 6 March 1918, Tulsa, Oklahoma
d. 17 July 1987, New York, New York
Trumpet. After participating in early bop performances, he joined Jazz at the Philharmonic in 1947 and was voted Best Trumpeter by *Down Beat* in 1949.

John McLaughlin
b. 4 January 1942, Doncaster, UK
Acoustic and electric guitar, composer. Sideman to Miles Davis in 1969, then leader of his own fusion group, the Mahavishnu Orchestra (1970–75, reformed in 1984). In this outfit and the smaller group Shakti (1975–77), he showed himself to be strongly influenced by Indian music.

Teo Macero
b. 30 October 1925, Glens Falls, New York
d. 19 February 2008, Riverhead, New York
Composer, record producer. He masterminded most of Miles Davis's recordings from 1957 onwards, but was also respected as a saxophonist and composer in his own right.

"Machito" (Raúl Grillo)
b. 16 February 1912, Tampa, Florida
d. 19 April 1984, London, UK
Bandleader. Brother-in-law of Mario Bauzá, he participated in the Latin jazz boom of the 1940s.

Albert Mangelsdorff
b. 5 September 1928, Frankfurt, Germany
d. 25 July 2005, Frankfurt, Germany
Trombone, composer. Eclectic performer who developed the radical technique of playing chords (multiphonics) on his instrument.

Shelly Manne
b. 11 June 1920, New York, New York
d. 26 September 1984, Los Angeles, California
Drums. Sideman to Stan Kenton and Woody Herman in the late 1940s, he founded Shelly's Manne Hole in Los Angeles in 1951.

Fate Marable
b. 2 December 1890, Paducah, Kentucky
d. 16 January 1947, St. Louis, Missouri
Piano, bandleader. Director of a jazz band on the Streckfus Line steamboats that plied the Mississippi River.

Branford Marsalis
b. 26 August 1960, Breaux Bridge, Louisiana
Soprano and tenor saxophone. Son of Ellis Marsalis. Sideman to Art Blakey, Miles Davis, Herbie Hancock, and his brother Wynton Marsalis in the 1980s.

Ellis Marsalis
b. 14 November 1934, New Orleans, Louisiana
Piano, composer. Father of Branford and Wynton Marsalis.

Wynton Marsalis
b. 18 October 1961, New Orleans, Louisiana
Trumpet. Son of Ellis Marsalis and brother of Branford Marsalis. He worked with Art Blakey and Herbie Hancock before becoming a prominent champion of traditional jazz values through a series of high-profile Columbia recordings in the 1980s. He is also a virtuoso on classical trumpet, and a noted music educator.

Warne Marsh
b. 26 October 1927, Los Angeles, California
d. 18 December 1987, Los Angeles, California
Tenor saxophone. Sideman to Lee Konitz and Lennie Tristano in the 1950s.

Lyle Mays
b. 27 November 1953, Wausaukee, Wisconsin
Keyboards, composer. Fusion artist closely associated with Pat Metheny since 1976.

Brad Mehldau
b. 23 August 1970, Jacksonville, Florida
Piano. Inventive improviser, celebrated for both acoustic trio and solo performances.

Pat Metheny
b. 12 August 1954, Lee's Summit, Missouri
Electric guitar, guitar synthesizer, composer. Leader of the hugely successful Pat Metheny Group since 1977, this versatile artist absorbed influences ranging from country and rock to avant-garde free jazz.

Palle Mikkelborg
b. 6 March 1941, Copenhagen, Denmark
Trumpet, composer. Danish player who came to international prominence when he composed *O* for Miles Davis in 1984.

Bubber Miley
b. 3 April 1903, Aiken, South Carolina
d. 20 May 1932, Welfare Island, New York
Trumpet. Sideman to Duke Ellington (1923–29) who developed the "growl" style of trumpet playing.

Darius Milhaud
b. 4 September 1892, Aix-en-Provence, France
d. 22 June 1974, Geneva, Switzerland
Composer. French composer whose ballet *La Création du Monde* (1923) contained jazz elements. He taught extensively in the US, where he numbered Dave Brubeck among his composition pupils.

Glenn Miller
b. 1 March 1904, Clarinda, Iowa
d. 15 December 1944, English Channel
Trombone, bandleader. Composer of "In the Mood" and "Moonlight Serenade." His hugely popular band reached its peak in 1939–42, before he formed a new band for the US Army Air Force and entertained Allied troops in Europe.

Charles Mingus
b. 22 April 1922, Nogales, Arizona
d. 5 January 1979, Cuernavaca, Mexico
Double bass, composer. Experimental composer who blended elements from bop and free jazz. His sophisticated bass playing was heard to best advantage in duets with Eric Dolphy in the early 1960s.

Thelonious Monk
b. 10 October 1917, Rocky Mount, North Carolina
d. 17 February 1982, Englewood, New Jersey
Piano, composer. Central figure of the early bop movement whose eccentric keyboard style remains inimitable. His compositions became a core part of the standards repertoire, and are characterized by harmonic and rhythmic unpredictability.

Wes Montgomery
b. 6 March 1923, Indianapolis, Indiana
d. 15 June 1968, Indianapolis, Indiana
Guitar. His sophisticated melodic improvisations were enormously influential on postwar guitarists.

Lee Morgan
b. 10 July 1938, Philadelphia, Pennsylvania
d. 19 February 1972, New York, New York
Trumpet, composer. Hard-bop performer who played with Art Blakey's Jazz Messengers (1958–61), then became a leader on the Blue Note label, where his successes included *The Sidewinder* (1964).

Jelly Roll Morton
b. 20 October 1890, New Orleans, Louisiana
d. 10 July 1941, Los Angeles, California
Piano, vocals, composer. The first jazz composer and intellectual, his group, the Red Hot Peppers, recorded polished music in the New Orleans style in 1926–27. In 1938 he emerged from obscurity to make a series of retrospective recordings for the Library of Congress.

Bennie Moten
b. 13 November 1894, Kansas City, Missouri
d. 2 April 1935, Kansas City, Missouri
Piano, bandleader. Pioneer of Kansas City big-band jazz and mentor of the young Count Basie.

Paul Motian
b. 25 March 1931, Philadelphia, Pennsylvania
d. 22 November 2011, New York, New York
Drums. Sideman to Bill Evans (1959–64) and Keith Jarrett (1966–77).

Gerry Mulligan
b. 6 April 1927, Queens, New York
d. 19 January 1996, Darien, Connecticut
Baritone saxophone, composer. After participating in Miles Davis's *Birth of the Cool* sessions (1949), he became a leading figure in the West Coast "cool" school when he formed a quartet with Chet Baker in 1952.

David Murray
b. 19 February 1955, Oakland, California
Saxophone, composer. Founder member of World Saxophone Quartet in 1977.

Ray Nance
b. 10 December 1913, Chicago, Illinois
d. 28 January 1976, New York, New York
Trumpet, violin. Sideman to Duke Ellington (1940–63).

Joe "Tricky Sam" Nanton
b. 1 February 1904, New York, New York
d. 20 July 1946, San Francisco, California
Trombone. Sideman to Duke Ellington (1926–46) who adapted the "growl" style of trumpet playing for use on the trombone.

Fats Navarro
b. 24 September 1923, Key West, Florida
d. 7 July 1950, New York, New York
Trumpet. Sideman to leading bop musicians, whose early death prevented him from reaching his full potential.

Jimmie Noone
b. 23 April 1895, Cut Off, Louisiana
d. 19 April 1944, Los Angeles, California
Clarinet, alto saxophone. He took the New Orleans style to Chicago in the 1920s and influenced the playing of Barney Bigard and Benny Goodman.

Red Norvo
b. 31 March 1908, Beardstown, Illinois
d. 6 April 1999, Santa Monica, California
Vibraphone, xylophone. Featured soloist with Woody Herman, Charles Mingus, and Benny Goodman. Married to Mildred Bailey (1933–43).

Joe "King" Oliver
b. 11 May 1885, Aben, Louisiana
d. 10 April 1938, Savannah, Georgia
Cornet, bandleader. Leader of King Oliver's Creole Jazz Band, his work in Chicago in the early 1920s laid the foundations for later jazz and provided an apprenticeship for the young Louis Armstrong.

Edward "Kid" Ory
b. 25 December 1886, La Place, Louisiana
d. 23 January 1973, Honolulu, Hawaii
Trombone, vocals. Exponent of the "tailgate" style of New Orleans trombone playing.

Tony Oxley
b. 15 June 1938, Sheffield, UK
Drums. Leading British drummer, well known since his appearance on John McLaughlin's album *Extrapolation* in 1969.

Walter Page
b. 9 February 1900, Gallatin, Missouri
d. 20 December 1957, New York, New York
Double bass. Bassist in Bennie Moten's and Count Basie's Kansas City bands.

Charlie "Yardbird" Parker
b. 29 August 1920, Kansas City, Kansas
d. 12 March 1955, New York, New York
Alto saxophone. The most revered and enigmatic character of the bop movement, a phenomenal improviser who influenced all subsequent reed players. He became as famous for his drug habit and its harrowing consequences as for his innovative playing.

Joe Pass
b. 13 January 1929, New Brunswick, New Jersey
d. 23 May 1994, Los Angeles, California
Guitar. His technical fluency made him an ideal partner for Oscar Peterson and other mainstream artists managed by Norman Granz in the 1970s.

Jaco Pastorius
b. 1 December 1951, Norristown, Pennsylvania
d. 21 September 1987, Fort Lauderdale, Florida
Electric bass. Member of Weather Report in the mid-1970s and early sideman to Pat Metheny, he led his own groups in the 1980s.

Gary Peacock
b. 12 May 1935, Burley, Idaho
Double bass. Sideman to Bill Evans (1962–63), Albert Ayler, and Paul Bley, and a member of Keith Jarrett's standards trio.

Niels-Henning Ørsted Pedersen
b. 27 May 1946, Osted, Denmark
d. 19 April 2005, Ishøj, Denmark
Double bass. Virtuoso sideman to Oscar Peterson in the 1970s and 1980s.

Art Pepper
b. 1 September 1925, Gardena, California
d. 15 June 1982, Los Angeles, California
Saxophones. Member of Stan Kenton's band (1946–51), who subsequently developed a bop-oriented brand of West Coast jazz.

Oscar Peterson
b. 15 August 1925, Montreal, Quebec
d. 23 December 2007, Mississauga, Ontario
Piano. A performer of staggering technical ability, with a prodigious recorded output, he made his name in trio work during the 1950s and was closely associated with Norman Granz from 1949.

Oscar Pettiford
b. 30 September 1922, Okmulgee, Oklahoma
d. 8 September 1960, Copenhagen, Denmark
Double bass. Sideman to Roy Eldridge and Dizzy Gillespie in the early 1940s, he moved to Europe in 1958.

Courtney Pine
b. 18 March 1964, London, UK
Tenor and soprano saxophones. Leading figure in the British jazz resurgence of the 1980s.

Jean-Luc Ponty
b. 29 September 1942, Avranches, France
Violin and electric violin. After working in John McLaughlin's Mahavishnu Orchestra (1974), he has played in all styles from swing to fusion and free jazz.

Bud Powell
b. 27 September 1924, Harlem, New York
d. 31 July 1966, New York, New York
Piano. Leading bop pianist and protégé of Thelonious Monk, he spent the period 1959–64 in Paris with Kenny Clarke.

Chano Pozo
b. 7 January 1915, Havana, Cuba
d. 3 December 1948, Harlem, New York
Vocals, percussion. Latin drummer who collaborated with Dizzy Gillespie in 1947–48.

André Previn
b. 6 April 1929, Berlin, Germany
Pianist, composer, conductor. West Coast pianist and Hollywood film composer who gained international fame as conductor of the London Symphony Orchestra in the 1970s.

Brian Priestley
b. 10 July 1940, Manchester, UK
Piano, writer. He transcribed Ellington's music in the 1970s and is popular in the UK as a broadcaster and author.

Flora Purim
b. 6 March 1942, Rio de Janeiro, Brazil
Vocals, guitar, percussion. Brazilian singer who worked with Chick Corea's band Return to Forever in the early 1970s.

Ike Quebec
b. 17 August 1918, Newark, New Jersey
d. 16 January 1963, New York, New York
Tenor saxophone. Bop performer who worked as A&R agent for Blue Note records, of which he became assistant musical director in 1959.

Gertrude "Ma" Rainey
b. 26 April 1886, Columbus, Georgia
d. 22 December 1939, Rome, Georgia
Vocals. Popular blues singer of the 1920s.

Dewey Redman
b. 17 May 1931, Fort Worth, Texas
d. 2 September 2006, Brooklyn, New York
Saxophones. Sideman to Ornette Coleman (1967–74) and Charlie Haden (1969 and 1982).

Don Redman
b. 29 July 1900, Piedmont, West Virginia
d. 30 November 1964, New York, New York
Saxophones, arranger. His collaboration with Fletcher Henderson in the 1920s laid the foundations for the big-band style of the swing era.

Django Reinhardt
b. 23 January 1910, Liberchies, Belgium
d. 16 May 1953, Fontainebleau, France
Guitar. Flamboyant gypsy performer who starred alongside Stephane Grappelli in the Quintette du Hot Club de France during the 1930s.

Emily Remler
b. 18 September 1957, New York, New York
d. 4 May 1990, Sydney, Australia
Guitar. Influenced by Wes Montgomery, she worked with Astrud Gilberto (1978–81) and was married to Monty Alexander.

Buddy Rich
b. 30 September 1917, Brooklyn, New York
d. 2 April 1987, Los Angeles, California
Drums, bandleader. Sideman to Tommy Dorsey (1939–42, 1944–45, and 1954–55), he moved smoothly from the swing to bop styles.

Lee Ritenour
b. 11 January 1952, Los Angeles, California
Guitar. Fusion artist closely associated with Dave Grusin and the GRP label.

Sam Rivers
b. 25 September 1923, Enid, Oklahoma
d. 26 December 2011, Orlando, Florida
Saxophones, composer. Sideman to Miles Davis (1964) and Cecil Taylor (1968–73).

Max Roach
b. 10 January 1924, Newland, North Carolina
d. 16 August 2007, New York, New York
Drums. Alongside Kenny Clarke, the most influential of early bop drummers. His work in the 1960s was associated with the Civil Rights movement in the US.

Charles Luckyeth "Luckey" Roberts
b. 7 August 1887, Philadelphia, Pennsylvania
d. 5 February 1968, New York, New York
Piano. Stride performer based in Harlem in the 1940s.

Marcus Roberts
b. 7 August 1963, Jacksonville, Florida
Piano, composer. Sideman to Wynton Marsalis (1985–91), before leading his own trio.

Red Rodney
b. 27 September 1927, Philadelphia, Pennsylvania
d. 27 May 1994, Boynton Beach, Florida
Trumpet. Sideman to Charlie Parker (1949–51).

Sonny Rollins
b. 7 September 1930, New York, New York
Tenor and soprano saxophones. Early bop work in the 1950s led to a brief collaboration with Miles Davis before he made his name as a leader. His playing formed a link between the styles of Charlie Parker and John Coltrane.

George Russell
b. 23 June 1923, Cincinnati, Ohio
d. 27 July 2009, Boston, Massachusetts
Composer. Theorist who formulated the procedures of modal jazz in the 1950s.

Johnny St. Cyr
b. 17 April 1890, New Orleans, Louisiana
d. 17 June 1966, Los Angeles, California
Banjo, guitar. Member of King Oliver's and Louis Armstrong's Chicago bands in the 1920s.

David Sanborn
b. 30 July 1945, Tampa, Florida
Alto saxophone. Fusion artist with a distinctively intense tone, whose album *Voyeur* won a Grammy in 1981.

Pharoah Sanders
b. 13 October 1940, Little Rock, Arkansas
Tenor and soprano saxophone, composer. A disciple of John Coltrane, with whom he played in the mid-1960s, he remained notorious for his strident tone colors.

Maria Schneider
b. 27 November 1960, Windom, Minnesota
Piano, composer. Her work was featured prominently in several US jazz festivals in the mid-1990s, and she later promoted it digitally via ArtistShare.

Gunther Schuller
b. 22 November 1925, Jackson Heights, New York
Composer, conductor, writer, French horn. His horn playing (which included work alongside Miles Davis in 1949) has been overshadowed by his conducting and writing careers. He is the author of the most thorough musical analyses of mainstream jazz yet to have appeared in print.

John Scofield
b. 26 December 1951, Dayton, Ohio
Guitar, composer. Sideman to Miles Davis (1982–85), and prolific leader from 1977 onward

James Scott
b. 12 February 1885, Neosho, Missouri
d. 30 August 1938, Kansas City, Kansas
Ragtime composer. With Scott Joplin and Joseph Lamb, he was one of the team of leading ragtime composers published by John Stark.

Ronnie Scott
b. 28 January 1927, London, UK
d. 23 December 1996, London, UK
Tenor saxophone, club owner. A participant in the British bop movement of the 1950s, his club in London remains the foremost UK venue for live jazz.

Artie Shaw
b. 23 May 1910, New York, New York
d. 30 December 2004, Thousand Oaks, California
Clarinet, bandleader. His band recorded its hit "Begin the Beguine" in 1938.

Woody Shaw
b. 24 December 1944, Laurinburg, North Carolina
d. 10 May 1989, New York, New York
Trumpet, flugelhorn. A member of Art Blakey's Jazz Messengers in the early 1970s, he also collaborated with Eric Dolphy, Horace Silver, and Chick Corea.

George Shearing
b. 13 August 1919, London, UK
d. 14 February 2011, New York, New York
Piano. Blind performer of "cool" jazz featuring a "locked-hands" style of block-chord playing.

Archie Shepp
b. 24 May 1937, Fort Lauderdale, Florida
Saxophones, composer. Free-jazz performer influenced by John Coltrane in the early 1960s.

Andy Sheppard
b. 20 January 1957, Warminster, UK
Tenor and soprano saxophones, composer. Sideman to Gil Evans and George Russell in the late 1980s, he has worked since the 1990s with Carla Bley and his own big band and trio.

Wayne Shorter
b. 25 August 1933, Newark, New Jersey
Tenor and soprano saxophones, composer. Sideman to Miles Davis (1964–70) and member of Weather Report (1970–85).

Horace Silver
b. 2 September 1928, Norwalk, Connecticut
Piano, composer. Leading hard-bop pianist,

long associated with the Blue Note label (1952–80).

Bessie Smith
b. 15 April 1894, Chattanooga, Tennessee
d. 26 September 1937, Clarksdale, Mississippi
Vocals. Her magnificently earthy singing earned her the sobriquet "Empress of the Blues" in the 1920s.

Clarence "Pine Top" Smith
b. 11 June 1904, Troy, Alabama
d. 15 March 1929, Chicago, Illinois
Piano. Boogie-woogie performer popular in Chicago in the late 1920s.

Mamie Smith
b. 26 May 1883, Cincinnati, Ohio
d. 16 September 1946, New York, New York
Vocals. Her blues recordings in 1920 were the first to be cut by a black jazz singer.

Willie "The Lion" Smith
b. 25 November 1897, Goshen, New York
d. 18 April 1973, New York, New York
Piano, composer. Stride artist and early mentor of Duke Ellington.

Elmer Snowden
b. 9 October 1900, Baltimore, Maryland
d. 14 May 1973, Philadelphia, Pennsylvania
Bandleader. His band The Washingtonians became Duke Ellington's first orchestra when Snowden was deposed as leader in 1924.

Tomasz Stańko
b. 11 July 1942, Rzeszów, Poland
Trumpet, composer. Sideman to Krzysztof Komeda in the 1960s, then notable as leader on the ECM label.

Rex Stewart
b. 22 February 1907, Philadelphia, Pennsylvania
d. 7 September 1967, Los Angeles, California
Trumpet. Sideman to Duke Ellington (1934–45).

Sonny Stitt
b. 2 February 1924, Boston, Massachusetts
d. 22 July 1982, Washington, DC
Saxophones. His fluent and expressive bop style was an impressive development of Charlie Parker's improvisation techniques.

Igor Stravinsky
b. 17 June 1882, Oranienbaum, Russia
d. 6 April 1971, New York, New York
Composer. He created modernistic distortions of the ragtime style in 1918–19, and composed *Ebony Concerto* for Woody Herman's Herd in 1945.

Billy Strayhorn
b. 29 November 1915, Dayton, Ohio
d. 31 May 1967, New York, New York
Piano, composer, arranger. Composer of "Take the 'A' Train" and "Satin Doll," he created many of Duke Ellington's finest scores in the period 1939–67.

Sun Ra
b. 22 May 1914, Birmingham, Alabama
d. 30 May 1993, Birmingham, Alabama
Keyboards, composer, bandleader. Colorful fusion artist whose Myth Science Arkestra was a potent force in the free jazz emerging in Chicago during the 1950s.

John Surman
b. 30 August 1944, Tavistock, UK
Baritone and soprano saxophones. Influenced by John Coltrane, his expertise first came to attention on John McLaughlin's album *Extrapolation* in 1969.

Ralph Sutton
b. 4 November 1922, Hamburg, Missouri
d. 30 December 2001, Bailey, Colorado
Piano. Modern exponent of the Harlem stride style.

Esbjörn Svensson
b. 16 April 1964, Skultuna, Sweden
d. 14 June 2008, Ingarö, Sweden
Piano. Leading light of the acoustic piano trio E.S.T.

Lew Tabackin
b. 26 March 1940, Philadelphia, Pennsylvania
Tenor saxophone. Married Toshiko Akiyoshi in 1970, with whom he led a successful big band from 1973.

Art Tatum
b. 13 October 1909, Toledo, Ohio
d. 5 November 1956, Los Angeles, California
Piano. Near-blind performer who revitalized jazz piano playing in the 1940s with a heady blend of virtuosity and harmonic daring.

Billy Taylor
b. 24 July 1921, Greenville, North Carolina
d. 28 December 2010, New York, New York
Piano, composer, educator. After a rich and varied performing career, he served as artistic director for jazz events at the Kennedy Center, Washington, DC, from 1994.

Cecil Taylor
b. 25 March 1929, New York, New York
Piano, composer. He worked sporadically in a free-jazz idiom throughout the 1960s, and gained greater exposure in the late 1970s.

Martin Taylor
b. 20 October 1956, Harlow, UK
Guitar. Sideman to Stephane Grappelli in the 1980s, he became a popular solo artist in the UK during the 1990s.

Jack Teagarden
b. 20 August 1905, Vernon, Texas
d. 15 January 1964, New Orleans, Louisiana
Trombone, vocals. After working in Paul Whiteman's orchestra in the 1930s, he formed his own big band and joined Louis Armstrong's All Stars in 1947.

Clark Terry
b. 14 December 1920, St Louis, Missouri
Trumpet, flugelhorn, vocals. Early work with Count Basie (1948–51) led to a stint with Duke Ellington (1951–59) and a close involvement with leading bop musicians.

Juan Tizol
b. 22 January 1900, Vega Baja, Puerto Rico
d. 23 April 1984, Inglewood, California
Trombone, composer. Specializing in the valve trombone, he worked with Duke Ellington (1929–44, 1951–53, and 1960–61) and composed "Caravan" in 1937.

Stan Tracey
b. 30 December 1926, London, UK
Piano, composer. Pianist at Ronnie Scott's London club during the 1960s, he played for Sonny Rollins's *Alfie* film score in 1966. His son Clark (b. 1961) is a drummer.

Lennie Tristano
b. 19 March 1919, Chicago, Illinois
d. 18 November 1978, New York, New York
Piano, composer. Blind performer who branched out from a bop background into an experimental brand of "cool" jazz in the 1950s.

McCoy Tyner
b. 11 December 1938, Philadelphia, Pennsylvania
Piano, composer. Member of the John Coltrane Quartet (1960–65), and a leader since the 1970s.

Naná Vasconcelos
b. 2 August 1944, Recife, Brazil
Percussion, vocals. Member of Collin Walcott and Don Cherry's world-music trio Codona (founded in 1978) and the Pat Metheny Group (1980–83).

Sarah Vaughan
b. 27 March 1924, Newark, New Jersey
d. 3 April 1990, Hidden Hills, California
Vocals. Early exposure with Billy Eckstine's band in the mid-1940s launched her on a solo career ranging from invigorating bop standards to lush arrangements of popular songs.

Giuseppe "Joe" Venuti
b. 16 September 1903, Philadelphia, Pennsylvania
d. 14 August 1978, Seattle, Washington
Violin. Duet partner of guitarist Eddie Lang in the late 1920s, he influenced Stephane Grappelli.

Collin Walcott
b. 24 April 1945, New York, New York
d. 8 November 1984, Magdeburg, East Germany
Sitar, tablā, percussion. Advocate of world music who specialized in traditional Indian instruments and formed the trio Codona with Don Cherry and Naná Vasconcelos in 1978.

Thomas "Fats" Waller
b. 21 May 1904, New York, New York
d. 15 December 1943, Kansas City, Missouri
Piano, organ, vocals, composer. Popular comic songwriter and virtuoso stride pianist of the 1930s.

Dinah Washington
b. 29 August 1924, Tuscaloosa, Alabama
d. 14 December 1963, Detroit, Michigan
Vocals. Membership of Lionel Hampton's band (1943–46) led to a wide-ranging solo career embracing blues and pop, in addition to jazz.

Grover Washington, Jr.
b. 12 December 1943, Buffalo, New York
d. 17 December 1999, New York, New York
Saxophones. His polished performances of soul-jazz brought him numerous chart successes from the mid-1970s onward.

Sadao Watanabe
b. 1 February 1933, Utsunomiya, Japan
Alto saxophone. Leading Japanese bop and fusion artist.

William Henry "Chick" Webb
b. 10 February 1909, Baltimore, Maryland
d. 16 June 1939, Baltimore, Maryland
Drums, bandleader. Hunchback bandleader who hired the teenage Ella Fitzgerald in 1934.

Eberhard Weber
b. 22 January 1940, Stuttgart, Germany
Double bass, composer. His group Colours met with critical acclaim in the mid-1970s when he became a key artist on the ECM label.

Ben Webster
b. 27 March 1909, Kansas City, Missouri
d. 20 September 1973, Amsterdam, Netherlands
Tenor saxophone. Sideman to Duke Ellington (1935–36, 1940–43, and 1948–49), he emigrated to Denmark in 1964.

Dave Weckl
b. 8 January 1960, St. Louis, Missouri
Drums. Dynamic member of Chick Corea's Elektric Band in the late 1980s, and leader of his own groups from 1990 onward. Proficient on both acoustic and electronic drums.

Kenny Wheeler
b. 14 January 1930, Toronto
Trumpet, flugelhorn. Based in the UK since 1952, he became an established ECM artist in the mid-1970s and has collaborated with Keith Jarrett and Jan Garbarek.

Paul Whiteman
b. 28 March 1890, Denver, Colorado
d. 29 December 1967, Doylestown, Pennsylvania
Bandleader. Dubbed the "King of Jazz," he promoted symphonic jazz by commissioning *Rhapsody in Blue* from George Gershwin in 1924. His bands produced polished dance music typical of the 1920s.

Charles Melvin "Cootie" Williams
b. 24 July 1911, Mobile, Alabama
d. 15 September 1985, New York, New York
Trumpet. Sideman to Duke Ellington (1929–40 and 1962–74) and Benny Goodman (1941), and a leader in his own right during the 1940s.

Clarence Williams
b. 8 October 1893, Plaquemine, Louisiana
d. 6 November 1965, Queens, New York
Piano, vocals. He collaborated with Sidney Bechet, Louis Armstrong, and Bubber Miley in the 1920s.

Mary Lou Williams
b. 8 May 1910, Atlanta, Georgia
d. 28 May 1981, Durham, North Carolina
Piano, composer. Her *Zodiac Suite* was performed by the New York Philharmonic Orchestra in 1946. She wrote scores for Benny Goodman and Duke Ellington, and was the first front-rank female instrumentalist in jazz.

Tony Williams
b. 12 December 1945, Chicago, Illinois
d. 23 February 1997, Daly City, California
Drums. A child prodigy, he joined Miles Davis at the age of seventeen and remained his sideman until 1969, also playing for Herbie Hancock. He formed the energetic fusion group Lifetime with John McLaughlin on his departure from Davis.

Cassandra Wilson
b. 4 December 1955, Jackson, Mississippi
Vocals. Strongly influenced by the blues, she made her highly acclaimed first album for Blue Note in 1993.

Teddy Wilson
b. 24 November 1912, Austin, Texas
d. 31 July 1986, Hillsdale, New Jersey
Piano, bandleader. Leading pianist of the swing era, famous for his work with Billie Holiday and Benny Goodman's chamber groups in the 1930s.

Kai Winding
b. 18 May 1922, Aarhus, Denmark
d. 6 May 1983, Yonkers, New York
Trombone. Along with J. J. Johnson, the foremost trombonist working in the bop style during the 1950s.

Phil Woods
b. 2 November 1931, Springfield, Massachusetts
Alto saxophone. Early work with Buddy Rich, Dizzy Gillespie, and Benny Goodman revealed his strong debt to Charlie Parker. He continued to top *Down Beat's* popularity polls in the mid-1990s.

Lester Young
b. 27 August 1909, Woodville, Mississippi
d. 15 March 1959, New York, New York
Tenor saxophone. Soulmate and frequent accompanist to Billie Holiday, he played in Count Basie's band (1936–41 and 1943–44) and was renowned for his light, clear tone.

Joe Zawinul
b. 7 July 1932, Vienna, Austria
d. 11 September 2007, Vienna, Austria
Keyboards, composer. His expertise with synthesizers in the jazz-rock group Weather Report (1970–85), which he coled with Wayne Shorter, enriched the soundscapes of the early fusion period.

John Zorn
b. 2 September 1953, New York, New York
Alto saxophone, bird imitations. Experimental free-jazz artist who began stamping his personal imprint on compositions by Ornette Coleman and others during the 1980s.

GLOSSARY OF MUSICAL TERMS

Acoustic
Live sound that has not been electronically enhanced. Used to distinguish an instrument from its electric version.

Acoustic recording
A recording made before the advent of the electrical process in 1926.

Atonality
The avoidance of a sense of key, generally through a consistent use of dissonance. The idea was imported into jazz from classical music, which began to dissolve conventional tonality in the early years of the twentieth century.

Backbeat
Placing a heavy emphasis on the beats of the measure traditionally regarded as the weakest (beats two and four in a four-beat measure).

Ballad
Any slow jazz piece characterized by melodic lyricism.

Banjo
An instrument developed by slave musicians in the nineteenth century from African prototypes, and common in jazz bands until supplanted by the guitar in the 1930s. The most popular model has five strings stretched over a circular body supporting a skin resonator; the strings are plucked with the aid of plectra. Six-string banjos were common in early jazz.

Bebop
A style of jazz developed in the early 1940s by small ensembles, characterized by virtuosic solo improvisations based on complex harmonic progressions and often promoting melodic angularity and metrical disruption.

Block chords
The parallel motion of chords, in which all underlying parts move in the same rhythm as the melody – a defining characteristic of the swing-band style of the 1930s and 1940s.

Blue note
A microtonal flattening of the third, fifth, or seventh note of the major scale for expressive effect, thought to be derived from African music. Blue notes sound noticeably harsher on acoustic keyboard instruments, which have no pitch-bending capability.

Blues
An improvised genre for solo voice, generally accompanied by a single instrument (e.g. guitar) in call-and-response patterns, which exerted a major influence on the development of jazz.

Blues progression
See TWELVE-BAR BLUES.

Boogie-woogie
A keyboard version of the blues, in which the harmonies are articulated by the player's left hand in repeated rhythmic figurations.

Bop
See BEBOP.

Bossa nova
Meaning "new wave," a jazz style popular in the 1960s that reflected strong Brazilian influences in its restrained and lyrical use of syncopation.

Break
A short improvised passage, usually performed by a solo instrument, inserted between adjacent sections of a piece by way of punctuation.

Cakewalk
A dance popular at the turn of the century and similar to ragtime in style, originally evolved by black communities to parody the pretentious behavior of white folk. The name derives from the tradition of awarding a cake to the best performer of the dance.

Call-and-response
A musical pattern of "question-and-answer," in which a short theme is passed rapidly from one performer (or group of performers) to another. The technique probably derived from the antiphonal singing common in slave working parties.

Changes
The repeating pattern of chords on which a conventional jazz improvisation is based.

Chord
The simultaneous playing of different notes to create a single harmony.

Chorus
In jazz, a single statement of the changes on which a piece is based. Solo improvisations are normally of more than one chorus in duration. The term can also describe the refrain of a popular song, preceded by a "verse."

Chromatic harmony
The chromatic scale employs all twelve semitones available in a single octave; chromatic harmony, therefore, utilizes chords with their root notes a semitone apart. The expression generally implies harmonic complexity and instability.

Combo
Jazz slang for a small instrumental group (cf. "combination").

Cool
The opposite of hot, usually applied to any style of jazz marked by emotional restraint.

Counterpoint
The simultaneous combination of more than one melodic line, sometimes referred to as polyphony.

Crossover
Any musical venture that transcends perceived stylistic or commercial barriers, e.g. idioms that synthesize jazz and rock (see FUSION), jazz and classical music, jazz and ethnic music, etc.

Cross-rhythm
The combination of rhythmic patterns to create displaced accents (see SYNCOPATION), which conflict with the main pulses of the meter.

Cutting contest
An informal competition between instrumentalists who try to outplay each other in a jam session.

Dissonance
A combination of notes that sounds "wrong" (or, more correctly, "discordant"). In classical music before the twentieth century, dissonances required resolution to "consonances;" in jazz, many milder dissonances have become standard elements of the harmonic vocabulary.

Dixieland
Early New Orleans ensemble jazz, as performed by white groups. The term "Dixie" refers to the southern states of the USA.

Electric piano
An electric keyboard instrument that imitates the sound of an acoustic piano. The metallic timbre of the Fender-Rhodes electric piano was popular with fusion groups in the 1970s, but now sounds dated.

Field holler
A work song (or shout) originated by slaves on US plantations.

Free jazz
Generic term for several styles of jazz, pioneered by the 1960s avant-garde, which abandon conventional harmonic, melodic, and rhythmic procedures in pursuit of greater musical freedom. At times, this dissolution of traditional musical grammar has consciously symbolized the black community's need for political and social freedom.

Front line
The soloists in a jazz performance (in early jazz usually a cornet/trumpet player, clarinetist, and trombonist), generally supported by a rhythm section. The term derives from the layout of marching bands in old New Orleans.

Funk
A term used in the 1950s to describe down-to-earth jazz styles (i.e. those characterized by powerful rhythms and prominent blue notes), especially in contrast to cool jazz. The term "funk" is synonymous with soul jazz, and should not be confused with its more modern pop-music derivative.

Fusion
A stylistic amalgamation of features from jazz, rhythm 'n' blues and rock music, first introduced by Miles Davis in the late 1960s. See also CROSSOVER.

Gig
Jazz parlance for a professional engagement.

Glissando
Sliding from one note to a higher or lower one by sounding the intermediate pitches. On a piano, all individual pitches between the two notes are clearly audible; on other instruments and in vocal technique a blurred effect is produced.

Gospel
Successor to the spiritual as the principal vocal genre in popular black religious music.

Growl
A manner of playing wind instruments intended to portray the rough sound of the human voice, or a manner of "dirty" vocal

production common in the work of blues singers.

Hard bop
A loose term usually indicating a development of bebop in the 1950s, in which the hard-driving rhythmic characteristics and blues mannerisms were intensified. Sometimes synonymous with funk and soul jazz, or used to indicate the importation of gospel features.

Harmon mute
A type of mute featuring a central stem that can be moved in and out to vary a brass instrument's timbre. Also known as a "wah-wah" mute, it became particularly associated with the playing of Miles Davis (who removed the stem altogether).

Harmony
The use of chords as a basis for musical textures, generally organized into a predetermined "chord progression" (see also CHANGES). Static harmony, which tends to avoid chord progressions, is a characteristic of some modal jazz.

Head
The statement of a theme at the opening and/or conclusion of a piece, before and/or after the improvised solo choruses.

Hot
A term popular in early jazz, referring to the elements of a performance that sound "jazzy" (e.g. swung rhythm, syncopation, blue notes, and expressive tone).

Improvisation
The spontaneous production of musical ideas by a performer, involving no conscious element of pre-composition.

Jam session
An informal group improvisation.

Licks
The characteristic (and sometimes idiosyncratic) melodic or rhythmic formulae habitually used by an individual player, sometimes referred to as "signatures."

March
A genre derived from military music, popular in America during the nineteenth century. Its multi-sectional structures and simple harmonic schemes provided the foundation for ragtime.

Meter
The organization of rhythmic pulses into regular stress patterns.

Minstrel show
A comic musical entertainment popular in America from the 1840s onwards, in which white performers blackened their faces and caricatured the behavior of black people. Later in the century, black musicians participated in such shows; many early jazz musicians began their careers in this way.

Modal jazz
A style of jazz, pioneered by Miles Davis and others toward the end of the 1950s, in which improvisations are based on modes rather than conventional changes. See also HARMONY.

Mode
Musical scale. In the twentieth century, both classical and jazz musicians grew frustrated with the major and minor scales that had dominated Western music for centuries, and began experimenting with less familiar modes. Some of these scales were inspired by the pre-classical music of the Renaissance, while others were borrowed from non-Western musical traditions.

Multiphonics
A technique used by avant-garde wind players to produce more than one note simultaneously.

Mute
A device inserted into the bell of a brass instrument to alter its natural timbre, generally resulting in a more subdued tone. Manufactured from a variety of substances, mutes are available in numerous designs, each with a different sonorous character.

Novelty
A popularized style of ragtime successful in the 1910s and 1920s, favoring pieces with fanciful titles and sometimes containing musical gimmicks.

Ostinato
Italian for "obstinate". A short musical motif subjected to more than one immediate repetition. See also RIFF.

Overdubbing
A studio technique in which additional tracks can be added to a recording in post-production.

Piano roll
A roll of paper which records a keyboard performance as a sequence of perforations. When passed through the mechanism of a player piano (pianola), an approximation of the original performance is produced.

Plugger
Employee of a music publisher responsible for promoting the company's latest issues.

Polymeter
A sustained application of polyrhythms in a layered musical texture, which suggests different meters are occurring simultaneously.

Polyphony
See COUNTERPOINT.

Polyrhythm
The superimposition of two or more conflicting rhythmic patterns.

Polytonal
The superimposition of two or more conflicting keys.

Pre-composition
Planning the structure and details of a musical work in advance of its performance, usually preserving them in the form of a notated score. The historical development of jazz has frequently involved a fruitful creative tension between varying degrees of pre-composition and spontaneous improvisation.

Professor
Informal title awarded to early jazz pianists who were capable of reading music.

Progressive jazz
A predominantly pre-composed big-band style promoted in the 1940s and 1950s by Stan Kenton as an amalgamation of jazz and modern classical music.

Race records
Recordings specifically aimed at the escalating black consumer market in the 1920s and 1930s.

Rag
Any piece in the ragtime style.

Ragtime
Early precursor of jazz, in which highly syncopated melodies were presented in solid musical structures borrowed from the march. Ragtime was pre-composed, and circulated in the form of songs, piano pieces, and orchestral dance music. See also CAKEWALK.

Reeds
Generic term for wind instruments that use a reed to generate their sounds, principally clarinets and saxophones (single reeds), and oboes and bassoons (double reeds).

Rhythm
The temporal organization of music as patterns of weak, strong, long, and short beats. Rhythms are usually governed by the constraints of a prevailing meter.

Rhythm section
Members of a jazz combo or big band responsible for maintaining the rhythmic and harmonic foundation of the music, and accompanying solo performers. A standard rhythm section comprises a harmony instrument (guitar, banjo, or keyboard), bass instrument, and drums.

Riff
Any short, catchy ostinato figure. Riffs were a common device in big-band music of the Swing Era, where they sometimes appeared as accompanying figures, or as the main melody. The device was retained as a prominent feature of the bebop style.

Rip
An exhilarating upwards glissando on a brass instrument.

Sampling
A technique in electronic music by which a segment of natural sound is extracted ("sampled") from a source, and then converted into digital information to provide the raw material for computerized transformations.

Scale
The arrangement of any group of musical pitches in ascending or descending order. See also MODE.

Scat
Singing an improvised melodic line to nonsense syllables, often in imitation of instrumental music.

Sequencing
The computerized repetition or juxtaposition of digitally sampled sounds.

Side
Before the introduction of long-playing records, a single recorded piece was often referred to as a "side" since it normally occupied one complete side of a 78rpm disc.

Sideman
Any player in a group other than the leader.

Signatures
See LICKS.

Soul
A brand of hard bop incorporating elements borrowed from black church music.

Spiritual
Vocal music of the African-American church, developed under the influence of European hymns in the late nineteenth century.

Standard
Any song melody forming part of the "standard" repertoire of themes used by jazz musicians as raw material on which to base their improvisations.

Storyville
Red-light district of old New Orleans, traditionally considered to have been the cradle of jazz in the early twentieth century.

Stride
The first important style of jazz piano playing, at its height in the 1920s and 1930s. It evolved directly from ragtime and took its name from the "striding" motion of the player's leaping left hand.

Swing
Type of (largely pre-composed) big-band dance music that was internationally popular in the 1930s and 1940s, which gave its name to the Swing Era.

Swung rhythm
The tendency of jazz performers to anticipate the main beats of a meter through syncopation, or to alternate notes of long and short rhythmic values. Both techniques propel the music forward with a strong rhythmic drive.

Symphonic jazz
Hybrid style combining elements of jazz and classical music, popularized by Gershwin and others in the 1920s and 1930s.

Syncopation
The accentuation of a weak beat to disrupt the expected stress patterns of a regular meter. See also CROSS-RHYTHM.

Synthesizer
Electronic instrument capable of producing a theoretically infinite range of sound colors.

Third stream
A modernized form of symphonic jazz, pioneered by Gunther Schuller from the late 1950s onward, in which jazz and classical-music elements are synthesized. Unlike symphonic jazz, Third Stream music involves improvisation, as well as pre-composition.

Tonality
The conventional system of major and minor keys prevailing in all Western music from the Baroque era until the twentieth century. See also ATONALITY.

Trumpet style
Melodic style of piano playing developed by Earl Hines in the late 1920s.

Twelve-bar blues
The most common harmonic progression in all jazz. It comprises twelve measures based on tonic (I), dominant (V), and subdominant (IV) harmonies, organized in the simple pattern I-I-I-I-IV-IV-I-I-V-V-I-I. Variety is injected into this configuration through the use of additional and substitute chords.

Unison
The simultaneous playing of exactly the same notes by more than one performer.

Vaudeville
A staged variety show popular in America at the turn of the century. Broadly comparable to the minstrel show, its musical content was important to the early development of jazz.

Vibrato
The creation of a rich tone color by the rapid oscillation between two notes of very slightly differing pitch. Various methods are used by vocalists and string, brass and wind players, but the technique is not possible on acoustic keyboard instruments.

Walking bass
An improvised bass line that fills the gaps between harmony notes by creating a purposefully striding melody, a device common in all jazz styles from the 1930s onward.

West Coast
A style of cool jazz originating in California during the 1950s.

INTERNATIONAL JAZZ FESTIVALS: A SELECT LIST

All festivals are held annually.

NORTH AMERICA

Canada

Edmonton International Jazz Festival, Alberta: June–July
Halifax Jazz Festival, Nova Scotia: July
Montreal International Jazz Festival, Quebec: June–July
Toronto Jazz Festival, Ontario: June–July
Vancouver International Jazz Festival, British Columbia: June–July

USA

Atlanta Jazz Festival, Georgia: May
Bix Jazz Festival, Davenport, Iowa: July
Blue Note Jazz Festival, New York, New York: June
BNY Mellon Jazz, Pittsburgh, Pennsylvania: year round
CareFusion Jazz Festival, New York, New York: June
Chicago Jazz Festival, Illinois: August–September
Detroit International Jazz Festival, Michigan: September
Greenwich Village Jazz Festival, New York: October
Jacksonville Jazz Festival, Florida: May
Jazz Appreciation Month, Washington, DC: April
JazzBoston Jazz Week, Massachusetts: April–May
Lionel Hampton International Jazz Festival, University of Idaho: February
Mary Lou Williams Women in Jazz, Washington, DC: May
Monterey Jazz Festival, California: September
New Orleans Jazz and Heritage Festival, Louisiana: April–May
Newport Jazz Festival, Rhode Island: August
Playboy Jazz Festival, Los Angeles, California: June
Sacramento Jazz Jubilee, California: May
San Francisco Jazz Festival, California: September–December
Tanglewood Jazz Festival, Massachusetts: September
Vail Jazz Festival and Jazz Party, Colorado: summer
Wichita Jazz Festival, Kansas: April
Xerox Rochester International Jazz Festival, New York: June

EUROPE

Austria

Jazzfestival Saalfelden: August
Jazz Fest Wien: June–July
JazzSommer Graz: July
Salzburger Jazz-Herbst: October–November

Belgium

Brussels Jazz Marathon: May
Dinant Jazz Nights: July
Gent Jazz Festival: July
Jazz Middelheim: August

Czech Republic

AghaRTA Prague Jazz Festival: Spring and Autumn
Bohemia JazzFest, various cities: July
JazzFestBrno: April

Denmark

Aarhus Jazz Festival: July
Copenhagen Jazz Festival: July
Vinter Jazz, nationwide: February

Estonia

Jazzkaar Festival, Tallinn: April

Finland

Imatra Big Band Festival: July
Jazz-Espa, Helsinki: July
Pori Jazz: July

France

A Vaulx Jazz, Vaulx-en-Velin: February–March
Europa Jazz Festival, Le Mans: March–May
Focus Jazz, Basse-Normandie: March–April
Jazz à Juan, Antibes Juan-les-Pins: July
Jazz à St-Germain-des-Prés, Paris: May
Nancy Jazz Pulsations: October
Nice Jazz Festival: July
Paris Jazz Festival: June–July

Germany

Deutsches Jazzfestival Frankfurt: October
Internationale Jazzfestival Sankt Ingbert: March
Jazzfest Berlin: November
Jazzfest Bonn: May–June
Jazz-Festival Moers: May
Jazzfestival Münster: January
Jazztage Dresden: November
Palatia Jazz, Pfalz: May–August
Women in Jazz, Halle: February

Greece

European Jazz Festival, Athens: May

Iceland

Reykjavik Jazz Festival: August–September

Ireland

Guinness Cork Jazz Festival: October
Sligo Jazz Festival: July

Italy

Crossroads Jazz Festival, various cities: February–May
New Conversations Festival, Vicenza: May
Pescara Jazz Festival: July
Umbria Jazz, Perugia: July
Verona Jazz Festival: June–July

Netherlands

Breda Jazz Festival: June
North Sea Jazz Festival, Rotterdam: July
The Hague Jazz: June

Norway

Kongsberg Jazzfestival: July
Molde International Jazz Festival: July
Nattjazz, Bergen: May–June
Oslo Jazzfestival: August
MaiJazz, Stavanger: May

Poland

Jazz na Starówce, Warsaw: July–August
Jazztopad, Wroclaw: November
Warsaw Summer Jazz Days: June–July

Slovenia

Ljubljana Jazz Festival: June–July

Spain

Barcelona International Jazz Festival: October–November
Heineken Jazzaldia, San Sebastián: July
Madrid Jazz Festival: November

Sweden

Gothenburg Jazzfestival: August
Stockholm Jazzfestival: June
Umeå Jazzfestival: October

Switzerland

Internationales Jazzfestival Bern: March–May
Jazz Ascona: June–July
Jazz Festival Basel: April–May
Lugano Jazz Festival: June–July
Montreux Jazz Festival: July

Turkey

Akbank Jazz Festival, Istanbul: September–October
Istanbul Jazz Festival: July

United Kingdom

Bath International Music Festival: May–June
Birmingham International Jazz and Blues Festival: July
Brecon Jazz Festival, Wales: August
Cheltenham Jazz Festival: April–May
Edinburgh Jazz and Blues Festival: July
Gateshead International Jazz Festival: March
Glasgow International Jazz Festival: June–July
London Jazz Festival: November
Manchester Jazz Festival: July
Oxford Jazz Festival: April

REST OF THE WORLD

Argentina

Buenos Aires Jazz: November
La Plata Jazz Festival, Buenos Aires: November

Australia

Australian Jazz Convention (different city each year): December
Melbourne International Jazz Festival: June
Wangaratta Jazz Festival: October

India

India Jazz Festival, Mumbai and Delhi: March

Indonesia

Java Jazz Festival, Jakarta: March

Israel

Red Sea Jazz Festival, Eilat: January
Tel Aviv Jazz Festival: February

Japan

Honmoku Jazz Festival, Yokohama: August
Tokyo Jazz Festival: September

Russia

Don Cento Jazz Festival, Kaliningrad: August
Le Jazz, Moscow and St Petersburg: April
Usadba Jazz Festival, Moscow and St Petersburg: June

South Africa

Cape Town International Jazz Festival: March
Joy of Jazz, Johannesburg: August

RECOMMENDED LISTENING

The following discography is organized broadly chronologically by musical style, in order to facilitate the selection of a personal anthology reflecting the historical development of jazz. Musicians within each section are listed in alphabetical order. Items are restricted to titles available on compact disc at the time of writing, although attention should be drawn to the flourishing (and sometimes expensive) trade in secondhand and deleted albums, both on vinyl and CD. Catalog numbers for individual classic albums are frequently subject to change, and such data is therefore not given below: the reader wishing to check the current availability, label, and catalog details of a particular album should be able to find this information quickly via an Internet title search. Dates, where given, refer to the year(s) of recording.

Many jazz studio recordings and live performances are widely available in the form of low- and mid-price compilations, which provide an inexpensive starting point for the listener wishing to build up a comprehensive collection. A more expensive introduction is the six-disc set *Jazz: The Smithsonian Anthology* (issued with an accompanying book), long regarded as a classic sampling of historic recordings and widely used as an educational tool. Inevitably, collections of this kind have been criticized by some jazz scholars for encouraging the formation of a jazz "canon" of classic performances, but the newcomer to the music in particular will undoubtedly find them an invaluable and informative resource.

Ragtime and Harlem Stride Piano

Eubie Blake, *Memories of You* (1915–73)
Dick Hyman, *Plays Fats Waller* (1988)
James P. Johnson, *Carolina Shout* (1917–25)
Scott Joplin: The composer's own recordings of his compositions on piano rolls are available on numerous inexpensive compilations; modern interpretations by Joshua Rifkin are also recommended
Morton Gunnar Larsen, *Fingerbreaker: Classics of Ragtime and Early Jazz Piano* (1999)
Willie "The Lion" Smith, *Willie "The Lion" Smith, 1925–37*
Ralph Sutton Trio, *Live at Sunnie's Rendezvous* (1969)
Fats Waller, *The Complete Recorded Works* (6 discs)

Blues and Boogie-Woogie Piano

Albert Ammons, *The Boogie Woogie Man: Original Mono Recordings, 1935–1943*
Pete Johnson, *Pete Johnson 1938–1939*
Meade Lux Lewis, *Meade Lux Lewis 1927–1939*
Ma Rainey, *Mother of the Blues* (5 discs)
Bessie Smith, *St. Louis Blues* (CD and DVD set)

New Orleans

Louis Armstrong, *Complete Hot Five and Hot Seven Recordings* (1926–28); see also under "Small Groups of the Swing Era" and "Mainstream Soloists" below
Sidney Bechet, *Sidney Bechet 1940–1941* and *King Jazz: Vol. 1* (1945)
Bunk Johnson, *Bunk's Brass Band and Dance Band 1945*
Jelly Roll Morton, *The Complete Jelly Roll Morton* and *The Complete Library of Congress Recordings* (1938)
New Orleans Rhythm Kings, *New Orleans Rhythm Kings, 1922–1925*
King Oliver, *King Oliver's Creole Jazz Band: The Complete Set* (1923–24)
Original Dixieland Jazz Band, *The Original Dixieland Jazz Band, 1917–1921*
Kid Ory, *Ory's Creole Trombone* (1922–44)

Symphonic Jazz

Aaron Copland, *Early Orchestral Works, 1922–35*; includes the Piano Concerto and *Music for the Theatre*
George Gershwin: Recordings of *Rhapsody in Blue*, *An American in Paris* and the Piano Concerto in F major are too numerous to list, but the composer's own 1927 recording of *Rhapsody in Blue* with Paul Whiteman is recommended. Complete recordings of the opera *Porgy and Bess* are widely available.
The Simon Rattle Jazz Album includes Darius Milhaud's *La Création du Monde*, Igor Stravinsky's *Ebony Concerto*, Leonard Bernstein's *Prelude, Fugue, and Riffs*, the original version of Gershwin's *Rhapsody in Blue*, and several vocal numbers in their Paul Whiteman arrangements.
Gunther Schuller's Third Stream movement of the late 1950s is well represented by *Birth of the Third Stream* (1956–58).
For Wynton Marsalis's large-scale jazz compositions, see *Jump Start/Jazz* (1993–95) and *Blood on the Fields* (1995). A Montreal performance of *Congo Square* (2007) is available on DVD.

Dance Bands of the 1920s

Bix Beiderbecke, *At the Jazz Band Ball* (1927–28)
Jean Goldkette, *Jean Goldkette Bands 1924–29*
Fletcher Henderson, *The Harmony and Vocalion Sessions* (1925–28)
Paul Whiteman, *King of Jazz 1920–27*

Big Bands of the Swing Era

Count Basie: Early work of the period 1936–41 is well represented on *The Essential Count Basie*, vols 1 to 3, and on *The Original American Decca Recordings* (1937–39). For later recordings, see *The Complete Atomic Mr. Basie* (1957).
Benny Goodman, *At Carnegie Hall 1938*, and *B. G. in Hi-Fi* (1954)
Lionel Hampton, *Lionel Hampton 1937–38*, and *Salle Pleyel, 9 March 1971*
Woody Herman, *Blowin' up a Storm!* (1945–47); includes Stravinsky's *Ebony Concerto*
Earl Hines, *Earl "Fatha" Hines: Piano Man, 1928–55*
Jack Hylton, *Jack's Back* (1935–39)
Harry James, *Harry James 1937–1939*
Glenn Miller, *RCA Original Masters: The Best of Glenn Miller 1938–1942*, and *The Army Air Force Band, 1943–44*
Bennie Moten, *Kansas City Orchestra (1929–1932): Basie Beginnings*
Artie Shaw, *Artie Shaw 1939*
Chick Webb, *Rhythm Man/Strictly Jive* (1931–40)
Excellent examples of the updated big-band sound of the late 1960s and 1970s are provided by the Thad Jones–Mel Lewis orchestra (*Live at the Village Vanguard*, 1967) and *The Toshiko Akiyoshi–Lew Tabackin Big Band* (1976).
See also under "Duke Ellington" below

Small Groups of the Swing Era

EUROPE:
Django Reinhardt, *Django Reinhardt 1935–1936*
Stephane Grappelli (with Django Reinhardt), *Quintette du Hot Club de France*
USA:
Benny Goodman, *The Complete Small Group Sessions* (1935–39)
Charlie Christian, *The Genius of the Electric Guitar* (1939–41)
Duke Ellington, *The Duke's Men: Small Groups* (1934–39)
Lionel Hampton, *Small Groups* (1937–40)
Esquire Jazz Concert (Metropolitan Opera House, New York, 1944), featuring Louis Armstrong, Art Tatum, Coleman Hawkins, Lionel Hampton, Billie Holiday, and many others

Duke Ellington

EARLY WORK:
Duke Ellington 1927–1929
Early Ellington (1927–34)
MIDDLE PERIOD:
Duke Ellington 1937–1938
Black, Brown, and Beige (1944–46)
Carnegie Hall Concerts
The Complete Columbia and RCA Victor Sessions
LATER WORK:
Ellington at Newport 1956
Three Suites (1960)
The Far East Suite (1966)
Second Sacred Concert (1968)
See also under "Small Groups of the Swing Era" above

Mainstream Soloists

Louis Armstrong: *Louis Armstrong 1947*, *California Concerts* (1951–55) and *Louis Armstrong Meets Oscar Peterson* (1957); see also under "New Orleans" and "Small Groups of the Swing Era" above
Ella Fitzgerald: For her early work, see "Big Bands of the Swing Era" (Chick Webb) above. Fitzgerald's celebrated *Songbook* series was reissued on eighteen CDs (see p. 195 for details of repertoire), alongside a single-disc sampler (*Best of the Songbooks*).
Coleman Hawkins, *Coleman Hawkins 1929–1934*
Billie Holiday, *The Quintessential Billie Holiday* (1933–42) and *Jazz Masters: Billie Holiday* (1952–56)
Art Tatum, *The Art Tatum Solo Masterpieces* (1953–55) and *The Tatum Group Masterpieces* (1954)
Sarah Vaughan, *Complete Recordings with Clifford Brown* (1954) and *Crazy and Mixed Up* (1982)
Ben Webster, *King of the Tenors* (1953)
Lester Young, *The Complete Aladdin Sessions* (1942–47)

Bebop

Kenny Clarke, *Klook's the Man* (1938–56)
Miles Davis: see *The Charlie Parker Story* (below); Davis's early bop recordings from 1947 are also to be found on *Charlie Parker Memorial*, vol. 1.
Dizzy Gillespie, *The Complete RCA Victor Recordings* (1937–49), *Pleyel Concert 1948* and *Gillespiana/Carnegie Hall Concert* (1961)
J. J. Johnson, *The Eminent Jay Jay Johnson* (2 discs; 1953–55)
Thelonious Monk, *Genius of Modern Music* (2 discs; 1947–48), *Art Blakey's Jazz Messengers with Thelonious Monk* (1957), and *The Thelonious Monk Orchestra at Town Hall* (1959)
Charlie Parker, *The Complete Savoy and Dial Studio Recordings* (1944–48), *Bird: The Complete Charlie Parker on Verve* (10 discs)

and *The Charlie Parker Story*, featuring Miles Davis, Dizzy Gillespie, Bud Powell, and Max Roach
Bud Powell, *The Amazing Bud Powell* (2 discs; 1949–53), and *The Genius of Bud Powell* (1956)
Max Roach, *Jazz in 3/4 Time* (1957), *Deeds, Not Words* (1958), and *We Insist! Freedom Now Suite* (1960)
Sonny Stitt, *Stitt/Powell/Johnson* (1949) and *New York Jazz* (1956)
The Quintet: Jazz at Massey Hall (1953), featuring Charlie Parker, Dizzy Gillespie, Bud Powell, Charles Mingus, and Max Roach

Hard Bop
Cannonball Adderley, *Somethin' Else* (1958), featuring Miles Davis and Art Blakey
Art Blakey and his Jazz Messengers: *Moanin'* (1958); see also under "Bebop" (Thelonious Monk) above
Miles Davis, *Walkin'* (1954), and *Cookin', Relaxin', Workin'*, and *Steamin'* (all 1956)
Dexter Gordon, *Doin' Alright/Dexter Calling/Go/Our Man in Paris* (4 discs; 1961–63)
Lee Morgan, *The Sidewinder* (1963)
Sonny Rollins, *Saxophone Colossus* (1956)
Wayne Shorter, *Speak No Evil* (1964)
Horace Silver, *Song for My Father* (1964)
The Best of Blue Note, a compilation including the title tracks of Morgan's *The Sidewinder*, Silver's *Song for My Father*, Blakey's *Moanin'*, and Coltrane's *Blue Train*

Cool Jazz and West Coast
Chet Baker, *Chet Baker and Crew* (1956)
Dave Brubeck Quartet, *Time Out* (1959)
Miles Davis, *The Complete Birth of the Cool* (1948–50)
Stan Getz, *Getz Meets Mulligan in Hi-Fi* (1957); see also under "Afro-Cuban, Latin, and Bossa Nova" below
Stan Kenton, *The Best of Stan Kenton* (1943–61)
Lee Konitz, *From Newport to Nice* (1955–80)
Modern Jazz Quartet, *No Sun in Venice* (1959) and *Dedicated to Connie* (1960)
Gerry Mulligan, *The Original Quartet* (1952–53) and *What Is There to Say?* (1958)
George Shearing, *Verve Jazz Masters: George Shearing* (1949–54)
Lennie Tristano, *Lennie Tristano/The New Tristano* (1955–62), featuring Lee Konitz

Afro-Cuban, Latin, and Bossa Nova
Mario Bauzá, *My Time is Now* (1993)
Stan Getz, *Jazz Samba* (1962) and *Getz/Gilberto* (1963)
Astrud Gilberto, *Verve Jazz Masters: Astrud Gilberto* (1964–66)
João Gilberto, *Amoroso/Brasil* (1977, 1980)
Dizzy Gillespie and Machito, *Afro-Cuban Jazz Moods* (1975)
Irakere, *Live at Ronnie Scott's* (1991)
Antonio Carlos Jobim, *Verve Jazz Masters: Antonio Carlos Jobim*; also available as part of the three-disc compilation *Verve Jazz Masters: The Bossa Nova Story*
Flora Purim, *Butterfly Dreams* (1973)

Modal Jazz
Bill Evans, *Everybody Digs Bill Evans* (1958)
Miles Davis, *Milestones* (1958) and *Kind of Blue* (1959), both featuring John Coltrane and Cannonball Adderley
Herbie Hancock, *Maiden Voyage* (1965)

John Coltrane
Blue Train (1957)
Giant Steps (1959)
My Favorite Things (1960)
A Love Supreme (1964)
See also under "Hard Bop," "Modal Jazz," and "Free Jazz"

Miles Davis
Miles Ahead (1957)
Porgy and Bess (1958)
Sketches of Spain (1959)
Kind of Blue (1959)
The Complete Concert 1964: My Funny Valentine and Four & More
E.S.P. (1965)
Miles Smiles (1966)
For other recordings from the 1940s and 1950s, see "Bebop," "Hard Bop," and "Modal Jazz" above; for jazz-rock recordings, see under "Jazz-Rock Fusion" below

Charles Mingus
Pithecanthropus Erectus (1956)
Tijuana Moods (1957)
Mingus Ah-Um (1959)
The Black Saint and the Sinner Lady (1963)

Free Jazz
Anthony Braxton, *For Alto* (1968) and *Three Compositions of New Jazz* (1969)
Art Ensemble of Chicago, *A Jackson in Your House/Message to Our Folks* (1969)
Albert Ayler, *Witches and Devils* and *Spiritual Unity* (both 1964)
Ornette Coleman, *The Shape of Jazz to Come* (1959), *Free Jazz: A Collective Improvisation* (1960), and *At the Golden Circle, Stockholm*, vols 1 and 2 (1965); see also under Pat Metheny below
John Coltrane, *The Major Works of John Coltrane*, including both versions of *Ascension* (2 discs; 1965), and *The Avant-Garde*, featuring Don Cherry (1966)
Chick Corea, *The Song of Singing* (1970)
Pat Metheny, *Song X*, featuring Ornette Coleman (1985)
Sun Ra, *The Magic City* (1965)
Cecil Taylor, *Jazz Advance* (1956) and *Unit Structures* (1966)

Piano Trios
Monty Alexander, *Full Steam Ahead* (1985)
The Bad Plus, *Give* (2002)
Nat King Cole, *Nat King Cole 1943–1944*
E. S. T. [Esbjörn Svensson Trio], *From Gagarin's Point of View* (1998)
Bill Evans, *Waltz for Debby* (1961), *Conversations with Myself* (1963), and *Trio '64* (1964); see also under "Modal Jazz" above
Erroll Garner, *The Original Misty* (1954) and *Concert by the Sea* (1955)
Tord Gustavsen, *Changing Places* (2002)
Hiromi [Hiromi Uehara], *Voice: The Trio Project* (2011)
Keith Jarrett, *Standards*, vols 1 and 2 (1983), and *Bye Bye Blackbird* (1991); see also under "ECM" below
Lyle Mays, *Fictionary* (1993); see also under "Jazz-Rock Fusion" below
Brad Mehldau, *The Art of the Trio*, vols 1 and 2 (1996–97)
Oscar Peterson, *Night Train* (1962), *Very Tall*, featuring Milt Jackson (1962), and *Satch and Josh*, featuring Count Basie (1974); see also under "Mainstream Soloists" (Louis Armstrong) above
Bobo Stenson, *Serenity* (1999)

Jazz-Rock Fusion
Chick Corea, *Where Have I Known You Before* (1974), *No Mystery* (1975), and *Elektric Band* (1986); see also under "Free Jazz" above and "ECM" below
Miles Davis, *In a Silent Way* (1969), *Bitches Brew* (1970), and *Jack Johnson* (1971)
Dave Grusin, *Harlequin* (1985), featuring Lee Ritenour
Herbie Hancock, *Head Hunters* (1973) and *Future Shock* (1983); see also under "Modal Jazz" above
Bob James, *One* (1974) and *Touchdown* (1978), including the theme from the American TV comedy *Taxi*
John McLaughlin, *Extrapolation* (1969) and *The Inner Mounting Flame* (1971), featuring the Mahavishnu Orchestra
Lyle Mays, *Lyle Mays* (1986) and *Street Dreams* (1988); see also under "Piano Trios" above
Pat Metheny and Lyle Mays, *As Falls Wichita, So Falls Wichita Falls* (1980); see also under "Free Jazz" above and "ECM" below
Pat Metheny Group, *Offramp* (1981), *First Circle* (1984), *Still Life (Talking)* (1987), and *The Way Up* (2004)
Lee Ritenour, *Color Rit* (1989); see also under Dave Grusin above
David Sanborn, *Voyeur* (1980)
Grover Washington, Jr., *Winelight* (1980)
Weather Report, *Black Market* (1976), *Heavy Weather* (1977), and *This is This* (1986)
Yellowjackets, *Greenhouse* (1991)

ECM
Arild Andersen, *Hyperborean* (1996)
Gary Burton, *Selected Recordings* (1973–86)
Chick Corea, *Solo Piano Improvisations/Children's Songs* (1971, 1983)
Jan Garbarek, *I Took Up The Runes* and *Ragas and Sagas*, featuring Pakistani musicians (both 1990), *Twelve Moons* (1993), and *Visible World* (1995)
Keith Jarrett, *The Köln Concert* (1975) and *Belonging*, featuring Jan Garbarek (1974); see also under "Piano Trios" above
Pat Metheny, *Bright Size Life* (1975) and *80/81* (1980), featuring Dewey Redman and Michael Brecker; see also under "Jazz-Rock Fusion" above
Tomasz Stańko, *Leosia* (1996)
Miroslav Vitous, *Universal Syncopations* (2003), featuring Chick Corea, Jan Garbarek, John McLaughlin, and Jack DeJohnette
Collin Walcott, Don Cherry, and Naná Vasconcelos, *Codona 1*, *Codona 2*, and *Codona 3* (1978–82)
Eberhard Weber, *Colours* (1975–80)
See also under "Piano Trios" (Tord Gustavsen, Keith Jarrett, Bobo Stenson) above

1980s to the Present Day
Geri Allen, *The Life of a Song* (2004)
Michael Brecker, *Two Blocks from the Edge* (1998) and *Pilgrimage* (2007)
Uri Caine, *Primal Light* (1996)
Béla Fleck, *Tales from the Acoustic Planet* (1995) and *Across the Imaginary Divide* (2012), with the Marcus Roberts Trio
Roy Hargrove, *With the Tenors of Our Time*, featuring Branford Marsalis and Joe Henderson (1994), and *Hard Groove* (2003)
Hiromi [Hiromi Uehara], *Duet* (2007), featuring Chick Corea, and *Time Control* (2008)
Soweto Kinch, *A Life in the Day of B19: Tales of the Tower Block* (2006)
Diana Krall, *The Girl in the Other Room* (2004)
Loose Tubes, *Dancing on Frith Street* (1990)
Branford Marsalis, *Scenes in the City* (1983)
Wynton Marsalis, *Wynton Marsalis* (1981), *Marsalis Standard Time*, vols 1 to 6 (1986–99), and *The Majesty of the Blues* (1989); see also under "Symphonic Jazz" above
Courtney Pine, *Journey to the Urge Within* (1986) and *Afropeans* (2008)
Joshua Redman, *Joshua Redman* (1992)
Gonzalo Rubalcaba, *Avatar* (2007)
Maria Schneider Orchestra, *Evanescence* (1994) and *Concert in the Garden* (2004)
John Scofield, *Still Warm* (1985)
Andy Sheppard, *Soft on the Inside* (1989)
Vienna Art Orchestra, *Art and Fun* (2003)
Cassandra Wilson, *Blue Skies* (1988) and *Blue Light 'Til Dawn* (1993)
World Saxophone Quartet, *W.S.Q.* (1980) and *Plays Duke Ellington* (1986)
See also under "Jazz-Rock Fusion", "Piano Trios" and "ECM" above

SUGGESTED FURTHER READING

Reference

Ian Carr, Digby Fairweather and Brian Priestley, *The Rough Guide to Jazz*, 3rd edn (London, 2004)

Leonard Feather and Ira Gitler, *The Biographical Encyclopedia of Jazz* (New York, 2007)

Barry Kernfeld (ed.), *The New Grove Dictionary of Jazz*, 2 vols (New York and London, 1988), single-volume reprint (1994), and online (oxfordmusiconline.com)

David Meeker, *Jazz in the Movies*, 2nd edn (London, 1981); see also Meeker's Library of Congress database, "A Jazz and Blues Filmography" (lcweb2.loc.gov/diglib/ihas/html/jots/jazzscreen-home.html)

Brian Morton and Richard Cook, *The Penguin Jazz Guide: The History of the Music in the 1001 Best Albums* (London, 2010)

Autobiographies and Memoirs

Louis Armstrong, *Satchmo: My Life in New Orleans* (New York, 1954)

Count Basie and Albert Murray, *Good Morning Blues: The Autobiography of Count Basie* (New York, 1985)

Sidney Bechet, *Treat it Gentle: An Autobiography* (New York and London, 1960)

Bill Crow, *Jazz Anecdotes* (New York and Oxford, 1990)

Miles Davis and Quincy Troupe, *Miles: The Autobiography* (London, 1990)

Duke Ellington, *Music is My Mistress* (Garden City, New York, and London, 1973)

Dizzy Gillespie, *To Be, or not ... to Bop: Memoirs* (Garden City, New York, 1979)

Benny Goodman and Irving Kolodin, *The Kingdom of Swing* (New York, 1939)

Woody Herman and Stuart Troup, *The Woodchopper's Ball: The Autobiography of Woody Herman* (New York, 1990)

Billie Holiday and William Dufty, *Lady Sings the Blues* (Garden City, New York, 1956)

Charles Mingus, *Beneath the Underdog* (New York and London, 1971; 2nd edn 2005)

Oscar Peterson, *A Jazz Odyssey: My Life in Jazz*, ed. Richard Palmer (London, 2002)

Horace Silver, *Let's Get to the Nitty Gritty: The Autobiography of Horace Silver*, ed. Phil Pastras (Berkeley, California, 2007)

General Histories

Joachim Berendt, *The Jazz Book: From Ragtime to Fusion and Beyond* (St. Albans, UK, 1976; rev. edn, 1992)

Samuel Charters and Leonard Kunstadt, *Jazz: A History of the New York Scene* (New York, 2nd edn 1981)

James Lincoln Collier, *The Making of Jazz: A Comprehensive History* (London, 1978)

Mervyn Cooke, *Jazz* (London, 1998)

Juliet Coryell, *Jazz-Rock Fusion: The People, the Music* (London, 1978)

Scott DeVeaux, *The Birth of Bebop: A Social and Musical History* (Berkeley, California, 1997)

Scott DeVeaux and Gary Giddins, *Jazz* (New York, 2009)

Ted Gioia, *The History of Jazz* (Oxford, 2nd edn 2011)

———, *West Coast Jazz* (New York, 1992)

Jim Godbolt, *A History of Jazz in Britain, 1919–50* (London, 1984)

———, *A History of Jazz in Britain, 1950–70* (London, 1989)

John Edward Hasse, *Ragtime: Its History, Composers, and Music* (New York and London, 1985)

André Hodeir, *Jazz: Its Evolution and Essence* (New York, 1956)

Leroi Jones (Amiri Baraka), *Blues People: Negro Music in White America* (New York, 1963)

Ekkerhard Jost, *Free Jazz* (Graz, Austria, 1974)

Stuart Nicholson, *Jazz Rock: A History* (Edinburgh, 1998)

———, *Jazz: The 1980s Resurgence* (New York, 1995)

Paul Oliver, *The Story of the Blues* (London, 1969)

Thomas Owens, *Bebop: The Music and its Players* (New York and Oxford, 1995)

Hugues Panassié, *Hot Jazz* (Paris, 1934; English trans. London and New York, 1936)

———, *The Real Jazz* (New York and Toronto, 1942)

Catherine Parsonage, *The Evolution of Jazz in Britain, 1880–1935* (Aldershot, UK, 2005)

David H. Rosenthal, *Hard Bop* (Oxford,1992)

Alyn Shipton, *A New History of Jazz* (New York and London, 2nd edn 2007)

George Simon, *The Big Bands* (New York, 1967; 4th edn 1981)

Eileen Southern, *The Music of Black Americans: A History* (New York and London, 2nd edn 1983)

Marshall Stearns, *The Story of Jazz* (New York and Oxford, 1956)

Barry Ulanov, *A History of Jazz in America* (New York, 1952)

Penny M. Von Eschen, *Satchmo Blows Up the World: Jazz Ambassadors Play the Cold War* (Cambridge, Massachusetts, 2004)

Geoffrey Ward and Ken Burns, *Jazz* (London, 2001)

Criticism

David Ake, *Jazz Matters: Sound, Place, and Time Since Bebop* (Berkeley, California, 2010)

Mervyn Cooke and David Horn (eds), *The Cambridge Companion to Jazz* (Cambridge, UK, 2002)

Krin Gabbard, *Jammin' at the Margins: Jazz and the American Cinema* (Chicago, 1996)

Krin Gabbard (ed.), *Jazz Among the Discourses* and *Representing Jazz* (Durham, North Carolina, 1995)

Robert Gottlieb (ed.), *Reading Jazz* (New York, 1996)

Bill Kirchner (ed.), *The Oxford Companion to Jazz* (Oxford, 2000)

Philip Larkin, *All What Jazz: A Record Diary, 1961–71* (London and New York, rev. edn 1985; original edn 1970)

Stuart Nicholson, *Is Jazz Dead? (Or Has it Moved to a New Address)* (New York, 2005)

Mark Tucker (ed.), *The Duke Ellington Reader* (New York and London, 1993)

Robert Walser (ed.), *Keeping Time: Readings in Jazz History* (New York, 1999)

Tony Whyton, *Jazz Icons: Heroes, Myths, and the Jazz Tradition* (Cambridge, UK, 2010)

Martin Williams (ed.), *The Art of Jazz: Essays on the Nature and Development of Jazz* (New York, 1959)

Martin Williams, *Jazz in its Time* (New York and Oxford, 1989)

Musical Techniques and Analysis

Paul F. Berliner, *Thinking in Jazz: The Infinite Art of Improvisation* (Chicago, 1994)

Michael J. Budds, *Jazz in the Sixties: The Expansion of Musical Resources and Techniques* (Iowa City, Iowa, 1978; expanded edn 1990)

Mark Gridley, *Jazz Styles* (Englewood Cliffs, New Jersey, 1978–85)

Barry Kernfeld, *What to Listen for in Jazz* (New Haven, Connecticut, 1995)

Ingrid Monson, *Saying Something: Jazz Improvisation and Interaction* (Chicago, 1996)

Lewis Porter, Michael Ullman, and Ed Hazell, *Jazz: From Its Origins to the Present* (Englewood Cliffs, New Jersey, 1993)

Ken Rattenbury, *Duke Ellington: Jazz Composer* (New Haven, Connecticut, 1990)

Gunther Schuller, *Early Jazz* (New York and Oxford, 1969)

———, *The Swing Era: The Development of Jazz, 1930–45* (New York and Oxford, 1989)

PHOTO CREDITS

a = above; b = below; c = centre; l = left; r = right

© ADAGP, Paris and DACS, London 1997 49, 53br, 59a.
Andy's Guitar Centre, London 127b.
University of Michigan Museum of Art, Ann Arbor 1948/1.103, © DACS 1997 114b.
Courtesy Jimmy Carter Library, Atlanta 191br.
By kind permission of BMG/RCA 115b, 161, 162.
Richard Braaten 21a.
British Council Collection. Courtesy of the Lefevre Gallery, London 10b.
Courtesy Capitol Records 237a.
Courtesy CBS Records 227a.
The Art Institute of Chicago. Lent by Archie Motley and Valerie Gerrard Browne 67b.
© William Claxton/The Special Photographers Library 12, 128a, 132, 159.
© Copyright 1932 The Copland Fund for Music, Inc. Copyright Renewed. Boosey & Hawkes, Inc., sole licensee. Reproduced by permission of Boosey & Hawkes Music Publishers Ltd 59b.
Corbis/Bettmann 6 (montage), 8, 9, 11b, 21b, 27, 41b, 45a, 46, 50, 52al, 54b, 63b, 65b, 75b, 761, 77c, 80a, 88, 100, 102b, 104a, 117b, 118, 133a, 142r, 171, 232, 240.
Corbis/Bettmann/Penguin 77r.
Corbis/Bettmann/UPI 6 (montage), 11a, 55l, 58a, 107b, 112, 113a, 121b, 122, 128b, 134, 140l, 141, 146, 150, 160a, 201l, 206, 208, 217.
© Corbis/Paulo Fridman 233br.
© Corbis/Rick Friedman 251b.
© Corbis/Star Ledger/Saed Hindash 246r.
© Corbis/Philippe Levy-Stab 226.
© Corbis/Joseph Schwartz 6 (montage), 123r.
© Corbis/Reuters/Mike Segar 245.
© Corbis/epa/Jason Szenes 234.
© Karl Dixon 7 (montage), 225r.
From MUSIC IS MY MISTRESS by Duke Ellington. Copyright © 1973 by Duke Ellington, Inc. Used by permission of Doubleday, a division of Bantam Doubleday Dell Publishing Group, Inc. 182r.
The Frank Driggs Collection 6 (montage), 15, 23a, 25a, 26, 28, 30l, 35, 36, 37, 40, 44, 47, 48, 51bl, 51br, 52ar, 52b, 53l, 56, 60, 61r, 62, 63c, 64, 66, 67a, 72b, 73, 77l, 78–9b, 80b, 82, 85b, 86, 91, 95, 98b, 99, 106, 107a, 109, 113b, 119a, 120, 124r, 186, 191bl, 209, (© Copyright, 1982) 111, (Photo Paul. J. Hoeffler) 151, (Photo Chas B. Nadell) 108, (Photo Popsie Randolph) 121a, 129a, 136b.
Courtesy ECM Records GmbH 177, 184a, 214bl, 228.
Courtesy EMI Records 6 (montage), 96b, 104b, 115a, 135a, 140r, 142l, 149a, 167b, 1681.
Courtesy Fantasy, Inc. 137, 184l.
Fender Musical Instruments Corporation 127c.
© Palma Fiacco 243.
Bradford Fowler 211al.
© Getty Images/AFP/Rafa Rivas 238.
© Getty Images/AFP/Kenzo Tribouillard 250.
Getty Images/Chicago History Museum 65a.
Getty Images/Frank Driggs Collection 45b, 57.
© Getty Images/FilmMagic/Stephen J. Cohen 225l.
© Getty Images/FilmMagic/Jason Merritt 242b.
© Getty Images/Jakubaszek 241l.
Getty Images/Michael Ochs Archives 87b.
© Getty Images/Redferns/Christopher Bierlein 241r.
© Getty Images/2011 C. Brandon/Redferns 7 (montage).
© Getty Images/ Redferns/2010 Peter Van Breukelen 7 (montage).
© Getty Images/Redferns/William Gottlieb 90.
© Getty Images/Redferns/Peter Pakvis 7 (montage), 246l.
© Gilles Petard/Redferns/Getty Images 83, 123l, 195.
© Getty Images/Redferns/David Redfern 244.
© Getty Images/Redferns/Frans Schellekens 237b.
© Getty Images/Redferns/Harry Scott 249.
© Getty Images/Redferns/Gai Terrell 216.
© Getty Images/Time & Life Pictures/Gjon Mili 224.
Photo Heidi Grassley, © Thames & Hudson Ltd, London 127b, 168r.
© Dani Gurgel, Brasil 235.
Photo © Skip Bolen for HBO® 253a.
Christian Him's Jazz Index 7 (montage), 199, 201r, 202, 203b, 210, 211b, 215a, 218b, 220, (© Photo Christian Him 1980) 178a, 194, (© Photo Nancy Clendaniel/Jazz Index) 214a, (M. Jones/Jazz Index) 78l, (© Photo Tim Motion/Jazz Index) 153, 203a, 221, 223, (© P. Symes/Jazz Index) 143.
Courtesy Randi Hultin 148a, 157a, 169, 200.
Courtesy Impulse! Records 242a.
Photo © Jak Kilby 2, 204.
© Herman Leonard/The Special Photographers Library 125r, 126, 131, 136a, 163l.
BFI Stills, Posters and Designs, London 69, 72a, 117a, 181a.
Courtesy Maher Publications 236r.
© Roberto Masotti 7 (montage), 192l.
Courtesy Monterey Jazz Festival 247a.
Courtesy Montreal International Jazz Festival 251a.
Joe Moore/Jazzportraits 247b.
© Muga Miyahara 231, 236l.
Institute of Jazz Studies, Rutgers, The State University of New Jersey, Newark 29a, 98a, 170a.
The Goodman Papers, Yale University Music Library, New Haven, used by permission 84, 154l.
Archive of New Orleans Jazz, Tulane University Library, New Orleans 4-5, 38.
Museum of the City of New York 31.
By Permission of Music Sales Corp., New York 182r.
The New York Philharmonic Archives 54l.
Public Library of Performing Arts, New York 85a.
Pablo Records 188r.
Bibliothèque nationale de France, Paris 39, 74.
© Succession Picasso DACS 1997 39, 43.
Player Piano Group, 93 Evelyn Avenue, Ruislip, HA4 8AH 32.
PolyGram Records, Inc., New York 157b, 163r, 179.
Popperfoto 103, 176.
Premier Percussion Ltd, Wigton, UK 119b.
Private collection 6 (montage), 10a, 18, 19, 23, 227b, 89r.
Reproduced with permission of Punch Ltd 58br.
© Redferns, London (Photo David Redfern) 7 (montage), 13, 149b, 155, 170b, 174, 178b, 182l, 187, 197, 198, 205, 207, 212, 218a, (Photo William Gottlieb/Redferns) 6 (montage), 75a, 97, 114a, 116, (© Redferns-William P. Gottlieb/Library of Congress) 42, 87ar, 101, 125l, 196, (Photo Max Jones Files/Redferns) 6 (montage), 61l, 94b, 138, (© Redferns. Photo Stuart Nicholson) 183, (Redferns/Michael Ochs Archives) 105, (© Redferns. Photo Andrew Putler) 165b, 175a, (© Redferns. Photo C. Stewart) 166.
© 1943 Republic Entertainment, Inc.® a subsidiary of Spelling Entertainment Group Inc.® Republic Pictures is a registered trademark of Republic Entertainment Inc.® All rights reserved 69.
Courtesy Rhino 253b.
Courtesy Riverside Records 51a.
Per Rønnevig 148b.
Courtesy Scandinavian Airlines 152.
Courtesy SONY Jazz 79a, 133b, 147, 173, 175r, 180a, 189.
Sotheby's Inc. 58bl.
© 1988 Sotheby's, Inc. Photo appears courtesy the artist and D. C. Moore 145.
Courtesy Barton Stabler, Westfield, New Jersey 215b.
Galerie der Stadt, Stuttgart. © DACS 1997 81b.
Courtesy Suntory Hall/Harmony Japan 7 (montage), 248.
TopFoto/Heritage-Images/Curt Teich Postcard Archives 41a.
© 1997 by Universal City Studios, Inc.
Courtesy of Universal Studios Publishing Rights. All Rights Reserved 72a, 181a.
HQ Music Service, RAF Uxbridge 94a, 102a.
© Geert Vandepoele 239.
Courtesy Verve 135b, 157b, 163r.
Photo Collection Viollet 24, 49r.
The Warner Collection of Gulf States Paper Corporation, Tuscaloosa, Alabama 17.
Library of Congress, Washington, DC 6 (montage), 16, 20, 29b, 30r, 59a, 89l, 92.
Library of Congress, Washington, DC/William P. Gottlieb Collection 229.
Library of Congress, Washington DC Prints and Photographs Division [LC-USZ62-49034 (b&w film copy neg.)] 22.
Courtesy Thelonious Monk Institute of Jazz, Washington, DC 233a, 233c.
© Val Wilmer 70a, 96a, 124l, 139, 154r, 156, 158, 164, 165a, 180b, 185, 188l, 190, 192a, 193, 213, 219, 222b.
Courtesy Yahama Kemble Music (UK) Ltd 33, 70b, 87c, 93.

INDEX

Numbers in **bold** type refer to pages on which illustrations appear.

INDEX